Something
Better for My
Children

Something Better for My Children

The History and People of Head Start

KAY MILLS

A DUTTON BOOK

DUTTON
Published by the Penguin Group
Penguin Putnam Inc., 375 Hudson Street, New York, New York 10014, U.S.A.
Penguin Books Ltd, 27 Wrights Lane, London W8 5TZ, England
Penguin Books Australia Ltd, Ringwood, Victoria, Australia
Penguin Books Canada Ltd, 10 Alcorn Avenue, Toronto, Ontario, Canada M4V 3B2
Penguin Books (N.Z.) Ltd, 182–190 Wairau Road, Auckland 10, New Zealand

Penguin Books Ltd, Registered Offices: Harmondsworth, Middlesex, England

First published by Dutton, an imprint of Dutton NAL, a member of Penguin Putnam Inc.

First Printing, April, 1998

10   9   8   7   6   5   4   3   2   1

REGISTERED TRADEMARK—MARCA REGISTRADA

LIBRARY OF CONGRESS CATALOGING-IN-PUBLICATION DATA:

0-525-94328-5
CIP data is available.

Printed in the United States of America
Set in Transitional 521
Designed by Eve L. Kirch

This book is printed on acid-free paper. ∞

CONTENTS

*Who dreamed for every child an even chance
cannot let luck alone turn doorknobs or not.*

—Miller Williams, "Of History and Hope"

Introduction

he face of poverty today is the face of a child. By the mid-1990s, more than one in every five American children under six years old—5,333,000, or 22.7 percent—was poor.[1] If that weren't bad enough, today these youngsters live in urban crowding or rural isolation where it is difficult to avoid debilitating drug use or alcoholism or teenage pregnancy. Overwhelmed schools fail to interest many young people in learning to read well enough to hold a job in a market that more and more prefers mental ability over muscles. Many jobs are no longer located in cities where the poor live, making finding work even more difficult. And too many times we read in our newspapers about random, unprovoked violence claiming the lives of children. Combating poverty is tough work that requires action on many fronts. Increasingly, however, government programs that could help are being cut, and private efforts are stymied by the enormity of the problem. Absent uplifting leadership, the country has descended into an anxious, punitive, and ungenerous mood. And the face of poverty grows younger still as a result.

This attitude did not always prevail. In the Great Depression, government led the way back to national economic health, putting people to work as it went. In the 1960s, poverty once again became more than a blip on the radar screen that is the American conscience. President Lyndon Johnson, who had learned about "the high price of poverty and prejudice" when he taught school in Cotulla, Texas, declared a war on poverty that engaged the country until the war in Vietnam drained off the resources. Senator Robert Kennedy traveled to Mississippi and ever after talked about the listless, defeated children whom he had seen in its shacks. Dr. Martin Luther King, Jr., was preparing to lead the Poor People's March on Washington when he was assassinated in Memphis. Young people, church people, dedicated people began to work in their own neighborhoods to try to change the lives of those on the margins; some stayed on the task even as the government increasingly bowed out.

Johnson's War on Poverty turned out to be a skirmish in what should have been a lifelong, countrywide crusade but never was. The poverty rate in 1995 among all Americans was nearly as high—13.8 percent—as it had been almost thirty years earlier.[2] That more do not live in poverty is no miracle; it is because the elderly now have better retirement benefits under Social Security and health insurance under Medicare and because the gap between the incomes of white and black families has narrowed.

One program has stayed the course. Head Start, the major remaining battalion from that original war on poverty, is still at work as a comprehensive child development program for poor children and their families at centers across the country. It has energized tens of thousands of Americans to educate themselves and to escape poverty. Head Start by itself clearly cannot lift families from poverty. By definition, money cures poverty. To get money, people need jobs that too often no longer exist. But Head Start has given many families a hand up and can continue to provide that boost, if the nation truly believes in the value of all families as well as in family values and is willing to help those families. Head Start is arguably the best investment America has ever made in its youngest citizens, although it definitely has areas that need improvement. Too many people, however, know too little about Head Start; that is why I decided to write this book.

Head Start had enough success stories to prompt me to travel around the country, trying to find out what worked and what didn't. From the open, rolling rangeland on a Montana Indian reservation to the tabletop flatness of the Mississippi Delta, from the streets of South Central Los Angeles to the hills of West Virginia, from migrant labor camps to enclaves of Vietnamese and Cambodian refugees, many Americans still live close to the margins. Yet in all those places, I met mothers who had seen what Head Start could do for their children—and for themselves. They got involved, and they started questioning not only how their children were being educated but also why their communities didn't have adequate housing or better health care or responsive politicians. In all those places, I met fathers who had realized that helping out in the centers wasn't just women's work. There were not enough of them, but those who were there came to know their own children better and guided others who may have had no fathers at home.

In this book, I tell the stories of many of the people I met—children, parents, teachers, and Head Start graduates. I tracked one Head Start center in the Watts area of South Central Los Angeles through a school year; throughout this book, you will watch the children's progress, as I did, from September to June. I wanted to show the human face of Head Start—to go beyond policy and show how Andre started learning to share and Maria became more adventurous, how Rachel Jones had enriched her journalism by recalling her own experiences, how Frankie King had been given that boost she needed to finish her education, how Ismelda Cantu found the confidence to run a Head Start center.

What I found in my travels was a simple but incandescent idea: Poor children can benefit from the same "head start" on learning that better-off parents can give their children. Head Start was designed so that not only would poor children start to count and to say the alphabet, they would also have their teeth checked, their eyes checked, their ears checked, just as middle-class kids routinely do. They would have the chance to get together with other children, the same way middle-class kids do, instead of remaining isolated on farms or in city slums. They would learn to ask questions, to listen to the answers or discover them for themselves, to help one another, and to see places in their community they might otherwise never visit. Simple but basic things other American children take for granted.

For adults, the benefits are clearer than for their children. They can tell you what or who changed their lives. Over and over again, parents with little education or opportunity told me how working with Head Start for their children's benefit led them to go back to school, to get better jobs, to learn to speak out, to escape an abusive relationship, to become politically involved. Many pulled themselves into the middle class because of the economic and educational encouragement they received in Head Start. And they could name the people who encouraged them. The adults' success stories are what I call the hidden hallmark of Head Start, revolutionary potential often realized but rarely trumpeted to the greater public.

What made this program a success in their eyes, I wanted to find out, when so many other efforts either failed or never had a chance to get in gear? Head Start was a potent combination of government leadership and government money mixed with local volunteer spirit, and that was certainly part of the answer. Was the secret to its endurance that it was built around children? Who, after all, can refuse to help a child?

More than thirty years after the program was hastily thrown together in early 1965, Head Start survives. The program's rules are more complex, and it serves thousands more children and spends millions more dollars. Head Start has enrolled more than 15 million children since it began. Its budget has grown from $96.4 million for the 1965 summer program to $3.98 billion in fiscal year 1997. But the program has never been fully funded and today serves only about 40 percent of the eligible children.

Head Start stands squarely in the middle of the contemporary version of a debate under way since the Republic was founded. How deeply should government involve itself in the lives of its people? We wanted roads west, protection for settlers, schools for our children—we wanted government to help secure our grandest dreams. But historically we have just as often moved on to escape increasing controls, we've hated paying taxes, and we've thought that the other guy was getting more than we did and that that wasn't fair. We're still wrestling with these contradictions. This American ambivalence has carried over to questions of how best to help the poor and how much to invest public resources in caring for children. The poor are shiftless, says one side. They're victims, says another. We want to be charitable to all the "deserving poor" but we show malice toward some whom we consider "undeserving." We've never been quite sure how to treat children, either. For a while we put them to work in brutal jobs; then we rescued them. Today, many politicians prefer prisons to preschools.

Whenever Congress has considered Head Start's money and its mandate, it never has had the will or the way to make the program what it could be: universal and of uniformly high quality. The public as a whole should be concerned; we all have an enormous stake in Head Start's future. The children in today's Head Start classrooms will be among the American workers and voters whose actions will affect how competitive our economy remains, how safe our neighborhoods can become, and how relevant to daily concerns our politics will be in the years to come.

At the same time, Head Start has not lived up to its potential by truly organizing parents to assume real authority over the program. Some communities never had Head Start programs with such involvement;

some did and saw it sapped. It is easier and far less time-consuming to tell parents how to do things than to help them do for themselves, but that should not be the point. Head Start has also done a poor job in letting the public know what it accomplishes, leaving itself vulnerable to critics who sound well-meaning but may not be.

Changes in welfare laws in 1996 also raise questions for the future of Head Start. Today the government appears more hostile than encouraging to the poor. Congress passed tough work requirements to cut the nation's welfare rolls, but without any guarantees that there will be enough money for quality child care as demand increases. Parents must be able to work secure in the knowledge that their children are not only properly supervised but also being well prepared for school. Head Start was already feeling the pressure from working parents who needed more than half-day programs; now it is truly squeezed. How effectively and creatively it meets this need will help determine how well it survives into the twenty-first century.

Now to the personal questions: Why Head Start? Why me? I started my journalism career in the mid-1960s, just as the injustices toward Southern black people were finally drawing national attention, outrage, and action. I wrote about Mississippi Summer and the first year of Head Start from a distance, preparing news copy for the broadcast section of United Press International. Later, I covered some of the early urban antipoverty efforts in Baltimore. Then I wrote editorials about Head Start and other education issues for the *Los Angeles Times*.

In the early 1990s I wrote a biography of Fannie Lou Hamer, the legendary civil rights leader from Mississippi. While the drive for voting rights stirred her greatest passion, she was involved in any program that would help poor people, black and white. She worked on the Head Start proposal for Sunflower County. She spoke passionately at protest meetings when Mississippi senators John Stennis and James O. Eastland sought to take Head Start's money away because it was going to the black community. And her husband made a living driving a bus for Head Start after losing his plantation job in retaliation for his wife's civil rights activity. As I looked for books to guide me in sorting out the Mississippi battles, I soon realized that any that had been written about Head Start were generally by participants—planners, local staff, researchers. No one from outside, no journalist, had yet told in any comprehensive way the lives of the people the program sought to reach. I long ago learned that it is the people out in the community, working day to day with the problems and recognizing the promise, who have the best insights into how policy translates into reality. Theirs is the human side of Head Start.

My mother reminds me that I have my own preschool story. I was an only child and a shy one at that, perhaps because of a speech problem. Only after years of speech therapy and practice could I be sure I could make myself understood to casual listeners. Maybe that's why I identify with the underdog. I attended a cooperative nursery school—not Head Start, but a program in which many of the mothers volunteered their time. Before I went to nursery school, I am told, I would often withdraw into myself if another child was getting attention. (No one believes that today, but it's true.) At that preschool program I learned that I would get my turn and the world would not end if another child was in the spotlight. My own memories of that age are dim—like some Head Start graduates, I do remember nap time and snack time for sure, and the teacher reading to us. I have always loved books and stories. I became a journalist and then an author to write them for others. Here, then, are stories of the history and people of Head Start.

Making the
Promise

Chapter One

The First Day of School at Watts Towers Center

our-year-old Janette walked in the door of her Head Start classroom on the first day of school and handed her teacher, Josephine Garner, a single morning glory blossom. It was 8:30 on a smoggy September morning, and Janette's sweet act of appreciation for her teacher was hardly the image that would come to your mind if I said, Watts, South Central Los Angeles, 1990s.

"Good morning, Raymound," Garner sang out in her strong voice as another child arrived at the Watts Towers Head Start, one of eleven centers run by Training and Research Foundation of Inglewood, California, and known within TRF as Site 05. "*Buenos dias,*" she added. Little Josefina hung her plastic Fancy Feline handbag in one of the cubbyholes for coats. The classroom on 105th Street, around the corner from the eccentric Watts Towers artistic landmark, was abuzz with children returning for the fall session. They were washing their hands, brushing their teeth, and getting their name tags pinned onto their shirts.

Garner, an ebullient African American woman of fifty-five and the site supervisor, looked like Gulliver amid the Lilliputians as she sat at one of the kid-sized tables, handing out toothbrushes. With her collar-length hair in ringlets, her shorts and sneakers and her energetic manner, you might not pick her out as someone who had had a grandson in Head Start some years ago. Garner had come by train to Los Angeles from Birmingham, Alabama, in 1962 when her oldest child, Angie, was a year old. Like countless other Head Start teachers, she started volunteering for the program in 1979, when her son was enrolled at Imperial Courts, where she lived. "I was just there. I came in at eight in the morning and left at four." While working with the children, "I said, 'This is what I want to be.'" Divorced, she had worked for fifteen years at an embossing-machine plant in Orange County but went back to school to take child development classes and had worked nights as a supervisor in several fast-food restaurants to support herself and her children in the past.

That first day of school, Raven, who had just turned four, arrived at the center with her mother, who wanted to bring a birthday cake to school. Diplomatically, Garner explained that they didn't have birthday parties because some parents could not afford such extras. The staff always blew up balloons and observed the children's birthdays by singing to them. This concern with what parents could afford was not an idle one. Children could enroll in Head Start that year if their parents earned $15,150 a year or less for a family of four. That's how the federal government officially defined poverty in 1995. In TRF's programs, more than 75 percent of the children came from homes with incomes of $12,000 or less each year. More than 55 percent of the families made less than $9,000 a year. Fifty-five percent of the children also lived with only their mothers. Just about that same percentage of mothers—53.5 percent—had not finished high school. You don't have to be an economist or statistician to link single motherhood and low education to low income. Forty percent of TRF's families were on welfare.

In Watts, it is important to remember these income figures because the neighborhoods don't look particularly poor—unless you have just driven through Beverly Hills or Bel Air, or even the middle-class, largely black neighborhoods off Vermont Avenue a few miles north and west. Wilmington Avenue, the main thoroughfare off the Century Freeway toward Watts Towers, is admittedly not a place you would go window-shopping. The first buildings you see as you head north of the freeway are a used-tire dealer and a liquor store. It is not the only liquor store in the mile and a quarter from the freeway to Site 05, and it was not uncommon to see several men with bottles in brown paper bags sitting on an abandoned sofa in a vacant lot across the street from it. Once you drive on across the railroad tracks, you see at least eight churches, most of them small storefronts, Jordan's soul food restaurant, a school, several minimarkets, and a motel, its windows barred.

Turn left at the Friendly Temple Baptist Church, R. J. Friend, Pastor, onto 105th Street and you'll pass a dozen or more one- and occasionally two-story stucco and wood houses on each side of the street on the way to the Head Start center. You may or may not get a civil hello from a woman sitting on a low wall having her morning bracer from a plastic cup. Other neighbors, some of whom have lived in the area all their lives, are far more willing to chat, even with a stranger. The neighborhood has a mix of Latino and African American families. The houses are small but serviceable. Rents run perhaps five hundred dollars a month for a two- or three-bedroom house; purchase prices hover around one hundred thousand dollars, low by Los Angeles standards. Several branches of one family may crowd into the houses so they can afford to buy or rent. Some yards are neatly planted with roses or bird-of-paradise plants; others have only a packed dirt surface and cars parked on the lawn. Drying laundry hangs on many of the fences early in the morning; some of the homes clearly house big families. On this street and around the corner on 106th, where some of the children live, there are fences around all the yards and bars on most of the windows. And dogs—big, barking, intimidating dogs.

Los Angeles's rapid-transit line cuts through the neighborhood on its run from downtown toward the Wilmington station. Through the narrow spaces between the homes on the south side of 105th you can see the structure that gives the Head Start center its name, Watts Towers. Simon Rodia, an Italian immigrant, started the towers in the yard of his home in 1921, constructing a latticework of steel, cement, and glass bottles, tiles, shells, and other salvaged materials. The tallest tower, resembling a medieval church spire, reaches about a hundred feet. Rodia finished his folk art tribute to his adopted city in 1954. His house burned down in 1955, and soon he moved away. His towers remain, maintained by the city of Los Angeles, the only tourist attraction listed for Watts in most guidebooks. The Head Start teachers occasionally walked the children around the corner to the towers when they needed a change of scene.

Training and Research Foundation, which operated the Watts Towers site and ten others, had been established in 1966 by Paul DeVan, an antipoverty agency administrator and former probation officer. It took its name from its original purpose, which was training parents, board members, and administrators to work with Head Start, not to run centers directly, and studying how to provide that training better. DeVan was later approached to take over two failing programs; TRF operated its first Head Start centers in 1975 and now has sites in South Central Los Angeles and neighboring Inglewood, Hawthorne, South Gate, and Huntington Park. It operated these centers as what Head Start calls a delegate agency, working as do other organizations under contract with the area grantee, the Los Angeles County Board of Education.

Elaine Atlow took over as acting director after DeVan had a stroke; she became director in February 1996, when DeVan retired and became a consultant for the program. Her story was like that of many other Head Start staff members around the country. Originally from Louisiana, where she had studied two years at Southern University in Baton Rouge, Atlow came to Los Angeles in 1961. Describing herself as an "overprotective mom" with two daughters, Atlow said that in Head Start she found a program "where I could be there and watch them." She started working with Head Start as an aide in 1965 and soon became a teacher and director for a program in Long Beach before moving to TRF.

In the year I was visiting its programs, TRF operated on a budget of $4.39 million, plus $279,000 from the child care food program that helped provide lunches for the children. It had thirty-five teachers, whom it generally paid from slightly under $20,000 a year to $36,000 a year, depending on whether they worked twelve months or nine and one half months a year, what amount of education they had, and how much experience they had. Other staff included almost the same number of teaching aides as well as education supervisors and a disabilities services coordinator; three women who worked with parent involvement; a nurse and two health assistants, a head cook, three assistant cooks and a nutrition driver; a warehouse clerk, a maintenance supervisor and maintenance workers; and several office staff members. These men and women supervised the teachers, linked children with counselors and other support services, checked immunization records and monitored children's growth, ran workshops for parents, prepared meals, repaired the buildings and kept them clean, and handled Head Start's mountain of paperwork.

I visited many of TRF's Head Start centers and got to know their teachers and other staff members on field trips, at retreats, and at other meetings. Many of their stories echoed those you will read in this book; I wish I could have included them all. I selected Watts Towers, Site 05, for my most regular visits because it was located in what seemed neither the toughest nor the safest of the TRF neighborhoods, because it had an almost equal mix of Hispanic and African American youngsters enrolled that year, and because it was in a neighborhood whose name was readily recognizable to people outside of Los Angeles.

I chose TRF's program as a whole because it was willing to open wide its doors to me. Some of the TRF centers, although not Watts Towers, were located in the congressional district of U.S. representative Maxine Waters, who had referred me to TRF. Waters, the outspoken head of the Congressional Black Caucus, has over and over again credited Head Start with focusing her talents. Originally from St. Louis, Waters had moved to Los Angeles in 1961 with her husband and two young children. In 1967, she got a job as an assistant teacher with a Head Start program. While working there, she attended California State University's Los Angeles campus and received a bachelor's degree in sociology. Eventually, she supervised local volunteer services and parental involvement for the Head Start program for which she worked. "We became advocates for continued funding, which brought us in contact with more politicians. We got to know them better, and that is, I think, perhaps the point that I see as my connection with politics and my real involvement beginning."[1]

Over the years, I had written several magazine profiles of Waters, so I turned to her when I was looking for a program in South Central that would let me be a fly on the wall for a year. She told me about TRF one Friday evening; the following Monday when I called, director Atlow said, "Oh, yes, the congresswoman said you'd be calling. How can we help you?"

Each time I visited Site 05, I would see parents, usually mom but sometimes dad, or grandma, walking children down 105th Street to the center. Some of the children arrived by car if they lived across Wilmington. Most walked, with some of the mothers pushing another child in a stroller or holding the hand of a toddler not yet old enough for Head Start.

By the first day of classes, many of the children had already had their medical and dental checkups, a regular Head Start feature, because they had been enrolled in the program for the summer as well. But Garner still had to nag some of the mothers to bring in their children's inoculation records. Marcus's mother said, yes, she had the papers and she'd bring them when she picked him up at noon. "You don't want me to meet you on that corner," Garner said in her best tough-but-caring tone to remind Mom that Marcus wouldn't be able to remain in the program unless she had his records. Marcus headed off to play and Garner warned, "I hate to do this but you have to pull that hat off in the house." Marcus took off his cap.

As several of the parents saw Garner sorting the toothbrushes—each with a plastic case around the bristles, and bearing a child's name—

they talked about how their children had cavities. Must be from too much candy, one lamented. Not necessarily, said Garner and her aides. The children may have been born with too little calcium in their bodies. Just then Travell headed for the front of the line to brush his teeth, and Garner intercepted him, telling him to wait behind Donisha. "When he gets to the big school," Garner said, "if he does that, they're going to tell him to sit down. He has to learn that."

Site 05 was one classroom about fifty feet by forty feet in a square gray, utilitarian stucco building. There were two doors, no windows. The center, surrounded by a high chain-link fence, had a grassy lawn with a swing set, a slide and jungle gym combination, a tunnel to crawl through, and a sandbox where the children often served up "apple pie" or "coffee" in little tin containers. Site 05 had both its morning classes— thirty-two youngsters—in the one classroom. Other TRF locations usually had separate rooms for each class, which reduced distractions and the noise level. No matter how many adults you have supervising, thirty-two squiggly four-year-olds in one room is a lot of four-year-olds.

The staff was one person short on opening day because an aide had been transferred. I asked Garner how she kept up her energy on days like this. "Pray," she said in her matter-of-fact manner. "Just pray for God to give me more strength. I'm short today. I can't go cry in the corner. I can't neglect my children. I just deal with it." Garner did have Veronica Perez, president of the center's parent policy council, on hand. The policy council members, elected by the parents, relayed information to other parents, went over the curriculum with the teachers, and often helped chaperon field trips and other special events. "She's like my right arm. She knows what I know," Garner said about Perez. The center would soon be assigned a new aide.

As Andre's mother signed him in, Garner called out, "Where's that TB test?"

"I got it," she replied as she pinned onto the back of Andre's shirt a large name tag giving his name and that of his Head Start center. "I'll bring it when I pick him up."

A certain calm had settled over the center by 9 A.M. as the twenty-eight children present sat down on a carpeted area in front of a bulletin board that held the month's theme, the community. Because the children had attended Head Start during the summer, they knew the drill. Their first-day crying was behind them, almost.

Anthony and Joshua squirmed the way four-year-olds squirm. Garner looked their way, saying, "Anthony, I'm going to excuse you. I don't think you're ready to come back to school." He went off to another part of the room but soon settled down and was ready to return. Several veteran Head Start teachers told me that the children they see today are much more active and less able to concentrate than children they saw twenty years ago. They aren't sure why. "We're getting all kinds of problems," Garner said, "and it's not just from families with single moms. These are kids with Mama and Daddy, sisters and brothers, the total *familia*. The techniques you used to use—just sit them down and let them have their cry—don't work anymore."

Some teachers said the children watch a lot of television, where nothing lasts for more than a few minutes, where shows cut frenetically in and out of action and to commercials lickety-split. The music their young parents listen to is also fast paced and loud. And their parents, who are in fact often young single moms, don't necessarily have long attention spans themselves, so concentration may not be reinforced or rewarded at home. Young parents don't necessarily know how best to toilet train their children, discipline them, or comfort them, so many of the children bring to Head Start whatever fears they have developed.

"Good morning, boys and girls," Garner called out. "Good morning, parents," she said as she seated herself on the floor, at the children's eye level. Garner's typical wardrobe on a teaching day was shorts or pants, a shirt, and sneakers to accommodate all that time on the floor or out in the play area. On many days this "circle time" would be the first time Garner sat down, because she put in busy mornings calling out greetings to parents as they crossed the yard, checking that they signed the children in and helped them find their name tags, giving parents work that they could do at home for the center, and generally preparing for the day ahead.

Everyone working at the center had her own style, and Garner's was usually the most forceful voice. Lupe Osuna, fifty-seven, the other teacher at Watts Towers for its two morning classes, was softer spoken but could be just as firm as Garner when needed. She, too, had started with Head Start as a volunteer when one of her five children was enrolled in a program in South Gate, a city adjacent to Watts. With these two veteran teachers, every move, every game, had a purpose. Garner started a Head Start standard: "Good morning, everybody, how are you?"

"Just fine," the children sang back.

"Good morning, Jesús, how are you?" Jesús sang back that he was "just fine."

"We are happy and we are gay. And we like to stay that way, so good morning to Janette, how are you?"

"Just fine." And so on until all the children had been greeted.

Michael, a big boy for his age, came in with his mother, Bianca. He was sulking. He sat behind the toy shelf, apart from the other children, saying nothing. Garner got up and peered over the shelf, singing out, "Good morning, Michael, how are you?" No response. Eventually she returned and led Michael into the circle for "Simon says, touch your head," and Michael touched his head.

"If you're happy and you know it, clap your hands," and twenty-nine pairs of hands clapped. "If you're happy and you know it, clap your hands. If you're happy and you know it, then your face will surely show it. If you're happy and you know it, clap your hands."

"If you're happy and you know it, stomp your feet," and twenty-nine pairs of feet stomped. "If you're happy and you know it, give a whistle," and twenty-nine children whistled—or made brave attempts. "If you're happy and you know it, slap your knee," and twenty-nine pairs of knees were slapped. "If you're happy and you know it, say hooray," and twenty-nine hoorays split the air. "If you're happy and you know it, do all five." Clap, clap. Stomp, stomp. Whistle, whistle. Slap, slap. Hooray!

Pointing to the bulletin board behind her, Garner said that today she was going to start talking about "community helpers" like the dentist. "If you don't brush your teeth, you get germs and you have to go to the dentist," she said. "This month we are going to be talking about the doctor. The doctor may need to examine your body parts so I want you to point out your head, your elbow, your knee" on this chart, which several of the children did. "Next week we are going to dress up with the stethoscope and be doctor," Garner told the children.

Garner put on a stethoscope and asked what the doctor checked with it. "Your chest," Shardae volunteered.

"Yes, they do that, but what else?"

"Your heart."

"These children have already been having their physicals so they know this," Garner said in my direction, one of her frequent asides during the morning.

"If he puts the stethoscope on your back, what does he tell you to do?"

"He gives you a Band-Aid," Joshua guessed.

"No, he tells you to what?" Garner said, coughing loudly.

"He tells you to cough," Ciara answered.

Ciara, a sturdy four-year-old with a mischievous grin, spoke up with regularity, and usually knew the answers. So did Shardae, a quick-witted, loving little girl who, as an only child, was a trifle headstrong (as even her mother admitted). Others among the children could barely be heard. Little Maria played quietly with the other children but rarely volunteered much information. Born with a tumor in her jaw, she looked as though she had the mumps. Garner and Osuna treated her just like the rest of the children to keep her from being self-conscious.

Every morning, Garner, Osuna, and their assistant teachers focused on preparing the children with the skills that they would need to succeed in school. Head Start's mission is not principally teaching children to say the alphabet and know their numbers—although it does do that. It helps in overcoming shyness. Getting over fears of being away from Mama or Grandma. Cooperating with one another and sharing. Learning to listen. Taking turns. Waiting in line. Understanding that your actions have consequences—for example, that it hurts somebody else when you punch them or bite them. It also helps children figure out how to hold a crayon, puzzle out answers on their own, develop good health habits, and try different and nutritious foods.

Head Start undertakes this mission in settings across the country ranging from Indian pueblos and reservations to migrant labor camps and Appalachian mining towns, from housing projects to pockets of poverty in affluent suburbs. Each center has a daily pattern that enables the children to become accustomed to the routine of school and prepare for what will lie ahead in kindergarten. The pattern was clear at the Watts Towers center: the children played on their own and ate a morning snack when they arrived; brushed their teeth; gathered for circle time; usually had some lesson about doctors or vegetables or some other topic of the day; colored pictures or strung beads or practiced writing their letters; played outside; washed their hands; ate lunch; and went home.

After talking to the children about what the doctor does, Garner started reviewing the days of the week and the colors—in English and in Spanish. *Lunes, martes, miércoles, jueves, viernes, sábado, domingo. Azul, verde, rojo, anaranjado, blanco, negro.* Teaching at the Watts Towers center was done almost entirely in English, but Lupe Osuna helped some of the children in Spanish and spoke to many of the Hispanic parents in their common language. Garner spoke a smidgen of Spanish as well—especially for purposes of keeping order among the children. Both teachers led many of the songs in Spanish as well as English. Fifteen years ago this site's enrollment was all black. On the first day of this class, sixteen out of the twenty-nine children present were Hispanic. That change reflected the flow of blacks out of South Central Los Angeles to suburban communities. They have been replaced by families who had left Mexico or Central America, settled elsewhere in the city, and then moved to Watts and other South Central neighborhoods to be nearer jobs or in pursuit of home ownership. In 1980, South Central was 14 percent Latino; today it is 51 percent and rising. Two-thirds of Watts residents are now Latino.

The ethnic composition of Head Start is changing throughout Los Angeles County. For the school year that I visited the TRF program, 1995–96, about 55 percent of the children attending its centers were of Mexican or Central American heritage, some 40 percent were African American, and a smattering came from other groups. Nationwide, Head Start students that year were 36 percent African American, 32 percent white, 25 percent Hispanic, 4 percent American Indian and 3 percent Asian. So this is not, contrary to some stereotypes, a program solely for poor black children, urban or rural.

A slight digression into history will help us better understand the cultures in which Head Start functions in Watts. We are told that there were two blacks among the group that settled the pueblo called Nuestra Señora de la Reina de Los Angeles (Our Lady of the Queen of the Angels) in 1781. These early settlers were outnumbered then by people whose roots were in Mexico, just as they are today. Few blacks lived in Los Angeles until 1880 because California was not a welcoming state. It had passed a harsh fugitive slave act and rejected the Fifteenth Amendment giving black men the right to vote. But by 1910 Los Angeles's black population started to grow substantially, from 7,599 (2.4 percent of the whole city) to 15,579 in 1920, 38,894 in 1930, and 63,774 in 1940, many of them railroad employees and their families. Migrants from rural Mississippi, Georgia, and Alabama had settled in Watts by 1916. By the 1940s, thousands of black migrants left farm work in the Old South, Texas, and Oklahoma, settling along Central Avenue. During World War II, 200,000 blacks arrived in the Los Angeles area to help build ships and airplanes and make steel and rubber. Many stayed, and by 1950, blacks were about 9 percent of the population.

Blacks found some jobs in the police and fire departments although few were able to advance. Teachers, preachers, lawyers, and doctors formed the backbone of a substantial black middle class in Los Angeles by the 1930s and 1940s, people who started chafing at residential restrictions and lack of progress both on the job and politically. Despite the explosive growth in the black population during World War II, the Los Angeles City Council remained firmly in the grasp of white conservatives into the early 1960s. There had been only one Hispanic councilman—Edward Roybal—and no black members of the council until Gilbert Lindsay was appointed to fill the vacancy created when Roybal was elected to Congress in 1962.

One who grew frustrated with his lack of progress in the police department was Tom Bradley, who went to law school at night and ran for city council in 1963 as the black community was developing its political muscle. Indeed, once they made their breakthrough, African Americans were able to elect city council members and state representatives, even members of Congress, in far greater numbers than could Mexican Americans who were entering the area. At every level of government, public-sector jobs opened up to black workers. Eventually, Bradley allied himself with liberal Jewish voters and became the first black mayor of Los Angeles, serving from 1973 to 1991.

Latinos also came to the city to work and also faced discrimination. The Mexican Revolution, which began in 1920, triggered large-scale migration. The bracero program—the importation of Mexican workers to pick crops in central California—also swelled the population. Once the growing season was over, white farmers wanted the Mexicans out of their area and either deported them or gave them just enough money to cross the Tehachapi Mountains, the gateway into the Los Angeles basin. Mexican Americans moved into East Los Angeles and were subject to prejudice, violence, and frequent deportations.

The most celebrated cases of bigotry and brutality occurred during World War II. In 1942, a young Mexican American's body was discovered near a swimming hole known as the "Sleepy Lagoon." The night before the body was found, there had been a fight there between two gangs. In the antiforeign mood of wartime, the police were looking for a pretext to clamp down on young Mexican Americans and so arrested three hundred of them; twelve were convicted of murder and five of assault. Law officers argued that Mexicans had a biological predisposition to commit violent crimes. An appellate court later threw out the verdicts. Historian Carey McWilliams, who was involved with the young men's defense, felt that the case marked a turning point for community organization as Mexican Americans rallied to help their own. The police also looked the other way when Mexican Americans were beaten during fights between servicemen and young men wearing the big-shouldered "zoot suits" on several nights running in June 1943. In these "zoot suit riots," sailors, later joined by soldiers and marines, beat bar-rio youngsters senseless, hauling them out of theaters and stripping them on occasion. One day there were forty-four arrests—all of Mexi-can Americans, all of whom had been beaten.

As the economy worsened in Mexico, jobs in the United States looked better and better; the population swelled in the bordering area of Southern California. Births, as well as immigration, contribute greatly today to the growth in the Hispanic community. Mexican Americans took jobs cleaning hotel kitchens and office buildings, mowing lawns, and sewing clothing in sweatshops. These immigrants had lower than average divorce rates and volunteered in high numbers for military ser-vice. But despite their patriotism, they couldn't flex the same political muscle blacks had demonstrated because many were unregistered to vote (they were in the country illegally or had not obtained their citi-zenship). It was the 1980s before the second Hispanic person reached the Los Angeles City Council and more Hispanics joined Roybal as members of Congress from Los Angeles. The presence of more Hispan-ics in what had been African American neighborhoods, the sense that Hispanics are landing many of the entry-level jobs, and the fact that African Americans still dominate the teaching ranks in many South Central schools with large Hispanic enrollments—all these factors have led to tensions that occasionally boil over, especially in the area's high schools.[2]

The discontents of both Latinos and blacks turned to rage—or in the words of some, rebellion—in the Los Angeles riot of 1992 after the acquittal of four white police officers who had beaten Rodney King, a black motorist they were arresting. That riot started several miles from Watts, but soon affected everyone living for miles around. Stores near the Watts Towers Head Start center were burned, and the center served as a distribution point for diapers and other supplies that par-ents couldn't obtain. But it was the earlier Watts riot of 1965—at that point the worst urban riot in more than two decades—that perma-nently etched this community's name into history. That riot, started again over the arrest of a black motorist, left thirty-four people dead and hundreds injured. More than four thousand people were arrested for looting, firebombing, and sniping; $35 million in damage was caused.

The 1965 Watts riot occurred in the context of increasing agitation for voting rights in the South and violent retaliation by police and whites threatened by change. The riot showed any white American who had not already figured it out that the problems of African Americans were not confined to the South. Local and national reports issued after the fact underlined the lack of jobs, poor schools, inadequate public transportation—indeed, the lack of almost every kind of social or economic service that would help people break through poverty and discrimination. Much has changed because of the public and private responses to the riots of both 1965 and 1992, but much has not. Many of the poorest citizens of Watts remain as cut off as ever from hope for a better life. Many a Head Start mother said she enrolled her youngsters because she wanted "something better for my children." As frustrated as Head Start teachers and administrators may be when parents are unable or unwilling to participate in center activities, those parents did take the initiative to enroll their children in this comprehensive program. Many others didn't.

On that first day of school in September, Ciara and Kimberly were saying their colors and Joshua was starting to learn to try to pay attention rather than squirming. After Joshua put his hand to his chin in puzzlement and it was clear he couldn't name the colors, Garner called on Marcus to help him. "Garner can't hear you," she said to the little boy because he spoke so softly. But Marcus had the colors mostly correct. Soon Garner separated two little boys, calling over her shoulder about children who play and distract the others' attention, "God knows they don't need to be together."

"Good morning, Mr. Joe," the children sang out as Joe Dancy, an assistant cook from the central kitchen in Inglewood, arrived with cartons containing lunch—ham sandwiches that day but normally a hot meal. Dorothy Stevenson, herself a parent of former Head Start students, supervised preparation of the lunches for nearly eight hundred children, plus teachers and volunteers, for all the TRF centers. When she started to volunteer at another Head Start program in 1968, she was asked if she would wash the dishes. "I could have done that at home," she said, remembering with a smile her reaction to the request, but she stayed on and later joined TRF in 1984. Now one of her sons who had been in Head Start was completing a master's degree at the University of California, Irvine.

After the food delivery was signed for, Garner reviewed the alphabet with the children. She let those who recognized the first letter of their name stand in line to go outside. Soon all the children were playing outside, some on the slide, others in the sandbox, others dashing about on tricycles. Still others were playing hopscotch with Garner, who said as she jumped from square to square, "It's been a long time since I've done this."

Veronica Perez supervised one of the children busily drawing at an easel. While keeping an eye open for youngsters riding tricycles too fast, she commented to the little girl on her artwork. Perez had three daughters, all of whom had attended Head Start. Janette was four, Diana, who had graduated that June, was five, and Cynthia was seven. Her husband worked at a plastics factory and the family had moved to the area across Wilmington about five years earlier because house prices were lower there. I wondered how people who could afford a house also qualified to send their children to Head Start—until I learned that several families lived in the house together. At one point there had been twenty-five people, including children, Perez told me.

"Watts has a bad reputation," she said. "At first I wouldn't go anywhere unless my husband could take me. Now I get out more. I talk to more black people." As the year would move on, Perez would be working with several of the African American mothers on the programwide parent policy council that represented families for the entire TRF program. A woman with clear leadership potential, she was at first hesitant about speaking at meetings.

Perez had hit upon another of the reasons I selected the Watts Towers center for my most intensive visits. I wanted to see how the longtime residents—the African Americans in the neighborhood—were getting along with the newcomers, the Hispanics. I knew I wouldn't see the interaction on the kind of day-to-day level that I would if I lived there, but I could see what kind of cooperation could occur when children were involved. This is an overlapping of two cultures that many in Los Angeles never see and of which many outsiders are not even aware.

By 10:35 on that first morning of school, the children were back inside to hear the story of Sylvester, a donkey who won't listen to his mother. As Garner was finishing the story, Osuna translated into Spanish. She was responsible for half the children and Garner for half. Later in the day, Osuna was head teacher for the afternoon class. The story was clearly one of the children's favorites, one they frequently requested. Sylvester's mother, it turns out, has warned him not to play with rocks and not to stay outside after dark. He does both and gets lost. His parents go to the policeman to see if he can help. Poor Sylvester. A lion turns him into a rock because he didn't listen to his mama, as clear a moral as one could hope.

Energy levels started to flag at this point, and several of the children snuggled up to Osuna while the group sang "Where Is Thumbkin?" Soon, however, they had washed their hands and were quietly seated at the lunch table, not eating until Garner led them singing, "Thank you for my lunch, *gracias por las comidas*." She explained to the children what they were having for lunch, and urged them not to eat their apples first. The apples would help clean their teeth.

One of the mothers who was volunteering left to pick up an older child in elementary school and her son Richard cried—often with no tears but with racking sobs—for an hour until she returned. Andre wanted to comfort him but Garner said he had to learn not to cry. Gradually, though, she moved near the child and urged him that, if he had to cry, he should at least "cry on a full stomach." He should eat his sandwich, she said, because no matter how much he cried, his mother still had to go to that school.

"Marcus, put that food in the trash," Garner called out. "You're not eating it, you're just throwing it." Early in the school year, as much food was thrown out as was eaten, until the children got used to eating away from home and eating food their parents might not prepare for them. Gradually, they ate more and more as the year progressed—although the children rarely finished everything on their plates. At 11:50 parents started arriving to sign out their children and take them home. Soon sixteen more children would come through the doors for the afternoon class and the routine would begin again.

Watts Towers:

In which Richard is a green dragon and Jenyffer a yellow sunflower. Josephine Garner reflects on her goals.

Halloween and costumes go together like parents and cameras. To the tales of goblins and ghosts, add safety tips and advice about the dentist and you have Halloween at Head Start. During most of October, Josephine Garner and Lupe Osuna, the teachers at the Watts Towers Head Start center, and the center's aides used Halloween as a focus for the children's work and play. When the children were learning their colors, they stressed orange and black, *anaranjado y negro*, just as they had learned about red and green, *rojo y verde*, when they had talked about traffic lights in September. When they worked on their motor skills—or muscular movements—the children colored pictures of witches. When they talked about going trick-or-treating, they anticipated the candy they might collect, but they also discussed safety and tooth decay.

"When you go trick or treating, what are you supposed to do?" Garner asked her three- and four-year-old charges one day in late October.

"Get candy," one of them piped up.

"No, you wait for your parents to check it. Should you get in a car with strangers?" she asked next.

"No, they'll cut your head off," one little girl chimed in.

"These kids see some scary shows," Garner called over her shoulder to me.

The lesson plans for the month called for a theme of health and safety. First, the children talked about firefighters, discussing fire equipment, playing the role of firefighter, and hearing a story about Lewis the Firefighter. Then they switched to the dentist, talking about their teeth and about germs and about fruit that would help keep their teeth clean. They cut and colored pictures of dentists. As Halloween neared, they learned about crossing the street safely as well as how to walk and jump like a cat. Their teachers read to them a story about "the witch next door." They practiced using scissors and they colored drawings of Halloween pumpkins.

The children may have been anticipating Halloween, but their teachers were already looking ahead to November. As Veronica Perez and Helen Nolan, mothers of children in the Watts Towers morning session, finished the minutes of the center parent policy council's first meeting, Garner talked with them about plans leading up to Thanksgiving. The children would learn about going to the grocery store and buying vegetables and fruit, they would talk about the Indians and the pilgrims and the first Thanksgiving, and they would learn about family traditions.

Garner was also chuckling a little about that first parent meeting. "Nobody wanted to run against anybody else," she said. "People don't want to run for office. They think they don't speak well enough. They think they don't write well enough. They think, '*I'm* not good enough.'" It's so difficult drawing people out at first, Garner added, evidently remembering some of her own emotions when she considered teaching for Head Start ten years earlier. She had been working as an assistant teacher, part-time, for the Los Angeles school district, she told me as she prepared lunch one day. "And I did this kind of work"—she was fixing hamburgers—"for ten years at night." She was reluctant to become a Head Start teacher. "I thought I wouldn't measure up." She was applying for a low-level job in the public school system, but when she took the reference form she needed to Paul DeVan, then the Training and Research Foundation Head Start director, he wouldn't sign it. He wanted her to work for TRF. He challenged her to try the harder teaching job, and she did it. She went to school at night while teaching during the day and earned her associate in arts degree from Southwest College.

Did she ever get frustrated, working so hard? "No, because I had a goal. At Southwest I had a teacher who was about sixty and she had such a presence. I said I wanted to be like her. I know it helped me when I went to school. And it helped my children see if I could do it, they could, too. Oh, yes, I'd get tired. I'd sit in the car between classes and I'd nod off like this," she said, letting her head rest on an imaginary steering wheel. "But I knew I wasn't doing myself any good just staying home. I need to take these fingers and do whatever I can with them."

Recollecting those days when she received public financial assistance, Garner added: "I praise Head Start. I was once an AFDC parent. Now I can send my son off to college. I can help him financially, mentally, educationally. It inspired me to go back to school. I want to go to Cal State, Dominguez Hills [for a bachelor's degree] eventually but I have to help my son first."

As they prepared for Halloween, parents worked during October to convert beer-bottle cartons into festively decorated candy carriers for each child. The idea was to give the children enough candy—but not too much—and have them parade around the neighborhood in their costumes so they wouldn't feel the need to go out at night for trick-or-treating.

The big day finally came. Little Marcus was a clown, and Richard, who had spent part of the first day of school crying, was a green dragon, seemingly quite content. Jenyffer brightened the overcast day in her yellow sunflower costume, and Yaneth was an orange pumpkin. "Raven, you *have* to go to dancing class," Garner sang out to Raven, who had on a pink ballerina outfit that, her mother explained, she was finally big enough to wear. "You know you have the legs to be a dancer," Garner said, and Raven, a small child who was always dressed well and who had already mastered an occasional coy look, nodded that, yes, she knew that.

The obligatory Mighty Morphin Power Rangers showed up, as did two Lion Kings, one Dracula, one Aladdin, a Barbie doll, and a slinky cat. Anthony was a firefighter seemingly straight out of the lesson plans with helmet, nifty yellow slicker, badge, and boots. Inevitably, there were children without costumes, but Garner and Osuna were prepared for that. "We were very poor when I was little," Garner said later as she served the lunch plates. "I remember wearing hand-me-downs and having the other kids laugh at me because they could tell the dress had been let down or taken up or they had seen the coat on somebody else six years ago. So for several days we went to the dress-up corner [in the classroom] and we showed the kids what we had and we dressed them up. So when today came, they didn't mind those clothes. They knew they were just as special as the store-bought costumes."

From the drawers and shelves, Garner and Osuna pulled out long white shirts that doubled as doctors' smocks as well as a Dracula cape, a waitress's uniform, an elegant rich witch's dress, and purses for two little ladies headed for the best shops. Edwin/Dracula had his face painted by teaching aide Deborah Chatman. Garner applied lipstick for Maria and Marisol and some of the other girls. Strings of beads dressed up two little witches. No child would be left behind this day.

Once everyone was outfitted, Garner had them pause before a full-length mirror to look at themselves as they lined up to go outside. "What's that woman's name? I saw her on TV last night," Garner said as one of the girls in a black outfit came along. "Elvira," someone called out. "Yes, come here, Elvira. Just look at yourself," she said to one slinky witch. "Now don't you feel good about yourself?" It's a phrase that you hear often in Head Start. It may look cloying in print, but it doesn't sound that way when said to a child who badly needs a dose of confidence.

The children went outside into the play yard, where Garner, costumed in a doctor's jacket with a stethoscope around her neck, grouped them for photographs to remember the day. Michael, the second Dracula, dashed off to go to the bathroom, so his partner, Travell, moved toward the back of the line to wait for him. Two by two, holding hands, the children stepped off behind Garner and Chatman. They led the way to the corner, where all the children stopped and passed between two of the adults, who were prepared to block traffic, had there been any. The children waved at a commuter train that whizzed by beyond a fence, then crossed the street to head back to the center. A UPS truck pulled alongside, and the driver waved to Garner and the children as he waited for them to cross. In the background, under scaffolding for repairs, was Simon Rodia's landmark Watts Towers.

Pausing for a few minutes in the churchyard next door to the Head Start center, Garner directed the children into a circle and got them to walk around inside it before they got back into a line—all part of learning shapes and learning to follow directions. By the time the thirty children (only two were absent) made the turn back into the center, Lupe Osuna and the mothers who had stayed behind had the tables set with Halloween pumpkin napkins that Garner proudly announced she had gotten on sale for only ten cents a package. Fall leaves and a little pumpkin decorated the middle of each table for eight. Garner took more photographs of the children holding the cartons of candy, all the while urging them not to touch any of it. That was a hard sell. Marcus's eyes were glued to the carton and its contents, but no one filched any of the sweets. It was surprisingly easy to convince them to leave the candy and wash their hands for lunch. The mothers and aides helped some of the children out of their costumes so they could eat.

Travell was wearing a crisply pressed camouflage outfit that had "US Marines" stenciled on his left pocket and "Travell" on his right. "Travell, we're going to have to take that hat off the corner of your eye. You can't be at the table with a hat on," Garner said as she took his fatigue cap and put it on her desk.

Garner served lunch and the children carried their paper plates to the table. A few had trouble pushing in their chairs, so Arcelia Acosta, Anthony's mother, helped out. A brunette with large expressive eyes, she told me in hesitant English that she had arrived in the United States seven years earlier from Guadalajara. Starting the day after Halloween, she would have two children in Head Start when César became old enough to join Anthony in the class. She proved one of the center's most faithful volunteers that year.

Several of the children were having difficulty keeping their hands off their food before the signal to eat, but Garner kept her eye on them. Rules are rules, even on Halloween. Finally, when all were served and seated, she sang with them, "Thank you for my food. Thank you for my food, tha-ank you. *Gracias por las comidas, gra-ci-as.*" Garner listed the menu: "We have mashed potatoes and turkey and spinach and bread and butter and milk and pears." Spinach, she reminded me, because it's rich in iron.

Turkey might not seem like a Halloween dish, but the bulletin board was already displaying pilgrim scenes and turkeys under the heading "Holiday Tradition." Garner explained to me that they had to put the next theme up on the walls whenever they had some spare time so that once Halloween was over, they could begin the November lesson plans. The next day they'd start fresh by talking about the color brown, discussing why there were leaves covering the lawns, learning about corn and turkeys, and understanding why Americans celebrate Thanksgiving.

The mashed potatoes proved a big hit for this Halloween lunch, but only a few of the children ate their spinach. Chatman and Osuna urged them at least to taste it. "I did already," Anthony told Chatman. "Let me see you do it again," she replied in her firm but pleasant manner. Andre was busy mixing his spinach and mashed potatoes, getting as much spinach on the table as in his mouth. One child spilled mashed potatoes on a Lion King's tail, but he didn't seem to notice. Finally it was time to hand out the candy. Marcus skipped out in delight and another Halloween at Head Start was history.

Chapter Two

Stonewall, Texas: How It All Began

 lashback to 1970.

Every schoolday four-year-old Elena Bravo and her little sister Lourdes, only three then, crossed the river near their Texas home to go to Head Start. There they would play and sing, start to count, and learn the alphabet. They also received help speaking English. They got their shots—"That was scary"—and sometimes, being little, they cried. It was hard for their mother, Socorro, to have her babies leave home each day, but the owner of the ranch where the family lived encouraged her. "He said it was important for us to go. It would help us and it was good that we go early, when we were so little," Lourdes recalled.

The river the children crossed was the Pedernales. The Head Start center was in Stonewall in the Texas Hill Country. And the persuasive ranch owner was, of course, Lyndon Baines Johnson. Five years earlier, as president, he had launched Head Start nationally. It took a bit longer for even this master arm-twister to convince his own conservative community to create a center, but in January 1969, just as Johnson was leaving the White House, Head Start opened its doors in a modest little building on the grounds of Trinity Lutheran Church. Today you can stand on the front step of the Stonewall Head Start and look a short distance across the river to the small, tree-shaded family cemetery in which Johnson was buried in 1973.

I was drawn to Stonewall because I had heard that Lyndon Johnson visited that Head Start center often after he left the White House. I wanted to write about the vision that Johnson and those who had planned Head Start had about trying to lift children out of poverty. What better point to start exploring that history than at the place where Johnson had the most personal contact with his creation? What had it meant to him, and would he have dreamed it would still be needed decades after his death?

During the Johnsons' White House years, it was Lady Bird Johnson, the president's wife and honorary Head Start chairman, who visited the centers. The president himself had less and less time for the war on poverty as the war in Vietnam absorbed his energy. Once back at the LBJ Ranch after he retired, however, he would often drop by the local Head Start program unannounced. The center is only a mile from the ranch house, a three-minute drive at best. Mary Beth Kendrick, often at the center because her mother taught for Head Start, remembered Johnson not as a celebrity but rather as the man who played with her and her friends when she was little. "He made us feel like we were the center of our world."

Elena Bravo Rodriguez, who later taught for five years at the Stonewall center, accompanied her Head Start class one Christmas to what everyone in the ranch area refers to as "the birthplace." That's a one-story white frame house on the ranch that was reconstructed on the site of the home in which Johnson was born in 1908. "We decorated a Christmas tree and hung ornaments in the house. Mr. Johnson came and people were taking pictures and he gave us all jelly beans."

He always had pockets full of jelly beans—so much so that a book was written about him called *Mr. Jellybean*. A far cry from the image that must have so wounded Johnson—no Vietnam War protesters there, with their chants of "Hey, hey, LBJ. How many kids did you kill today?" This was a lifelong politician with an intense desire to leave his mark on history, and he was saddened to see the programs he had created shunted off and sometimes completely shuttered by his successor, Richard Nixon. So it was all the more natural for him to seek contact with one of his programs that worked. Sometimes the former president's arms were loaded with toys for the children when he went to the center. Most often he showed up by himself, not for photo opportunities, but to see how the program was progressing. "He was in and out. He knew what we were doing," one former teacher said, but she added that "he never, ever tried to tell us how to do our work."

Sometimes Johnson, whose hair had grown long by then, would ford the Pedernales in his white Lincoln Continental, call out to the children to "pile in," and off they'd go up the ranch road to Weinheimer's grocery store to buy candy. That he was the former president was not an issue to these children. "He was a nice, jolly man who liked to come and play with us," Kendrick said. "He'd come by himself, and we'd say, 'There's Mr. Johnson, let's go play.'"

"When he came, everyone crawled all over him like a grandpa. All teaching stopped. We didn't interfere, though, because we thought that was important, too," said Kendrick's mother, Mary Lindig, who taught at the center at the time. She had started taking Mary Beth with her when her daughter was two years old.

Johnson "kept up with every single detail," Lindig said, recalling one example. She had previously taught high school English, history, and music, and had decided she needed some brushing up on early-childhood education when she started working with Head Start. She was taking a course several afternoons a week at the University of Texas in Austin. She also ran an afternoon program for about twelve of the children whose parents worked at the LBJ Ranch, the vast Hill Country retreat on which the former president raised prize cattle and which he had used as the Texas White House while he was in office. Austin is more than an hour's drive from Stonewall, so Lindig regularly arranged for a substitute to look after the children in her absence. Evidently she had mentioned taking the class to Johnson because not long after one of his visits to the center, Lindig received a telephone call. "Miss Mary, this is Luci," said the former president's younger daughter, who was living in Austin. "My daddy says you have to go to school and he wanted me to come and sit with the children this afternoon."

Knowing the children could be a handful, Lindig tried to protest. "But Luci, I have to be there by one o'clock." The president's daughter said that was no problem; her father had assured her she could get there. "He ordered the helicopter and the helicopter flew her in and she did well." The minister from the church came over to help and everyone had a fine afternoon.

In those days, the Head Start program was housed in what had been the church's choir and Sunday-school room across from its sanctuary. It was a small, old, drafty building with linoleum floors. On one of his visits, Johnson took a look at the linoleum. "You need something warm on this floor," he announced. A few days later a truck drove up loaded with a rug with long, looped—and impractical—pile. Down it went. "It was a rug and it was warm and that was what was important," Lindig recalled, "but we lost many a crayon down in that pile."

Johnson always had his eye out for what the little center needed because he had helped set it up. Head Start had been overwhelmed with applicants when the program began in the summer of 1965, but community organizations in Stonewall weren't among them. Gillespie County was heavily conservative and the president had to do a selling job to get the community to buy into a government antipoverty effort. By 1968 there was still no Head Start center although there were many poor white and Mexican American children in the area who qualified for the program.

Meantime, Trinity Lutheran Church, just off U.S. 290 near the ranch, had a pastor who was starting his ministry, Norman Truesdell. Johnson enjoyed his company, occasionally attending his church and often having Truesdell and his wife, Marlene, come to the ranch for dinner, riding, or a movie in the converted hangar. The subject of Head Start came up during the visits in that summer and fall of 1968. Truesdell felt there was a need for the program locally; his wife, who had been a kindergarten teacher, agreed. The Reverend Wunibald W. Schneider, the priest at St. Francis Xavier Catholic Church, also in Stonewall, often was involved in these conversations at the ranch as well.

Truesdell took an informal survey that confirmed his feeling that there were children in Stonewall and down the road in Johnson City who could benefit. He told Johnson about his findings one night at dinner. The president was more than receptive; it was *his* program, after all, and he obviously wanted a center for the children of workers living on his ranch, too. "Well, if you lit a match," Truesdell said of Johnson, "look out, he was going to get a gallon of gasoline and get the fire started." Application forms were delivered the next day. When Truesdell looked over the papers, he realized he didn't always understand what information was being sought. So Johnson, still in office then, took Truesdell, his wife, and Father Schneider to Washington in mid-October to meet with the people at the antipoverty agency who had written the forms. The Truesdells and Schneider stayed several nights at the White House, then said good-bye in the Oval Office and headed home to gear up for Head Start. Trinity Lutheran's congregation donated the space.

By mid-December, the local weekly newspaper headlined joint church services dedicating the Stonewall Head Start program "in an atmosphere of ecumenism in keeping with the Christmas season."[1] With the Johnsons sitting in the fourth-row pew at Trinity Lutheran, more than three hundred people heard Truesdell and Schneider offer prayers and Scripture readings. Higher-ups from the Lutheran and Catholic churches shared the pulpit as well. The Reverend James Otterness, a vice president of the American Lutheran Church, paraphrased the apostle Paul, saying that if the Mexican American children who would attend the new Head Start program "can go to school and learn just five words, it is better than hearing 10,000 words they don't understand." Noting the poverty in the area, Otterness added: "Here you are right next to the ranch of the President and you wonder if these things exist here. And I'm afraid they do."[2]

Stonewall's was the first Head Start center in the immediate area. "Once the community saw Stonewall and saw that we weren't going to collapse the churches, Fredericksburg and other areas got Head Start, too," Truesdell said.

The center opened in January, just two weeks before Johnson left the presidency. Marlene Truesdell was the center's first teacher, and about twenty children enrolled. "President Johnson was extremely interested," she recalled. "Once, I mentioned to him that it would be really nice to get a sandbox. He had an architect design us a beautiful stone sandbox. I doubt there was any other center had as nice a sandbox."

Johnson also cajoled his daughter Luci into expanding to Stonewall the vision-screening program that she had organized in the Austin area by about 1970. "He said I was screening every other child in Texas but not 'his'—they were always 'his'—and was I discriminating against them?" Luci Baines Johnson said. Even though Stonewall was beyond the geographic range of the Austin program, "it was easier to do it than to not."

Luci Johnson had helped conduct vision screenings in inner-city Washington during Head Start's first summer, when she was eighteen. The auxiliary of the American Optometric Association had established the Volunteers for Vision program there and in other Head Start locations. Luci volunteered not only because the program was an initiative of her father's administration but also because she had had a vision problem herself. "My life was completely salvaged by having that developmental vision problem solved. I went from an unsuccessful, unhappy, frustrated student to eventually a very successful college career." Her experience made her realize that if she, the daughter of a president of the United States, could have this problem and suffer from it, what about the children of other parents? "It was an ideal way for me— Luci—to support Head Start. I'd been there. I knew the price. I knew what having a poorly functioning visual system meant."

Head Start, for the Johnsons, was "a family affair. It was a bit like working on the family farm," said Luci Johnson. "Instead of raising corn and alfalfa, we raised hopes and opportunities. My father thought that the passport out of poverty was education. If you started school on an uneven plane, it was like starting a race with your shoelaces tied together. . . . If you had your physical, emotional, and psychological distractions resolved, you could take advantage of those educational opportunities afforded to you. If not, you would be defeated before you ever began."

Lady Bird Johnson has reminisced that some of her husband's happiest hours in retirement were spent dropping in on the little Head Start center across the river from the ranch. Head Start brightened his days in other ways. "I remember one really hot day when everything was going wrong at the ranch. We hadn't had any rain for weeks and none was in sight. The irrigation system had broken down and all day men had been trying to get the heavy irrigation pipes through the fields. Lyndon was thoroughly exasperated, and exploded, 'This has been an awful day!'

" 'Oh, no, sir,' one of the men who had been helping spoke up. 'This has been a wonderful day. My little boy came home from Head Start today and he has already learned how to write his name.' "[3]

By 1996, there were fifty children, Anglo and Mexican American, attending the Stonewall center. The majority were enrolled in Head Start, but there were also several in a community preschool program that Johnson insisted be set up so that all the children in the area could benefit from the center; those children paid a modest tuition. There were four teachers and four aides. One of those teachers was Lucy Bravo, who had attended Head Start not long after her older sisters Elena and Lourdes. The original building now houses the program offices; the center also has a small building and the church's large fellowship hall for its four classrooms on the grounds shaded by live oak and pecan trees. The center backs onto a state park and Trinity Lutheran's own small cemetery. It is a place of rural tranquillity utterly different from the streets of Watts or Kansas City or Baltimore. Cars pass only occasionally on the narrow ranch road. Across the river, cattle graze on the LBJ Ranch.

"The setting is part of our success. It's like going to Grandma's house," said Margie Sultemeier, executive director of Head Start programs at Stonewall, Fredericksburg, and Harper. Sultemeier herself has ties to the LBJ Ranch. She married a ranch hand who worked for the

Johnsons; their wedding gift from President and Mrs. Johnson was a honeymoon at the White House. She had volunteered at the center years ago and became the program director in 1990.

In one of the Stonewall classrooms one morning, a little blond boy was getting special attention from his teacher as he drew a picture while the aide was reading a story to his classmates. In another room, children were making pumpkins out of orange Play-Doh. In a playroom, children were having their recreation period indoors because of a misty rain and fog covering the Hill Country. They danced around in a circle with their teacher and aide. Later all the children gathered around little tables outside the gleaming kitchen and had a lunch of burritos, corn on the cob, and an apple that the cook had cored and sliced for each of them.

"When I started here," Sultemeier said, "I realized that we had some children who were second-generation Head Start. At first I was quite excited about that"—that their parents had seen the need for the program because they had been in Head Start themselves. "But then I said, 'Hold on, that's not a good sign. Head Start is supposed to help families out of poverty.' But today both parents work and the family is still not out of poverty. I came to realize that they are still poor, but they are better off than when they were children." It was a refrain I heard in Alabama and elsewhere around the country. It reflects the realization that poverty may be deeply entrenched but it can be alleviated. Many can even escape its grip.

History sometimes seems serendipitous: at the right time, trends and tasks, leaders and money, just come together. The effort against poverty and the president who led it reflect a touch of that almost accidental good fortune. It is also true, however, that American attitudes and policies regarding education and the welfare of young children and the poor had evolved over decades so that all was in readiness by the mid-twentieth century: an ambitious man, an economy for the moment robust, and public concern coincided in an unprecedented attempt to lift all boats. To continue the nautical metaphor momentarily, the ship foundered, but not because it was unseaworthy; it sank under fire from real torpedoes in a real war. The economic seas also were not as well charted as anticipated.

What was the context for the task the Johnson administration undertook? In education, in policies concerning young children and the poor, it took the relentless, often inspired work of many men and especially women in public-spirited organizations to change attitudes and enact reforms. Yet in each policy area there was also deep ambivalence toward the power of government. We Americans, for example, have never been quite sure how much we want the federal government involved with our children's educations. We usually say, "No, thanks," except when we really can't—or won't—do something ourselves. Many of our forebears settled on this continent, after all, because they didn't like all-powerful kings and fiats from far away.

In the early days of America, most children who were taught at all were taught at home. Children needed to do basic sums and be able to read the Bible for themselves if the economic independence and religious freedom the colonists sought were to be maintained. Only a few—and generally only boys—received much formal education, however, because children were needed to help their parents raise crops, store food, and make clothes and household necessities. By the time America started expanding westward, however, the settlers wanted to better themselves; that meant more schools for more children. Land— 98.5 million acres of federal land—was given to states to support public schools.[4] Even with this major federal support for public schooling, each community hired its own teacher; education at the classroom level was never considered a national government function. The significant and unfortunate exception was schooling for American Indian children, which after the 1870s and well into the twentieth century often took them to boarding schools away from their homes, their languages, and their cultures.

As public schooling expanded, several groups remained on the margins. Education for black children was provided in grossly inferior settings, especially in the racially segregated South. Girls often were not encouraged to finish high school or to aspire to college, nor were the poor, who often lived in communities that could not afford good schools or many textbooks. At the same time, though, education was considered the way to Americanize the European immigrants entering the country in the early days of the twentieth century. Many of them were steered toward vocational rather than academic courses.

The federal government paid more attention to education during World War II because the military found an alarming level of illiteracy among its potential troops. (Even in 1963 the President's Task Force on Manpower Conservation reported that 40 percent of draftees rejected for service were high school dropouts; another 40 percent had never even reached high school.)[5] The Lanham Act of 1940 also provided federal aid to "impacted areas"—school districts near military bases that didn't pay taxes but did swell the attendance rolls. Military policy continued to influence government involvement in education after the war; the GI Bill for federal scholarship aid gave returning service personnel the chance to go to college. Then in 1957, the Soviet Union launched its first Sputnik satellite. The public clamored to know why the nation's cold war enemy had gotten into space first. In the name of national security, Congress passed the National Defense Education Act in 1958 to increase financial support for teaching math, science, engineering, and foreign languages.

In 1954, the Supreme Court issued a major ruling that altered the course of American education. Separate schools for black and white students were held to be inherently unequal and could no longer be maintained. That decision profoundly affected American politics as well as its schools. By reason of political longevity, Southern Democrats held key chairmanships on Capitol Hill and thus had critical parts to play in congressional consideration of presidential initiatives. Their resistance to the decision in *Brown v. Board of Education* would affect their votes on measures concerning the federal role in education and other aspects of public policy for several decades.

But the world they were helping govern was changing. In the twenty years after World War II ended, 80 million babies were born, putting enormous pressure on local school systems and making communities more receptive to the possibilities of federal aid to education. Thus, when John F. Kennedy entered the White House in 1961, there was a growing sense that the federal government could play a larger role in public schools despite powerful Southern resistance. In 1961 and 1962, Kennedy unsuccessfully sought congressional passage of legislation that would provide federal aid for public school construction and teachers' salaries. In 1963 he introduced a more targeted education package that directed some of its aid not only to overcrowded schools and construction on college campuses but also to disadvantaged areas, both rural and urban. One key part of that legislation, the Higher Education Facilities Act of 1963, was making its way toward final passage when Kennedy was assassinated. Education experts have pointed out that even though federal aid to public schools and many other elements of Kennedy's legislative package failed that year, momentum was finally developing toward a new federal role in education. Kennedy's death would provide a surge of support for his initiatives in that direction, as it also did for passage of civil rights legislation. His proposals represented the first time since World War II that major federal aid to education was not based on national security interests.[6]

America frequently changed its mind about children's welfare as well. In early America, working-class children were often apprenticed to tradesmen with little consideration of their wishes or their physical well-being. Later, when production left the homes and small shops for factories, children were put to work for long hours and under grueling conditions in textile mills, garment-industry sweatshops, and coal mines. In the South, slaves' and later sharecroppers' children picked cotton or tobacco when they were barely large enough to carry a sack.

As more immigrants moved to America's cities, settlement houses—the most famous being Hull House in Chicago and Henry Street in New York—opened to provide education, health care, and recreation for the families as well as to crusade against their exploitation. Established in 1895 by Lillian Wald, the Nurses Settlement at 265 Henry Street, for example, sent public-health nurses into neighboring homes to provide care for those not ill enough to need hospitalization or to help convalescents released from hospitals. Care for infants and their mothers increased markedly after Congress first created a federal Children's Bureau in 1912, then passed the Sheppard-Towner Act in 1921. That law, based on mortality statistics gathered by the bureau and on public concern its leaders fostered among women's organizations, provided money for states to run clinics for pregnant women and mothers with infants. The development was all the more remarkable because preventive medicine did not receive the focus then that it does today.[7] The clinics soon ran afoul of organized medicine and the law expired in 1929, but the program showed what gains could be made. It could be considered a precursor of Head Start's emphasis on health care for children.

During this period, Congress passed two laws to reduce child labor, both of which a conservative Supreme Court declared unconstitutional. A proposed constitutional amendment to override those decisions was never ratified.

For the youngest children, care was almost always provided in the home, almost always by their mothers or older sisters and brothers—except in the case of the well-to-do, who hired nannies, and the very poor, who sometimes found care for their children in day nurseries or gave them up for adoption. The nation's first kindergarten—for German-speaking children—was established in Wisconsin in 1855 by Mrs. Carl Schurz, wife of the U.S. general and newspaperman. Five years later,

Elizabeth Peabody and her sister, Mary Mann, began a kindergarten for English-speaking children in Boston. By 1880 there were four hundred kindergartens in thirty states. But when Head Start began in 1965, only half of American children had kindergartens available to them. Nursery schools, for even younger children, had begun to develop in the early decades of the twentieth century but often were attached to universities or formed by parent cooperatives; few were available for the poorest children.

The federal government, ever wary of intruding into a realm of families and communities, crossed that line first because of economic crisis and then because of military necessity. In 1935, during the Great Depression, Congress passed the Social Security Act, which included aid to the states for children's health and welfare. In addition, the Works Progress Administration set up day care programs aimed more at providing jobs for out-of-work teachers than at helping child development. Nonetheless, they were *federal* day care centers; by 1934, 75,000 children were enrolled in 1,900 WPA nursery schools. Many were later closed as teachers once again found jobs, but during World War II production needs dictated that some of these centers be kept open for the children of working women. The Lanham Act sent money to local communities, many of which ran child care centers in public school buildings. Some 3,100 centers served about 140,000 children. All but a few of these programs were closed at war's end even though there still were 16 million women in the work force—2 million more than when the war started.[8]

The third strand of policy to explore in understanding how the antipoverty program developed is, of course, that involving the poor themselves. Americans have long divided the poor into two broad classes: those who cannot work and earn money because they are too young, too old, or too ill, and those who we feel should work but don't or won't. We try to help the former and often blame the latter for their situation. Over the centuries, private charities have given alms while public institutions have built poorhouses.[9] Missionaries moved into American slums with fervor during the country's Great Awakening before the Civil War to try to put the poor on the path to economic well-being by encouraging them to lead moral lives. Later, social workers probed into the lives of the poor in a country that otherwise enshrined the privacy of the home. Families have been supported, then broken up, then supported again, all in the space of a few decades as policies have changed.

Even during the Great Depression, ambivalence toward the role of government remained: President Franklin D. Roosevelt transferred relief programs back to states once the crisis abated, and the Social Security system that Congress passed exempted agricultural and domestic workers, two of the poorest groups who needed it the most but who had the least political clout. The jobs that Roosevelt created were generally intended to tide people over who had had work; the programs neither provided permanent employment nor trained people who lacked job skills. Nonetheless, the Roosevelt administration's program to combat the depression set a precedent for collective action when rugged individualism could not overcome economic hardship.

After World War II, the nation focused on European recovery as well as on its own prosperity. By the early 1960s, however, it became clear that many, especially black Americans, farmworkers, and children, did not share in the country's wealth. The 1960 census showed that 37 million Americans—one-fifth of the population—were impoverished; one-third of the poor were children. Nearly half of all nonwhites lived in poverty.[10]

John F. Kennedy had shown some readiness to focus on the question when, during his campaign for the presidency in August 1960, he used the phrase "war on poverty" during a speech at Hyde Park, New York, marking the twenty-fifth anniversary of the Social Security Act. In his inaugural address, Kennedy let the word go forth about the domestic as well as the foreign policy attitude of his administration, declaring: "If the free society cannot help the many who are poor, it cannot save the few who are rich."

Kennedy had seen the poverty of unemployed coal miners in West Virginia. He knew the economic statistics. And he and many other opinion leaders read the writers and thinkers who were spotlighting *The Other America*, as author Michael Harrington called it.[11] Harrington humanized poverty. He described people for whom struggle and sacrifice only made life worse, not better, people so beaten down that they saw a different America than the middle class knew. These were people who were illiterate, ill housed, poorly fed, often sick, out of work; their children died in infancy and their parents died too young. Their futures held only more of the same. Harrington's book, published in 1962, received a broader audience when it and others were reviewed in a *New Yorker* article, "Our Invisible Poor," by social critic Dwight Macdonald. "That in the last half century," Macdonald declared, "the rich have kept their riches and the poor their poverty is indeed a scandal." His conclusion: "The federal government is the only purposeful force—I assume wars are not purposeful—that can reduce the numbers of the poor and make their lives more bearable." Not only should the federal government stimulate the economy by increasing its spending, Macdonald wrote, it should also intervene directly to help the poor. "We have had this since the New Deal, but it has always been grudging and miserly, and we have never accepted the principle that every citizen should be provided, at state expense, with a reasonable minimum standard of living regardless of any other considerations."[12]

Throughout the 1950s, as Daniel P. Moynihan, who later became a U.S. senator, pointed out in his critique of the antipoverty program, intellectuals had been writing about the breakdown in community, the alienation of young people, the isolation of individuals, the sense that something was very wrong in the country and that government might be the only sufficiently large and powerful agent for change.[13] Also contributing to the climate of opinion, Moynihan wrote, was the growing role of philanthropic organizations—especially the Ford Foundation—in financing direct-action projects aimed at social change. Ford sponsored a four-and-a-half-year planning process designed to help local communities combat juvenile delinquency. That planning yielded a blueprint that in many ways, especially with its emphasis on community action, resembled the Economic Opportunity Act that launched the federal war on poverty.[14]

One of the last triggers for Kennedy administration action may have been a Homer Bigart article in the *New York Times* in October 1963.[15] From Whitesburg, Kentucky, Bigart wrote that the only ravages seen by people hurrying through this area where so many were out of work might be the damage strip mining had done to the land. "But to the sociologist, the erosion of the character of the people is more fearsome than the despoiling of the mountains," Bigart wrote, adding that the miners displaced by automation and changing fuel needs had a "native clannishness" that made moving to the city and adjusting to it painfully difficult. Bigart's article reminded Kennedy of the despair he had seen in Appalachia, and projects were quickly initiated for job training, food distribution, housing, and even a Christmas-vacation program using college students as a domestic Peace Corps in eastern Kentucky.

In preparing for his 1964 budget message, Kennedy decided that attacking poverty would be a keystone of his legislative program. He asked Walter Heller, his chief economic adviser, to study potential antipoverty programs. Where to lodge any program was a key question because of bureaucratic turf wars. What to call it was another because some people in the administration wanted to avoid the word "poverty." As a result, according to a history of the agency that emerged to lead the fight, "the war on poverty began as a 'prosperity' program." Pockets of poverty should be called "targets of opportunity."[16]

The civil rights movement arrived on Washington's doorstep in August 1963 when Dr. Martin Luther King, Jr., led the March for Jobs and Freedom, conceived by union leader A. Philip Randolph. In addition to the march, two more books—*Night Comes to the Cumberlands* by Harry Caudill and *The Wasted Americans* by Edgar May—underscored the problems of rural and urban poor. On October 21, 1963, Kennedy suggested that he might visit an impoverished area to give the issue more national visibility. His cabinet met October 29, and Kennedy left behind a memo pad with the word "poverty" written six times and the word "coordination" underlined twice and enclosed in a penciled box. Walter Heller last talked to Kennedy three days before he was assassinated in Dallas. Kennedy urged continued action to help government agencies reach a consensus on an antipoverty program. Did he want that measure to be part of his 1964 legislative program? Heller asked.

"His answer was an unhesitating 'yes,' " Heller said.[17]

Lyndon Johnson became president when Kennedy was shot to death November 22, 1963. The next day Heller asked Johnson if he wanted to continue the effort against poverty. "His immediate response was 'That's my kind of program. It's a people program,' " Heller said.[18]

Johnson had a particular affinity for the program, one holdover from the Kennedy administration said. "It's close to his roots. Where Kennedy may have had only an intellectual appreciation of the need to eradicate poverty, Johnson had a 'gut' reaction to the basic idea."[19] As a boy growing up in Texas, he and his family had known hard times when his father's ill-conceived venture into growing cotton went bust. At twenty, Johnson had had to drop out of college to earn money to pay for his education. He did so by teaching at the Welhausen Elementary School amid the shanties in Cotulla, sixty miles north of the Mexican border. Teaching the Mexican American children there, the president said many years later, taught him "the high price of poverty and prejudice." For too long, he said, America's conscience had slept "while the children of Mexican Americans have been taught that the end of life is a beet row or a spinach patch."[20] Johnson wanted to make a difference for children like those he had known in Cotulla. What long experience had brought firsthand to Johnson, Senator John F. Kennedy, the son of a rich man, had had to go to West Virginia to learn.

Johnson also wanted to undertake a program that would be his own and would set his administration apart from Kennedy's. As he told his old friend Elizabeth Wickenden not long after he took office, "I have a very difficult problem. I feel a moral obligation to finish the things that JFK proposed. But I also have to find issues that I can take on as my own." So, Wickenden added, "he came to this poverty program—making it nationwide. He didn't go into what it would do specifically. He said, 'I have to get re-elected in a year and a half, so I have to do something of my own.' "[21]

In his January 8, 1964, State of the Union speech, Johnson formally announced what would be his major domestic effort. "This administration today here and now declares unconditional war on poverty," he told the nation's lawmakers and its people, "and I urge this Congress and all Americans to join with me in that effort. It will not be a short or easy struggle—no single weapon or strategy will suffice—but we shall not rest until that war is won. The richest nation on earth can afford to win it. We cannot afford to lose it." To find the money for an anti-poverty program, Johnson told Defense Secretary Robert McNamara to cut defense production costs. He also called for a hold on federal jobs so that the money could be shifted to the new projects.[22]

The president had to quash turf wars within his own administration because the Department of Labor and the Department of Health, Education, and Welfare each thought it should run parts of the new program. But Johnson felt that "the best way to kill a new idea is to put it in an old-line agency." He wanted his War on Poverty to have coordinated leadership and direction.[23] Johnson soon convinced Sargent Shriver, Kennedy's brother-in-law and head of the Peace Corps, to take on the job as his "personal chief of staff in the war on poverty" as well.

That very day, Shriver invited Michael Harrington to come to Washington. At lunch, Shriver said to Harrington: "Now you tell me how to abolish poverty."

Ever the critic, Harrington replied, "You've got to understand right away that you've been given nickels and dimes for this program. You'll have less than a billion dollars to work with."

"Well," said Shriver, "I don't know about you, Mr. Harrington, but this will be my first experience at spending a billion dollars, and I'm quite excited about it."[24]

That was Sargent Shriver. Quick. Positive. And flying by the seat of his pants for the next few weeks as a task force he assembled tried to answer the question he had asked. That the task force included no representatives of the people most directly concerned—the poor—and was composed almost entirely of white men underscores the sea change in American attitudes and practices that has occurred since then. In no small measure that change was spurred by the antipoverty program that emerged from that task force. On March 16, 1964, President Johnson proposed the legislation that would establish a Job Corps, authorize community action programs, provide loans to farmers and to businesses that would hire the chronically unemployed, create the Volunteers in Service to America, and set up the Office of Economic Opportunity to direct these initiatives.

The War on Poverty attacked symptoms more than causes. From within the Johnson administration, Labor Secretary Willard Wirtz thought there should be more emphasis on jobs; they produced income, and he could see little income and few lasting jobs in the community action program.[25] At one cabinet meeting at which Wirtz presented his viewpoints, Johnson ignored him, made no response, moved right on to the next item on the agenda.[26] Following Wirtz's approach would have meant taking a hard look at an economy that was on the surface looking good.

From the outside, organizer Saul Alinsky thought too much power would still reside in city halls, banks, and corporations. Changing that alignment would have meant taking a hard, and politically offensive, look at their concern for the poor. The victims—poor people—weren't exactly being blamed in this case, but it was they who would have to change, not the system.

Political momentum, however, was on Johnson's side. He was still seen as the successor of the slain young president, grappling with a major issue. Republicans were hard-pressed to oppose a war on poverty in an election year. They did contend that the plan was a stale rehash of programs that had been considered before and rejected, but those programs had not been submitted by Lyndon Johnson. No one knew how to work the legislative process better than this former Senate majority leader. Conservatives said poverty was the fault of the poor and couldn't be fixed. "The fact is," said Senator Barry Goldwater of Arizona, who would be the Republican presidential nominee that fall, "that most people who have no skill, have had no education for the same reason—low intelligence or low ambition." In American society, Goldwater went on, people receive rewards by "merit and not by fiat."[27]

Despite this grumbling, the House passed the Economic Opportunity Act, 226–114, on August 8, 1964, and the Senate followed, 61–34, three days later. On August 20, Johnson signed the measure, his first major legislation passed by Congress since he had taken over the presidency. Congress appropriated $800 million for the effort and the Office of Economic Opportunity (OEO) began its formal operation October 8.

Head Start, one of the few survivors of this war on poverty, was not among its original troops. It was not mentioned in the Economic Opportunity Act, but there could be no question of the need for a program for children. The estimates were that one-third of the nation's poor were children; 6 million of them were six years old or younger.

Today, when many more people have television sets and so can see more of the world even if they do not share in its wealth, it is hard to conjure up the isolation and desolation of many poor children and their families in the 1960s. They often did not know how others lived or to what they might aspire. They lived in homes with no heat and with holes in the roof or the floor. Their drinking water came from a metal drum outside that collected the rain—and with that drinking water came disease. Urban or rural, they might never have seen a doctor, nor had their mothers while they were pregnant. They lived amid peeling paint in big-city tenements or pesticides sprayed on nearby cotton fields. They cried themselves to sleep at night because they were hungry, and their parents wept, too, at the sound. Often their mothers and fathers had little schooling, so they could not read to their children; sometimes they rarely talked to them. When children started school, they might be unable to see the blackboard because no one had ever checked their eyesight. They might not be able to hear the teacher well because no one had checked their hearing. And with necessities missing at home, there was no time or energy or money to encourage the joys of learning. Head Start planners heard early on of many children who had "never used cut-out scissors, looked at a picture book, or scribbled with a crayon, been told a fairy story, been coaxed into completing a simple task successfully, or been talked to as human beings."[28]

The Freedom Schools operated in Mississippi by civil rights workers in the violent summer of 1964 showed the hunger poor people felt for this head start. Black children of all ages attended classes where their teachers helped them shape their aspirations and learn that they could challenge white America for not sharing the nation's abundance and opportunities. The schools gave these young people a chance, often for the first time, to voice their own ideas and form their own questions.

The teachers sensed a rising excitement about learning. While Freedom Schools taught children from toddlers to teenagers, not just preschoolers as Head Start would do, there can be no doubt that they showed poor people what they could do themselves. They created possibilities in lives that had had few, and they helped pave the way for Head Start.

As Shriver met with senior staff at the Office of Economic Opportunity in the fall of 1964, he was concerned that there would be no concrete program in place by the following summer to show the press. "From the moment the War on Poverty had begun . . . there were many elements in the Congress and everywhere else attempting to shoot it down," Polly Greenberg, one of the staff assistants, recalled.[29] Shriver looked at a pie chart of the nation's poverty population and saw that the biggest chunk was children. He realized that if there was a War on Poverty "and we don't have programs specifically aimed at children, nobody can say we're having a war to help the most numerous victims of poverty. It's just as if you had a war to conquer Germany and you didn't drop any bombs on the German soldiers—you wouldn't be conducting the war intelligently."[30]

No matter how intelligent a policy may seem in the abstract, there are almost always personal reasons as well that individuals take up a cause or a program. Shriver was no exception. He had served as president of the school board in Chicago, where he had seen "how the cards are stacked against kids in the slums in a huge number of ways."[31] Shriver and his wife Eunice also had worked for years on issues involving mental retardation. Her sister Rosemary Kennedy had been institutionalized because of mental illness. The Joseph P. Kennedy, Jr., Foundation, with which the Shrivers were associated, had financed a project by Susan Gray of the George Peabody Teachers College in Tennessee which showed that early intervention with three-, four-, and five-year-old retarded children living in underprivileged areas could raise the children's IQs. Shriver was also aware of research showing that malnutrition affected mental development. He wondered, therefore, if early intervention and better nutrition would help children who were not mentally handicapped but retarded by virtue of their poverty, so he asked Richard Boone of the OEO staff to look into that question.[32] Boone quickly pulled together a planning committee headed by Dr. Robert Cooke of Johns Hopkins Medical School, the Shriver family pediatrician.

It is worth noting the makeup of that committee because it greatly affected the direction Head Start took toward a comprehensive program involving health and social services as well as education:

- Dr. Robert E. Cooke was the chief pediatrician at Johns Hopkins Hospital.
- Dr. Mamie Phipps Clark was executive director of a New York City child development center and the wife of noted educator Kenneth Clark.
- Dr. George B. Brain was dean of the School of Education at Washington State University and former superintendent of schools in Baltimore.
- Dr. Urie Bronfenbrenner was a social psychologist at Cornell University.
- Dr. Edward P. Crump was professor of pediatrics at Meharry Medical College.
- Dr. Edward Davens was acting commissioner of health in Maryland.
- Mitchell I. Ginsberg was associate dean of Columbia University's School of Social Work.
- Dr. James L. Hymes, Jr., was chairman of the early childhood education department at the University of Maryland.
- Dr. Reginald S. Lourie was director of psychiatry at Children's Hospital in Washington.
- Dr. Mary King Kneedler was an assistant professor at the Development Evaluation Center at Western Carolina College.
- John H. Niemeyer was president of the Bank Street College of Education.
- Dr. Myron E. Wegman was dean of the University of Michigan School of Public Health.
- Sister Jacqueline Wexler was president of Webster College.
- Dr. Edward Zigler was a Yale University psychology professor and chaired his department's child development program.

As Shriver was learning, the field of child development on which many of these professionals concentrated had undergone marked changes in perspective in the twentieth century alone. By the early 1960s researchers such as J. McVicker Hunt and Benjamin Bloom had put to rest the theory that heredity determined intelligence, which therefore was immutable. Scholars saw that a more nurturing environment, as well as education in which parents were deeply involved, helped children increase their achievement and develop the self-confidence that can lead to success in school. Susan Gray's project in Nashville was one of several showing the value of early intervention with young children.[33]

The Cooke committee met diligently, with Jule Sugarman, an administrator who had been on the task force that drew up plans for OEO, shepherding the process. Shriver was also talking to experts. One suggested that the best the government might realistically hope to bring off and evaluate was a program for 2,500 children; even that might be a stretch because of the difficulty in finding qualified teachers. That recommendation discouraged Shriver. "It would be stupid for us to try to reach only 2,500 children, considering the size of the population we were dealing with," he thought. "We were talking about a million children nationwide who were living in poverty. . . . We had to devise programs that could have mass application, mass effectiveness."[34] Not only would a program for 2,500 children have been too small to have any big impact on poverty; it would also have been unable to garner political support in the communities that didn't win any grants. Shriver knew his boss well enough to know that Johnson wanted big and bold programs that would "hit the whole nation with real impact."[35] And Shriver knew his politics well enough to know that a highly desirable program for children might divert some of the criticism already being leveled at the new community action agencies, which were seen as a threat by mayors and other local politicians. Head Start would also be a way to "overcome a lot of hostility in our society against the poor in general and against black people who are poor in particular, by going at the children."[36] Shriver, the master political salesman, always spoke of Head Start, and of the entire War on Poverty, as offering the poor "a hand up, not a handout."

In only a few weeks the Cooke committee reported that a comprehensive program for preschool children was not only needed, it could be done and should be started that summer as the first step toward a full-year program. Reporting to Shriver, the committee suggested launching about 300 programs serving 100,000 children. When Shriver received the report, he asked Sugarman what it would cost.

"Of course, we hadn't figured the cost at all," Sugarman recalled, "and I said, 'Well, I'll look into it and let you know.'

"He said, 'Fine, you have an hour!' So another fellow and I sat down over lunch, and we figured out what Head Start was going to cost in the summer." They estimated $180 per child for the summer; the program that summer averaged $186 per child.[37]

What the planners underestimated was the size, because they under-estimated how heartily the public and the president would embrace the program. Shriver wrote to school and welfare officials around the country telling them about the program, and responses trickled in. Soon, however, a mailbag full of cards was dumped on the table. "Instead of 300 communities, we had that summer over 3,300 communities involved in the program," Sugarman said, "and instead of 100,000 children we had 560,000 children."

Nobody had a name for this new program. Shriver had been talking about a "kiddie corps," and Judah Drob of the training staff suggested Head Start one day at a brainstorming session.[38] Shriver knew that many children started school having never been in a school building before. They might not have the right clothes or the right haircut, and they hadn't been away from home or held a piece of chalk. It was frightening, and no wonder they fared poorly. "We figured, we'll get these kids into school ahead of time," he said; "we'll give them food; we'll give them medical exams; we'll give them the shots or the glasses they need; we'll give them some acculturation to academic work—we'll give them . . . a *head start.*"[39]

Lady Bird Johnson became directly involved with Head Start from the outset. She and Shriver met with a small group of social workers at the White House in January to discuss the concept. That night Mrs. Johnson wrote in her diary: "The Head Start idea has such *hope* and challenge. Maybe I could help focus public attention in a favorable way on some aspects of Lyndon's poverty program."[40]

On February 12, 1965, Mrs. Johnson hosted a tea in the Red Room of the White House to help launch the program. Prominent women from business and entertainment attended, as well as a number of governors' wives. "Do you think we can make it work?" she asked the group. Health, Education, and Welfare Secretary Anthony Celebrezze answered with a story about the effects of taking extra effort with young people. Years ago in Cleveland, he said, there had been a group of boys who could easily have gotten into trouble but a teacher formed them into a club. They played basketball and had debates on civic issues. " 'In the years since then,' " Mrs. Johnson recalled Celebrezze saying, " 'one of the men has become a judge, three are lawyers, one is an architect, one a doctor, one a dentist, two are CPAs, and one was the mayor of Cleveland and now sits in the president's cabinet.' You had only to look at Mr. Celebrezze to know he had lived this story," Mrs. Johnson recalled.[41]

After her guests left, Mrs. Johnson was asked by Shriver to be honorary chairman for Head Start. Yes, she replied, but she wanted to be more than a figurehead. She wanted to work at it, which she did by helping corral volunteers, visiting Head Start centers, and focusing press attention on the program.

Given the inadequate news coverage of Head Start today, it is interesting to note that early stories about the program often ran on what were then "the society pages." That placement helped create the image of "an acceptable, nice program in the public mind," Jule Sugarman recalled. "While community action . . . was being bloodied every day on the front page, Head Start was receiving glowing tributes in the society and community-news pages from local establishment leaders."[42]

Mail was pouring in. The program's small staff faced selecting the areas that would operate Head Start centers, and finding or training teachers who could work with young children. Shriver recruited Dr. Julius B. Richmond, a pediatrician who had just been named dean of the medical faculty at the State University of New York in Syracuse, as director of Head Start. Richmond's work had come to Shriver's attention because of a program he and Dr. Bettye Caldwell had set up in Syracuse. They had noted that all children seemed to develop at the same pace in their first year of life, but then poor children's development declined once they started trying to use language and explore their surroundings. With early intervention in a stimulating environment, Richmond and his colleague found, the decline could be prevented.[43] Richmond and Jule Sugarman, who became Richmond's deputy, set up shop in the basement of the only space that could be found—a condemned brick hotel building, long since torn down, across from the Madison Hotel in Washington, D.C. Bushel baskets full of applications covered the floors.

Although Head Start wasn't mentioned in the legislation that launched the fight against poverty, it fit easily under the section establishing community action agencies. These agencies received preference in deciding who should run the local Head Start centers. Richard Boone, the Office of Economic Opportunity's director of policy planning and development, had gotten a phrase requiring "maximum feasible participation of the poor" written into the Economic Opportunity Act, and he was its principal advocate. As Polly Greenberg, who worked for OEO, has written, "Sargent Shriver was unarguably Head Start's primary parent. But Head Start had two parents. Because CAP [community action program] people, most of whom were devout believers in maximum feasible participation of the poor and the importance of providing varied and plentiful opportunities to people poised to benefit from them, did the staff work for Sargent Shriver, they wrote into the Head Start plan requirements for heavy parent participation at every program level—on the local government board, in program planning, as volunteers, and in paid jobs through the program." That emphasis, she added, made Head Start a maverick. "And a political survivor." Boone has never gotten the credit he deserved for his role, Greenberg contended, because he later fought against efforts to destroy a pioneering Mississippi program (see chapter 3).[44]

Over the years, community action agencies have continued to run many Head Start centers, keeping alive the planners' notion that this program was broader than education, as vital as that was. Today only about 19 percent of Head Start programs are operated by local school systems. The vast majority are run by nonprofit, nongovernmental agencies in settings as varied as church basements, well-equipped new buildings, or former stores in cities and rural areas, on Indian reservations, and in migrant labor camps. From the outset, the program included health care, social services for families, and attempts to involve parents more closely in children's education. In short, it was a community action program, not solely a school program. In 1965, some school systems were not interested in operating integrated programs or receiving federal money with strings attached. Some also had little in the way of kindergarten, let alone preschool programs; others were viewed as distinctly inhospitable places for fostering parent participation. Head Start's planners felt that freestanding community programs offered greater flexibility than did school systems with cumbersome layers of bureaucracy.

Facing a mountain of applications that spring of 1965, Head Start nonetheless wanted to be sure its centers were located in areas "that were really poor, places where federal programs never seem to get started," Sugarman said. There was no time for painstaking community organizing because the first grants were to be announced in a few months. So Head Start asked 125 young management interns from various federal agencies who were willing to give up their weekends for six weeks "to go out to the 300 poorest counties in the United States to help them write an application." Head Start provided a crash course at night to train the interns in what communities needed to know about budgets and management of the program, then paired them with university professionals and paid their way to sit down with local people and prepare their proposals. "As a result, 225 of the 300 poorest counties were actually in the program that summer." Mrs. Johnson helped out by generating interest among cabinet and congressional wives, who used their contacts around the country, calling and staying on the phone until they found someone willing to talk about Head Start.[45]

The process generated 3,300 applications, which had to be processed in six weeks. "We couldn't hire several hundred people to do this processing and then keep them employed in Washington indefinitely," Richmond said. "There'd be no need for them after we got the programs funded. We thought, where do you get people who could work on a short-term basis that intensively? And I think it was Jule who got the idea, and it turned out to be a brilliant one, of tapping into the substitute teachers in the District who were generally not fully employed." One night after a meeting, Richmond took a professional associate back to the office where the "processing line" was hard at work on the grant applications. "The lights were blazing and people were working and things were really revved up by then. By this time it was about eleven o'clock at night." His friend's eyes popped. He hadn't seen anything like that since World War II.[46]

As the numbers of programs swelled, so did the need for teacher training. It was late March already, but Head Start signed contracts with 140 universities to establish six-day training programs, which that summer trained about forty-two thousand people.[47] Thousands of teachers were needed because of a small but significant decision, one that has stayed in force virtually unchanged. The suggestion had been made that Head Start have the same number of children per teacher that elementary schools had—about one teacher for twenty or thirty children. "No, we can't have that," Richmond said. He thought one trained teacher and two teaching assistants for each fifteen children was more appropriate, but his staff said, "You've just more than doubled the budget for teachers." To which Richmond replied, "Well, if it's necessary that we do a program for half as many children this first year, that's what we ought to do. I don't know whether we'll succeed if we have one teacher per fifteen children with two assistants, but I know we'll fail if it's one teacher with twenty or thirty children. One of the most important things about a new program is that it succeed and demonstrate success."[48] Today the ratio is generally one teacher and one aide to sixteen or seventeen three- and four-year-olds, with fewer children for teachers working with infants and toddlers.

Head Start did not need to reduce its scope because of Richmond's decision; money was not an object in those earliest days. The nation's economy was booming: profits had been up for four years in a row, auto sales were better than ever, and the gross national product had jumped 6.5 percent in 1964. The economy was enjoying its longest period of peacetime expansion—forty-seven months—in the nation's history.[49] So each time Richmond would up the ante, he would go to Shriver. "He'd say, 'Well, let me talk to the president,' and the next day he'd say, 'Fine.'"

"That illustrates one of the fantastic aspects of OEO," Shriver said. "I increased the funding by myself! I didn't have to go to Congress; I didn't have to go to the president; I didn't have to go to the Bureau of the Budget. Congress had appropriated money, and if I wanted to spend it on Head Start, I could spend it on Head Start. If I wanted to spend it on the Job Corps, I could spend it on the Job Corps. There are very few occasions in government history where any administrator of a program ever had the kind of freedom and power I had at OEO."[50] The legislation submitted to Congress had been vague because its drafters wanted to keep the program flexible; they had no idea what problems they would encounter. They also didn't want to make enemies on Capitol Hill by being too specific in what they would and would not do.[51] This landmark legislation was also enacted in what today would be record time. From submission to enactment, the Economic Opportunity Act was passed within five months. Many sections of the law had little or no legislative history, thus giving little direction to OEO and much discretion to its director.[52]

Today Head Start is moving toward working with children at younger and younger ages. But in those early days Richmond and his advisory committee faced the question of whether they wanted Head Start to cover children from birth to school age. No, they decided. They would concentrate on children in the year before they started school. "Not all schools across the country entered children at the same age because some had kindergartens and some didn't," Richmond said. "Only about half the children of the country at that time had kindergartens. So in some instances we were dealing with the four-year-olds where there were kindergartens, and other places we were dealing with the five-year-olds. . . . We felt that even though our resources were fairly good, if we distributed them thinly over all of the preschool years, we wouldn't have an impact on any one age period." Richmond also believed "that if we were going to impact on the children with a carryover to the school years, that it would be better if there were not a gap between the time they were in the program and the time in the school."[53]

The processing line did its job, and Head Start was ready to announce its first grants. On May 17, 1965, in a Rose Garden ceremony at the White House attended by four of the children who would be enrolling in Head Start, President Johnson stepped before reporters and cameras and proudly announced the new program. As many as one-half million children would receive preschool training and medical and dental attention that summer. Their parents would receive counseling on improving the home environment.[54]

> This is a very proud occasion . . . because it was less than three months ago that we opened a new war front on poverty. We set out to make certain that poverty's children would not be forevermore poverty's captives. We called our program Project Head Start. The program was conceived not so much as a federal effort but really as a neighborhood effort, and the response we have received from the neighborhoods and the communities has been the most stirring and the most enthusiastic of any peacetime program that I can remember. . . .
>
> I believe this response reflects the realistic and wholesome awakening in America. It shows that we are recognizing that poverty perpetuates itself. Five- and six-year-old children are inheritors of poverty's curse and not its creators. Unless we act these children will pass it on to the next generation, like a family birthmark. This program this year means that 30 million man years—the combined lifespan of these youngsters—will be spent productively and rewardingly, rather than wasted in tax-supported institutions or in welfare-supported lethargy.
>
> I believe that this is one of the most constructive, and one of the most sensible, and also one of the most exciting programs that this nation has ever undertaken. I don't say that because the most ardent and most active and most enthusiastic supporter of this program happens to be the honorary national chairman, Mrs. Johnson. We are taking up the age-old challenge of poverty and we don't intend to lose generations of our children to this enemy of the human race.
>
> This program, like some of the others, will succeed in proportion as it is supported by voluntary assistance and understanding from all of our people. So we are going to need a million good neighbors—volunteers—who will give their time for a few hours each week caring for these children, helping in a hundred ways to draw out their potentials. We need housewives and coeds. We need teachers and doctors. We need men and women

of all walks and all interests to lend their talents, their warmth, their hands, and their hearts. The bread that is cast upon these waters will surely return many thousandfold.[55]

Johnson could not know that he had just summed up several of the reasons Head Start would last well beyond his own lifetime. First, it allowed for local initiatives on the kind of programs communities wanted. Second, by involving parents it would not be seen as interfering with family prerogatives but rather as providing family assistance. And third, by incorporating parents and other community people as volunteers, it would build its own lobby that would take action when future administrations threatened cuts or major changes in the program.

More broadly, Head Start would last because President Johnson got it out there while the getting was good. He had come into the presidency in his own right with a landslide vote and a heavily Democratic Congress the previous November, and he knew there was a limited time to put programs into place. Indeed, in the 1966 congressional elections, some forty-five supporters of the antipoverty program in the House were defeated.[56] The magnitude of Head Start's accomplishment was borne out years later when former cabinet secretary John W. Gardner commented that its revolutionary impact had never been fully appreciated. "We will never, never go back to the pre–Head Start delusion that we can provide all children with equal opportunity by simply enrolling them in first grade at the age of six. We now know that by that time some children have fallen irreparably behind. That is an advance in our understanding that never will be reversed."[57]

At the same time, however, the president in his address launching the program may have also planted the seeds of future discontent by overpromising the results. Because of one summer program, thousands of children were not suddenly going to emerge from poverty. Once the program was lengthened and solidified, they would, as will be seen in this book, have a head start on learning and prospering, but there could be no guarantees. Broader, more lasting strategies for combating poverty would be needed, and with them, greater national will to do so.

As Johnson spoke at the White House, Head Start centers across the country were enrolling children, hiring teachers, finding classroom space. Head Start's art director designed a flag with a big arrow pointing upward (he favored ladders and arrows, rejecting flaming torches and flexed arms as "totalitarian heroic"). The suggestion was made that

Mrs. Johnson raise one of the flags on the south lawn of the White House to help kick off the project on June 30. Such a flag-raising ceremony would, however, create a precedent, so the president was asked whether he approved. Showing how minutely involved the president could be—especially with programs he cared about—Johnson wrote on the bottom of the memo reporting the suggestion: "Who made request?" Two days later Johnson received word that Shriver had made the request and Liz Carpenter, Mrs. Johnson's press secretary, had approved. In the president's black pen he marked "OK," but soon there was a memo to Carpenter saying that the president preferred that Mrs. Johnson merely present the flag, not raise it.[58]

Head Start had decided to make June 30 a symbolic occasion to launch its program nationwide. The new flags were hastily distributed around the country. The night before the big day, the wife of the program director in Providence, Rhode Island, called, frantic. The ceremony was set, the mayor was coming, the navy band was going to play—but the flag hadn't arrived. "I've got to have a flag," she said. "Somebody's going to have to tell me what it looks like and I'll sew one tonight." Someone did, and this modern Betsy Ross went to work.[59]

The next day—National Head Start Day—Sargent Shriver presented the program's new flag to Lady Bird Johnson at the White House to help kick off the program. Now, like her husband, she could speak of her hopes for the program.

"What a beautiful flag!" the First Lady exclaimed. "I like the design of the arrow pointing upward, which symbolizes the lifting of spirits, not only of 40 million families whose children live in poverty—but of those of us more fortunate who have this specific way to do something lasting for them." In hundreds of cities and towns over the next few days, half a million children would have "their first chance to meet crayons and books—to plant a seed—to visit the school where they will begin the first grade next year—to learn about their community— perhaps see the zoo, or the fire station or a park. They will learn to communicate with the world about them," she said.

Before presenting a Head Start flag to the director of one of the first summer programs—for ten children in East Fairfield, Vermont—Mrs. Johnson expressed optimism about what Head Start could achieve, tempered with more caution than her husband had shown. "I have great hopes that this program will be the big breakthrough we have been seeking in education—the insurance against school dropouts— the insurance for a smaller welfare roll," she said, adding, however: "I do not need to tell you that such an ambitious program is filled with pitfalls and disappointments. And there will be doubters who are quick to point them out. But we are not working with people who live neat and tidy and secure lives."[60]

She was right. In Mississippi, where Freedom Schools the previous summer had planted one seed for Head Start, those doubters would soon pounce. Determined parents and teachers would rally to keep a unique dream alive for as long as they could.

Chapter Three

Mississippi: The Fight for Control

 ven at seventy-one, Clarence Hall, Jr., stood ramrod straight. A farmer, he was equally straightforward about the significance of Head Start for the poor people living in his Mississippi Delta community. It helped them examine their condition, set goals for the future, and learn what to do to achieve them, Hall said. "Head Start opened up the whole thing—the political process—and people learned how to go about achieving these goals. They learned how you get things done at the local level up to the state level on up to the national level."

This awareness was a move, if not toward holding power for themselves, at least toward insisting that the powerful be accountable. That scared and angered the powerful in Mississippi and nationally, setting off a struggle that has ongoing reverberations. That struggle must not be forgotten because it shows that a program many think of today as only a nice little preschool activity was once at the heart of a national controversy. It is also a reminder of what can happen when the powerful attack an effort to help the powerless, for that happens again and again. And it shows the commitment of the poorest of people to open new doors for their children. If we do not know of their struggles, we rob their story of its triumph.

For poor black Mississippians, securing the vote was vital but abstract. Seeing what they could do for themselves through Head Start—that was a reality. To understand why this political and economic change was so threatening, you have to know the Mississippi Delta, which covers the northwest corner of the state and remains home to some of the nation's poorest people. It is another country, today as yesterday. Two-lane roads run ruler straight across miles of unrelentingly flat fields, the landscape broken only occasionally by a farmhouse and its surrounding shade trees, a cotton gin, or a catfish pond. Slaves helped create the Delta's wealth, which had then been maintained by exploiting sharecroppers. Little was spent on educating black children in Mississippi, and particularly not in the Delta. In the 1950s and 1960s resistance to school desegregation and then voting rights for its black population was virtually absolute among white Deltans; the White Citizens Council was born in Indianola, the seat of government for Sunflower County in the heart of the Delta. This massive resistance set the Delta and all of Mississippi back by decades so that the state ranks at the bottom on many measures of health, education, and welfare. That hurts not only the people, but also their economy.

In 1955, Emmett Till, a black teenager visiting from Chicago, was murdered in the Delta for allegedly flirting with a white woman. His death was hardly the first lynching, just the best publicized. Blacks in the Delta, like many across the state, lost their jobs and sometimes their lives for crossing the lines whites drew around them, especially for trying to secure their civil rights. In short, it was dangerous to be black in the Delta, yet that region produced many of the heroes of the Mississippi civil rights movement, some heralded, others lesser known but no less courageous—Fannie Lou Hamer from Ruleville, Amzie Moore from Cleveland, Unita Blackwell from Mayersville, Jake Ayers of Glen Allen, Mae Bertha and Matthew Carter of Drew.

Where once you might have seen hundreds of people chopping or picking cotton in the Delta, today machines do the work. When I last visited Mississippi in October 1995, green monster cotton-picking machines were crisscrossing the land, swirling the dust in the dry fields and plucking the cotton out of the bolls. Rows of cotton "modules" lined the picked-over fields like beached whales. Instead of hauling cotton off to the gin in lumbering cagelike trailers as was the practice the last time I was in the state at picking time, workers now packaged the cotton in large rectangular blocks, covered them with yellow or blue or black tarps, and wrote in large black letters on the side of the module what field it came from. And a few more jobs bit the dust.

Wisps of cotton still dot the shoulders of the roads but, more and more, the people who once did the work have left. Issaquena County, where Clarence Hall lives, not far from the Mississippi River on the far western side of the state, has only 1,875 residents, down from 2,737 in 1970. After the seasonal work was finished, unemployment could run as high as 23 percent, as it did in the winter of 1997.

In the Mississippi Delta of the 1960s it was not uncommon for people to have no electricity, no indoor plumbing, little or no heat in the winter. Poor children living in "the rural" rarely, if ever, saw doctors or dentists. The demands of the cotton crop set the school schedule for black children, who had to work in the fields alongside their parents to help make ends come anywhere near meeting. You didn't even need to go inside the black schools to see how inferior they were, said Mae Bertha Carter, whose family fought against their segregation.[1] The black schools had only the "raggedy books" handed down from the white school; the teachers sometimes had little more education than their students or were so beholden to the white superintendent for their jobs that they made no waves. Mississippi had no kindergarten, and the idea of any public preschool for black children would have been preposterous.

But the Delta was stirring. Throughout the 1950s a few intrepid souls had signed memberships in the National Association for the Advancement of Colored People. Through NAACP meetings, they kept up on news of the Montgomery bus boycott, the student sit-ins, and the freedom rides. Then in 1962 young people from the Student Nonviolent Coordinating Committee (SNCC, pronounced "Snick") came to the Delta. When two of the young men arrived in Mayersville, Unita Blackwell knew they weren't local; they were walking too fast. They had to be "freedom riders."

These young people, joined by native Mississippians, undertook the painstaking work of convincing sharecroppers, maids, and ministers to register to vote. In 1964, aided by college students from around the country, many of them white, a black third party mounted a challenge to the state's all-white delegation to the Democratic National Convention in Atlantic City. That convention opened only days after the bodies of James Chaney, Andrew Goodman, and Mickey Schwerner, three civil rights workers who had been missing for forty-four days, were found buried in an earthen dam. The Mississippi Freedom Democratic Party challenge, unsuccessful in the short term, nonetheless helped organize many areas of the state and set the stage for the entry of Head Start into Mississippi.

Clarence Hall had been the Freedom Democrats' vice chairman in his county; Henry Sias was the chairman. Sias went to Atlantic City;

Hall did not go then, but he was a member of the integrated Mississippi delegation seated by the Democrats at their 1968 convention in Chicago. Hall was one of the many black veterans of World War II who returned home to find he could not register to vote. He had joined the Army Air Corps at seventeen, made sergeant at eighteen, and helped haul the bombs and ammunition that supported the D-day invasion. He landed on Omaha Beach. Hall stayed in the service until 1946. He tried several times to register to vote but "failed" each time he was asked to interpret one of some two hundred clauses in the Mississippi constitution. "A lot of the registrars couldn't interpret them either," he recalled, "but it was just a means to keep us from registering." It took Hall until 1965, after passage of the Voting Rights Act, to register.

Spurred in part by the accelerating civil rights movement, the Johnson administration launched its war on poverty in 1964. During the following winter and spring, the Office of Economic Opportunity prepared a program that would give poor children a boost toward success in school. "We got the word and we were already having meetings every week," Hall told me. The Freedom Democrats had selected three representatives from each of the five county government subdivisions as part of their organizing efforts. "It was easy to get the word out about where we should have centers and how many children we would need."

Hall lived, then as now, on a farm in the Valewood section of the county. I had thought the highway going to Mayersville was rural, but the road going back to Valewood was more so. When Hall was looking for a place to house the first local Head Start program, the minister at his church, St. John Missionary Baptist Episcopal, agreed to let the program use the church building, a move involving considerable risk. "He was all for it. He wanted things changed in life," Hall recalled. "We had about fifty members of our church then. About one-third of our members left. I guess they were afraid." Outsiders tend to think of Freedom Summer 1964 as the time of high tension in Mississippi, but the summer of 1965 was no less so. Passage of the Voting Rights Act and pressure from the federal government for the state to move on school desegregation showed that change was coming, and change had bitter enemies in Mississippi. The Ku Klux Klan threatened parents in the Delta who sent their children to Head Start.

In Rolling Fork, not far from Valewood, Frances Alexander and her husband had one of the first Head Starts in their home. Crosses were burned in front of the house and shots fired into it. "Folks had to sit shotgun at night to keep them from burning the place down." A week before the schools in Rolling Fork were to be integrated that summer, someone went down that lonely rural road to Valewood and burned Clarence Hall's church. No one was ever caught for the crime. "The officer who investigated said it must have been caused by lightning," Hall said. "It had rained earlier that night but I remember how clear it was. You could see the moon. There wasn't any lightning." The Head Start program finished the summer in a big tent sent in by the Child Development Group of Mississippi, its parent agency. "The idea was to try to frighten people but instead of frightening them, more people went to register their children for school," Hall said. "Instead of frightening them, it drew them closer together. It didn't matter because people were determined."

They were going to need that determination. Not only did Head Start and its friends have enemies in Mississippi, they also had powerful forces arrayed against them in Washington. Most notable was John Stennis of Mississippi, chairman of the Senate Appropriations Committee, which determined how much money the antipoverty program would have to spend. Stennis was no friend of civil rights. He was indignant that massive amounts of federal money were going into the black community in Mississippi, bypassing local governments to which he had many political ties. He had the investigative means to make life very hard for the Child Development Group of Mississippi, and he used them.

The Child Development Group of Mississippi—which everyone referred to as CDGM—was at first the beloved child of the national Head Start office. It was extraordinarily innovative, reaching into communities with some of the greatest need in the nation, and it deeply involved parents, without whom it could never have gotten off the ground. Each of those attributes eventually became a negative in the eyes of some beholders.

Like Head Start nationally, CDGM started life as a modest idea— preschools in perhaps five or ten communities for about one hundred children, with a sixty-five-thousand-dollar budget. Like the national program, CDGM grew because there were both massive needs and a seemingly bottomless pit of money, at least at the outset. Dr. Tom Levin, a New York psychoanalyst, had worked in the Mississippi Freedom Schools during the summer of 1964 and wanted to try the concept for young children, especially the children of people who had committed themselves to civil rights. In the spring of 1965 he met in New York to explore the idea with a small group that included the Reverend

Arthur Thomas, director of the Delta Ministry, the Mississippi arm of the National Council of Churches, deeply involved in civil rights; Jeannine Herron, who with her photographer husband Matt had moved to Mississippi to participate in the movement (they were teaching their children at home); Dr. Sol Gordon, who wanted to teach reading by using parents and older brothers and sisters as the instructors; and Polly Greenberg, who had worked at the U.S. Office of Education and was one of the first Head Start staff members. Greenberg eventually went to Mississippi to work for CDGM, the organization that emerged after this meeting, and later wrote a detailed and invaluable history of the energy and the intrigue surrounding the program, *The Devil Has Slippery Shoes*.[2] Even among this committed group, there was reluctance to take federal money and possibly deflect the movement from its goal of securing basic rights. Immediate need won out over idealism.

Established quickly and often chaotically, like the rest of Head Start, CDGM provided an eight-week program for six thousand children in eighty-four centers in twenty-four counties during the summer of 1965. By channeling its $1.4 million grant through Mary Holmes Junior College in West Point, Mississippi, a small black school run by the Presbyterian National Board of Missions, the Office of Economic Opportunity avoided the veto of Mississippi's governor to kill the program. CDGM, however, would be headquartered at Mount Beulah, a small abandoned college west of Jackson that had also housed civil rights organizations, a decision that would cause problems down the road for CDGM and for OEO.

Despite the popularity of the Head Start concept with the local Freedom Democrats like Clarence Hall, the party's leadership and that of the increasingly militant SNCC workers were chilly about the idea. They thought, not without foundation, that the antipoverty program would buy off the poor without creating real change.[3] Meantime, white political leaders at first saw Head Start as another sign of federal interference and so were slow off the mark in trying to establish programs that they could control. Only the poor people seemed to care.

Local CDGM centers started with virtually nothing. Parents and teachers—often one and the same—scoured church buildings, found crayons and paper, and signed up the children. "Maids, mothers, and field workers developed into beginning nursery school teachers," Polly Greenberg observed.[4] Greenberg, who had become one of CDGM's two program coordinators, felt the group's track record was mixed in terms of the quality of its programs. "By the end of the summer we had found nineteen out of eighty-four centers that were pretty terrible. In contrast to these, there were twenty-two centers that were generally felt to be excellent," with the remainder falling in the middle. "Holly Grove, nestled in the hills of Holmes County, was an example of an excellent center."

Holly Grove was one of those hard-to-find places that dot rural America and especially Holmes County, where I've gotten badly lost myself. ("Turn right at the puddle," which had dried up, Greenberg wrote about trying to find it during a 1965 visit, "turn left at the dairy farm," which seemingly had no cows, and "go a ways," which turned out to be ten miles.) "When I finally bumped through the pits and potholes and pulled into the dusty parking patch next to the old church," Greenberg added, "I found all the children outside playing in the pine woods. Sad piano music floated out the church windows, and a hearse was drawn up to the door. The resource teacher, a vivacious and marvelous local teacher named Mrs. [Doris] Clarke, hurried over, motioning me to hush, and whispered that a funeral was in progress. It was for a baby girl who had starved to death that morning.

"She said it was 'recess' anyway, and 'class' would resume momentarily. Meanwhile, the children romped and frisked on a lovely playground which they called 'the park.' The community had made it in a pine forest." Soon the children had lunch of corn bread and fried chicken, peas, beans, salad, mashed potatoes, canned peaches, milk, and cake on a table underneath shade trees outside. The men of the community were building a kitchen for the program, but hadn't gotten it wired yet. Later, people who lived in the area would donate pots and towels to equip the kitchen. The women made rag dolls for the children to play with.

Writing to the CDGM office later that summer, one of the Holly Grove teachers reported:

> From a mass of withdrawn, repressed pre-schoolers who had never ridden a seesaw, worked a puzzle, drawn a picture, we have, with few exceptions, a happy, cohesive group of kids full of vitality (and now, at last, food) who spend their day creating, pretending, playing, singing, looking, listening, and wondering. We don't pretend to be a super educational machine at Holly Grove—the children didn't learn to read and write in our eight weeks. However, we did expand their limited view of life; we did provide a chance to test their intellectual and physical muscles; we did provide a transition between mother and school as the children learned to work and

play with others. Finally, and perhaps the most important of all, we tried to show these children that they were important—that we cared about what they had to say, what they did, what they made. Some of our kids can't read a word—some can't count to ten—but almost all have a measure of human dignity that they didn't have before.[5]

Head Start's national director, Dr. Julius Richmond, visited CDGM toward the end of that summer. "The program really was exciting. We traveled from community to community, often with cars loaded with rednecks following us, talked to some of the young people who had come from the North as volunteers in the program who would be standing guard at night over their buildings with rifles and things of this sort. It was really a tense situation. One of the most beautiful programs we saw had been operating out of a wonderful little black church . . . and it was burned down the day after we visited the place." Richmond had been to Clarence Hall's church at Valewood.[6]

With the program barely under way, Senator Stennis sent an investigator from Washington and charged that federal money was subsidizing civil rights activities. It was the first of many barrages; in time, Stennis would claim that money was being grossly mismanaged, and that nepotism was practiced. There was sometimes a glimmer of truth to his charges, so CDGM soon was placed on the defensive, especially because of Stennis's power over OEO's appropriation. Yes, some of the CDGM staff also worked on civil rights—how many other people were willing to go to work on a program to help poor blacks in Mississippi in the summer of 1965? Yes, some money was not properly accounted for—how many poor black people dared ask white suppliers for receipts in 1965? Yes, the staff of the Head Start center in a small town named Richmond Grove were all related because all the people in Richmond Grove were related.

After his visit to Mississippi, director Richmond said he was surprised that Stennis's auditors found only twenty-six thousand dollars for which there were no receipts. "I was a little taken aback that it was that low. We had cautioned people about getting receipts and documenting everything because we knew that sooner or later this kind of thing would come up. But to me, that was a ridiculously low figure not to have receipts for when you're expending a million and a half dollars and particularly under those circumstances. So I viewed this as kind of a Star Chamber proceeding."[7]

Stennis was not CDGM's only powerful enemy. Mississippi governor

Paul Johnson called the program "an effort on the part of extremists and agitators to subvert lawful authority in Mississippi and to create division and dissension between the races." With staggering hypocrisy, Johnson wrote Sargent Shriver in June 1965 that people in his state were amazed that the U.S. government "would finance this type of undertaking and therefore cripple the Head Start program in Mississippi which could have been one of the finest things to which the Federal Administration could point." The governor enclosed a letter from a black minister who said he had visited CDGM's Mount Beulah headquarters and claimed to have seen "liquor and evidence of drunkenness" and had heard reports of "lewd behavior."[8]

Under fire, CDGM's grant for the second year of operation was in some doubt. OEO chief Shriver testified before Stennis's committee in October 1965 and defended his agency's supervision of the program. CDGM staff and community allies were, of course, involved as charged in civil rights activities, but at that point Shriver said he had no problem with that as long as it was on their own time. "The impression . . . has been created that something un-American has been going on here (in CDGM) because somebody, when they are not working in the child development center, has participated in some civil rights activity. . . . As far as I am concerned, I didn't know that there was something un-American or illegal about participating on your own time in activities of that type. Frankly, I have done this on my own time."[9]

OEO sent its own investigators to Mississippi before the summer ended and also tried unsuccessfully to get the CDGM staff to move from Mount Beulah to Mary Holmes Junior College more than 150 miles away in the northeastern section of the state. The staff rebelled but eventually did move into a Jackson office. Late in the summer the CDGM board removed Tom Levin as director, not, it said, at the behest of the government but obviously with the intent of trying to save the program. Levin's successor was John Mudd, a white twenty-six-year-old graduate student with no administrative experience but who had run a summer program for Tougaloo College students in Jackson the previous summer. He was working on his doctoral dissertation and helping set up a cooperative in Batesville in the northern part of the state. And he was a friend of Marian Wright, the young civil rights attorney who was an influential force on CDGM's board (and who, as Marian Wright Edelman, later established the Children's Defense Fund).

At summer's end, communities wanted to keep their Head Start centers operating, but CDGM had no more money. The volunteer spirit took over. "In those days, when the money didn't come in, people fed the children from their own freezers, refrigerators, and gardens," said Westean Young, one of the Valewood community people who helped keep the centers operating. Clarence Hall had given her her first job—driving the children to the center—because her father had a truck. Today Young is the director of the Guiding Light Head Start center in Mayersville.[10]

Pauline Sias, who lives about five miles off the main road through Mayersville, was involved early and deeply in Head Start. When the money for Head Start was cut off, she said, it was "pretty rough." Sias, who had eleven children of her own to feed, always kept two freezers of food from her garden. "My oldest son says that I would can everything and then look around for the bush, too. All the ladies that had deep freezes, we would bring something every morning to feed the children. Beans, peas, corn, you name it." One white man in the area would donate food but the rest of that community was resistant.

"Lord have mercy, it was really bad," how poor the children were that year, Sias said. Some came to the center wearing dirty, shabby clothes. One woman cut up an old gathered skirt to make children's clothes. "You'd be very surprised how many clothes you can get out of a gathered skirt," Sias said with a chuckle. "We made panties, little shirts, little dresses." Somebody gave the program a zinc tub and the teachers bathed the children and put clean clothes on them because their parents hadn't been washing their clothes. "If you've got just two garments, you *could* wash them. Some of them were lazy."

No one was getting paid, but Clarence Hall and Unita Blackwell, another Freedom Democratic Party activist, were traveling around the country, trying to raise money so that the staff might receive ten dollars every two weeks. "Most of us were together and fought through it," Sias recalled. They had to stick together because once people became involved in Head Start, local banks often would not give them loans. Only one store would give the Siases credit, and they often could not get seeds for their crops when they needed them. "I held my ground," said Sias, who worked for Head Start for twenty years. "I got into the movement with my whole heart, soul, and mind. I always wanted something better for my family. There was so much if you were willing to learn."

Communities could not keep their programs going forever without money. CDGM submitted its formal application for full-year federal funding in November 1965. Weeks went by, with promises from Washington but no money. Still, the Head Start centers kept on going. "Having tried the official channels with no result, CDGM decided to try some on-the-spot lobbying. On February 11, 1966, forty-eight five-year-olds and twenty-five teachers, nurses, and parents boarded two chartered buses and rode 1,100 miles from Mississippi to Washington. A Bethesda, Maryland, church found people who would pick up and house small groups of children and teachers when they arrived late at night. The next day they marched into the Wedgwood and walnut hearing room of the House Education and Labor Committee to hold class, complete with their little chairs, carrots and juice for snacktime, even a live mouse for a science demonstration. "Glory, glory, hallelujah, we want our Head Start school," they chanted, and spread out their crayons and paper on the deep pile rug.

The children and their teachers were greeted by five members of Congress, although none was from Mississippi. One of them said he hoped CDGM's grant would be approved "before too long." The children also toured the White House and, on Lincoln's Birthday, stood on the steps of the Lincoln Memorial and sang "We Shall Overcome" and "Happy Birthday to You."[11]

Eleven days later a grant for $5.6 million came through—a huge amount of federal money being poured into Mississippi's black communities. That stirred Stennis and Senator James O. Eastland even more. The next day, Stennis charged that the grant would "play into the hands of extremists" and add credibility to those who said the poverty program was "devoting millions of taxpayers' dollars to special groups and individuals who use the money for their own selfish purposes."[12]

Despite the indecision and carping from Washington, CDGM was not only functioning, but growing and having an economic impact in the communities where it operated. By June of 1966, it was serving 12,145 children at 121 centers in twenty-eight counties. All but about 1 percent of its employees in the centers across the state were Mississippians, a point CDGM made in rebuttal to charges that outsiders had invaded the state yet again.[13] Eighty percent of the central office staff were Mississippians, although several of the top jobs were in fact held by outsiders. CDGM teachers were earning thirty-one dollars a week more than they had before starting their jobs with CDGM (remember, those are 1966 dollars in a desperately poor state). About one thousand poor people had helped make the decisions governing these centers.

Collie Barnes bore witness to the personal side of CDGM's impact.

By 1995, she was the director of the True Light Head Start center in Anguilla, a dot of a town on the route from Vicksburg north toward Greenville. She remembered well the excitement when Head Start began: "People would teach their own children and we were going to get paid for it! I forget what the minimum wage was then but it was better than the three dollars a day we got for chopping cotton."

Teaching jobs were available, but Barnes was married then to a man who didn't like the idea of women going out on their own, so she couldn't go away for the training. "But they still needed a janitor. It paid five dollars and it was in the shade. The other was in the sun from sunup to sundown. The choice was very clear." Soon she became center coordinator, then administrator, some years doubling as a lead teacher when the budget was tight. Since then she's had three years of college, but more than that, she said she had grown so much and met all kinds of people—"not to mention the economic impact on my life. I've reared three children and had a good job. Thirty years ago that was beyond my wildest dream and that's what it was—in my *dreams*."

Another 4,365 children were being taught at "voluntary" centers; despite having no federal or CDGM money, they were nonetheless among the largest Head Start programs in the country. Many of these centers were part of a political tug-of-war between groups that had been associated with CDGM and community action agencies hastily being set up by county governments. These local powers-that-be had finally awakened to the potential of the programs—if they could control them. In Bolivar County—where local Head Start advocates had tried unsuccessfully to get the all-white board of supervisors and school system to cooperate—1,300 children were learning how to draw and sing and acquire other skills in a program entirely staffed by volunteers during the spring of 1966. People who earned about $450 a year in the Delta communities of Shaw, Rosedale, and Cleveland gave their time free. They took up collections to buy paper and paints and transported children to the centers in whatever cars and trucks they could find. These people did not feel that the county's newly established community action agency adequately represented the poor and so refused to cooperate with it.[14]

The same struggle was occurring in neighboring Sunflower County, home of both Fannie Lou Hamer and Senator Eastland. Hamer had been jailed and brutally beaten for her voting rights activities, and became nationally known for her moving testimony at the 1964 Democratic convention. She had helped write the grant application for the local grassroots Head Start program. Later she was deeply involved in negotiations to keep that poor people's effort alive. Local people pitched in in Sunflower County, just as they had in Bolivar, when the federal government decided that its money should go to the county-organized agency, Sunflower County Progress, Incorporated. This "community" antipoverty agency was headed by a former Indianola police chief, Bryce Alexander. That meant OEO was financing a group led by someone who had broken up voter-registration meetings and arrested civil rights workers. He soon resigned because black objection was so strong. The agency's board, however, was composed of ten white men, seven African American teachers (dependent on whites for their jobs), and one landowner whose wife was a teacher. The board president was a former member of the White Citizens Council, formed to fight school integration.[15]

The county-run and grassroots programs coexisted for several years, but not without a struggle. One hot August day Hamer led a protest at the county's air-conditioned antipoverty offices over lack of pay for her group, saying, "We just plan to sit here. We got plenty of time and this place is more comfortable than home for most of us." Local people had begun Head Start, she added, and it had proved to be a program that could lift people up by their bootstraps. "The boot is being taken away from us and the strap, too."[16]

The fight drained energies that might have been better devoted to the two programs' children, but it was an important fight for political power. It was, as one OEO inspector wrote, "a Civil War among poverty warriors . . . rather than an outright attack on the problems of the poor."[17]

Meantime, on the statewide level, CDGM's leaders felt that their program was only serving about 7 percent of the eligible children. So in July 1966 CDGM requested $41 million to run a full-year program for thirty thousand children. The request was promptly rejected as massively out of line; CDGM was told that it could operate a program for only the same number of children it had previously served. OEO also questioned the group's expenditures, administration, and civil rights activities.

In September 1966 the federal government decided not to refinance CDGM as it was then constituted. In addition to specific fiscal irregularities, the report accompanying the OEO decision questioned what it called CDGM's "go-it-alone policy" instead of cooperating with other community groups.[18] No sooner had the government turned CDGM down than it handed out two grants to new Head Start sponsors: $1.2 million to Rust College in the northern part of the state for a twelve-month program in two counties for 600 children, and $713,000 to Southwest Mississippi Opportunity Incorporated for programs for 935 children in three counties over eight months. In an article headlined "Manna from OEO Falls on Mississippi," *Washington Post* reporter Nicholas von Hoffman wrote that Rust's grant was announced before OEO had received its formal application. "The college's president, Ernest A. Smith, said he hoped to complete by today an application explaining how the money he has been given would be spent."[19]

Three thousand people gathered on the campus of Jackson State University in the state capital on October 8, 1966, to protest. Fannie Lou Hamer was one of the principal speakers. "I feel sorry for Sargent Shriver," she roared, "because he ain't ever had a mess like the mess he's going to have when all of us sit down in front of his house. People from Harlem, people from Watts are sayin', 'Tell us when, honey, and we'll come with you.' "[20] Sounding a theme she often stressed, Hamer added: "We aren't ready to be sold out by a few middle-class bourgeoisie and some of them Uncle Toms who couldn't care less."[21]

If the Mississippi picture was not already complicated enough, while CDGM was fighting for its life a new organization was being set up—some said with White House help, others denied that—to run many of the state's Head Start programs. On October 11, OEO awarded this group, Mississippi Action for Progress, Incorporated (MAP) $3 million for a full-year program for 1,500 children. MAP's board of directors included Aaron Henry, who had worked tirelessly for civil rights through the NAACP and who had chaired the 1964 Mississippi Freedom Democratic Party delegation. Board members also included several prominent whites, including Hodding Carter III, editor of the *Delta Democrat-Times* in Greenville, which regularly provided the only comprehensive coverage of the Mississippi movement, and Owen Cooper, president of the Mississippi Chemical Company and the Mississippi Economic Council. Henry's participation stunned CDGM, whose leaders considered him a Judas. Henry had no problem with the federal government requesting regular financial accounting or reports on the use of automobiles, he said. "We had to take the pressure off of Shriver, because Stennis and Eastland and the whole damn gang" wanted to cut off the child development grants.[22]

Shriver soon met with church officials protesting the decision against CDGM. He denied the mounting charges of political pressure.

OEO's review, he said, had found that CDGM had neither the capacity to manage the grant nor the willingness to use existing community facilities, thus harming the program because classrooms were not adequately supervised, health programs were inadequate, and buildings and equipment were substandard. The review concluded "that further funding of CDGM would not be in the best interest of a strong well-managed program of the type which OEO intends to see continued in Mississippi."[23]

The political war escalated with a full-page advertisement in the *New York Times* headlined: "Say It Isn't So, Sargent Shriver." The ad, paid for by the National Citizens Committee for the Child Development Program in Mississippi, charged that Shriver had bent to political pressure from those who saw CDGM as a threat.[24] Shriver retorted that "for over two weeks I have been saying that it isn't so, that it hasn't been so, and that it will not be so. But some people are unwilling to listen. It is shocking to me that any Americans, and especially members of the clergy, should rush into public print impugning the motives of a public official before ascertaining the facts." CDGM's project constituted in many ways "one of the more promising chapters of the history of the poverty program," a wounded Shriver added, pointing out that it had received one of the largest Head Start grants in the country—$5.6 million—the previous February.[25]

The ad had deeply upset Shriver. "I'd never really seen him as moved and as angry as he was," said Jule Sugarman, the Head Start administrator who was a key figure in dealings with CDGM. "It was a terrible reflection on his personal integrity. It was one of those situations in which quite well-meaning people on both sides of the argument completely lost, in my judgment, perspective, and were so engaged in fighting with one another that they couldn't stand together against what was really a common enemy."[26]

Gradually, OEO and CDGM agreed to enlarge the group's board of directors, to tighten financial controls, and to make clear to employees that they could not participate in political or civil rights activities during working hours. That accomplished, on January 30, 1967, OEO gave the program its third grant for $4.9 million to serve 5,900 children in fourteen counties.

Polly Greenberg wrote that CDGM's spirit seemed to give out even before its grant ended the following December, this time never to be renewed. Thanks to the politicians and bureaucrats, she said, "CDGM had lost its splendid Pegasus qualities. It had achieved a nearly perfect parochial point of view." And no wonder, she added—Head Start's budget had been cut nationally and in Mississippi, and an amendment sponsored by Congresswoman Edith Green had stripped community action agencies of freedom from local political control.[27] But CDGM had shown poor people what they could do, had pushed Head Start nationally to be more aware of parents' potential, and had probably made Mississippi whites sit down with blacks to run local community action agencies sooner than they would have done on their own. Indeed, Greenberg believed that OEO shot down "its best Head Start, in order to wrest power from the poor and rapid reformers, and try to get it into the hands of moderate Mississippi whites" to reinforce their hand in opposing the more rigid segregationists.[28] CDGM was the cutting edge of the War on Poverty in Mississippi. Next to the supposedly radical CDGM, other innovative programs for young children looked safe and so may have benefited from the comparison. CDGM had been a short, sometimes messy, often brilliant attempt to alter the future for Mississippi children, and it focused national attention on the problems they faced in a way that has rarely been possible since its demise.

Nothing is easy in Mississippi. Today more than one-third of its children under five live in poverty. Many lack health insurance. Their families deal with an increase in drug abuse and teenage pregnancy and a decrease in jobs for people with few skills. Today twenty-five organizations provide Head Start services across the state for more than twenty-four thousand children, placing Mississippi among the top ten in enrollment even though it ranks thirty-first in total population. Yet 65 percent of children who are eligible cannot be enrolled because of lack of money.

Among today's Head Start programs is that run by a spiritual descendant of CDGM, an organization called Friends of Children of Mississippi (FCM). When the federal government cut off CDGM's grant in October 1966, Friends of Children got its start helping poor people run their Head Start centers on their own while trying to convince OEO it was wrong. When OEO gave CDGM its last grant the following January, it left out five of the counties that CDGM had served. Representatives from those areas, plus one other county that had been running a voluntary program, met in Jackson and decided to prove the government had been wrong by operating their own independent program. They were friends, they said, and their purpose was to serve children, so they decided, why not call ourselves Friends of Children of Mississippi?[29]

For eighteen months, unfunded, this organization ran twenty-nine centers for 1,500 children. The centers received only about thirty cents per child a week from FCM for meals, and local people provided the rest. "Tomorrow I'll try to bring some greens" to feed the children, one woman would say, as women had been saying before all over the state. "I'll try to bring some meat," another would volunteer. "Many a day I walked out the back door with the last piece of salt pork to take to the center," said Lorene Starks, who was working at a center in the Delta. "This lasted for months and months." FCM appealed to the Field Foundation, which provided $425,000 to aid the new organization for about fifteen months. "We'd get ten dollars a week" then, Starks recalled. "Oooh, that ten dollars a week was *money* for us." Eventually, FCM became a federally funded delegate agency through Tougaloo College, then in 1980 received a Head Start grant in its own right. Friends of Children now serves almost three thousand children in fifteen counties through the midsection of the state, including Issaquena County, where this story started.

Highly visible among those working for Head Start—and everything else—in Issaquena County has been Unita Blackwell, for many years mayor of her small hometown of Mayersville and later awarded a MacArthur Fellowship, known popularly as a "genius grant." Over the years that I have been going to Mississippi, she has become a friend, so when I first got to Mayersville, I paid her a visit. Sitting in her cluttered back room as she struggled to organize her own memoirs, she thought back on how Head Start had affected her life. When Head Start began in 1965, she was already deeply involved in civil rights activity, having gone to Atlantic City as part of the Mississippi Freedom Democratic Party delegation the year before.

"Head Start started out to be about the children but it turned out to be about all of us because it developed all of us as better community leaders. It opened up another realm for us to look at. I got more training." She went to Harvard to learn problem-solving techniques. "It opened up the door. You start a process of going back to school and you continued. I was always learning things but this was organized learning.

"It expanded people to want a house. They patched up their houses. They wanted their shacks to look a lot better. Their children came home clean. They found out that they were supposed to change their clothes. It opened up so many learning avenues for the families." People had been reluctant to go to Head Start meetings because they were disgusted with the school system whose teachers thought they were ignorant. But when they did go, they found they had much to give, that they could help run things.

"You don't know what you're giving a child. You don't know who you're molding." Blackwell was clearly thinking about her own teacher, Mattie Mae Cotton Franklin of West Helena, Arkansas, who had recently died. Lighter-skinned children than Blackwell were always favored in school and in church, pushed forward to do things, but this teacher told her she, too, could recite. "She gave me the courage—even though I was scared to death—to give these little speeches." And Blackwell stood up with her hands together and a schoolgirl's look on her face as though she were about to recite. "Head Start does the same thing. It starts children to be ready for the next opportunity. Head Start is your foundation to say you can do it.

"We didn't know that it was going to be this profound. I didn't know we were doing profound things. We were just trying to survive."

Watts Towers:

The children learn new foods and old traditions. Lupe Osuna and Gloria Heyman tell their stories. A crisis is resolved. Raymound starts to participate. The teachers cope with paperwork, and the parents join in a Thanksgiving potluck.

"What do we celebrate this month?" Lupe Osuna asked the Watts Towers Head Start children one brisk morning in early November.

"Halloween!" piped up one of the four-year-olds.

"No, Halloween was last month. What do we celebrate this month?" There was a pause and the children seemed genuinely stumped.

"Thanksgiving!" said Osuna. "What do we eat?"

They weren't certain about that one, either. It was early in the month, early in the lesson plan. So Osuna explained that some people would have turkey. "Some mommies have tamales because they don't like turkey."

"I like tamales," said one little voice.

Halloween behind them, the children were learning about fruits and vegetables. On top of the toy shelf were some pumpkins, squash, and brown and yellow corn. In one corner, there were books on *Where Food Comes From* and place mats with the vegetable group, the meat and protein group, and the grain group. Near the area where the children had circle time was a low round table set with plastic versions of potato and roast beef at one place, pasta and sauce at another, a hot dog at a third, and a chicken leg, carrots, and peas at the fourth.

Once the children were seated in the circle, Maria, as shy as ever, came in, had her name tag pinned on, and walked over to sit next to Karina, who greeted her with a hearty, "Hi, senorita!"

Osuna held up a cutout of a strawberry and asked what it was. Then she held up a cherry cutout, then corn. "Monday we eat co-orn. Monday we eat co-orn, yum, yum, yum," she sang, and the children followed along. "Today is Tuesday. Tuesday we eat strawberries. Yum, yum, yum." On Wednesday the song had the children eating cherries, Thursday string beans, and Friday an ice-cream cone. *"Yum yum yum!"* the children fairly shouted at that one. Then Osuna went over the colors of the fruits. She had the children get up from their places and pick up a fruit and tell her what it was. Maria identified a *piña* (pineapple), Richard an apple, and Jenyffer a melon. One by one, they went over the fruits in English and Spanish. "Pineapple, *piña*. Cantaloupe, *melón*. Apple, *manzana*. Banana, *plátano*. Pear, *pera*."

Osuna had developed a knack for drawing the children's attention toward her for the lessons or the singing despite the fact that she had been extraordinarily shy when she first started teaching years earlier. "Oh, it was awful," she said. "Every time I would talk my face would get red."

How did she get over that?

"Just the years, I guess. I still feel a little embarrassed sometimes. I really don't know how to sing," she said, but she did it anyway. Osuna got her start with the program in typical fashion: the middle three of her five children had been in Head Start, and she volunteered every day when the youngest of those three, Carlos, was enrolled. She even helped the staff clean up at the end of the school year in June, washing the walls and packing the equipment. The next September she went to volunteer again. The teachers urged her to apply for an aide's job. "They said, 'You're here every day. You know what to do.' But I was so uncertain it took me until October to apply." As he had done with Josephine Garner, Paul DeVan, then the Head Start director, insisted that Osuna try. He liked to bring people in at the grassroots level and watch them grow, and his successor, Elaine Atlow, adhered to the principle he established.

"My husband didn't talk to me for a month after I started working," Osuna said. "My mother-in-law told me, 'Don't let it worry you. Keep on working. One day he'll leave you and you'll have a job.' She was right." He did start talking to her again when he finally decided she wasn't going to stop working, but indeed he left her three years later.

She had to go to school at night, and remembered: "It would be hard in the winter when I had to get the bus in the rain to go to East L.A. College." Sometimes she had to take two buses. She would have classes from 7 to 10 P.M. after working all day, get home at 11 P.M., do what she needed to do to prepare for the next day's work and her children's school day, then finally go to bed. Her daughter helped with the younger children. "The good thing," she said, "was that I was getting my education. I was learning more about how to work with kids and getting new ideas for projects I could use with them." She moved from teacher's aide to teacher five years before I paid my visits to Watts Towers.

Osuna especially enjoyed her arts and crafts classes and constantly was pulling the parents, especially the Spanish-speaking mothers, together to work on candleholders or souvenirs or knickknack containers made from old glass bottles or baby shoes or cigar boxes. She liked the fact that Head Start and its craftwork gave the women the opportunity to get together socially and to have a sense of accomplishment for having made something. She knew full well that some of their husbands weren't keen on the women being away from home, but they could do it in Head Start's case because it involved their children.

After Osuna finished that morning's conversation about fruits and vegetables, the children colored outline drawings of cabbages or carrots while some played outside. Andre looked at teacher Josephine Garner, wearing a black dress with a white design instead of her usual shorts or slacks, and asked, "Where are you going?"

"See, he noticed." She said she'd had a good day at church that Sunday so she decided to wear the same dress to class. Fortunately, it had big pockets into which she was constantly reaching for a pen or a crayon.

Ciara shuffled through a stack of folders looking for one with her name on it so she could put her paper in it. She realized hers wasn't in one pile and found it in another stack on the floor. Some of the children could recognize their name by that point in the year, but many still could not.

"Ciara, you're so good. You're so sweet today," Garner said, as she frequently did, rewarding the children with praise when they completed tasks or showed particular thoughtfulness. "Shardae, you're doing a beautiful job." Turning to one child who spoke very softly, she told him, "Anthony, I want you to open your mouth and talk. You're going to kindergarten next year. You have to talk."

She picked up a book to show the children what lettuce looks like. "You put lettuce on your hamburger when you go to Big Boy. You use cabbage for cole slaw. Your mama makes soup out of cabbage." After she flipped through the pictures, she showed several of the children how to hold a crayon, to which some clung as though it were a dagger. "I know that's hard for some of you children," she added patiently.

"Anthony, that's beautiful," she said. "*Que bonita!* César, you're doing a beautiful job but let's not put the crayon in your mouth."

Each child had his or her own goals as part of an individual education plan—IEP, in the jargon—that the teachers drew up and went over with parents. For example, Garner hoped that building Andre's self-esteem would help him feel more confident so he wouldn't cry every time things didn't go his way. She had told his mother what she could do at home to help him, and earlier that morning he had been playing more cooperatively with the other children. She had also spoken to Marcus's mother about letting him put his own shoes on and learn to tie them. It takes him too long, his mother had responded. But he had to develop self-sufficiency, Garner replied, and wouldn't if she kept doing things for him. She was trying to share with parents "the tricks of the trade, as the kids say."

The children were quietly listening to stories as a lunch of tacos and beans, fruit cocktail, and milk was being prepared. But the calm was short-lived. In one of the reading groups, Andre hit Jenyffer and she hit him back and Andre bit her. He wailed more than she did. Garner put alcohol on Jenyffer's arm—"The skin wasn't broken but you can't be too careful"—and filled out an accident report. She called the parents of both children as she was required to do. Andre continued to wail while Jenyffer was calm and even tried to wipe away Andre's tears. "He knows he's going to get punished," Garner said. "I'm sorry. I can't help it. He has to learn you can't bite people."

Wayne, meanwhile, was lying on some carpet squares. His mother had wanted to keep him home but he wanted to go to school. Now his cold seemed to have settled in his ears and he was crying softly. Garner put cotton in his ears and called his mother as well. She held Wayne on her lap and put her sweater around him. "Whatever you all have, I refuse to get it," she said to the world in general. "I refuse to let you rain on my parade."

By the time Andre's mother arrived, he had stopped crying and was eating lunch. Garner had him tell his mother, a petite woman with large brown eyes that Andre had inherited, why he had bitten Jenyffer. It was hard to make out what he was saying because he had started to cry again. Finally, Andre and his mother walked down the steps and toward the front gate to go home. Jenyffer left with her mother not long afterward. "Whew," Garner said. "There for a minute there was a crisis."

It was developing into one of those days every teacher knows too well. Later that day a plastic bag containing the leftover beans tilted, and the beans ran down the side of the counter. The children's clamor seemed to be rising: "Miz Garner, *Miz Garner!*" The center became one big Excedrin headache. Finally, Garner realized she needed a break.

"When I get like that, they know just to let me go." When her lunch hour came, she headed off to Burger King to collect herself.

Each morning either one of the two teachers or two aides conducted the circle-time activities, gently encouraging the participation of some of the shyer children but never forcing it. "Praise the Lord," Garner would say when Marisol or Jenyffer spoke up, as they were beginning to do. "*No habla?*" she asked Raymound. "You don't have to," she added. When Raymound, the tallest child in the class, first enrolled, he said nothing. When the class went on a field trip during the summer, he stuck close to his mother. He wanted to decide what he would do and when he would do it. By November, he still didn't participate much, but when Garner or Osuna led the game Simon Says, and Simon said "Stand up," Raymound stood up. When the children walked or flew or waddled like ducks around in a circle in time to a recording, Raymound was right there, walking or flying or waddling with them. I started to see the little changes that Head Start makes.

"What are these?" Garner said one morning, pointing to a paper turkey tacked to the bulletin board.

"Chickens!"

"No, these are turkeys. What time do we have turkeys?"

"At the beach."

"No, we don't have turkeys at the beach. We celebrate Thanksgiving in November and we have turkeys."

The children were regularly drilled on their colors, and by this point Marcus knew most of them and was speaking louder. He handed the pointer to Raven—"Don't stick it in her eye; just give it to her"—and she rattled off, "*Azul. Rojo. Verde.*" And then she did them in English.

"All *right*, girlfriend!" Garner sang out. "You came in here speaking English and you'll leave speaking Spanish."

Then the children sang a song about little ducks who went out to play, and Raymound did some of the motions. He was saying some of the words, almost to himself.

Watching the children draw, I could see the levels of skill change as well. As they stood at an easel set up outside the classroom, some drew big sweeping lines; Maria carefully drew little circles barely the size of a quarter. "What's that?" I asked her. "A happy face," she said with a trace of a smile. She brightened a bit more each time I spoke to her. It wasn't just me, of course; the teachers were noticing that she was slowly becoming less wary.

The teachers also knew by that time in the year who could color small designs and who still needed to learn the larger, sweeping motions. While aide Deborah Chatman was laying out pictures for the children to color one day, Garner suggested a few changes. "Don't give him that," she said of one. "You could give him the ship"—which was larger—"and he couldn't hit it" because he hadn't fully developed his motor skills.

By two days before Thanksgiving, the sign-up list that had been posted on the center door for a holiday potluck was full—mostly with names of the Hispanic parents. Osuna was already starting to cut out pictures of foods with a Christmas theme, and parents were working on outlines for the children to color in December—snowmen, Hanukkah candles. In the month to come, the children would learn about how Christmas is celebrated around the world as well as talking about other observances during the period such as Hanukkah and Kwanza. Garner wanted them to learn about different customs "so that if they go to another school and meet other children they won't be surprised like I was. We do this so kids can understand other cultures. When I was little, I didn't know Jehovah's Witnesses didn't get Christmas presents and I gave a little boy a present. His father was insulted that I even offered it."

By potluck day, November 22, Veronica Perez was hard at work on red-and-white Santa Claus hats for each of the children. As one unit neared its end, preparations were always under way for the next. The morning of the potluck, the children busied themselves playing with puzzles, blocks, and spools or brushing their teeth. Andre came over to me with what resembled a pocket with a zipper on it. He didn't say anything—just handed it to me—so I was stumped as to its purpose. Deborah Chatman explained that the children could use these items to learn how to zip zippers, button their buttons, and snap any snaps. So Andre and I practiced zipping.

Even on a festive morning, there was paperwork to do. At meeting after meeting I would attend that year, across the country as in Los Angeles, there were rumblings about the records that had to be kept. When children enrolled, teachers had to check that they had inoculation records, birth certificates, and income verification, either from the welfare department or an employer. The teachers and aides recorded attendance, kept meal counts, set up and saved the daily sign-in sheets, noted the number of parent volunteers and their hours, prepared lesson plans, wrote referrals for children with possible problems, observed the children and took notes on what they observed, drew up individual education plans and went over them with the parents, and did assessments of the children's progress twice a year. "If you keep it up daily, it's not so hard," Osuna said, but it could take a half hour out of each day. Part of the paperwork load occurs because Head Start teachers wear many hats. In the public schools someone else enrolls the children and keeps those records. In the public schools someone else serves the meals and keeps those records. In the public schools a nurse writes up the report if a child is hurt and keeps those records. Head Start staff members do all that in addition to their teaching. The Training and Research Foundation needed to keep the records to satisfy the county government that it was doing what was required to run a safe and sound program, and the county government needed the records to satisfy the federal government. Still, it was always a difficult balance between maintaining the accountability of the teachers and their programs and allowing them the flexibility—and the time—to do the rest of their jobs.

Gloria Heyman, twenty-seven, took the circle time that morning; new as an aide that year after six years of volunteering at Imperial Courts, she wasn't as sure of herself as the teachers or the more veteran Chatman. Head Start is often a learning experience for its staff as well as its children, and Heyman told me later, "I've got a lot to learn." She'd had a rough childhood—thrown out of the house when she was twelve and becoming a mother at sixteen—and she liked learning how children should be raised. "What I got" from volunteering, she added, "I wanted to give back."

Heyman worked with the children on learning their colors—what was red and what was blue and what was pink. Maria spoke very quietly as she walked along the squares of color that hung below the bulletin board, naming most of them correctly, still mostly in Spanish. Andre didn't seem to know the colors, although Garner said he did, he just wasn't concentrating. When one of the children didn't recognize white, Chatman, sitting nearby, asked her what color were her tennis shoes. "White." So what color is that? "White." Chatman had started walking along the board with the children and Garner gently moved her away. Just give Heyman moral support, she added. "She'll never know how much she can do unless you let her do it."

Garner had called Andre's mother because of his prolonged whininess that day. When she arrived, she stooped down and talked to him quietly, then left. Andre stayed. Behind him the children were singing a song about popcorn popping, hopping in time with the music. Ray-mound was hopping with the rest, smiling broadly.

It was time to set the tables for lunch and have the children play out-side. Since the grass was wet, Garner decided to take the children for a walk around the block. We headed toward Wilmington, carefully stay-ing on the sidewalk until we reached a moving van that was blocking the way. Garner walked out into the street and directed the children around the van. At the corner of 105th and Wilmington, two men with their beer cans in paper bags respectfully let the children pass. Garner pointed out that here was where Josefina lived, and Maria, and Marisol at a house with a van out front. She had been to many of the houses on one of several home visits the teachers must make each year.

The walk was designed to help the children learn to cross streets safely and to follow directions—such as walking in line and keeping their fingers away from the fences so that the many dogs along the street wouldn't bite them. The walk ended at the church play yard, where Garner let the children charge around the blacktop. "Let them be children," she said. "They have to grow up soon enough." She espe-cially wanted them to run and play because some of them would be cooped up in apartments over the holiday for Thanksgiving. Raymound and Janette tore after each other while Maria, Fabiola, and Yaneth walked along a painted line in single file as Garner had taught them earlier.

Soon it was time for the children to go inside. While they waited for Garner to serve their lunch—chicken, dressing, gravy, greens, cranberry sauce, and spice cake—Osuna kept the children's attention. She had a calendar with pictures of fruit that she would slyly hide as she turned each page and then ask the children which fruit was shown for each month. The children were puzzled over the picture of sour cherries be-cause they'd never heard of that variety. One by one, the children were called away to get their paper plates—hold them with both hands, please—to have their lunch. After they ate, the parents moved the ta-bles together and covered them with the orange-and-brown center-pieces they had made of leaves and doilies and orange paper. By noon mothers and one father came in with bowls of vegetables, dishes of turkey, and plates of desserts—including a sinful yellow cake with chocolate icing and Toll House morsels on top. The tables brimmed with food, including many Mexican dishes for the parents' lunch.

Garner joined the parents, and all held hands in a circle around the table as she led a grace and then sang as she always did with the children: "Thank you for my luh-unch, *gracias por las comidas,*" and everybody laughed. Soon about fifteen or twenty parents, mostly Hispanic but a few African American, were sitting around the table, eating and chatting. Ciara's mother, who was taking a class at Trade Tech leading toward office management, came in to pick up her daughter and stayed for lunch.

"Seeing this," said Garner, "people breaking bread together—it makes my day."

Meeting the
People

Chapter Four

Fort Belknap, Montana: A Powwow to Preserve a Culture

Winston Morin pulled his small Head Start bus up in front of a pink Quonset-hut classroom at the Fort Belknap Agency and traded friendly insults with Barbara Long Knife, a veteran teacher, as she climbed aboard for the late-morning pickup run. The two-way radio hanging above Morin's left hand crackled as he started the engine; one of the children on his route wouldn't need a ride that chilly morning. The bus passed between the Kwik Stop and the information center run by the tribes on this Indian reservation in north central Montana and turned south.

The ride was my introduction to a handful of the children served by 134 Indian Head Start programs in twenty-eight states. The 168 three- and four-year-olds enrolled at Fort Belknap and the other Indian children nationwide that year made up 4 percent of Head Start's total. The experiences of these children dramatically underscore not only the impact of this federal program but also some of its problems. Indian Head Start programs also show the expanding scope of this attempt to give poor children a better start on success in school. The poverty that drew the attention of the Johnson administration was that of Appalachia, of the Mississippi Delta and rural Alabama, of inner-city Los Angeles, and of course that of the Texas Hill Country, Johnson's home. But no poverty is more intractable than that on some of the nation's Indian reservations. These children, too, have drawn Head Start's focus, as have those of migrant workers, Hispanic immigrants, and Cambodian refugees as well as physically or emotionally handicapped children who are impoverished. Each represents variations on the common theme.

That morning in Montana, Morin drove through eight miles of virtually treeless rolling hills, spotting two antelope for me, before he picked up his first customer, a shy little girl who headed for the back of the small bus. Long Knife moved along behind her to make sure her seat belt was buckled. Then we turned back north to pick up ten more children from two neighborhoods. We were less than an hour from the Canadian border in the vast open rangeland known as Montana's "high line" for the railroad that runs across the northern part of the state.

One mother came to her door when Morin pulled up in front of the modest house and honked the horn. Waving the bus away, she called out, "She's sick," as her daughter tugged on Mom's sweater. It was 11:30 in the morning and at some houses both Mom and Dad were home because unemployment officially stood at about 52 percent on the reservation—some say 75 percent because only the people who signed up for benefits got counted. Of those who had work, 40 percent earned less than seven thousand dollars a year. This is not a reservation rich from oil royalties or gambling revenues.

Morin, who doubled as a custodian for the Fort Belknap program, dropped the children off at the recreation hall, where later in the week they would rehearse for that Friday's Head Start powwow. It would be a major occasion on the reservation, the chance to start the children dancing their tribal dances. But on this day, when the children streamed off the bus, they headed for small tables that Panna Garrison, the cook, had set for lunch. That may be the only balanced meal for some of the children. Critics may consider Head Start glorified baby-sitting, but Garrison, who has had children and grandchildren in Head Start herself, would dispute that notion. Not only do the children get at least one nutritious meal a day, but they start learning their letters and their numbers and naming colors and shapes. "They are more sociable" with other children, she added.

Sociability, mingling, self-confidence: whatever the words the parents and grandparents use for it, it's a condition not to be taken for granted at Fort Belknap, the reservation for members of the Gros Ventre and Assiniboine tribes. Some children live in such isolated farm and ranch areas, thirty and forty miles from the agency, as the main part of the reservation is called, that they rarely get to town. And when they do, they are in Harlem, Montana, population 882. Harlem has two grain silos along the railroad tracks and a Main Street shopping area of two blocks. The biggest town in the immediate region—Havre, pronounced HAV-ver, population 10,000—is another forty-two miles west.

It is the land, not the towns, for which the people served by the Head Start program at Fort Belknap feel special kinship. If you are going to know about the land, you must spend a lot of time in a car. Early one evening the program's director, Caroline Yellow Robe, and I drove fully half an hour along the road south to Lodge Pole without seeing another car going in either direction. There are few other main roads on the reservation; it's mostly green or tawny rangeland, depending on the season. Reservation boundaries contain more than 650,000 acres stretching forty miles north to south, twenty-six miles east to west. I was reminded that when I had asked Yellow Robe over the telephone whether the drive from Great Falls to Harlem was a pretty one, she had replied dryly: "If you like prairie." Later I learned what she meant—the land seemed to go on forever, often without a house or barn or any sign of human habitation, even though 3,091 people live scattered around the reservation. Starkly beautiful with flat, grassy plains at the north end, the reservation land rises to about six thousand feet in the Bearpaw and Little Rocky Mountain ranges in the south. I could always sense the higher land around me even if I couldn't always see it. After driving through a landscape with so few people, I saw the approaching lights of the main agency section, where most of the population lives, entirely differently than I had perceived them when I left a few hours earlier. Now they represented a comparative metropolis.

Over vast sections of the reservation, there is little to see but telephone poles stretching off to the horizon, with Snake Butte rising abruptly from the flatland in the background. Fort Belknap, established by federal law in 1888, was named after William W. Belknap, who had been secretary of war. One of its principal tribes, the Gros Ventre, from the French for "big belly," came originally from the plains and were associated with the Algonquian-speaking Arapaho and Cheyenne. Once they had lived in Minnesota, then migrated west through North Dakota into Montana. They called themselves the White Clay People because they washed their clothing with a clay substance that turned their buckskins white. The other tribe, the Assiniboine, speak a Sioux dialect and once lived in an area from Minnesota west to the Sweet Grass Hills of northwestern Montana.[1]

Fort Belknap Agency is near the Milk River, a tributary that flows east and south into the vast Missouri River, which crosses Montana not far south of the reservation. This is Lewis and Clark country. After you drive across it for hour upon hour, you can return to their journals with a healthier respect for their trek up the rivers and over the mountains. Indeed, Lewis noted the day that the expedition first saw the Milk River—May 8, 1805, after a spell of cold, blustery weather much like I encountered the same week in early May 190 years later. "The water of this river possesses a peculiar whiteness," the journals recorded, "being about the colour of a cup of tea with the admixture of a tablespoonfull [sic] of milk, From the colour of it's [sic] water we called it Milk river."

Later in the nineteenth century, long after Lewis and Clark passed by, land in the area grew more attractive to white settlers when the Great Northern Railroad from St. Paul, Minnesota, to Seattle, Washington, was completed in 1893. The railroad's push west from North Dakota had begun in 1887 and reached Harlem on August 24 that year. That siding was finished in two days. The story goes that local folks along the rail line were upset that their sidings—and thus their communities—were identified only by numbers. They made a pilgrimage to railroad headquarters where an office worker, blindfolded, spun a globe. The cities around the world on which his finger landed became names on the raw Montana landscape—Havre, Harlem, Glasgow, Zurich, Malta. At about this same time, gold was discovered in the Little Rocky Mountains at the south end of the reservation, and the towns of Landusky and Zortman developed tough reputations. Mining still goes on today at Zortman, just over a ridge from the reservation. There a modest church stands sentinel above a wooden bar and restaurant building that doubtless dates back to the hell-raising days. The mining has been controversial because the Gros Ventre and Assiniboine have contended that it has poisoned their water supply.

Homestead acts early in the twentieth century opened the land to wheat farming and stock raising; sufficient rain between 1910 and 1918 encouraged these efforts. Dry years "left many settlers trying to find enough money to leave their shack full of dreams," as a local history puts it. The population of Blaine County, in which most of the reservation is located, peaked in 1940 at 9,566. By 1990, it was less than 7,000. Better roads, better cars, better jobs—indeed, any jobs—took people and businesses away from the county and from little towns like Harlem. Today the Fort Belknap tribes are the biggest employer in the area; others are the local schools, the one remaining local grocery store, and a few other small businesses. Grain silos mark every railroad town in this area, and there are two in Harlem, one of which is owned by the Japanese, a resident told me with some disdain. Tumbleweeds blow through the streets, sometimes seeming to outnumber pedestrians, and a hand-lettered sign on the door of Harlem's senior citizen center cautioned the elderly to "hang onto the door when the wind is blowing."

Going to north central Montana held appeal because I could learn about a rural Head Start program in a part of the country totally new to me, a part unlike the tourist attractions I had visited in Glacier National Park or along Flathead Lake in the western part of the state, unlike the comfortable college town of Missoula, with its bookstores and coffee shops. This is land people see from the train on their way to somewhere else, a place to which the Indian people (and that's what those I met usually called themselves in conversation, not "Native Americans") return to be with family.

Despite the interest I developed in the history of the Fort Belknap region, I had really been drawn there to interview Caroline Yellow Robe. Initially, I was attracted to her story because of the beauty of her name, the description inherent in it. Yellow Robe. I took with me to Montana a fascination with place names and people's names, names that conjured up memories from my childhood reading—place names like Snake Butte, Wolf Point, Rocky Boy, and people's last names like Long Knife, Stiffarm, Horse Capture, Weasel, and Yellow Robe.

But it was more than a name that led me to Caroline Yellow Robe. I was in search of personal histories that tell the tale about Head Start better than policy papers and sheets of statistics. I knew only that Yellow Robe had gone from motel maid to master's degree holder and Head Start director; I wanted to know more. As I heard her story and countless others over the weeks and months that followed, I learned about an America that escapes the headlines, that puts one foot in front of another every day to help its own families and those of its neighbors. I listened to people tell how they struggled out of a poverty I cannot imagine; the lamp that lit their path was Head Start.

Two months before I visited Fort Belknap, Yellow Robe's second husband—her first marriage ended in divorce—had died. Despite what must have been moments of deep sadness, she was persevering. She had a wry sense of humor plus a grin that brightened her round face and could light up a room. Yellow Robe, in her mid-fifties, spoke in what can only be described as a lilting manner, with a slight inflection at the end of a sentence, not quite but almost a question mark. Almost a Canadian accent, or Minnesotan. Short sentences. She had a grandma's warmth; seeing how she held on her lap a child who announced at the mini-powwow that he felt sick, I knew she was in the right line of work.

Yellow Robe had graduated from an Indian school in South Dakota that had given her no sense of any future other than returning to the reservation and raising a family. In the 1950s, the federal government moved Yellow Robe's family to California as part of its relocation efforts to find Indians jobs off the reservations. At first her husband had a job in the electronics industry in Scott Valley near San Jose, but then he had to have surgery for a hernia, so he was out of work. As an Indian woman, even one with a high school diploma, Yellow Robe found it hard to get work. She picked strawberries and other crops in the Watsonville area, part of California's agricultural heartland. She went to work early in the morning, when it was still cool, because it was easiest to pick the strawberries cleanly then. You had to get the stems, she remembered, because if you didn't, the foreman wouldn't pay you for that basket. Without the stems, the strawberries grew moldy more quickly. "We had to do a duckwalk through the field, bent over." It was right about then that she decided that she had to do something else for a living. She also decided to move back to Montana, where she had grown up, because her children were little and she didn't want them to become involved with the gangs that were attracting young people's attention. Her husband was an alcoholic, she said, and some years later they were divorced.

Yellow Robe was working as a motel maid and one of her children was in Head Start its first year—1965—when a staff member kept after her to volunteer with the program. She wasn't much interested but eventually relented because the woman knew her mother. Yellow Robe hoped that she could satisfy the persistent woman by helping children get their physical examinations one Saturday. She kept working because she could see the program helped poor people. "We were poor, but there were others so much poorer. I remember one family—the mother had run off and left the father with all these little kids," she said, gesturing with her hand to show how small the children were. "We picked them up on the school bus—they had on no shoes, no socks, and some had no underwear."

First she volunteered. Then she became a teacher's aide in the Havre Head Start program run by the local community action agency. She was hooked. She was making $1 an hour, was picked up and dropped off, and could even take home the leftover milk, she said, smiling at the memory. And she was going back to school because she had found that she could earn $2.50 an hour as a teacher. Head Start insists that aides take training so that they can learn more about working with children and can move up to better jobs. She enrolled at Northern Montana College in Havre. She took her children to her mother's home at 7 A.M., went to class from 8 to 9, worked at Head Start, picked up her children and fed them dinner, then took them back to her mother's, went to class, and studied. She was often bone weary.

Yellow Robe had never been on a college campus before attending a Head Start workshop and, once enrolled, she felt the sting of discrimination. "Some of them made you feel you were in the way. They had lots of misconceptions about Indians. They thought you had no morals, that you didn't know what soap and water was, that you took sex where you could find it, that Indians didn't know how to settle anything without fighting. That was one of my professors, a psychologist, who said that."

After six years of this, she was a junior. Offered the chance to join the Teacher Corps, Yellow Robe was reluctant to sign up because she'd already been in school for so long; she'd have to commit herself for two more years. Then came mention of a stipend to go to school and help support her children. That sold her. She went to Utah, and finished her bachelor's degree in early childhood education at Weber State College in Ogden in 1975. She insisted on doing her internship at an Indian school. By 1978 she had also earned a master's degree at Eastern Montana University in Billings.

The night we were riding out to the small Head Start center at Lodge Pole for a parent meeting (for which only one parent showed up—one of Yellow Robe's ongoing concerns), I asked her whether she had ever been frustrated all those years she was in school. Sure, she said; "my grades were like a graph of how I felt—up and down." She was determined to finish, however. She desperately needed the additional money that a fully certified teacher would earn. Yellow Robe inherited a certain stick-to-itiveness. She remembered the determination of her great-grandmother, who used to drive a horse and buggy hundreds of miles from Montana into Wyoming. Why, I asked, did she do that? "I don't know. Maybe to see relatives. She would drive through the park [Yellowstone]," over the Continental Divide. Yellow Robe knew that if her great-grandmother could do that, surely she could finish school.

After finishing college, Yellow Robe taught for five years at Hays, where even on the reservation she encountered discrimination. Young teachers, fresh from college, would be hired from out of state, enticed by the offer of free furnished housing. Just when the teachers had gotten some experience and started to know what they were doing, they'd be let go after three years—before they could get job security. New teachers would be hired and the cycle repeated. When Yellow Robe was hired, the school board passed a rule saying that no one who lived within fifty miles was eligible for the housing. That meant her. She agitated for change, as she had learned to do while working for the community action program that ran Head Start in Havre, and she and her allies ousted the school board majority. The new members didn't renew the superintendent's contract. Yellow Robe got her housing.

In 1979 she was named director of the Head Start program. She also emerged as a voice for Indian Head Start programs on a national level, serving on the boards of the National Head Start Association and the Indian Head Start Directors Association and testifying in 1994 at the first hearings ever held by Senate committees on Indian Head Start programs. During the summer of 1996 she was named to the first class of Head Start Fellows, allowing her to spend a year in Washington. She also took the two-week management training course sponsored by Johnson & Johnson at UCLA's Graduate School (see chapter 15).

Starting with a staff of eight at Fort Belknap, she built it into forty-three, adding parent involvement coordinators, a social service coordinator, a health coordinator, and a special education teacher. She hired Wilma Matt, a Chippewa from Canada married to a local Gros Ventre, as a parent involvement coordinator. When construction of the center for which Matt was to coordinate parent activity was delayed, Yellow Robe asked her to start a home-based section of Head Start. Matt, who has a bachelor of fine arts degree from the University of Montana and a master's degree in education from Harvard University, made the rounds of about twelve children once a week—children whose parents didn't want to send them to a regular classroom either because they'd been ill, because they might not have been as mature as other children or had been too isolated to work well with other children, or because the parents simply wanted them taught at home. There were also some who just didn't want to part with the children yet. Matt trained the parents to work with the children on their colors, their coordination, and other activities during the week before she visited again.

A day in the life of the Fort Belknap Head Start program was full of experiences that the children's parents said helped their youngsters when they started elementary school. School readiness, more than actual academic accomplishment, is Head Start's aim, but many of the children did start learning to count, to recognize colors and shapes, and to say the alphabet. They took field trips to places they might not otherwise see—the buffalo preserve near Snake Butte, for example—and they rode the train the eighty miles from Malta to Havre, a first for many of the children. In addition, health screenings as the youngsters enrolled helped find tooth decay and vision and hearing problems.

The examinations also helped turn up attention deficit disorders or cases of fetal alcohol syndrome, caused because the child's mother was alcoholic. With information from the screenings in hand, the Head Start staff could start to work with those children and try to head off problems that could lead to inattention and failure in school for years to come. While I was at Fort Belknap, John Weasel, who lived on the reservation, had just been hired as an aide, especially to help two children who had particular difficulty concentrating on their work or playing well with the other youngsters. Although he worked with all the children, he was particularly the strong presence for the children with behavior problems as they walked to rehearse for the mini-powwow or tried to scamper behind the bleachers instead of eating lunch. The men on Head Start staffs are often bus drivers or maintenance workers, but at Fort Belknap another young man was training to be a teacher. He liked children, he explained, and the work was more regular than fighting fires.

Head Start catches some children's problems so that they can get help before they are in second and third grade and making straight F's, Holly Allen-King, a guidance counselor and teacher at Hays/Lodge Pole School, told me. The holder of bachelor's and master's degrees, Allen-King, daughter of Fort Belknap's first Head Start director, Minerva Allen, was based in Hays, at the south end of the reservation. She had been enrolled in Head Start herself during the first summer program in 1965.

For the children on a reservation, Head Start also marks "the first time the kids are out of their family circle—away from aunts and uncles and grandparents," Allen-King added. The children gain independence and become more responsible. "That's the first step toward maturity, toward going to school. They get used to being with other children and they learn what's expected of them in school when they start."

Head Start is hardly perfect—not here, not anywhere. Yellow Robe said her program has been "written up"—held to be out of compliance—periodically because of poor attendance. Head Start programs must maintain 85 percent attendance, not always possible at Fort Belknap in winter because the youngsters catch all the childhood ailments and don't have ready access to doctors, few of whom are willing to work in such a remote spot. When it snows, sometimes the buses can't get through. And some people live so far out—Lodge Pole, for example, is forty-eight miles from agency headquarters—that if they have to make a trip to town, they take the children because they wouldn't be home in time to look after them when the half-day Head Start program ends. The buses that Head Start uses to transport the children cost money, an expenditure the budget writers far away in Washington don't always understand. For example, Yellow Robe allotted about 10 percent of her $795,000 annual budget for bus maintenance, gasoline, and drivers' salaries for vehicles to serve the Head Start centers near agency head-quarters, in Hays and in Lodge Pole.

Yellow Robe was also disturbed by the shortage of training money. "They set programs and staff up for failure without providing adequate training. Twenty years ago you could send your staff to some college for half the summer. They'd come back better prepared to go into the classroom. There was money that helped with tuition. We don't know where it went to."

Fort Belknap staff members who were working to obtain their child development associate (CDA) credential did so by attending satellite broadcasts on the reservation every Friday afternoon. It took longer to earn the CDA this way, but there was no nearby alternative. It's a con-stant battle to keep trained staff because people either get promoted out of the classroom or leave for better-paying positions with public schools. No one goes to work for Head Start to make money. Yellow Robe paid her teachers with bachelor's degrees between $9,000 and $12,000 a year when I visited in 1995. They could make $21,000 in the public schools. Nationwide, salaries for Head Start teachers averaged $17,341 in 1996 if they had the CDA, up from $10,000 in 1990, and $21,541 with a college degree. Fort Belknap Head Start staff also had no health insurance; the Indian Health Service was supposed to care for them. Despite their salaries, Yellow Robe said, Head Start teach-ers are being asked to do more today. They have to know about drug abuse, alcohol abuse. "Head Start is such a comprehensive program. You don't just learn about children. You have to learn about dealing with parents, about dealing with the community, about dealing with health problems."

Indian Head Start programs—and others in rural areas—have difficulty recruiting teachers because of their remote locations and low pay. They share another problem: Head Start was set up to be run as cheaply as possible, not to pay for bricks and mortar, so its programs always had to rent or renovate existing buildings. Until the law was changed in 1994, Head Start programs could not use federal money to build any centers; even now they must jump through many hoops before being allowed to undertake construction. Tribal leaders say few buildings are available on the reservations either for rent or renovation, so they are forced to turn to prefabricated modular units, which Yellow Robe said are too hot in the summer and too cold in the winter.

Yellow Robe went through two years of bureaucratic delays trying to start a new center for children in the Dodson area, thirty miles from agency headquarters and too far for daily bus transportation. A farmer had donated two and a half acres of land to Head Start, hoping a center would open in time for his grandson to attend. By the time money was approved for a modular building, the price had increased beyond what Fort Belknap could afford. Then there was a hassle over whether the log building that the community wanted met the definition of a modular building or whether it was new construction. Finally, during a visit by Montana's lone congressman, former representative Pat Williams, one parent complained about the delay in getting the center. Williams intervened, and three weeks later the parents had their approval. A local Mormon church donated the labor and ground was broken in mid-May 1995—with one shovel of dirt being turned by the little boy, who was by then ready to begin kindergarten. The saga wasn't over, however. Even though twenty-five children were set to attend the new center, they could not do so because the money to equip it ran out. Then the program found it hadn't gotten all the right-of-way legal papers signed that it needed. So those twenty-five children had a home-based program until the center could open.

This tale is not unusual. The Oneida tribe in Wisconsin received $185,000 for a modular classroom unit. "The modular is essentially four pieces of tin, and, of course, arrived unassembled," Oneida vice chairwoman Loretta V. Metoxen told a Senate hearing in 1994. "The tribe had to pay (from its own funds) a contractor approximately $200,000 to 'construct' the modular. Then the tribe had to pay for 'extras' such as heating units, flooring, landscaping, fencing, sidewalks, a handicap entrance ramp, a driveway, a security system and an overhead sprinkler system."

For the $605,000 total spent for the modular, Metoxen added, "we could have built a brand new, structurally sound, state-of-the-art facility. Instead, we have what the community calls 'the chicken coop,' " with problems with the heating, tile, and linoleum, a sagging ceiling, and a lack of rain gutters.[2]

These are headaches that occur out of range of the children. At Fort Belknap Head Start, their lives follow the seasons—the start of classes in the fall, from 8 or 8:30 A.M. to 12:30 for one group, with breakfast and lunch, and from 11:30 to 3:30 for another, with lunch and a snack. As the year progresses, the children learn about various national holidays and local heroes, about the changes in the weather, and most of all how to deal with one another. One morning I visited Jari Werk's class of four-year-olds, dropping in as they were finishing a breakfast of cereal, toast, milk, and banana. Then Werk's teacher aide and the classroom's foster grandmother—half the classrooms have older adults, paid under the federal foster grandparent program, who work with the children—cleared the breakfast food and dishes. The children played with dinosaur toys and plastic building blocks while their teacher corralled them, one by one, to brush their teeth. This is an important part of the Head Start day, as teachers emphasize the benefits for the children of caring for their teeth and washing their hands.

Later the children sat at their kid-sized tables to color, cut out, and decorate drawings of Indians. Like all children, they worked at different speeds and in different styles. Some colored within the lines and others didn't. Some followed directions and some didn't. Some got more glue on their hands than on their Indians, but eventually they all finished. Letting off steam in the play yard, the children gathered around aide John Weasel, who found what looked like a Montana-sized mosquito hopping around in the grass. Across the yard, little Cecil played on the tubular slide, yelling "Geronimo" as he zipped along. I asked him if he knew who Geronimo was and he looked at me as if I must be daft. "Of course," he replied, "an Indian! *Ger-on-i-mo!*" he cried even more emphatically as he took off down the slide again. In a few minutes the children paired up and walked, in mostly orderly fashion, to the gym to practice dancing for the mini-powwow that Head Start was sponsoring later in the week.

That powwow was a highlight of the Head Start year—and certainly of my visit. It carried great significance for the tribes. "Head Start helped bring back our culture," Caroline Yellow Robe said. Under government guidelines, Head Start programs must be responsive to the culture of the people they serve, and her program serves mostly Indian children, plus a few white children from town whose parents have chosen to enroll them. (There is no Head Start program in Harlem.) Yellow Robe easily recalled days of open hostility toward Indian people in local businesses and schools. Restaurants had signs declaring: NO INDIANS OR DOGS ALLOWED. Her grandmother would never take her family to restaurants on any trips because she remembered too well being kept out of them. Instead, she would buy sandwiches and they would sit and eat in whatever shade they could find. Once, long after I had taken photographs of Yellow Robe at her desk and at the mini-powwow, she told me she had always been uncomfortable around cameras. "When I was growing up," she said, "my gramma made us hide when people came around with cameras. We lived near the highway and people wanted to stop to 'take pictures of the Indians.' "

Looking back at Indian history, Yellow Robe added that "the public schools and mission schools tried to erase our culture. When my mother and grandmother went to school, they couldn't talk their language. They couldn't sing their songs. They couldn't dance their dances. They were made fun of. My people couldn't practice their religion. The elders had to practice it at night in secret." Head Start allowed the culture to reemerge, she said. "We didn't have to hide."

The Friday night I was at Fort Belknap no one was hiding. Parents and children streamed into the recreation center at the agency, drawn by the prospect of seeing the children dance, the chance to socialize among themselves as they sat on the bleachers and in lawn chairs they had brought from home, and the opportunity to win a VCR or a popcorn maker or a handmade purple satin star quilt in a raffle. The event raised money for extras for the children and the program. Sitting at a table near the emcee's platform, Yellow Robe shook her head with a wry little laugh. "Remember those meetings and how many parents came?" she asked me, looking around at hundreds of parents and children.

After one of the tribal elders gave a prayer in his own language, many of the parents circled the gymnasium floor with their children, who were beaded, bangled, and befeathered. John Weasel, emcee for the evening, introduced the tribal singers who would provide the music, including one group of teenagers who were all Head Start graduates themselves. One or two of them gave Yellow Robe big winks or shy smiles. "Pick a slow tempo," Weasel urged the singers. "This is the first time many of these children have danced for us." And dance they did, most with high animation, some with deep gravity, others sharing giggles with their friends, a few plodding along as though they'd rather be home watching television. At the end of the evening, as the youngsters started to fade, a handful of men in elaborate regalia performed strenuous dances. One wee little boy, costumed himself, joined them. When one of the men would put his ear to the ground, the child would put his ear to the ground in perfect mimicry. When one stepped especially high, the little boy would step especially high. The child was oblivious of all but the dancers.

Some families presented gifts to teachers who had helped their children that year or toys for children's special friends. When the second or third round of presentations began, I asked Yellow Robe when this custom started. "Oh," she said in her dry way, "it's gone on for years. But the gifts used to be tepees and horses." A little later the three Head Start centers on the reservation—at the agency, in Hays, and at Lodge Pole—each crowned their prince and princess of Head Start, designations earned in a fund-raising contest. "See how we take some things from the English—prince and princess?" Yellow Robe said in an aside, inflection rising.

One of the dances that night honored Yellow Robe. Staff member Wilma Matt took the microphone to tell the audience how Yellow Robe had been honored the month before in Washington. Too often, Matt said, people were more recognized away from home than at home. Not that night. The staff presented Yellow Robe with a shawl showing the three existing and one prospective Head Start centers and with DIRECTOR written in one corner. After her coworkers draped the white scarf around her shoulders, most of the tribespeople attending started walking slowly, steadily, one or two abreast in a large circle around the gym floor. As Yellow Robe moved along with her staff (and, I believe, fought back a tear), young and old would greet her with a handshake or a hug.

I had first met Yellow Robe in Washington at the ceremony that Wilma Matt described, before my visit to Montana. She was being honored by the National Head Start Association as one of its "stars," one of its success stories. She was up there on the stage with Johnson administration antipoverty director Sargent Shriver, Congresswoman Maxine Waters, Head Start director Helen Taylor, and various Head Start founders. Hers was the most emotional moment of the night when some of her staff walked to the apron of the stage and handed up to her an eagle plume, a symbol of spirituality in Indian religions.

Recalling that moment, I asked her about a pole with a row of eagle feathers that I saw hanging in her office. She explained that years and years ago it had been the custom to give such feathers to veterans of wars. Her supervisor said, "Teachers are veterans," and that it was appropriate to give them each an eagle plume. So each of the nine plumes hanging from the beaver pelt on the staff mounted over the window had been given to honor one of her Head Start teachers. "It depicts that they are leaders in the community," she told me. It's also another way to incorporate tribal culture into modern programs.

Indian Head Start programs across the country feel the urgency of saving their cultures. As Linda Kills Crow, past president of the Indian Head Start Directors Association, put it: "We often have to teach our children they are Indian. . . . They think that Indians are in 'Dances With Wolves,' but don't realize that they, themselves, are Indian, and we try to teach pride in who we are. This is very important in our communities if we are going to preserve them."[3]

Many Americans may not care whether the children of Fort Belknap and other Indian programs know their culture—although their parents care deeply. Where the Fort Belknap program is typical of those across the country, though, is in its encouragement for parents to become involved in their children's education and to change their own lives. That's why there are parent involvement coordinators in most programs of any size. It is their job to aid teachers in showing parents what they can do to help their children and the program, and to help them organize events so that they can get to know one another and work together. If there is an element of Head Start programs unknown to the general public, it is the change that Head Start has made in parents' lives.

Parents are urged to volunteer in their children's Head Start classrooms, to learn what their children should be able to do at each stage of their development, and to advocate for their kids, says Dawn Bishop-Moore, a tall, bustling woman in her mid-thirties who was president of Fort Belknap's parent policy council when I visited. When the children get to the public schools, she said, it's different. "There you have to go to the office, you can't go to the classroom. You turn 'em over in the morning and you get 'em back in the afternoon."

Bishop-Moore was a teenager herself when her first child started Head Start—the kind of parent who went to the meetings but sat in the back and didn't say much. "But through the years I got more confidence in myself, my self-esteem went up." Then a single mother on welfare, she went to the teacher of her second-oldest daughter and told her she was going to treatment for an alcohol problem; they held her child's Head Start slot open. "I went to treatment and I came back. I started feeling more confidence in myself. . . . I started basically moving up those rows of chairs, and pretty soon I was sitting in the front and I was voicing the things I would sit there and think about."

Later she not only helped set policy for her local Head Start program but saw the national picture as well as the Indian parent representative on the national board of the National Head Start Association. "Our parents have to see that there is a wider world," she told me one night as we sat over a meal at Deb's Diner and Ice Creams on the highway in Harlem. "They think nobody pays attention, but they do. They can make a difference."

Her daughter, the first of five who were in Head Start, was in the National Honor Society in high school. Because of the job her mother got as postmistress in Hays in 1993, she didn't qualify for college scholarship aid and worked in the Americorps program to try to earn a voucher to attend college.

Dawn Bishop-Moore had listed her Head Start volunteer experiences on her application for that post office job. "I feel that Head Start has had a major role in my accomplishing that." She's hardly alone. Panna Garrison, once briefly on welfare, has paid off her house and a pickup truck. Holly Allen-King worked for the school system. Reese Gray, the young man who had fought forest fires and worked in a honey factory, was training for a teaching certificate. Perry Main, bus driver and custodian at the Hays Head Start center, told me that his wife saw the value of going back to school after working as a Head Start kitchen aide; she was studying natural resources at Fort Belknap College. These are ordinary people doing ordinary jobs—paying ordinary taxes. Their stories, like Yellow Robe's, are common; virtually every Head Start director in America can tell you similar stories. And none of these people are sure where they might have been but for Head Start.

No one says it more clearly and candidly than Caroline Yellow Robe. "I probably wouldn't even be here. Where I was living, so many people have become alcoholics. I'd be six feet under from cirrhosis or whatever. That was all there was to do. You go where you feel comfortable. I went back to some of those [cocktail] lounges in Havre, and some of the people I grew up with, they're still there. . . . What my first boss did was give me the feeling I'd accomplish something—that my opinion counted for something."

Chapter Five

Auburn, Alabama: Reaching Beyond the Classroom

 uestion:
Which of these activities involves Head Start?

(A) A woman sets as her goal obtaining a commercial bus driver's license, succeeds, and then aims at a new target—taking the test for her high school equivalency diploma.

(B) A child sees a commitment to service in some of the adults around him and ultimately decides to join the Peace Corps. Later he finishes a doctoral degree in Arabic studies.

(C) A woman who dropped out of school in eighth grade nonetheless has a yearning for more education, so she earns a high school equivalency diploma, then completes bachelor's and master's degrees. She and her husband see their six children through college.

(D) A family can't pay its rent or buy food because someone got sick and there was no health insurance. They call a federally financed community services program seeking help.

(E) Thirty-six families move into new two- and three-bedroom apartments on the edge of a university town.

(F) Twin girls have their height and weight checked and wince as they have blood drawn so that it can be tested for lead and iron levels.

The answer, in Lee County, Alabama, is "all of the above."

The Alabama Council on Human Relations (ACHR) is a private, nonprofit agency that for many years has run two Head Start centers serving some three hundred children—in Opelika and in Auburn in one of the state's easternmost counties. But it does more than prepare children to learn and so to succeed in school, although that is certainly the part of Head Start's mission with which the general public is most familiar. In Lee County, the Head Start staff has learned that when one of its families is homeless or hungry, or parents are jobless or unschooled, Head Start itself must try to address the problem rather than pass it off to a state or local government agency. Program director Nancy Spears outlined her guiding philosophy this way: "You cannot talk to a poor family until they have food in their mouths, housing, and aren't worried about other things. Then you can say, 'Okay, now your kid needs a good education.' "

This emphasis on social services stems in part from Head Start's history in Alabama. When the program opened its doors in 1965, the state government and many Alabama citizens cared little about helping their poor black neighbors, who in the main were the ones who enrolled their children in Head Start. Out of prejudice, poor whites rarely did so. That first summer, as the ACHR's Head Start staff recruited children, they found mentally retarded black youngsters who had been locked in back rooms because their parents hadn't known what to do with them. Neither the state nor the public schools had programs then to help these children, so Head Start worked with them until much later, when the state assumed responsibility. Even when state or local programs were established to help low-income people obtain education or housing, government employees often treated the poor themselves as the problem. When Head Start staff members tried to work with these agencies, they were often frustrated. Because their program was under the umbrella of a broad-based human relations agency, one that had existed *before* Head Start and not only *for* Head Start, they could work directly on finding food, housing, and appropriate education and job training for families.

Nancy Spears came by this concern for others early on. Raised largely by her aunt in Rome, Georgia, Spears attended the white school near her home while the black children went to a separate school virtually across the street from hers. One day some of the white children were throwing stones at the black children. Her aunt told her that was wrong. "She said, 'God made everybody equal' and for me to never forget it! And I never forgot it." Years later, Spears had married a university psychology professor and was living in Auburn, Alabama, when she started working with the Alabama Council on Human Relations. An outgrowth of the Southern Regional Council, an Atlanta-based group seeking to improve race relations, the ACHR had helped arrange the talks that first brought together Montgomery, Alabama, city officials and leaders of the 1955 bus boycott by thousands of black citizens refusing to accept segregated seating. The Reverend Martin Luther King, Jr., who emerged as a leader during that boycott, said the council was Montgomery's only biracial group at the time that "alone . . . brought the two races together in mutual efforts to solve shared problems."

When Head Start was gearing up for its first summer program in 1965, federal planners sought agencies that would run integrated centers. Lee County officials weren't interested on that basis, so the ACHR was asked to step in. Spears operated the program out of her basement and then astounded her bosses by proposing that the agency keep running Head Start. Over the years since then, Spears has applied with regularity for any new grants or programs that will help Head Start families.

Before undertaking the program, Spears, who has a master's degree in child psychology, had read about what Head Start proposed to do. "I said, 'My God, this is the answer for a lot of these poor kids.' This was going to help children who had suffered all those years." After that first summer—which Spears has called a "horrible-wonderful" time because it was both chaotic and creative—she saw that Head Start has been only that, just a start toward all the services poor families needed. "They needed much, much more," she said, so she wrote a proposal for a federal grant for follow-through action. "They gave me a grant, believe it or not, and we went into the homes, helping families with food stamps, even though their kids were not in class" for Head Start at that point.

Parent involvement, you will hear over and over again in this book, is critical to Head Start. In those early months of Head Start in Lee County, no parent got more involved, none saw her life and the prospects for her family change more than Frankie King. A tall, handsomely dressed African American woman of fifty-seven when I met her, King was shy in those early days of Head Start. Spears first hired her as a clerk-typist although she admittedly "couldn't type a lick," and she was hesitant even to answer the office telephone, which was one of her duties. Spears would leave the room so that King would be forced to answer the phone.

King had dropped out of school in the eighth grade. She had only attended every other day anyway because she and her sister had to take care of the younger children in her family. She recalled that when her mother told her she was going to have another baby, she cried and her mother asked her why. "It's not that I didn't want her to have that baby but I just knew I would have to watch it." Married at sixteen, she had six children herself. "I was country as grits when I got married, and my father told my husband that my idea of cleaning was shoving stuff under the bed." But soon King was working as a maid, cleaning other people's homes. She worked from 8 A.M. to 2 P.M. so that she could be home when her children returned from school. She had promised her father that she would finish her education but had no idea how she was going to do that. "I dreamed of going to school but I couldn't get up that muddy hill."

One night she went to a PTA meeting. Jerry Roden, Jr., from the Alabama Council on Human Relations was telling people that the council was going to sponsor a basic literacy class. King asked what could be done for people like her who could read but still didn't have the education they needed. Roden said if there was "enough interest," the ACHR would run a class for them, too. King went door to door and recruited more than thirty people in a week. She attended the classes from 6 to 8 P.M. four nights a week at the high school for eighteen months. Her son Tim told me that the people taking the class often wore their church-going clothes—"that showed us how much it meant to them." King was "deadly afraid" of taking the test for her general equivalency diploma. "I counted up and my arithmetic told me what I had learned in two hours a night four nights a week for eighteen months was not equal to the tenth, eleventh, and twelfth grades. I told myself, 'I have not learned enough.'" She took the test. "They didn't have anything on there that I didn't know." She passed.

Meantime, a friend wanted to learn nursing at an area trade school, attended then only by white students, so King accompanied her to pick up her application. Told they could only get the application from the principal, they found he was never there—or at least people at the school *told* them he wasn't there. Finally, they asked someone who knew the principal to telephone him so he would be there on their next visit. King went to pick up the applications and the man spun them down a table in her direction and said, "People like you make me sick."

She decided that if she made him sick just by getting the application, "I would make him good and sick by going to his school."

In those days, "there was one place for blacks and one for whites and I had had no problem with that. That was the way it was done. No one was ever ugly to me, probably because I was always where I belonged. That was the first time anybody was ugly to me. It made me more determined. I don't like somebody telling me what I can't do. If that never happened, perhaps I wouldn't have been so determined to go there. I knew he wasn't going to drive me away from that school. I'm thankful for things that make it a little tougher for me. It showed me I can do it. You just have to step around or over or under those folks."

Head Start reinforced her lifelong interest in learning. "Lee County Head Start truly involved us in the program. Head Start asked us to share. That's the key to anything you are going to do—you have to believe that you can do it. Everything centered around that Head Start child. I loved books anyway. When I was little, I spent a lot of time by myself and I would read to the mops and the brooms. So what they were saying in Head Start helped reinforce what I already liked. What was important for me was that somebody else cared as much about it as I did."

King started to work for Head Start in the fall of 1965 and soon discovered that if you were a teacher, you could get money to go to classes. So she became a teacher, and Head Start helped her fulfill her promise to her father. At one point, she and two of her children were in college at the same time. King earned a bachelor's degree from Shaw University in 1975 and in 1994 got a master's degree from Alabama A & M in Huntsville.

"Not having other people I knew doing this, understanding it, was hard. The Head Start family and my own family understood, but otherwise there was not a lot of encouragement. People would ask, 'Why do you want to go to school? You have your GED, you have a good job. I wouldn't do that.' They'd say, 'Do you know how old you're going to be when you get a degree?'

" 'If I live,' I'd say, 'I'm going to be that old anyway, I might as well have a degree.' " Later she realized that "nothing could stop me but me. All I had to do was want to do it."

For a year, she commuted most weekends to Atlanta, a 120-mile drive, to take courses at a branch of Shaw University. Usually, she took her three youngest children with her. That way she'd know what kind of schoolwork they were doing and have a chance to spend more time with them. Her children saw her with books all the time and knew that if she had to study, so did they. "It was good for me and good for them. I never had the problem folks have with children who don't want to go to school."

King did have one bad experience when she was taking a sociology class at Auburn University. The professor would stand up before the seventy-five or one hundred students, all white except for King, and "she would say some things black folk did that weren't true." King preferred not to challenge the teacher in front of the full class, so she went to her office and asked, "Where did you get your information?" It stereotyped blacks and was not in the textbook. The instructor suggested that King was wasting her time in the class, to which she responded, "You're paid to teach and I'm here to learn. It's my time to waste. You teach and if I get it, I get it." That was the only D grade that King received during her college career. About six years later she recognized the woman at a Western Sizzler restaurant. She hadn't gotten tenure. She was a cashier.

"People didn't understand why I wanted to go to school. Because I liked it. I had this drive within me. I used to have nightmares and I would wake up because something was stopping me from getting to that school." One friend said she didn't want to go to school to read about "dead white folks" like John Quincy Adams. Later that same friend said she was proud of King and went back to school herself. All the travel and all the studying while working never frustrated her, King said; it was just what she had to do. "I never talked to folk who were negative. You knew who they were after a while and I stayed away from them. I was so excited. I'd say to myself, 'I'm going to get a college degree.' I was the first one in my family to get a college degree."

Frankie King and her husband, who worked for the produce department of the Winn-Dixie grocery store for thirty-four years, instilled that love of education in their children, all six of whom are college graduates. Several hold advanced degrees. Son Tim runs a Head Start program in Baltimore (see chapter 10).

Tim's brother Stephen attended Head Start its first full year and remembered the bus picking him up and dropping him off at home. Through Head Start, he got to go to children's movies at the local theater, an activity that "made the white-owned and operated cinema and normally white-patronized cinema less intimidating to a five-year-old black kid." The program's medical and dental checkups "sent a clear message that an area outside my regular family cared about my well-being."

In 1990 Stephen King told a congressional committee in Washington what Head Start meant to him and his family. Perhaps more than any other factor, he told the lawmakers, "I am a believer in Head Start because I remember it as an enterprise in which blacks and whites overcame much of the racial conflict. In very segregated Auburn, Alabama, blacks and whites could work and learn together. The adults I met through Head Start, teachers, nurses, administrators, volunteers, cooks, and others were of African American and European American and other backgrounds. The center I attended was housed in a Quonset hut which was also a Sunday school area of an all-white Catholic church. . . . There were many mornings when I woke up to find my mother and the Head Start director talking or working at my house. It was unusual to find a white person in a black neighborhood, but since we had no phone, that was the only way the program director could talk with my mother on weekends or early mornings when she wanted to. I thought of it as normal that people from various cultural groups could be colleagues and friends."

Seeing the commitment to public service of his mother and her Head Start colleagues influenced Stephen King's decision to join the Peace Corps. He served three years in Morocco, met his wife there, and in 1997 received his doctoral degree in Middle Eastern politics.

During her early days with Head Start, Frankie King also served on its parent advisory council. "One of the things that Head Start does is recognize that parents have an interest in their children but they don't know where to start and how to do it. It gives you that hope" that you can change things for your family. "I dare say that if it had not been for Head Start, I don't know what I'd have been doing. I didn't see any light anyplace. It offered that light."

In those days, she was a very quiet person. "You wouldn't know I was there," King said, although if she had questions, she would force herself to ask them. As a result of this shyness, King has empathy for others who need to be brought out of their shells. As ACHR Head Start coordinator for human services and parent involvement, she has always looked at the people sitting in the back at a meeting and not saying anything. She learned to see whom you could depend on, who would do what they said they'd do. "What I've found is that you don't overwhelm the parents. Be sure what you give them to do is something they can do. They may get tired of it but by the time they are sick and tired, they're hooked. You have to get them addicted to you."

Lee County, in which Spears, King, and the others on the council staff operate the only two Head Start centers, is the first Alabama county you reach when driving southwest from Atlanta on Interstate 85 toward the state capital, Montgomery. The county had 91,360 residents in 1995, more than one-fourth of them in rural areas. The population was one-fourth African American. Although the unemployment rate was comparatively low at 4.5 percent in 1996, many of the blue-collar jobs were in nonunion mills or were service jobs at Auburn University, and thus low paying. Seasonal layoffs were common for at least one of the county's large employers.

There are Head Start centers in Opelika and Auburn. Opelika, with 22,122 residents, used to be principally a farm community. Now it has an Ampex tape factory and a Diversified Products plant that makes exercise equipment. It's not unlike many Southern towns: two miles from the rundown housing near the Head Start center—the weather-beaten homes you see in pictures of how the poor live in small towns—are substantial, comfortable Southern homes. Old money. Auburn, linked by the Opelika Road (U.S. 29) on the north and Interstate 85 on the south, is a university town. Amid its 33,830 citizens, it too has substantial pockets of poverty. Overall, almost 20 percent of Lee County's children eighteen or under lived in poverty in 1990 and 21.6 percent of its children lived in single-parent families, which almost invariably have lower incomes than two-parent families.[1]

"It is amazing that poor people survive in Lee County," one Alabama Council on Human Relations report said. "AFDC payments, if one can get them, are woefully inadequate. There is no public feeding facility (soup kitchen), and Food Stamps are difficult to get. Only 41 percent of area schools participate in the school breakfast program. Auburn dropped its participation several years back, despite the 40% poverty rate in the city of Auburn."[2] To try to combat this indifference, the council started a hunger coalition that not only serves people who are hungry but lobbies representing those who want to see hunger end. In its efforts to serve poor families, the council also began a child-care feeding program enabling family and group day care homes to obtain money and nutrition advice for providing breakfast, lunch, snacks, and sometimes even supper for several hundred children a day; renovated and staffed a shelter—called Our House—with four bedrooms upstairs and two small apartments downstairs; and operated a day care center for infants and toddlers.

In addition to its focus on hunger in the wider community, the council's Head Start programs also made sure the children enrolled there ate nutritious meals. The morning that I visited the sprawling redbrick Darden Head Start center in Opelika, the kitchen staff was hard at work preparing taco salad for the 189 children attending that day. The cooks planned meals with foods that, among other things, were rich in iron, such as liver, spinach, and beets. Poor people usually eat lots of starches because they're cheaper, so Head Start tried to correct for any dietary deficiencies.

The Darden center, like its counterpart in Auburn, was housed in a building that was once the community's all-black school. It had closed when newer consolidated and integrated schools were built, and the council rehabilitated the space for use by Head Start. Until the ACHR obtained this school building, its Head Start programs were scattered at area churches and other smaller sites. Spears wanted to bring them under one roof to eliminate duplication of services and cut maintenance costs.

ACHR aide Michelle Pugh took me to the Darden center that day. Pugh, an energetic young white woman, was herself a former Head Start mother who had become the program's jack-of-all-trades, from hanging drapes to substituting as a bus driver. First on our agenda was a check on the health screenings that are an integral part of Head Start. Twins Lakasha and Alisia wore little hospital gowns like grown-ups do as they were weighed and measured and the information was recorded on their growth charts. I followed the twins and their mother down a corridor that years ago would have been filled with high school students changing class and heading into the lunchroom. That day a phlebotomist was working alone at a table in the large room, drawing children's blood so that it could be tested for lead levels, iron content, and sickle-cell anemia.

By the time enrollment was completed, three hundred children were expected in the thirteen classrooms at the Darden center. In addition to teachers and aides, most of the classrooms had foster grandparents, who received stipends under a separate federal program. They often comforted children who might not be too happy to be in school that day, took the children to use the toilet and wash their hands for meals, and helped supervise the outdoor play periods.

Parents want their children to learn their numbers, to be ready for school, but "what they want their children to be ready for is what they remember about school," said Faye Crandall, education coordinator for the Lee County Head Start programs. "They remember sitting in little desks, learning their numbers and letters. There's so much more to it than that." One of her knottiest problems was how to deal with parents' expectations while subtly altering them to help their children. "I want these children to succeed academically. But life is also about getting along with your neighbors and thinking through solutions. How do I talk to a parent about what they want their child to be about at twenty-five? It's not necessarily about reading and writing but about feeling good about yourself, about learning that if I can't do something here, how can I get to the place over there where I can do something?"

One of the downsides of the consolidation of Head Start sites into one large center in Opelika has been that direct parent involvement with children's education in a classroom setting—a key part of Head Start's mission—became difficult because so many families lived far from the centers. They lacked transportation, and the children came by school bus to the centers. Crandall encouraged parents to talk more with their children at home and help them learn to find answers to their questions themselves rather than having their parents tell them what to do. She and the teachers she supervised also started sending material—called RAGS, or Reading Activities and Growth for Success—home to help parents work with their children. The activity during my visit centered on having children learn about money. "Many of the children haven't dealt with money," Crandall said. "Let them count your pocket change," she would tell parents. "If you go to a store, tell them how much something costs and let them give the money to the clerk so that they see there is an exchange." She wanted parents, many of whom had little education themselves and who might be unused to talking to their children, to increase their interaction with them. "Growth and knowledge come from experience," Crandall added.

Her own experience included working the night shift at one of the local textile mills—where she soon learned she didn't want to do that all her life. She returned to school and received her master's degree at Alabama A & M in Huntsville. Asked why she wanted to work with Head Start children, Crandall, who is white, explained that she came from a poor family herself. Her father milked cows, then worked in a mill. "I've always been big, always been heavy," she said, "and people tended to think you couldn't do anything. I guess that put a fighting spirit in my heart. Having that sensitivity myself as a child made me want to do something with children that the rest of the world overlooked."

Down the hall from Crandall's office at the Opelika center was its family services center, an outgrowth of a Republican administration initiative to improve Head Start. A nationwide pilot project, of which the ACHR program was a part, showed that the families of many Head Start children needed intensive help to improve their literacy and employability as well as to combat drug abuse and other problems.

Lori Bethune, an employability specialist with degrees in psychology and counseling, was hired in January 1992 to work for the three-year family services center demonstration project at Darden. There were forty such centers in the country. She helped people on both the practical and the psychological levels. Some had no idea how to fill out a job application, what an employer would look for in an interview, or how to behave on the job so that they could remain employed. Bethune worked with them on those practical matters and helped them set short-term and long-term goals, to look for occupations based on their values and their interests so they would be less frustrated with problems at work and more likely to stay on. Some of the people, mainly women, who worked with her found jobs in day care, nursing, and food service. Bethune, like most others in Head Start, said her job would be easier if funding for the program were stable and predictable. She also wanted to see a supportive employment program established so that people could indeed be placed in jobs at training wages once they were ready for full-time work.

The ACHR's staff had tried to refer Head Start parents who wanted to take classes toward their general equivalency high school diplomas to a county program. "But some of the women had topped out at third grade," said Kay Butterfield, a literacy specialist, yet the pattern in the GED classes "was to give them a book and hope they learned. Going to class almost ended up being a punishment to get their welfare checks." So the council started its own GED classes tailored to the women's needs.

Any teacher knows that you may have to deal with what has gone on outside of class as well as the subject matter within class. "We've tried to make this a safe place for the people to come in and talk," Butterfield said. And there's always something to talk about: the day before my visit two men had fired shots at each other near the area's elementary school, so that was topic number one the next morning. How, the women were asking, could they ever hope to protect their children?

You cannot necessarily measure success by how many of these adults earn their high school diploma, Butterfield told me. So many people had so far to go; the reading level in her classes averaged fourth grade. One-fourth of these adults read below second-grade level. Some didn't read well because they couldn't see well. Butterfield noticed some of the people in her classes were holding their papers close to their eyes and moving them away or they were squinting. "All those people with low levels of reading needed glasses," Butterfield said. "And so many of their other problems are connected with their doing poorly in school. What if their vision problems had been caught earlier?"

One of Head Start's bus drivers, Teresa Frazier, was among the women in Lori Bethune's class the morning I visited. She had attended Head Start herself twenty-nine years earlier. I had heard other parents say that they had been in Head Start and now their children were. I found myself wondering, "If this is such a good program, if this is supposed to help lift people from poverty, why are people's children following them into Head Start?" So I asked Frazier that question.

Her mother had been on welfare, she told me. "People live like their mothers." But she didn't want to do that. She had had a job with the East Alabama Medical Clinic in Opelika but couldn't keep it because she didn't have her GED. She had set as one goal passing the commercial driver's test—although she was scared about taking it—and she had done that. So she had a better job driving and doing office work for Head Start, but she still wanted that diploma. Her thirteen-year-old daughter was helping her prepare for the essay part of the GED exam, the section that intimidated her most. Frazier's example provided one answer to my question: She may still be poor but not as poor as her mother.

There are other answers as well. "You don't do 100 percent of the job on any family" in the amount of time a child is in Head Start, or even in one generation, Janet Burns, the ACHR's administrative coordinator, said. Despite the success of a Frankie King, who has a master's degree as do several of her children, "you just could not get every family to that point in one generation," Burns added. When she started to work for the program twenty years ago, a vast number of the families had no one working at all. Burns had recently pulled some statistics and found that only ninety of the children now have parents who don't work. "Now we are serving the working poor," she said. "If you could get one more generation in," they might be able to move out of poverty programs altogether.

Among the other programs that started under the Alabama Council on Human Relations' umbrella to help these families are a weatherization effort that has cut home heating bills and reduced energy consumption; a community services block grant providing emergency food and housing when people lose their jobs or face other financial disasters; and construction of low-cost housing.

People want quiet, safe places to raise their children—and poor people are no different than others on that score. Students dominate rental housing in Auburn, so builders have chosen to cater to their needs rather than build many apartments for low-income people, especially those with children. Nancy Spears hired Bonnie Rasmussen as housing coordinator and handed her a grant approval for the ACHR to construct and co-own (with the construction firm) a $1.9 million project with a loan to be paid back to the government over twenty years. The city of Auburn helped by donating six acres of land for the forty spanking new two- and three-bedroom apartments that opened for tenants in the summer of 1995. Rents were kept lower than normally would be the case for housing of its quality. To qualify for the housing, tenants could earn no more than $18,000 for a family of four, although if they started making more money once they moved in, they could stay.

Veronica Jackson, a no-nonsense young woman, supervised the gracefully landscaped complex for the management firm hired by the ACHR. She held tenant meetings where she told residents there would be no loud music and no hanging out. "I've told the people about wanting to keep the place nice. If they don't like it, they can go back to the projects."

Shelter. Food. Child care. Job counseling. Basic education. Head Start. It would seem that the Alabama Council on Human Relations had its hands full in Lee County. Why, then, open a Head Start center in neighboring Russell County, as the ACHR did?

To visit Russell County, southeast of Auburn, is to step back into 1960s poverty. The statistics paint a grim enough picture: Of the 13,418 children in Russell County in 1995, almost 28 percent lived in poverty. Virtually the same percentage lived with one parent. Of live births in the county, 13.5 percent were to unmarried teenagers.[3] Those, as I say, are the facts. My abiding image of Russell County, however, lingers from a ride that Nancy Spears, Michelle Pugh, and I took down a country road just outside the small town of Hurtsboro. In one yard sat abandoned cars; a pig chowed down amid children at play. Down the road an elderly black man sat in a wheelchair in the doorway of a sagging white frame house. At least he's getting a breeze, Spears said sadly. He had no place to go and not much of a place in which to stay. The scene was pure Dorothea Lange, but I could only capture the scene in my mind, not on film as she had done during the Great Depression. Stopping the car to take a photograph would have been an outrageous invasion of the old man's privacy, which was about all he had left.

Hurtsboro, where the council rehabilitated the old high school to serve as a Head Start center, may be a bit like that old man's house: not many places to go and not much to make one stay. The rural area of the county—and it is largely a rural county—had never had Head Start. The county seat, Phenix City (notorious as the vice haven that lured soldiers from Fort Benning, Georgia, in the 1950s before it was cleaned up), ran a program for the town children; the rural superintendent hadn't cared to have Head Start, Spears told me. A few of the local black leaders and a nun who worked there urged Spears for years to go into Russell County, but she wouldn't because there were too many things undone in Lee County. "I don't believe in taking on too much because you fail. You just can't do all the things this program wants to do."

By the time of my visit, Spears and the council had won the support of a new rural school superintendent. Head Start would have four classrooms for about seventy children; an adjoining wing of what had been the black high school would be a senior citizens center. There was a gym next door and a large old building in the back that Spears hoped one day could be a family services center.

On January 16, 1996, Marian Wright Edelman, an attorney for the first Head Start programs in Mississippi in the 1960s and a strong defender of them today as president of the Children's Defense Fund, cut the ribbon opening this new Hurtsboro center named in her honor. The center gleamed and Edelman and her friend and ally Nancy Spears beamed. Down the hall, little Anganique sat shyly at a table in what the next day would become her Head Start classroom. Another chapter in the story of Head Start and the Alabama Council on Human Relations was about to begin.

Watts Towers:

Debra Alexander describes how she makes ends meet and what Head Start has done for her daughter Shardae.

Many a morning on the Watts Towers playground, I would hear someone crying out from the swing set, "Push me, Miss Kay" or at lunch, "Sit by me, Miss Kay." No one ever called more insistently than my four-year-old friend Shardae. She had been named by her grandmother, who said Shardae was African for "God has made a crown." Her middle name is Diamond—"a little jewel that needs polishing," as her grandmother had put it. Her grandmother died on Christmas Eve several years ago, but Shardae's mother, Debra Alexander, has kept working with her only child, helped in the polishing by the many hands of Head Start at Watts Towers.

The children and parents of Head Start are individuals, not case histories, not categories, so there is no way of knowing whose story is typical or indeed if there is any such thing as typical. Some of the mothers I interviewed revealed little of their own lives or were so young they had comparatively little to reveal. Some were clearly not talkers, at least not to strangers. Shardae's mother, on the other hand, was older, at forty-four, than most, and more open. She had a work history and a religious base, often answering her telephone with "Praise the Lord." She was being tested by life and she remained upbeat. "I'm a very spiritual person. Somehow God opens a door and in comes something." A tall, broad-shouldered, robust-looking woman, Alexander smiled easily and spoke earnestly.

As for Shardae, she was a frequent hugger, strong willed and bright. "She's quick," her mother said, and "she has exceeded beyond my wildest dreams. I am trying desperately to keep her in this realm" of success in school and a sunshiny happiness in life. Shardae was enrolled in a Christian school kindergarten the year after Head Start instead of attending the local public schools as her mother had done. Alexander thought it provided a better environment for her daughter.

Shardae and her mother lived in a white wooden duplex in some need of a paint job about ten blocks from the Watts Towers center.

Debra Alexander greeted me warmly, showing me into her clean and tidy house, the front room filled with philodendron plants. Shardae's books were neatly lined up on a shelf near the television. The *Encyclopaedia Britannica* and a *Roget's Thesaurus* were also shelved on either side of the TV. An array of bright prints hung on the walls, and Deb Alexander showed me with a smile how she had put them up "over the holes in the wall." We don't have much, she said, "but we have what we need. We make do with what we've got."

Alexander grew up in the neighborhood and attended Grape Street Elementary and Jordan High School. She trained at the Jordan-Locke Community Adult School and worked as a practical nurse and then a licensed vocational nurse for twenty years. She didn't intend to become pregnant. Shardae's father, unemployed when I interviewed Alexander, lived not far away; Alexander said he played an active role in his daughter's life.

Six months after Shardae was born, Alexander was riding a city bus to work when the driver stopped abruptly. She pitched forward but was holding the bus pole and dislocated her shoulder. She said that she had had surgery but the ligaments did not mend properly and the shoulder still would get dislocated. She couldn't lift over twenty-five pounds. "That ended my nursing career." She went from disability payments to the Aid to Families with Dependent Children program. "I did not want to get on the county for anything in the world. I get $433 a month and I have to make it work."

Putting Shardae in Head Start when she was three years old was a blessing. "I don't know what I would have done without Head Start. It gave her time away from me so she could get her little mind working and gave me time to regroup each day." When we spoke, Alexander was taking business English and typing at the Maxine Waters Employment Preparation Center. She attended classes to be "reskilled," as she put it, from 8 A.M. to noon every Monday through Thursday. Each morning she would take Shardae to the house of the child's grandfather, who took her to Head Start by 8:30 or 9 A.M. Then he or Alexander would pick her up at noon.

"Sometimes it gets rough" on $433 a month, especially when Alexander had been "making good money—$900 to $1,000 every two weeks" when she was a nurse. "That change put horrendous pressure on me economically." Alexander regularly walked to area churches when there would be food giveaways—mainly bread—and collected bottles and cans to turn them in for the deposit. That's how she said she would get the $25-a-month tuition for Shardae's kindergarten. "Anything I can get helps." She had also received extra milk, juice, eggs, cheese, beans, and peanut butter through the Women, Infants and Children (WIC) federal nutrition program, but that ended once Shardae started kindergarten, so more money had to be put aside for milk. Once Shardae left Head Start and did not enroll in public school, she no longer received a free lunch, so Alexander fixed that meal for her every day.

She also was receiving $169 in food stamps each month. There would be times during the month that she had to limit the vegetables she bought, depending instead on giveaways from the church. She would buy only small amounts of meat and depended on churches or charitable organizations for turkeys at the holidays and for Christmas parties for Shardae. Then, too, the stamps didn't come at the same time as the AFDC check, so sometimes she had to stretch. "Just another way they try to make us uncomfortable," she said matter-of-factly. "I rely on the church and friends to pass me clothing. Every two months Shardae needs new shoes and Payless is the cheapest thing going. Most of her clothes come from the secondhand store."

The support system in her neighborhood has helped her every step of the way. "I have a landlord who is extremely lenient and loving. And the neighborhood is great. If I need a ride, I go up the street and I can get a ride. When I wanted to take a word-processing class at Shardae's school, I needed fifty dollars for it. You can't get a school loan for that. The man who owns the liquor store loaned me the money, and I pay it back a bit at a time."

As we sat in her living room talking about making ends meet, I calculated roughly that she received less than ten thousand dollars a year. When I said that, she nodded at me. "I live below the poverty line."

She took a deep breath: "It would be easy for me to sit here and collect a check. I have five things in my wardrobe. I wear each one day a week. I keep them clean. I don't spend time at the nail shop. I don't spend time on my hair at the hairdresser. I do my own hair." Older people provided emotional support for her but sometimes she felt ostracized from women her own age. Perhaps she made them feel inferior although they weren't, she said. "When you feel bad about yourself, you want somebody else to feel bad, too. They could do the same thing I'm doing but they have a different agenda than I do, so I'm an oddball. That's okay with me. All I want to do is go to school and take care of Shardae."

Head Start helped Shardae on a variety of levels. A blood test that was part of her Head Start physical revealed that she had lead poisoning, which can affect children's learning ability and is the kind of problem parents might not spot until too late. "This is an old house. It's in the air, the dirt." So Alexander learned that she needed to give Shardae an iron-enriched diet. Through Head Start Shardae also received her immunizations against smallpox, polio, measles, mumps, and other diseases. The state's MediCal program for low-income people covered Shardae's physical, and Alexander worried about whether she would be covered by health insurance when she returned to work. "I want to return to work but I also want my child to be able to see a doctor. That's what worries so many people on AFDC—not losing the cash grant, not the food stamps, but the health care. They killed national health insurance," she said. "Everybody needs to be healthy to be productive. If not for us, let's at least have national health care for the children.

"Politicians say children are our great resource," she added, building up a head of steam. Alexander was *very* well informed about politics. "Well, don't we protect our resources? Don't we cultivate our resources? We have made our children vulnerable. Each person is born with some attribute. If that attribute is not cultivated, then it will rot away. One of these children may grow up to make a law that governs me." Shardae might become mayor or governor, her mother said, "and she would make decisions on what kind of health care I get as a senior."

We talked about race relations. Parents pass some of the racial tensions they feel on to their kids, she said, and that's natural. The children haven't known other kinds of kids, so some of the Hispanic children hang back from mingling with the African American children. "But some of the Spanish kids who didn't play with Shardae last year play with her now." Josephine Garner was teaching each group the other's culture and history, Alexander said, and she liked that. "When you are able to do that, then you start understanding their history" and who they are.

She complained, though, that some parents sent their children to Head Start just to get rid of them, not to help their development. "Miz Garner has the children's best interests at heart. But she needs more parent involvement, people who have had hard lives themselves and who understand what the children are up against."

What, I asked Alexander, frustrated her the most about her situation as she was going to school and trying to raise a daughter, in Watts, on AFDC?

"The whole bureaucratic system has become insensitive to the needs

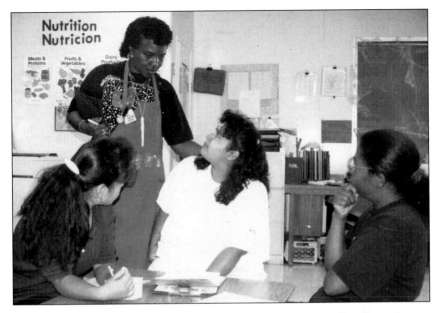

Watts Towers site director Josephine Garner *(standing)* talks about lesson plans with parents *(left to right)* Arcelia Acosta, Veronica Perez, and Helen Nolan.

Maria graduates from Head Start as teacher Lupe Osuna looks on.

All photos by Kay Mills except as noted.

Even lion kings have to brush in Head Start.

Fabiola, Yaneth, Raymound, and his pal Anthony sing a Head Start favorite, "If You're Happy and You Know It, Clap Your Hands."

Shardae hugs mom, Debra Alexander, in front of their home in Watts.

Ciara delves into a book during a break at Watts Towers.

Head Start field trips take children to science museums, like this one in Los Angeles, to see eye-catching displays.

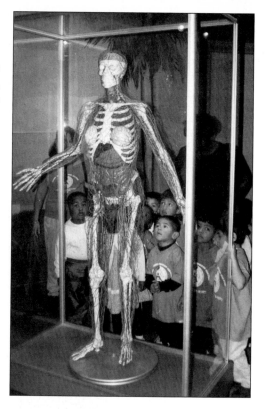

Andre enjoys his ride on a Head Start visit to Green Meadows.

Aide Deborah Chatman comforts a tearful Jesus.

Shardae shows her artwork to aide Gloria Heyman.

Josephine Garner helps Marcus string macaroni as his classmates practice their hand-eye coordination.

Andre and his cousin Raven are all smiles, and Andre's mom is proud of them both at Head Start's graduation at Watts Towers.

Luci Baines Johnson tests Wendy Lindig's vision in a 1982 screening at the Stonewall, Texas, center. Wendy is training to be a physical therapist, and her mother now teaches at the Stonewall center. FRANK WHITE, *courtesy of Brenda Lindig*

Kevin likes the books that, as part of the asthma education project for Boston's ABCD Head Start, help his teacher, Donna Coleman, explain how asthma and allergies affect him and other children.

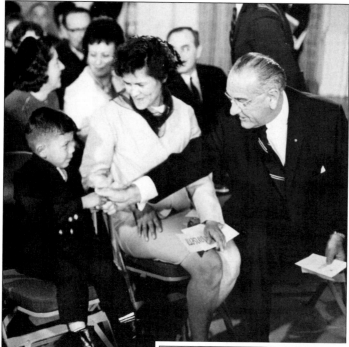

Above: President Lyndon Johnson congratulates "Pancho" Mansera as the California boy visits the White House with his mother *(center)* for the screening of a film about his Head Start experiences. ROBERT KNUDSEN, *from the LBJ Library Collection*

Right: Today, Frank "Pancho" Mansera is a machinist in his hometown, where he lives with his wife, Lorraine, and sons Frankie, Gabriel, and Steven.

Henry Gentry, with his son Taylor, credits Head Start for creating the sense that "learning is fun." He attended the program in Kansas City, Missouri, in the late 1960s.

Rachel Jones, Head Start graduate from Cairo, Illinois, reports on issues that affect children. JOHN FICARA, *NEWSWEEK*

Head Start graduate Tami Torres runs a boutique in her hometown of Merced, California. JAY SOUSA

Ismelda Cantu, site director for the migrant Head Start program in Westley, California, checks the day's attendance.

A father weary from working all day in the fields near Ceres, California, picks up his daughter at the Head Start center.

Migrant Head Start programs have long cared for infants, such as these children Josefina Martinez supervises in Westley.

Pearlene Reese, director of the migrant programs in Stanislaus County, California, recalls how Head Start encouraged her to earn B.A. and M.A. degrees.

Clarence Hall, Jr., helped raise money for Head Start programs in the Mississippi Delta during the struggle to keep centers open in the late 1960s.

The children at the Crum, West Virginia, Head Start center learn sharing as well as painting.

Frankie King *(left)* and Nancy Spears check the Auburn, Alabama, program scrapbook. King and Spears have worked together since the program got underway.

Outdoor play helps children in Opelika, Alabama, get their exercise.

Hmong children Maika *(left)* and Mae tell aide Erica Clark that "this is an apple." Clark is a graduate of the Parents in Community Action parent-training program in Minneapolis.

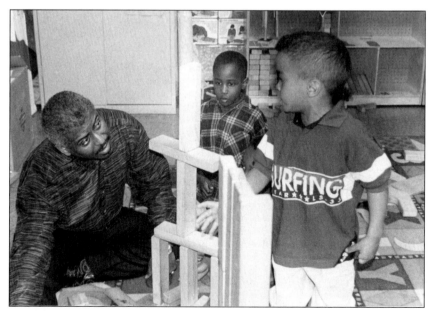

Dwayne Crompton, director of the KCMC Child Development Corp. in Kansas City, Missouri, and a former teacher himself, pays a visit to one of the full-day centers his program established.

"Mr. Bill"—William Silverman, who runs a nearby apartment complex—volunteers regularly with Head Start children in Rockville, Maryland.

Nisseth Sath *(third from left)* translates for a Cambodian father during a conference with his daughter's kindergarten teacher in San Jose. Sath worked for a project that helped children make the transition from Head Start to elementary school.

Caroline Yellow Robe *(second from left)*, Head Start director from Fort Belknap, Montana, shares a word with former War on Poverty director Sargent Shriver as Antonia Lopez, Congresswoman Maxine Waters, Dr. Marjorie Bakken, Dr. Ansel Johnson, and Sarah Greene participate in a National Head Start Association awards program.

Rick Weasel helps son Bow Horn with final touches before the Fort Belknap mini-powwow, where Head Start children learned tribal dances.

of people," she replied. "No matter what road you take, it's not enough for some people. The media and others group us all together. We're all lazy and shiftless. I'm not on drugs, the worst habit I have is cigarettes. I don't drink. What else could I be doing at the moment? . . . Sure, the media needs to report fraud and crookedness but they don't tell the positive things that we're doing and, trust me, it is a struggle to get off. Me, I have a work history. Just imagine the fear that some women who haven't worked must feel."

Shardae had been listening to us talk as we sat on the living-room couch during my first visit and she was starting to squirm. She wanted to hear a story. I told her the story about my book on Head Start; that clearly wasn't what she had in mind. As even her mother acknowledged, Shardae tended to be bossy. Her mother hoped that meant she would be a leader. "She wants to call the shots." Shardae picked out a book and started to read aloud. Her mother asked her to take a toy car and go outside, but to stay in the front yard. She did, after extracting a promise from me that after her mother and I talked, she would have my undivided attention. I kept my word. Shardae put a tape into a little tape recorder and wanted to dance. She especially wanted to do an elaborate ballroom dancing–type sweeping dip, so there I was in a little house in Watts, playing Fred Astaire to Shardae's Ginger Rogers.

"Shardae loves to read, too," her mother said. "She acquired that from Head Start." I added that perhaps she got some of it from her mother as well. "Well, they cultivated it. Head Start allows me to challenge Shardae, to help her with things that are above her. I want her to reach when she goes to school. Garner and the other teachers encouraged her."

I asked Alexander if her neighborhood had a lot of crime. "Yes," she replied. Much of it is drug related and she has told Shardae of the harm drugs can do. "Maybe I'm trying to scare the hell out of her about drugs." Alexander didn't feel uncomfortable herself because she had grown up in that neighborhood. "Maybe I feel safe here because everybody knows me. But I wonder sometimes if somebody out there shoots—as they do every night—what if the bullet penetrated the house and hit Shardae? What if it hits me and Shardae doesn't have a mother? So much of the crime is committed by juveniles. They just disregard everybody. They have no conscience."

The young people haven't had a positive nudge early in life, she said. "So much of it is in the home. If you know nothing, you can teach your child nothing."

Chapter Six

Westley, California: Seasons on the Soil

The fields and orchards of California's San Joaquin Valley were still cool, quiet, and dark at 5 A.M. as mothers and fathers in long-sleeved shirts, work pants, and heavy shoes hustled into the Westley Child Development Center, their children wrapped in light blankets and asleep in their arms. Soon enough it would be one hundred degrees amid the rows of tomato plants or at the canneries where these migrant laborers worked. For the moment, though, a sliver of moon and one or two stars lit the flat, lushly green landscape, and a bird sang softly outside the one-story brown buildings. The children barely stirred as their parents and teachers laid them on foam-rubber pallets and covered them. For the moment, all one could hear, despite the presence of several dozen children, was the hum of the washing machine in the hallway and the rare cry of a child who didn't want Mama to leave.

Elvira Garza, Sofia Gonzales, Elvira Tamez, Maria Cabrera, and other teachers and aides were at work settling the children. Tamez was tuning a radio in her classroom, futilely searching for some soft music. One teacher spoke quietly to a father in a seed-company cap about some business that needed attention. Another caught up on paperwork as the children slept. When the parents signed their children in at 5:05 and 5:10 and 5:20, they wrote on a clipboard where they were working that day, in case of emergency: Turlock Fruit Company, Tri M Farms, Salinas, Stanislaus Foods. Some had hour-long drives ahead in the gathering light; others needed only to go toward nearby Patterson or toward

Modesto, where green beans or ripening tomatoes were being cultivated or apricots picked. Many of the families lived in the trailerlike low-rent housing in the Westley camp that encircled this migrant Head Start center. Less than five miles away, truckers and vacationers sped up California's midsection along Interstate 5, barely blinking at the Westley exit, its two motels, three restaurants, and overpriced gasoline.

In the infant-care building, Cabrera or other staff members carefully checked over each arriving child for diaper rash, insect bites, scratches or bruises, or other possible health problems. Especially on Mondays, after weekend trips, the little ones often had diaper rashes, which usually cleared up quickly. Parents brought in a change of clothing for their children, turning over the little plastic carrying cases to one of the teachers and receiving them again at the end of the day. One mother in a tomato-speckled T-shirt dropped her baby off at the end of her 11 P.M. to 6 A.M. shift at Stanislaus Foods so she could sleep while her husband worked. Like the older children, these youngsters would sleep until 7:30 or 8 A.M., then be given their bottles of milk or fed around low crescent-shaped tables by several of the six or seven women who cared for them during the day. Thirty-eight infants were enrolled in this part of the Head Start program, and by 6:30 A.M. fourteen of them had been dropped off. Many fathers brought in or picked up their children, more than at most urban centers, although only one showed up at the evening parents' meeting.

Opening at 5 A.M. (or almost that early) and caring for infants and toddlers distinguish migrant Head Start centers from most other Head Start programs. Programs for migrant families also require that the children's parents earn half their income from agricultural work and have moved in the twenty-four months before the child is enrolled. Just as migrant farm labor has changed over recent decades, so, too, has care for the children of those who work in the fields. Head Start for migrant workers' children follows their parents' seasons on the soil. Some farmworkers may move less frequently today because in some communities better housing has been built for them (better, but not always good). Nonetheless, a Head Start survey showed that two-thirds of the families served made two or three moves a year. Today, if they arrive at a migrant labor camp in time to secure housing, many stay put and drive to various jobs in the area as the crop seasons change, at least in central California. The more experienced among them work every season at nearby canneries.

In the past, parents either took their youngsters into the fields with them or left them in their cars, under a shade tree if there was one. Now in communities from Laredo, Texas, to Sunnyside, Washington, and from Winter Haven, Florida, to Presque Isle, Maine, there are migrant Head Start centers in many areas where crops are being picked. For example, across the country from the Westley center, parents were dropping their children at the Head Start in the basement of St. Paul's Lutheran Church in Biglerville, Pennsylvania, before heading out to harvest apple and peach crops. To qualify for infant and toddler care there, both parents must be working. "There's not one family we have that's on welfare," said Jane Nutter, a deputy director of the agency running the Biglerville migrant Head Start. "They are families—nuclear families—mom and dad—together raising their children. I bet I could count on my hand the number of single parents in our program."

Nationwide, the bulk of Head Start students are three- and four-year-olds. When Congress extended the program's life in 1994, it authorized creating pilot projects to provide the program's comprehensive services for infants and toddlers—from newborns to three years old—at selected Early Head Start centers. Of necessity such care has long been part of the migrant program: in more settled communities working parents might have someone to care for their babies, but among the migrants that's not as likely. Migrant Head Start thus needs more teachers and aides because the ratio of staff to infants is one to three, where in classrooms for older children it's one to eight. Westley, for example, had 90 infants and toddlers under three years old at the peak of the 1995 season, as well as 150 children from three to five years old. Three-fourths of Biglerville's total enrollment was infants and toddlers.

There are other differences between migrant and regular Head Start programs:

▪ Head Start programs usually follow the traditional September-to-June school year and run half a day. Migrant Head Start programs open when the families arrive in an area. For example, the Westley center generally opens in April and runs through November or early December as parents pick cherries and apricots, then tomatoes, melons, cauliflower, and green beans, and later walnuts and almonds. The Biglerville program opens in late July and runs into November. All but a few centers are open at least eight hours a day, often receiving children before dawn and not closing until the parents return from the fields or orchards in late afternoon.

▪ On the West Coast, migrant Head Start programs are operated regionally whereas one agency—the East Coast Migrant Head Start

Project—oversees programs from Florida to Maine. It delegates the actual center operation to agencies like Rural Opportunities, Incorporated, a private nonprofit corporation that during the 1995 season served almost 900 children in Pennsylvania, Ohio, New Jersey, and New York. Overall, the East Coast Migrant Head Start Project has grown from 380 children in three states with a $500,000 budget in 1974 to almost 8,000 children (two-thirds of them under three years old) and a budget of $35 million in twelve states. In California, the Westley center is part of the Stanislaus County Child and Infant Care Association, one of the agencies that runs Head Start in a seven-county central California regional program.

■ Families working in the fields move often on the East Coast, so these programs work to pass children's records from program to program and provide some continuity in the activities that help the children develop their skills. In California, however, Hal DeArmond, director of the seven-county regional migrant Head Start program headquartered in Modesto, said that transferring the records didn't work as well. The centers have a 70 percent rate of families returning each year, but one year, out of 795 forms parents had been given the previous year, "we got back two. After four years of that, we just had to stop." However, use of new technology, including the Internet, holds great promise for record transfer.

Every Head Start center has its routines, and migrant programs are no different. The routines just start earlier. By 7 A.M. at Westley there was a cool breeze blowing outside and the sun was up. Inside the larger of the center's two buildings a few children who had just arrived were awake. In one of that building's seven classrooms, several children sat coloring at a kid-sized table while seven four-year-olds still slept on the blue pallets on the floor. Across the hall, twenty toddlers were asleep when Elvira Tamez and her colleagues turned the lights on at 7:15 and started gently waking the children, changing diapers that needed changing. By 7:30 A.M., the whole center was astir. Tamez was putting children's shoes on, one after another, calling out, "Next!" as an aide combed a little girl's hair. Shortly before 8 A.M., the remainder of the staff streamed in, punching the time clock in the front office near longtime secretary Estella Martinez's desk.

By 8 A.M. everybody was eating pancakes prepared in the large kitchen down the hall. After the four-year-olds in Elvira Garza's classroom brushed their teeth, she gathered them around for the traditional Head Start circle time—mostly but not entirely conducted in Spanish at Westley. The twenty-two children sang a song about washing their hands and combing their hair, then lined up to go outside. Across the hall, in the toddler classroom, little Roberto, not yet three, was fitting plastic cutouts of a cat, a boat, and a fish into matching frames. He knew the words *gato, barco,* and *pescado.*

In the infants' area, one teacher was working with six little ones who were getting used to different shapes and textures, in this case, macaroni. They pounded it, threw it, and put it in their mouths—everything in such exercises has to be edible for that reason. Gardenia, an eight-month-old with big eyes and a knockout smile, was stacking blocks with the slight help of one of her teachers. At 10:15, the infants had a lunch of mashed peas and bananas, having been there, after all, since 5.

Outside, Miguel was stringing orange and green macaroni with teacher Elvira Tamez and several of his classmates. She explained that she was working with the children on hand-eye coordination. For a two-year-old, Miguel was doing quite well. The day was growing pleasantly warmer, not wickedly hot yet, and little knots of children and their teachers sat under trees around the play area. Tamez pointed proudly to a young woman across the playground and said, "That's my daughter. She was in Head Start here. Now she's an aide."

Christina Barajas, almost twenty-five, had been an aide for six years and sometimes substituted as a teacher. It's hard for grown-ups to remember much about their own childhood experiences in Head Start, but Barajas did recall that she would cry when the cots came out because she didn't like to take naps. Married at fourteen, she, too, picked crops, as her husband still does. Eventually, "I said to my mother, 'Please help me get a job there. I don't want to work in the fields anymore.' "

Soon Barajas, her mother, and other teachers and aides herded the children inside for lunch, then nap time. By 2:15 or 2:30, everyone was up again and having a snack. A few of the parents who had dropped off their children when the center first opened started picking them up. One father had dirt caked on his pants to his knees; a mother collecting her infant son had an orange kerchief under a cap to help keep her head and neck cool in the heat, which had reached one hundred degrees. The teachers who opened the center had left by then, and the breeze was hot.

Teachers and aides were methodically changing the babies' diapers, washing their faces, and combing their hair in preparation for their parents' arrival. Jennifer, who explored everything, started to stand up in a little chair, and a teacher swooped over to help her down so she wouldn't fall. After 4 P.M., those children who hadn't been picked up yet were all taken to one of the classrooms in the main building so that the other teachers could prepare for the next day. Some of the parents who came in at this point had been home to shower and had on fresh shorts and shirts.

Children of migrant workers bring with them to Head Start the needs of any poor youngsters who move frequently. These often are medical problems because parents have had no access to health care or no time to tend to infections. "I never saw so many ear infections until I started working for Head Start," said Pearlene Reese, executive director of the Stanislaus County Child and Infant Care Association, who had been with Head Start since its earliest days. "I saw children with pus running from their ears. So many of these parents have to make do. The children had parasites or untreated teeth. They were not thriving."

Today children entering the program in Westley most frequently have problems with their teeth. When families are on the move or are exhausted when they come in from the fields, it's often easier to pop a bottle in the children's mouths than to feed them healthy vegetables and fruit, said Noni De La Rosa, Westley's health aide. The sugar in the milk eats at the enamel on the children's teeth. Two area dentists donate their time to check the children's teeth. In addition, a local Elks Club provides a technician who does vision screenings and a Lions Club helps pay for glasses that are needed. Teachers had noticed, for example, that one little girl had trouble finding things; it turned out she needed glasses, and had just received them when I visited.

The children at the Westley center and other migrant programs also faced emotional uncertainties. It's hard enough on some children to be left with strangers first thing in the morning even when they have settled lives. For the youngster whose family uproots itself often, that can be particularly traumatic. One morning little Ruben, new to the center and wearing an oversized Dallas Cowboys cap, would sit only with his mother, who stayed in the classroom with him that day. The next day she had to go to work, and he cried and cried. He'd run to the window and look out and cry. Anyone who came in the classroom door picked him up; he'd be quiet for a moment, then start to cry again. Elvira Garza and the other staff members spoke gently with him and let him walk hand in hand with them as they moved around the classroom. As the children played outdoors, Garza put Ruben on a seat at the back of a tricycle; he managed to flash a wan smile as another child pedaled him down the walkway. He smiled a bit more as Garza ran sand through his fingers and helped him fill a small pail. Later he ate his snack quietly, but his big eyes still held the look of a lost little boy.

Ismelda Cantu, an energetic woman in her late thirties who is the Westley center supervisor, knew all those uncertainties. Her own family, which spent each winter in McAllen, Texas, followed the crops into Illinois, Colorado, or California until she was about eleven years old. She would go to the fields with her parents and stay in the car with some of her brothers and sisters. "They'd pack two lunches—one was for us—and tell us not to get into theirs. Sometimes we couldn't help it—we did—and we'd get into trouble." Often the family worked in nearby Patterson, where Cantu now lives with her husband, Gerardo Barrera, an auto mechanic, and their daughter Nelly.

"I remember we'd go into a school and be there maybe two days. There was no work and we had to move out." In other places, "you'd finally make a friend and then you'd be gone."

Sometimes, when they were in Patterson, Cantu and her younger brothers and sisters attended Head Start. She was the middle child—the seventh—of thirteen. The younger children in her family, who had gone to Head Start, generally finished high school and some even started college. Then, Head Start was housed in barracks-like buildings; today there is a gleaming new infant and toddler center in Patterson, complete with a spotless diaper-changing area, comfortable chairs, cribs, and colorful toys. Around the corner is a new Head Start center for older children.

These buildings represent a bright spot for the migrant workers and their children, whose life centers around long hours in the flat, hot, dusty fields. "Christmas in July" and other festivities at which families can socialize at the center are popular events. The center meetings don't draw as well—about twenty parents attended a 6 P.M. session during one of my visits—but at that meeting parents learned what to do about problems on the job, what mammograms are like and where to get them, as well as how to enroll in classes to learn English. Manuel Jauregui, who had become active when three of his seven children were in Head Start in Turlock, about thirty miles away, came to the Westley center to urge its parents to become more involved. "Being a parent is a lot of responsibility. This is one," he said in Spanish to a group composed almost entirely of women. "If you are involved, you know what your child is doing and you can encourage their education," he added. *"Por favor, hagan que sus esposos vengan"*—Please, make your husbands come.

Many of the parents were young, as Cantu had been when she got involved. She had dropped out of high school in tenth grade to help support her family. Even earlier, she remembered she was cutting asparagus in Illinois or picking potatoes in Idaho. By fifteen, she was in the fields full-time, thinning tomato plants or picking tomatoes. "We'd be at work not long after five a.m.—as soon as you could see anything. You were lucky if you still lived at home because your parents would make your lunch. Once I got married, I made the lunch and I'd have to wake my husband up and tell him they were blowing the horn for us to go— they wouldn't wait."

As a teenager, she didn't mind the work. She'd have a radio and her friends there with her. When the day was over, she said, "You'd come home and slather Noxzema on your red face because your boyfriend was coming over" and then you'd be back at work the next day. She'd go to work as early as possible and stop by early afternoon. "In the heat, the tomato plants would flop over and you couldn't work as well. Then when we were picking tomatoes, even with the machines, we'd have to pick by hand the ends of the rows—*las cabezeras*—where the machines would turn. Sometimes my husband and I drive along and I see the people out in the fields and I tell him when I look at that that we are so lucky we aren't there anymore. I really feel for these parents."

Like Cantu, most of the staff at the Westley center once worked in the fields. Secretary Estella Martinez, who had been with Head Start twenty-three years, started picking crops when she was ten years old. She remembered moving her little brother in a hammock from under one tree to the next tree when the family would be picking fruit or nuts. "I hated to pick grapes. The vines were sticky and spiders hid in them. You used a little knife to cut off the whole bunch of grapes and if you didn't watch out, you'd cut yourself, too. I told my mother I would work anywhere—just please don't make me pick grapes." Martinez, who began with Head Start as an aide, helped open the Westley center each morning. Clearly an ardent supporter of the program, she asked cheerfully, "What other secretaries go to work at five a.m.?"

Workers of Mexican origin have long been a mainstay of the labor force in the San Joaquin Valley, whether braceros imported years ago to pick crops and then be sent home, or today's families of migrants, some of whom remain in the United States in the off-season—often in Texas or Arizona—while others return across the border. They may be poor, but the land on which they work is rich. And full of contrasts. On one side of the highway, those drivers roaring up Interstate 5 pass a seemingly unending flat sea of green trees and fields made possible by irrigation. Rising abruptly on the other side of the interstate are rolling, grass-covered hills, turned a tawny brown in the summer heat and looking from a distance like misplaced sand dunes—if dunes ever had a string of power lines running down them.

Westley, a town of five hundred people, elevation eighty-five feet, was settled in 1888 around land owned by John Westley Van Benschoten. It is on the northwest end of the San Joaquin Valley, which lies between the Sierra Nevada on the east and the Coast Range to the west. San Francisco is north and west of the valley, Sacramento due north, and Los Angeles due south. Originally inhabited by the Yokut and Miwok Indians, the area drew little attention until after the gold rush because neither the Spanish nor the Mexicans established missions in the area. Cattle ranches and wheat farms were established after the gold rush, and the area often saw battles over water rights. The federal government's Central Valley Project, begun in the 1930s, crisscrossed the area with irrigation canals, allowing farmers to diversify their crops. In Westley today there is a warehouse, a grocery store, a hotel and restaurant, a post office, and a few car-repair shops. The nearest city is Modesto, the county seat, about half an hour's drive.

One day Cantu drove me into the nearby fields to see if we could find the kind of tomato machine she rode as a young woman. A suburbanite, I had never heard of tomato machines, and my ignorance astounded and amused Cantu's coworkers. Not far from the Westley camp we saw a clump of parked cars, which always meant crop work in the area. Obligingly, at just that moment, there came one of the machines that picked the tomatoes, plant and all, and conveyed them to workers riding on the truck along either side. Wearing hats and often plastic sheeting or garbage bags to protect them from squirting tomatoes and ever-present dust from the fields, the farmworkers cleaned and sorted the tomatoes, which were then conveyed into trailer trucks traveling alongside. Toilet or water breaks were few, and the conditions were clearly exhausting. More than one Head Start staff member told me that she began working with young children after deciding that she did not want to spend the rest of her life riding a tomato machine.

Married at eighteen, Cantu had a daughter, whom she enrolled in Head Start. She started to volunteer for the program, "probably because I didn't want to let go." She started wondering, "What does it take to work here?" Soon she began substituting as an aide for the program and became motivated to earn her high school diploma. "Somebody out there is telling you there is something else you can do and you're realizing that you could do it." Even so, Cantu found going off to Modesto Junior College "the scariest thing," especially her first class in child development. "There were several of us and when we got our first papers back, they were full of red marks, mainly for the grammar. But they helped us. The college got us a tutor who went over our papers with us before we turned them in. So when that was over, I thought, 'I survived this. I think I can do another.' " Now she's only a few courses shy of receiving her A.A. degree and hopes to attend California State University, Stanislaus, in nearby Turlock.

"My life was in the fields," she said. "My parents had maybe a fifth-grade education. They didn't discourage education but they never encouraged it. For us, making a living, putting food on the table, surviving, was more important." Working in the fields was "all we knew. That was the norm."

Head Start staff showed her how to apply to become an instructional aide and prodded her along the way. "People believe in something that you never believed in. The people in Head Start could do things your parents couldn't do for you," she said, her eyes starting to mist over. For that reason, she has overcome hesitancy about public speaking and has talked with local high school students about having a plan for the future. There are things you can do, she told them. "They need to know that."

One of the Head Start staff who encouraged Cantu—sometimes pushing her to do jobs she feared she couldn't do—was Pearlene Reese, who was the Westley center supervisor before running the countywide program. When Reese left Westley, she asked Cantu, who had moved quickly from aide to teacher to head teacher at Patterson, to take over for her. "She was the first one to tell me I had all this potential," Cantu remembered, adding, "I think I told her no at least six times. I was afraid. I didn't want to fail. I liked what I was doing." But Reese ultimately wore her down, and she's been Westley's supervisor since 1991.

Reese had needed similar prodding years earlier. The oldest of eight children, she came with her family to the agricultural town of Dos Palos in Merced County in the 1930s. Her father had ridden a freight train from Arkansas to see whether he could find work. Over the years a small black community developed in Dos Palos as relative followed relative.

"Cotton is king over that way," Reese said. She had dropped out of school in the tenth grade to work in the fields.

"In 1965, Head Start came to town. We had never heard of anything like this before. We thought it was almost too good to be true. It was going to provide all these services for children. And there were no jobs in this little town. We were excited to think about having a year-round job. I was thirty-two and never had had a year-round job at that point."

Reese radiated enthusiasm when she talked about Head Start; it had changed her life. In 1965, she applied to be a community aide because she felt she had no skills and so could not be a teacher. The superintendent of schools, who sat in on all the Head Start job interviews, noted that she had been a regular volunteer at the health clinic at the George Washington Carver Center and thought she had promise. She could be an instructional aide, he said—on the condition that she go back to school. "There's not a choice," she remembered that he had told her.

Reese took classes in child development and finished junior college after years of work. She hadn't really known what she was doing, she explained, and because of that lack of focus she had far more credits than she could transfer to the university. She received a bachelor of arts degree from what was then Stanislaus State and in 1986 earned a master's degree in education from California State University, Sacramento. Often she would work from early in the morning at Westley, then drive either to Turlock or eighty miles each way to Sacramento to take evening classes. "I had the feeling that someone could see something in me that no one else had. At home I just helped with the work. I was the oldest and I was just the workhorse. You didn't get a lot of strokes. You just did what you did. Head Start let you try to stand on your own and was there to support you."

Head Start encouraged the parents of Dos Palos to get involved and, in tending to their children's needs, they realized that the community needed running water so the youngsters could take baths. Churches got involved in the program, too. "If Head Start never came," Reese said, "I don't know where my life would have gone. More than what it did for the children, it's what it did for the adults."

Reese has applied the same lesson she learned from that long-ago superintendent in dealing with others unsure of their abilities. Angelita Aguiniga, Westley's head teacher, started volunteering when one of her younger children was in Head Start and, like so many others, thought, "Why can't I work here instead of working out in the fields?" By then she had had nine children (eventually she had twelve), so going back to school was difficult. Her husband worked nights at a packinghouse and she worked days as an instructional aide.

"Then Pearlene asked me to become a teacher," Aguiniga said. " 'I don't think I'm ready,' I told her. 'You're either ready or not. You're either going to be a teacher or you're out. There's no reason for you not to,' Pearlene told me. I was scared. I didn't think I could do it. But it was a good decision. She helps you along."

Reese told her that there was " 'no need to be put in one spot for the rest of your life.' She would not take no for an answer." Aguiniga showed her own determination once she started back to school. "My family didn't have much education," she said, thinking about her father, who came to the United States under the bracero program. Every one of her children got an education, she said proudly—they've all graduated from universities and one has a master's degree from the University of California, Berkeley—so she decided she could get an education, too. Seventy years old, she needed three more classes to receive her associate of arts degree. "I have until the year 2000 so even if I do retire, that's what I want to do. I will have accomplished my goal."

Despite Pearlene Reese's obvious fervor for her job, the migrant Head Start program she headed was hardly without its problems. Turnover among teachers in Head Start anywhere is high because of low pay, and that is especially troublesome in the small communities that migrant Head Start programs serve or in the isolated areas where some Indian reservations are located. How many people want to live in Westley or on the prairies of central Montana? A beginning Head Start teacher in the Stanislaus program earned $8.50 an hour for an eight-hour day in 1995. Teachers could count on working about 165 to 170 days a season, which translated into $11,220 a year. Reese estimated that her program lost about 25 percent of its staff each year. She could finally offer them health, dental, and life insurance—but still no retirement benefits—so she was able to retain some of the more qualified people.

"But we often don't attract the caliber we need because migrant Head Start still is not viewed as mainstream. . . . We are the stepchild of the child development community. The families you serve don't have any status, so you don't. There's not a lot of value placed on what we do. Our programs are often unseen. Nobody knows they're out there, tucked away in farm labor camps." At one particularly remote center, she said, she lacked enough aides to handle the number of children for which the program was licensed, so some twenty children were going without Head Start services.

Reese was critical of the rush to expand Head Start to serve more children without adequate preparation time. Between 1989 and 1993, for example, Republican president George Bush presided over an expansion of the program from one that served 450,970 children at the beginning of his administration to one that enrolled 713,903 when he left office. Because of the expansion, Reese said, migrant Head Start found itself competing for staff with other local Head Start programs. Nationally, Head Start needed to do more to address the problems of training staff and providing benefits such as health insurance and retirement income, said Reese. "We need to stop and do what we do well. Maybe we can't serve more children." In addition, "people truly question what kind of educational program we offer when we open at five a.m. They think it's just baby-sitting. People also have problems with our serving infants and toddlers and having a shorter year."

What these doubters may not know is that babies are constantly learning. Everything is new; everything becomes experience. "The first thing the children learn is to be social, to be able to detach from their mothers," Angelita Aguiniga told me. "They learn to trust us, to depend on us to take care of them. They have brothers and sisters, sure, but they need to learn how to socialize with other children and with children their own age. Then they start being self-sufficient and feed themselves. They learn how to swallow, and first they eat with their hands and then they learn how to eat off a spoon. We also introduce them gradually to different varieties of food, such as rice and meat and other table food. They are also learning a routine. We mothers lay them down when they want because it's one-on-one, but they need to learn a schedule, such as not having a bottle all the time. They develop fast. If the mothers bring the infants [to Head Start] constantly, they adjust better."

Some people might say that children should learn all these things at home, that the state is taking over the parents' role, I suggested. "Some of the parents are so young, they don't know what to do," Aguiniga replied. "We had a girl twelve years old in here the other day to register her baby in the program. Twelve years old! A baby with a baby. Having a baby is the easiest thing. Taking care of it is something else." It's hard just to survive, Aguiniga said. "I know. We used to follow the carrots. We worked in the Imperial Valley before we settled in the Turlock area. You don't have time when you've worked in the field all day; you're so exhausted. If you have five or six kids, you don't have any energy. I can see how they need this program. I drive from Turlock every day and I see those women already out in the field and I think, 'Dear Lord, thanks to God, I'm not out there.' That gives me more energy to do what I do."

She needed that energy when the children woke up from their afternoon naps. Little Jennifer circulated through the whole room, pulling out toys, examining books, and exploring every nook and cranny. She and several of the other children, all under a year old, held on to a banister and climbed up four steps to a wooden slide. All the while Aguiniga or one of the other teachers sat on the little steps to lend a steadying hand and make sure no one took a tumble. In the infant-care center, each staff member had three children that she particularly observed and for whom she had the prime responsibility. But the center was open such long hours that some teachers came in early and left early, so the children had to get used to being tended by several adults.

Several aides had quit because Westley was too far from Modesto, where they lived and where their children would be starting to school. Because of Westley's location and low pay, Cantu had difficulty finding staff that had already earned six class units in child development as required. "I told Pearlene I need to hire people—and fast. The children are here and the parents need these services." So Cantu had hired seven parents in entry-level jobs as aides, and they were getting on-the-job training as well as special classes at the center. "These parents deserve a chance. Obviously someone has to train them because even though they're parents, they still need some teaching on how to care for children," she said. "I'm being selfish if I say, 'I don't want to do it.' Somebody did it for me. It's more work and you're risking the quality of what you're working for." But, in the end, she felt she had no choice but to take that risk.

First and foremost, these new aides needed to learn about the health and safety of the children. Cantu and Aguiniga also stressed that anyone working with these children—especially the infants—really had to love kids because otherwise the children could quickly get on their nerves. One young woman said after the first day that it seemed as though there were one hundred kids in the center. The second day her stress level was better and it only seemed like seventy-five. By the third day she was doing fine.

"They also have to be observant," Aguiniga said. "They have to have eyes in the back of their head. I tell them to sit somewhere that they can have a view of the whole room. They have to see what kids are doing where they might get hurt and head it off. Everyone is really responsible for all the children. Safety is the biggest part. Then feeding them enough to make sure they're healthy. I tell them the paperwork is the last part. I'll help them with that.

"They also have to use the toys as teaching devices. A toy is not a toy if the child doesn't know how to work it. They also have to learn to help children. Some of the little ones don't know how to sit up. Their parents live in little houses or tents and they don't want to put the child on the floor, rightly so. So they put the child in a car seat or one of those child seats. They don't develop any back strength that way."

Aguiniga, Cantu, and other senior staff were doing what Head Start leaders must do—creating their own staff—because the program rarely has trained teachers flocking to its doors. Working with Modesto Junior College and helped by financing from the state, Head Start teachers can receive money to cover tuition and books for some classes they need. The Stanislaus County Office of Education, the grantee that oversees the seven-county migrant program, also offered intensive teacher training twice a week. One aide said the training helped her both in dealing with the parents and in understanding the children. With infants and toddlers, she said, they can't tell you what they feel, so "every clue they give you, you have to keep in mind."

At first it was hard going back to school, many of the teachers said. Elvira Tamez, whose toddler class I visited, told me that she started at Westley in 1974 as an aide. She was eighteen then. She had eloped at thirteen and had had three children in Head Start. She, too, had worked on the tomato machines. Her daughter Christina, the Head Start aide, "helps me with the commas in the papers we write because I only went to fifth or sixth grade."

Three Stanislaus County centers, including Westley, have been selected to help provide training for teachers from migrant Head Start programs around the country. Teachers and directors come for a week at a time and, after an assessment of what they need to work on, they observe classrooms through one-way mirrors and with audio headsets and confer with mentor teachers.

The regional programs also offered literacy training for parents and older children. Several days each week Anthony Butera wheeled the "literacy van"—a Winnebago with books for children and parents and four computers on board—down the valley's back roads to Head Start centers. One afternoon I followed him to Los Banos, where several parents came with their youngsters to borrow books. One little girl stayed for almost an hour, going through one reader after another. Meantime, Allan Espinoza and other older children worked on reading comprehension and sentence structure on the two IBM and two Macintosh computers in the rear of the van. Butera, a literacy specialist, said his fond dream was to get an encyclopedia on CD-ROM for the young people to use, which he did a few months later. It was clear from looking at the housing in Los Banos—measuring perhaps twenty feet by ten feet, just big enough for sleeping and some cooking—that no one had any encyclopedias. There was no handy library, yet children often had school assignments for which they needed reference materials.

In another approach to literacy, Juan Lezama, who runs the Merced Migrant Head Start Services, also part of the seven-county regional effort, started a program teaching illiterate parents how to read and write in Spanish. Then they would be better able to learn English. "I saw that some of them had trouble even filling out our forms. They had either no education in Mexico or second- or third-grade educations." Nationally, fewer than one-third of the migrant Head Start parents speak or read English well; almost half did not finish elementary school. Lezama's program provided both basic literacy training and secondary-school work for those parents working toward their high school equivalency diplomas. "My goal is that as soon as they finish these elementary-level courses, if they get into ESL [English as a second language] classes, their English will be better."

One of the teachers in the Merced literacy program was Miriam Ortega, whose daughter, Jahdaiz, graduated in August 1995 from Head Start in the Planada migrant labor camp outside Merced and then started kindergarten. Ortega, who was encouraged to become active by Planada's social worker, Mary "Sukie" Contreras, had been president of the local and regional parent policy councils. She also enrolled in college in Blythe, California, where her family spent the winter.

"When I started working with Head Start," Ortega told me as we sat in the program office in Merced, "I had a lot of trouble with my family, with my husband. When I would go to meetings, to classes, my husband would get mad. Today he pushes me to go to school." Two years ago he also started back to school to learn more English. Ortega, a slender woman in her thirties, has traveled to Washington twice for Head Start meetings and once to San Diego. The year after I met her she became a Head Start aide, continuing to work with the program rather than picking crops because, she said, "I'd like to give back all the things they gave me. I feel close to the program. I love this program."

Involving parents who have worked in the fields all day can be difficult, but the Head Start staff has found that if programs are built around the children—like the Planada graduation—parents will come. They also like picnics and other programs involving food. Sukie Contreras, in her twentieth season with Head Start, said the most effective means of involving parents is "to make them welcome, to make them feel good about themselves. They always have something to teach me."

Parents flocked to the Planada Head Start graduation that I attended. Mothers and fathers, grandmas and grandpas, little brothers and sisters all put their folding chairs along the edge of a concrete basketball court at the migrant labor camp early on a Friday evening after the day's work in the fields was done. Inside the Head Start center there was a swirl of activity as parents brought in dishes of enchiladas, frijoles, *ensalada*, tortillas, and other food for the potluck supper that would follow the graduation. Some of the graduates, about twenty in all, walked carefully around the room in their little caps and gowns so as not to lose their caps; others delighted in darting around. With everyone assembled outside, the children marched to their seats in small chairs opposite their elders. Head Start teachers nudged reluctant two- and three-year-old performers onto center stage to sing short songs, and then the graduates paraded up to center supervisor Anna Moreno to receive their certificates.

In Head Start, you never know what has made an impression during any particular day or season. Is it a graduation like the one at Planada? Or maybe a ride on the back of a tricycle at Westley, or nap time, or a trip to the local elementary school and the first meal at the cafeteria? What sticks in a child's mind?

Ismelda Cantu remembered. When she was in Head Start as a youngster in Patterson, the center had some clothing someone had donated. "There was a red velvet dress that made me feel so good. I used to like to come in and put on that little dress. I loved it. But I didn't know what I looked like in it because we didn't have mirrors in the classrooms then. One day a teacher knew how I felt about that dress and walked me to the bathroom and held me up to see myself in the mirror in that little red dress. You remember when somebody made you feel special."

Chapter Seven

Montgomery County, Maryland: Head Start in a Suburban School System

Montgomery County, Maryland, is one of the richest counties in the United States. Bordering the nation's capital, its neighborhoods are a suburbanite's delight: azaleas and dogwoods bloom lavishly in the spring, children zip around on bicycles or skateboards on humid summer evenings, maple and oak leaves create blazes of fall color, and snow falls often enough in winter for sledding and snowmen (as well as notorious traffic snarls). Houses routinely sell for more than $200,000 to families whose median income is nearly $70,000 a year. It is a well-educated county with slightly more than half of its population over twenty-five having at least a college degree; many have one or more advanced degrees. Nearly one-fifth of its population works for the federal government and about another tenth for state or local government. County schools, which regularly send almost 60 percent of their students to four-year colleges and another 15 percent to community colleges, were supported to the tune of $882 million in 1995–96, or $7,591 per student.

But as the Bible says, the poor are always with us, and Montgomery County is no exception. More than 5 percent of the county's 795,600 people (it has a larger population than six states) earn less than $15,000 a year. Another 13 percent earn under $30,000 annually in a county with high housing costs. The Montgomery County school system, which runs Head Start, traditionally has operated its program generously, turning the usual ratio of greater federal than local support on its head by providing $2 for every $1 in federal money. It has also allowed the working poor—families of four earning $25,000—to enroll their children in Head Start; most programs limit eligibility to annual incomes under $16,000.

But the county Head Start program reached a turning point during the 1995–96 school year. It enrolled 1,554 children but had to place another 300 on a waiting list at the beginning of school because it had neither the teachers nor the space for them. The following spring, county officials applied the brakes when Head Start officials asked for the money to avoid another massive waiting list by serving additional children. "If we can't afford the Jaguar, what model can we afford?" one county councilman asked. Couldn't Head Start cut existing expenses in order to serve these children? Why not, another council member suggested, explore contracting the program out to a group using lower-paid staff? The Head Start program received its money that spring, but the council planned to experiment with a small pilot project through the county community action agency to operate a full-day Head Start program with teachers who did not have bachelor's degrees.

The national Head Start program has a system in which it often channels its money through what are called grantees, in this case the Montgomery County Community Action Agency, an arm of the county government's Department of Health and Human Services. From the outset, the community action agency worked with Montgomery County public schools as the agency delegated to operate the Head Start centers. Head Start began in Montgomery County with a six-week summer program for 545 children in 1965. Some Head Start grantees run the centers themselves; many do not. In Los Angeles County, for example, the board of education received the federal grant to run Head Start and delegated that authority to agencies such as service sororities and other nonprofit groups like the Training and Research Foundation whose sites I visited. What difference, I wondered, did it make when public school systems themselves ran Head Start centers?

Seeking an answer, I went home to Montgomery County, whose public schools have long been among the best in the United States. I know; I attended them from kindergarten through high school. I was well prepared for college. I had read history and literature, played clarinet in the band and catcher on an intramural softball team, planned school assemblies, worked on the junior high and high school newspapers, and learned how to study. My parents valued education; both were college graduates.

When I attended Montgomery County public schools in the late

1940s and 1950s, virtually all my fellow students were white. A much more Southern-seeming state then, Maryland did not integrate its schools until after the Supreme Court said segregation was unconstitutional. Even then, only a few black students enrolled in the schools in the part of the county near Washington, D.C., where we lived. The few Hispanic or Asian children with whom I took spelling lessons or played dodgeball were diplomats' children or longtime residents. Among my classmates a refugee was someone who had fled Greece after World War II or Hungary when its revolution failed in 1956. Today the county schools have added students whose families came to the United States from wars in Vietnam and Laos, famine in Ethiopia, political unrest in El Salvador, and poverty in Mexico. Many came with little money and sometimes little education. By the mid-1990s, the county Head Start enrollment was 43 percent black, almost 37 percent Hispanic, nearly 11 percent white, and 9 percent Asian. Almost thirty languages were spoken, including English, Spanish, Vietnamese, Chinese, Korean, Creole, and Cambodian.

And when I was in elementary school, the fathers in my neighborhood went to the office and most mothers were homemakers. At 5:30 P.M. I could count on some of those fathers getting off the bus at the end of our street and buying some lemonade from me at my little stand in front of our house, where it was perfectly safe for me to play storekeeper. In our neighborhood, drugs were what you took when you were sick (and yes, doctors made house calls). People often left their doors unlocked, and the only guns were old service weapons stored in trunks in the attic. Today mother and father alike drive to work; more of the young couples with children live farther out in the county, where the new schools and new town houses have been built on land that once was dairy farms or woods. High-tech companies have created jobs along a corridor leading out of the District of Columbia, but most of the employment goes to the well-educated. Pockets of poverty are left behind or created as immigrants arrive seeking jobs in the growing service industries, such as lawn care for the suburbanites who got there first. Increasingly, Head Start serves many of these immigrants' children, providing the first school experience for them and others whom the changing economy or the vicissitudes of life have left behind. It helps them learn English, exercise their curiosity, and find a safe haven.

I quickly discovered the most obvious features of the Montgomery County school system's operation of Head Start: all the centers are in public school buildings and all their teachers are credentialed. That is, they have at least bachelor's degrees and often master's degrees. Nation-wide, while many Head Start teachers have college degrees, many others do not; they hold the child development associate certificate. Cre-dentialed teachers are usually better paid than the average Head Start teacher—often a former Head Start parent—nationwide. A full-time Head Start teacher—one who had classes in both the morning and afternoon—earned $28,933 annually in 1995–96 in Montgomery County compared with the average beginning Head Start teacher, who earned $17,341 a year, or $21,541 with top experience.

Many Head Start programs either cannot pay the higher salaries of teachers who are college graduates or prefer to train as teachers moti-vated parents who have had children in Head Start themselves. They feel that these people—usually women—have greater understanding of the lives of poor children than a middle-class, college-educated teacher might have because they've been there themselves. Within the Head Start hierarchy, there is not much debate on the question: the program has preferred hiring parents who show promise and will undergo the necessary training. The risk is that unless local administrators always keep the good of the children uppermost in their minds, Head Start can become more of a community-employment program than one for child development. In the broader early-childhood-education world, what kind of training is best has been a widely debated issue. There is sup-port for both points of view—that teachers with college degrees may have a greater base of knowledge while those from the neighborhood may know better the context in which the children live. "You have to have both" backgrounds mixing in your program, one expert told me. "If you don't have the knowledge, you won't be as good a teacher. If you don't have the context, you won't stay. You'll be looking to get out."

Good teachers and bad teachers exist in all settings, can be products of the best colleges or no college, may be those who receive high pay or hardly any pay. In my travels, I saw teachers whose poor grammar was no model for young children and aides who took little initiative beyond making sure children were safe and quiet. I also saw creative teachers of all backgrounds making a lot out of a little, piquing children's curiosity, bringing shy children out of their shells and helping insecure children learn to share, spotting potential health problems, and engulfing their charges in love. Some of the most effective teachers had bachelor's and master's degrees; many did not.

I saw two pros at work on a visit to the Montgomery County Head Start: Ana Ramos, since retired, and Sheila Levine. Their teaching styles differed but the results in both cases were classes of exuberant children, learning about everything from computers to vegetables while sharing, caring, and being cared for. I also met some of the social service aides who worked with Head Start families and helped change their lives and who had had their own lives touched as well. As I would also see in San Jose, in Dallas, in Kansas City, and elsewhere across the country, it was often these aides who made Head Start more than "just" a preschool education program. They and the health and parent involvement specialists were the people who could make Head Start truly a holistic family program—or not.

First I visited Ana Ramos's classes at Rosemary Hills Head Start. A primary school, Rosemary Hills is a one-story redbrick building not far off one of the main thoroughfares in lower Montgomery County. Although the school is on a street of 1950s and 1960s two-story suburban brick houses, it also draws from apartments along East-West Highway and Sixteenth Street, where many immigrants live. One sign along a nearby walking path was in Spanish. That's normal for California or Texas, but I had not seen that sign of change in Montgomery County before.

Ana Ramos had been with Head Start for twenty years—the first fourteen as an instructional assistant—and had a master's degree in early childhood education from the University of Maryland. To her thinking, it was beneficial to have Head Start in the school system because of the training the teachers were required to have, because the classes had sufficient space and materials, such as books, art supplies, and computers, and because the staff drew credentialed teachers' salaries.

As her morning class came into the large classroom, many of the children hugged their teacher, and Ramos had quiet conversations with several of the parents, including one father from Guinea. A sedate, soft-spoken woman, she sat in a chair, not on the floor, for the usual Head Start opening, called "circle time." She had sixteen children in her morning class and fifteen in the afternoon, so she was a full-time teacher at full-time pay. The morning class included children whose parents were from Ethiopia, Guinea, Jamaica, Haiti, and El Salvador.

Families whose children attended Head Start at Rosemary Hills often shared apartments or houses because of high rents, especially in the area near the Silver Spring Metro bus and subway station not far from the school. With so many people living in one place, that often meant children might have difficulty sleeping because someone was always awake and stirring around the house. Once the children reached school, they were cranky or restless. One child's mother worked nights, so various relatives took care of him during the day. He had no routine, as was the case with many of the children who didn't have regular bedtimes, often sleeping wherever they dozed off. Her afternoon class, Ramos told me, was calmer because even if the children went to a baby-sitter in the morning, they had had more rest. Often families were in the United States illegally. "They hide in the shadows all the time. They don't take their children to the public library" or many other places. "They don't take them to doctors," often because they lack health insurance.

Part of Ramos's morning routine was to select volunteer helpers for the day: line leader, caboose, weather reporter, and children to help set the lunch tables, water the plants, and check the calendar. Ashley had calendar duty and announced that today was Thursday. Michelle had weather, went to the window, looked out, and came back to say that the sun was shining. Somebody asked why it was shining and why it hadn't been shining yesterday. The consensus: because of the clouds "way up there."

Ramos quietly called on various children. If several were eager, she told them who would be next and who after that so they would learn to take turns. The children went over their day's schedule. They would have circle time, work time, cleanup time, outdoor play, art, and lunch; then they'd brush their teeth and hear a story. Then it would be time to go home. They were learning to establish routines for learning. The day before, the children had been learning about apple seeds, so Ramos, who had gone to the grocery store to get foods that might have seeds in them, held up several green beans. "Do you think this has seeds?"

"Can we bite them and see if they have seeds?" Shamani asked.

"What is this?" Ramos asked.

"A carrot," one child guessed incorrectly. "It looks like a snake," says another. "They are called string beans," said one of the children.

"Do we eat some of these for lunch sometime?" Ramos asked, just as one child interrupted that her uncle loved them.

"Hello, the teacher's talking!" little Shamani called out to the offending child.

One of the children grew restless, so Ramos asked him to do a "magic five." The children knew that meant to sit down and cross their arms and legs—their teacher's way of having them be quiet. As Ramos cut open the vegetables with a knife, several of the children warned her not to touch the sharp part.

After playtime the children went to art class, where that instructor read to them about planting bulbs in the fall and showed them how plants develop.

"What are these called?"

"Hairs?"

"No. They are roots."

The teacher read from a book illustrated with blooming flowers of red, orange, and green, and she had the children tell her what the colors were. After the story was over, the children "planted" real seeds by pasting them on a sheet of paper and coloring an area of dirt and grass over them. Then they glued on its "root," a piece of yarn. "Cool!" said one child. Then they drew pictures of the plants growing up from the seeds and roots.

"How come we don't get to paint?" one of the children asked.

"This is crayon day," the teacher explained. "Next week we can dive into clay." The children were working in a classroom used solely for art. Each week each class spent twenty minutes each in the library, in a computer room, and with special physical education, music, and art teachers, options made possible because Head Start is located in school buildings and because Montgomery County schools have been particularly well financed over the years. In the art room, for example, supplies included crayons, glue, paper, finger paint, plastic cartons of markers, boxes of scissors and yarn, tins of paintbrushes, boxes of colored pencils, and rolls of different colored paper. I realized that another of the small luxuries was having a sink in that room solely for cleaning brushes and paint-covered hands; in the self-contained Watts Towers classroom in Los Angeles such cleanup had to be done at the same sink where the children washed their hands or brushed their teeth.

When the children returned to their classroom—about the size of the whole Watts Towers building—they exchanged the books they had taken home so their parents could read to them. They carried them in little cloth book bags that senior citizen volunteers had made for them. Ramos read them a story, then before lunch had them do the "body rock"—they danced and rocked their hips, knees, arms, and head as she called out the names of each body part for them. These kids had all the moves.

Then it was lunchtime. As they lined up to wash their hands, Fareed was bothering Jennifer, so Ramos asked, "What do you say to him?"

Jennifer looked at the teacher shyly with no answer. "You say, 'Stop it.' "
So she did. After eating, the children lined up to brush their teeth.
Around the room and out in the hall were cutouts of their families
mounted on sheets of construction paper—most were mommies and
daddies (one just had mommy). Ramos told me later that one little girl
had said matter-of-factly that the teacher wouldn't see her daddy on a
home visit because he was in jail. "He shot a man," the child had said.
The children went home by bus, so they soon lined up with their back-
packs adorned with Minnie Mouse, Looney Tunes, Pocahontas, Bat-
man, the Orlando Magic, the Lion King, or Barney.

At 12:20 P.M., the second group of children came in with aide Antia
Cacoilo, who herself had had four children in Head Start. These children went through the same routine of picking helpers—Unique would
water the plants, Glenda and Adrian would be lunch helpers, and
Franklin wanted to be line leader. Ramos told the children that that day
they would go to see Mrs. Traxel in the computer room. While they
were exchanging books before lunch, Franklin asked Ramos if she
would please tie his shoes. "You used my favorite magic word," she said.

Then the children ate their lunch quietly, brushed their teeth, and
had a lesson looking for seeds. Ramos cut open an apple and Unique
said the seeds were in a star pattern. "What is this?" said Ramos, holding up a yellow piece of fruit.

"*Banana!*" little Unique called out in her biggest voice. She was new
in class and didn't know the routine. "Unique," Ramos responded, "my
ears work very well. If you yell, you might hurt my ears." They all took a
small piece of banana to see if there were seeds in it. Ramos had
Glenda, a shy child, take a sack around for all the children to put their
banana peels in and urged her to say, "Put the banana peels in here" to
each child. But Glenda spoke to only one or two and then very softly, at
which point Charles said: "I can't hear you."

Soon the children walked down the hall and around the corner to the
computer room. There teacher Gail Traxel asked the children how
many knew how to write their names. Perhaps half did. Traxel settled
them all at computers to find each of the letters in their name. Jenny
worked enthusiastically on her own, while Glenda and Cindy helped
each other and Sally typed diligently. When each child finished, Traxel
helped him or her print out the work. "Give yourself all a pat on the
back," she said as the children finished. A roomful of computers, sufficient for each child's use even for twenty minutes at any one time, is a
luxury (or necessity) that many Head Start programs do not have.

None of Ramos's students that day had severe behavioral problems. She was fortunate because Head Start teachers around the country say they are seeing more emotionally disturbed and therefore disruptive children than ever before. They don't feel that they know how to cope, and they seek special training on dealing with these children so the classroom isn't unbearable for their classmates. Montgomery County Head Start has set aside resources to try to work with these children.

"Behavioral problems are extremely significant in our population," said Winnie Johnson, Montgomery County Head Start's disabilities co-ordinator at the time of my visit.[1] "Kids come to us with lives that are not pleasant. They see police come into their homes. Their parents or neighbors may use drugs. They have teenage mothers who haven't had any parenting themselves so they don't know what to do." She pulled out a consultation referral form and said, "I'm getting a lot more of these and for things much more serious. This is serious stuff. It's not just 'Johnny's having a bad day.' This is unsafe behavior"—fighting, kicking, biting, swearing, yelling, jumping around, constant belligerence.

Montgomery County has established four diagnostic learning centers at schools with Head Start programs. These centers have smaller classes—no more than twelve each—and teachers experienced in dealing with behavioral problems. A team of teachers and specialists meets once a month. "That's why it's so important to have a comprehensive program," Johnson said. "You can't just have behavior management programs in class. The family and other services have to be involved. We are nowhere with just one person doing it all."

Such an approach is not without its own problems. Johnson was trying to determine how classes could be made smaller and therapeutic help could be built in without having to give the children a label. "Unless you have a disability, you don't get any services," she said, but many parents fear transfer to such programs will stigmatize their children for the rest of their school years. If classes for these children are kept small, other classes have to be larger, and new behavior problems are created.

"There is a real lack of therapeutic support for children and families in crisis," Johnson said. "Those supports have to be there if education is going to work. If it doesn't work for these kids [with behavioral problems], then it disrupts education for all the others. If children are acting in unsafe ways, it's scary. Head Start shouldn't be scary. It should be a safe haven, but some of these kids are making it not safe."

Not all the children in these smaller Head Start classes are children with behavior problems or disabilities. In the one that I visited, there were three children who had been specially referred for help out of an enrollment of ten. One of the youngsters spoke little, but his teacher said he was making progress; twice a week he had a session with a speech pathologist in the same building as his Head Start classroom. Another seemed hyperactive, but again the teacher was a calming influence, often channeling his activity so that he would stay busy building a house with blocks or helping to set the table for lunch. The third child's development was seriously delayed; he was five years old and could not walk well without assistance, he didn't talk, and he may have been autistic. The other children were aware that he was not like them but they weren't shy about playing with him, which he enjoyed. When the teacher gave each child a streamer and told them to swing them up and down, he could follow those directions. At one point he wrapped himself around my legs with a loving hug.

The other children were not without traumas in their own lives. In this class, one child's father had been killed, one's mother had cancer, another's uncle had cancer, and one's father had committed suicide just the weekend before my visit—"just out of ten children," their teacher said.

These classes provide a more structured environment than other Head Start classes do. With sometimes chaotic lives at home and no regular bedtimes, the children need to know what's coming. They learn that the expectations don't change from day to day, for example, that they will have a snack every day when they arrive, they will share experiences at circle time, and then they can work and play until lunchtime. Their teacher, who had a master's degree, had long experience teaching, including sixteen years with Head Start. She and an instructional aide moved frequently from child to child, giving each of the ten some individual attention and always speaking quietly and positively to them, even when one of the boys balked at helping to clean up blocks he had scattered on the floor.

Head Start and its parents don't always succeed. Sheila Levine, the teacher I visited the day after seeing Ana Ramos's classes, recalled one student who was so out of control he literally had to be pinned down. At home, "his mother would smack him and he'd smack her back. She eventually gave up and the boy now lives with his father" out of the area.

Many young parents don't have the skills they need to raise children, Levine added. That means they don't follow up on what they say. They make threats they don't mean or they make threats when something else would work. They don't know how to get their children to go to bed. "There's no rhyme or reason to their day, no structure in the home. There's no control over what the children are watching on television. Violent movies are brought in to play on the VCR. As a result, we're seeing a lot of angry kids. There's a lot of violence and acceptance of it in their lives. It's very normal."

Levine's Head Start class at Maryvale Elementary in Rockville, Maryland, the county seat, must therefore be an oasis for these children. A ten-year veteran at Maryvale with bachelor's and master's degrees from Brooklyn College, Levine gave her students structure—and hugs. She liked teaching in Head Start because of the variety of talents it called upon. She and her aide, Gretchen Chase, a former Head Start parent, formed a particularly good team "because she has insights I don't have," Levine said. Among the children Levine and Chase taught were nine or ten who lived in a shelter for the homeless. Their program began at 7:40 in the morning and ran for six hours. Some of the children stayed for after-school care provided by the city of Rockville because they weren't able to get into the shelter until 6:30 P.M. each evening.

After the children saluted the flag and practiced marching to the tune of "You're a Grand Old Flag," Levine asked them questions about the story that had been read to them the day before, "Goodnight, Moon." Then she asked Tanya to check the weather. "It is cloudy. It is not cold," Tanya reported precisely. Levine told me later that Tanya spoke no English when she started Head Start. "She's really getting a handle on it."

The class counted the number of boys and the number of girls present—in English and in Spanish. Then they talked about the seeds they were going to plant in little cups and pantomimed a flower growing. "How does it grow?" Levine asked as the children unfolded their arms like emerging blossoms.

"Big!" they shouted.

Flowers remained the theme during art time. One little boy who was slow to develop in terms of speech and vocabulary but who loved art was painting flamboyantly—and quite well. His flower had a giant red-and-yellow blossom and green leaves. Across the room two parents worked with children who were planting seeds.

Bill Silverman—"Mr. Bill" to the children—was helping a child select the crayons she wanted to use to color a flower. A silver-haired man who ran a forty-unit apartment complex nearby, he told me that he had some extra time and wanted to do something for the community, so he had sought volunteer opportunities. First he tried Children's Hospital, but they told him he would have to deal with kids who might die. "I told them I couldn't handle that," so then he tried Head Start after seeing an ad for volunteers in a local weekly newspaper. He applied and passed the screening by Head Start's coordinator of volunteers, Patti Stefanelli, who asks two obvious questions—whether people have disabilities that would inhibit their working with children and, of course, whether they have been convicted of any crimes. Some volunteers from the community make puppets, knit caps and mittens, or sew for the Head Start centers at home while others work in the classroom. "I wonder why more men don't do this," Silverman told me. "These kids are starved for attention from men."

Several parents joined their children in the classroom and stayed for lunch—pizza, celery, carrot sticks, milk, and orange sections. Then it was nap time. "At the end of the month when the moms are running out of money, we find that even more come here," Levine said. "Some even take naps with their children," as two did that day. The program had been adopted by a group of retired nuns who had made pillows for the children to use at nap time. Levine gently rubbed the backs of several of the children to help ease them into resting.

For her part, Levine was quite clear about the advantages credentialed teachers have in the classroom. "You have a better background in child development from taking the graduate courses. You pick up anything new—and there's a lot—from reading the literature. You devise strategies from semesters and semesters in the classroom. You have to keep up with your education. It's a requirement for certification." She felt that it was also a plus to have the program physically within the schools. Many of the children would go to kindergarten in the same building where they attended Head Start, so they were used to the place and to having lots of bigger kids around. Levine knew and consulted regularly with their teachers. If a question came up two or three years after she had a child in Head Start, she was there to consult with the current teacher and the child's parents. Making the physical transition into kindergarten was thus not as big a deal as in some other Head Start programs (see chapter 13).

In addition to having teachers like Ramos and Levine with college training, Head Start in Montgomery County drew on the knowledge of parents whose children had been in the program. They served as either classroom aides or social service workers. They could tell parents from firsthand experience how they dealt with the same circumstances the children or families face today, and they could point them to sources of help elsewhere in the county.

Head Start's caseworkers—called social service assistants—usually work at four or five sites and may have caseloads of from seventy to one hundred families. All of them have had children in Head Start themselves and, like Toni Floyd, have strong personal reasons for doing what they do. That they do it for a school system shows the influence of Head Start.

"My youngest child's Head Start teacher seemed to see something in me that nobody had," Toni Floyd told me. "She didn't have me do cut-and-paste things. She really did have me do curriculum." Fresh from a divorce, "it turned out I may have needed the children as much as they needed me." She worked as an aide and would have been content to stay in the classroom "but I saw so much being lost from Friday to Monday. I saw something I could give back to the program."

She had been married to a military man and had four children from that first marriage. Before she remarried, she said, "I was in that category of working poor. I would pray somebody would ask my kids to dinner because I had only one package of hot dogs. I know what these families are going through. I was living it. I lived overseas for three years so I also know the feel of not knowing the language."

Floyd started working with Head Start in 1979 and became a social service assistant in 1981. She worked with parents who needed help finding apartments, searching for jobs, and handling their children. In many cases the parents, especially mothers, were so beaten down that they didn't know how to make things happen for themselves, she said. They also needed some reality checks—they might want a job that required a master's degree when they didn't have a high school diploma, or they thought, "If I can just get divorced, everything will be fine." She knew from experience that there were still many things to deal with as long as children were involved, and her own experience helped her win the confidence of the parents so they would open up with her.

"Head Start not only put me on a job track but what it did even more was give me self-esteem. I didn't realize I didn't have an identity. I was very happy being somebody's wife, somebody's mom. I didn't have an identity crisis—I didn't have one to begin with. Head Start showed me, 'Hey, I can do this. I'm really good at this.' Head Start took my strengths and utilized them."

* * *

While there doubtless are those in Head Start who chafe within the school system, the Head Start program run by Montgomery County was among the best that I saw in my travels. It should be. The teachers seemed well trained and highly motivated, the facilities ample and safe, the needed supplies available, the social services accessible, although caseloads per worker were clearly too high for maximum impact. The program was trying to help children with behavioral problems while serving their classmates as well. It was working on the transition between Head Start and elementary-school classes. If all school systems were like Montgomery County's, I would have less concern about proposals to turn Head Start over to the states, where they would doubtless be administered by the education establishment. But of course all school systems are nowhere near as comprehensive in their outlook as Montgomery County's and not nearly as well financed.

But it did have disadvantages. One downside was the extra layers of bureaucracy that Head Start encountered by being part of the school system. It took longer to initiate programs or respond to new situations because more people had to be consulted, more had to sign off, more had to get enthusiastic. Creative ideas may get lost in the maze, and some children overlooked in the shuffle.

Head Start in Montgomery County ultimately receives many of its funds from the county council, a political body in a very politically attuned community. So not only must its Head Start program sweat out congressional decisions, it also faces county political and budget maneuvering. So far Montgomery County has done well by Head Start. However, I've seen too many other school boards and county commissions across the country to whom I'd feel distinctly uncomfortable entrusting Head Start's future, especially given that the poor are not a popular constituency.

Head Start is enriched by having some of its programs run by public school systems like that in Montgomery County. But it also benefits strongly from the diversity of the agencies that operate Head Start centers: groups that were active in the fight for racial justice in the South; Indian tribes sensitive to the needs and customs of their own children; broad-based nongovernmental community action agencies that can help families with job training and housing concerns as well as early-childhood education and care; organizations staffed by people who used to pick crops themselves and know what it takes to escape that life.

Watts Towers:

Gunfire erupts near a TRF center. The parents talk about future lessons. A popular counselor arrives. Andre's mother comes for a conference. And the children learn about Christmas, Kwanza, and Hanukkah.

Aide Deborah Chatman hung up the telephone one winter morning just after I arrived at the Watts Towers Head Start and told me that there had been a shooting near the Imperial Courts center the day before. The staff had been reassigned for the day, so I shouldn't go there. I didn't need to be told twice. In my initial swing around many of the Training and Research Foundation centers, I had been at Imperial Courts Head Start the first day of school when we heard five or six gunshots in the distance. It was a tossup who moved faster, site director Annette Russell in closing the door, or me in getting out of the way. The day of the latest shooting, staff members from a gym near the Imperial Courts center had gone to the two Head Start classrooms around lunchtime to warn the teachers that a feud among several young men from the neighborhood could well lead to violence. Children arriving for the afternoon Head Start session were sent home quickly. Not long afterward, one young man was shot and killed; another had been severely wounded.

The incident gave me pause, especially because the staff and children at Imperial Courts were no longer anonymous to me. After Watts Towers, I visited that site most often; the two centers were only a mile apart. I had gotten to know Russell almost as well as the staff at Site 05. In the interconnected world of Head Start, she had taught Josephine Garner's grandson and Garner later taught one of Russell's grandchildren. LaShunda and Yolanda Davis, Deborah Chatman's daughters and students at UCLA when I met them, had attended the Imperial Courts Head Start. Gloria Heyman's daughter had attended Imperial Courts Head Start, and Garner had been a parent volunteer there.

Russell, fifty-seven, had come to Los Angeles from Mobile, Alabama, in 1956. She started working for TRF in 1975 and earned a child development associate certificate, a requirement for teaching at Head Start.

She had been Imperial Courts supervisor for five years. Her style in working with the children appeared more casual and grandmotherly than Garner's, but she was no pushover. She reprimanded children who swatted others or who ran in the classroom, warning that they could get hurt. But then she consoled them and held them on her lap when they bumped a head or skinned a knee. She spent hours the first day of school trying to figure out how to help a three-year-old stop crying. "On the first day of school, we used to have a lot of crying," she said, a touch ruefully. "There's still some but we don't have much of that anymore. These children are too used to being on their own." The first day I had visited her, Russell told me the staff found a three-year-old girl wandering around the projects, untended.

Russell would shake her head in disbelief when she told me about such incidents. She was a woman of blunt opinions. Too many of the people in Imperial Courts had money but did the wrong things with it, she complained. The drug PCP had been the downfall of many. "They don't work," she said. The pre-Christmas fatal shooting was not unusual, either. During the summer, Russell said, "we heard shooting and we had to gather all the children and come inside and hit the floor. Sometimes they walk around with guns just like the Old West."

If I had trouble settling down to watch the children at the Watts Towers center after hearing about the shooting, I had to wonder how it affected youngsters to whom gunshots were not so rare. Had any of the children I knew seen the shooting?

With some difficulty, I swung my focus to a curriculum meeting that Watts Towers site director Josephine Garner was having with several parents elected to serve as officers for the local center. Helen Nolan arrived first, her baby in a carriage. Daughter Jameisha gave her a kiss on the cheek, then joined the other children playing on the floor. Under the bulletin board, Christmas stockings bearing the children's names were all hung with great care. Garner explained the plans for the next month to the parents while Lupe Osuna settled the children into their morning routine. The children would be discussing how the weather had changed since fall and why they were wearing warmer clothing.

"We definitely won't see snow in California. We know it doesn't snow" in Los Angeles, Garner said. To show the children something resembling snow, the teachers would put ice and rock salt in a glass and scrape the resulting frost off the outside. They would display summer and winter clothing and talk about the differences. And always they would incorporate numbers, shapes, colors, the alphabet.

In the middle of January the children would learn about Dr. Martin Luther King, Jr., and observe his birthday holiday. "We end up with a number of kids wanting to be Dr. King when we have the children portray various black history figures in February," Garner said. "I remember one Mexican child being King one year—he's still walking around feeling so proud."

Garner explained to the handful of parents that the teachers would be starting to teach the children handwriting; their main focus would be on the alphabet. With both the alphabet and numbers, Garner said she was concerned that the children not just recite by rote but also recognize letters or numbers out of sequence. The alphabet booklets they were planning to make would allow parents to reinforce the work at home. They'd teach the alphabet even using the King holiday—K is for King.

Helen Nolan commented that Jameisha knew her colors but sometimes confused them. Nolan talked with her about the cartoons she watched on television, asking her what she remembered about them to check her level of concentration. Of Martin Luther King, she said she wanted Jameisha to know "he was somebody who worked for our people," to understand "about the march [on Washington] opening the door for black people." And she wanted her to know that "he was a man of God."

Garner interjected that King "did not only march for blacks. He worked for all mankind." When they reached February and Black History Month, Garner added, they would have other examples besides King of noted African Americans—inventors, scientists, politicians, musicians. For example, they would learn about George Washington Carver and the development of the peanut—peanut butter being ever popular among the children. Over the years Garner had gathered curriculum books that helped the teachers deal with African American and Mexican history and culture for young children.

Soon Veronica Perez, president of the center's parent group, arrived with her two older daughters, Cynthia and Diana. Garner filled her in about the alphabet book and the handwriting exercises, adding that many children didn't know how to hold a pencil. Perez said that she had noticed that, too, a few days earlier, when the parents and teachers were helping children sign a card thanking someone who had donated books to the center. "Only about four could write their names by themselves."

"You can't make a W if you can't stroke up and down," Garner said. "So we work on these skills. But we can't focus enough on this part of the work if there aren't parents volunteering. You have to get the children to sit down and you can't concentrate on the teaching if you are dealing with their wandering."

I asked if they found that the children were more hyperactive now than a few years ago. Yes, they agreed, although Perez reminded the group that the year before, when the Power Ranger cartoons were popular, there had been more fighting and kicking as the children mimicked the Rangers. "This year they don't listen," Perez said. "You can tell them something five times and they don't pay attention."

If that's a result not just of lack of concentration but a deeper problem, counseling and other special help is available in a range of situations:

- A child acts up to the point of being a danger to himself or to other children.
- A child is a slow learner or rarely says anything.
- A child's family has had a trauma—death, illness, alcoholism, drug abuse. Or the child has seen an act of violence, like the Imperial Courts shootings.

The Training and Research Foundation worked through the Los Angeles school system, which wanted to identify children with potential learning problems early and which contracted out for the counseling services. I saw some counselors who were good, and some who seemed unable to connect with the children. None had enough time to spend at any one center to make a real impact. Spotting trouble early is one positive aspect of Head Start, but too many programs are not able to follow through with the thoroughness they would like or that children deserve.

Some of the four-year-olds at Site 05 focused intently on what they were doing; others were easily distracted or roamed the room. Some, like Ciara or Kimberly, spoke up loud and clear; others mumbled or barely spoke at all. Julie Kammerer worked for the Child and Family Services agency, one of the agencies that contracted to help TRF; she had a real rapport with the children. But she would also be the first to admit that she couldn't spend all the time with each one that she would have liked. (The following year when I returned to the center, the counselor who succeeded Kammerer, who was earning a master's degree, had been assigned to spend twice as much time with the children. You could see the impact of that extra attention.)

If a Head Start teacher spotted a child with speech problems, she would fill out a referral form and give it to the TRF disabilities co-ordinator. Then Kammerer or one of her colleagues would visit the center to screen the child on speech and language skills. They would also assess social skills such as joining in play, sharing, and helping themselves, as well as motor skills such as grasping a crayon or catching a ball. Once the Head Start teachers received Kammerer's report, they drew up a plan to help the child. Then the child's parent was asked to meet with the TRF Head Start disabilities coordinator, Lidia Vargas; a school official, Addie Moore; and the Head Start teacher. If the parent didn't want the child to have any special intervention, "that is something we need to respect," Kammerer said. "We are here to do what the family wants." That happened once at the Watts Towers the year I was visiting—the teachers thought a little boy in the afternoon class needed work on his speech but his mother declined, saying he would grow out of the problem. Sometimes, the teachers told me, parents won't admit that their child has a problem and so turn down any extra help.

Kammerer commonly found children who had problems speaking clearly or even talking at all. Many were from Spanish-speaking families and were in school for the first time—faced with other children, adults they didn't know, and a language they couldn't speak. "They commonly go through a six-to-eight-month silent period. They're assimilating what's around them. Ninety-nine percent of them are speaking beautiful English by June."

Others, though, had problems making the emotional adjustment from home to school. Some had suffered traumas such as seeing a shooting or being molested. In other cases, no one talked much to the children at home or listened to them. They simply didn't get much practice talking. Kammerer viewed this early detection of potential learning problems as one of Head Start's main strengths. When she visited centers, she would do whatever she could to get the children talking—work with flash cards, accompany them on the playground, push them on the swings—anything to discover what they might like to talk about.

One day while I was at Watts Towers, Kammerer came through the door and many of the children called out, "Hi, Miss Julie!" She was clearly a favorite visitor. Joshua gave her a big hug. Kammerer also worked with Marisol, who rarely spoke but pointed at objects or at other children doing something she didn't like. I learned that Marisol's sister had Down's syndrome and sometimes communicated by pointing, not talking, so Marisol may have been imitating what her sister did. Her mother said Head Start helped give her the confidence she needed that she knew the right words for what she wanted to say.

Another December morning while I was at the Watts Towers center, Addie Moore from the Los Angeles school district arrived with Lidia Vargas to consult Garner and Andre's mother. Before the conference began, Moore told me that she wanted to help children see themselves as learners. Too often, she said, parents limit their children by doing something for them because they think that they can't do it themselves. If that's the case, the child isn't learning. I thought back to Marcus's mother putting his shoes on for him because she said he took too long doing it.

Andre's mother arrived on her way to her job at a hamburger shop in downtown Los Angeles. "Is it all right if I sit in on the conference?" I asked her. Fine. Normally these meetings were confidential.

Andre and his mother lived then with her sister, Raven's mother. Andre loved his little cousin, and he was having to learn to share her attention with others and indeed to share toys or books as well. When Andre was on the playground, he might be riding a tricycle and see another child enjoying a Hula Hoop. He'd decide that's what he wanted to do, right then and there. Once he got the Hula Hoop, sometimes asking, sometimes taking, he'd want to do something else again. If he didn't get his way, he would sulk or cry. Moore suggested to Andre's mother that she always assure him that he would get a turn if he shared. Garner told the group that Andre was learning to get along with other children. He would put up his hand, saying, "Stop! I don't want to hit you."

When discipline changes between home and school, that poses a problem for children. Moore told both teacher and parent that they had to be consistent. "If something's a no-no today, it has to be a no-no tomorrow." The consequences needed to be the same. "We as parents often send the wrong signal," she added. "They know if they keep bugging us, then we'll give them what they want to get rid of them. Do that once and they think they can do it again. If it's no, it's no."

Andre's mother said that she could tell what her son was learning in Head Start about crossing the street safely or about shapes such as squares and triangles. She had also been impressed when he counted for her in Spanish. Moore urged her to tell him that what he had learned was good, to reinforce what he was picking up in the classroom.

Sometimes Andre did not follow directions. "When you ask him to do something and he's just standing there, you may have to restate it because he may not have understood the vocabulary you used," Moore said. Children often understand questions asking "what" first, she added. "If you ask what they had for breakfast, they'll tell you," but if you ask *when* they had it, they may tell you *what* again. "We cannot assume that because we tell him that he gets it."

The question now: what next? Moore told Andre's mother that they could recommend that when he entered kindergarten, he receive special education. Some parents fear special education, she explained, because they think it will label their child. But no money comes for help without a label. Teaching social behavior doesn't fall into the categories covered by special education, but teaching language and speech—that is, helping a child understand what is expected—does. The women explained to Andre's mother what official forms would follow him to kindergarten. This committee of school staff, Head Start staff, teacher, and parent needed to decide whether Andre should have the service and whether it should be continued into kindergarten. Andre's mother said yes to both, and Garner nodded in quiet agreement. As the meeting broke up, Andre came over to give his mother a good-bye hug, and she headed off for her job.

Andre and the other children at Head Start loved Christmas, loved singing "Jingle Bells," loved their teachers. Travell would jump up to hug teacher Lupe Osuna around the knees—then so would Clintisha-beth, then Wayne, then Marcus. As they scampered back to their seats in the circle, Osuna said to the children, "Good morning. What day is today?" Some guessed Saturday.

"I don't come to work on Saturday," Osuna replied. "Today is Thursday." After they went over the days of the week, they talked about Christmas. Osuna explained that Christmas was not just about receiving. "It's about giving, too. You have to give your love to your mama." The lesson plans called for studying how holidays are celebrated around the world—not just Christmas but also Hanukkah and Kwanza. With the help of a recording, the children had been learning their numbers one to ten in Swahili as preparation for Kwanza. The books around the room reflected the seasonal focus as well: *The Sweet Smell of Christmas, Seven Candles for Kwanzaa, The Story of Christmas,* and *Rudolph the Red-Nosed Reindeer Shines Again.* Having lots of books around is important at Head Start so they're there whenever the children want to pick them up; there might not be many in their homes.

The crafts period, in which the children developed their hand coordination, focused on making a Star of David for Hanukkah. Garner produced two triangles out of sticks "like the doctor uses to make you say 'ah,' " and then placed them together as a six-pointed star. "Do not put it in your mouth. Do not stick someone," Garner told the attentive children.

Maria was starting to talk more, and in English. I asked her what she had done that day. "I made a star," she said, and counted with me the number of sides on each triangle she had used.

After one morning's craft activities, Osuna read to a small group of children from a book picturing ducks in the snow. "Who has seen snow?" she asked these California kids. "Who has touched it? What does it feel like? Is it cold or hot when it snows?" Both Osuna and Garner explained in detail the stories they were reading. They worked to involve the children in counting or identifying the animals they could see and naming the colors, trying all the while to link the story however they could to the children's own lives. When they finished, they asked the children what they remembered.

At playtime, the teachers took the children for a walk around the block. I walked with Michael, a stocky, powerfully built child who dwarfed my other hand-holding pal of the day, little Jameisha. Michael wasn't saying much in class at that point, but both he and Jameisha talked up a storm on our walk. Jameisha told me her house was decorated for Christmas. We passed many dogs, and Michael told me he had a dog. Some of the center's neighbors were outside decorating their houses and they waved at the children or chatted with them. It was a peaceful preholiday scene, and hard to believe that only a mile away a Head Start center was shut down because of a fatal shooting.

Chapter Eight

Where Are They Now?

P ancho Mansera was a listless five-year-old. He wasn't growing. "The sun bothered his eyes and he used to scream all the time," his mother recalled. He was frequently ill, and his face and neck were bloated. He spoke very little and rarely smiled. His parents, Simon and Mercedes Mansera, lived in the farming country between San Luis Obispo and Santa Maria in central California. They had taken Pancho to doctors but nothing they did seemed to help.[1]

In the summer of 1965, Marie Burt, a nurse, suggested that the Manseras enroll Pancho in a new program called Head Start, where he would get a complete physical and whatever follow-up help was needed. Dr. William Tibbs, who was giving the examinations, found that Pancho had a thyroid condition that was treatable by medication. When photographer Jim Vestal from the *San Luis Obispo County Telegram-Tribune* came to the center, he snapped a shot of Pancho sitting by himself while the other children played. By the end of the summer, Pancho was starting to pay more attention to his surroundings.

His medical treatments took much of his time away from kindergarten, so he wasn't ready for first grade with his classmates and returned to Head Start for a second summer. By then he was running and playing—he never sat still, his Head Start teacher said. Over that year, he had grown five and a half inches. When the *Telegram-Tribune* photographer returned, he found Pancho and his younger brother Tino in the midst of all the activity. "Medical authorities state that if Pancho's problem had not been identified and he had not received thyroid treatment at this early age," the newspaper reported, "he would have been malformed, mentally dull, and had difficult psychological problems, that is, if he had lived at all." His teacher that summer, Henry Grennan, told the newspaper that Pancho would be well equipped to handle kindergarten classes that fall.[2]

Pancho became Head Start's poster boy—featured on the cover of a brochure about the program and then in a short film. The twenty-five-minute color documentary showed Pancho selecting a book for Grennan to read to the class and cupping his hand to his ear as though he were listening to the sea. In the film, Grennan took the children for a nature walk, and Pancho ran happily alongside his teacher. At the end of the documentary, Pancho hugged his teacher, and the movie concluded with the message that Pancho was "completely alive, with life and loving life."

President and Mrs. Lyndon Johnson invited Pancho, his parents, his teachers, the doctor, the nurse, and others to the White House, where they showed the film in the East Room at a March 13, 1967, event honoring Head Start. Henry Grennan, who retired in 1996 after more than thirty years as a teacher and school principal in Santa Maria, California, remembered that he and Pancho had made a greeting card to give the president. When Johnson saw it, he said, "Hey, this is for me," and leaned over to shake Pancho's hand. Grennan also took some California poppy seeds to Mrs. Johnson because of her interest in wildflowers. Pancho nibbled on fresh strawberries dunked in powdered sugar at the reception in the State Dining Room, and later went to the zoo, saw John F. Kennedy's grave, and posed on the steps of the Lincoln Memorial with his dad.

Lady Bird Johnson especially thanked Pancho for coming to the White House. "To have a movie named for you is quite an honor even for a movie star, you know. I have never heard of a movie named 'Spencer,' or 'Marlon,' or 'Kirk.' But I think you especially deserve the honor for, as a star, you cast a bright light of promise for us all."[3]

Sargent Shriver, head of the antipoverty program, introduced President Johnson, saying, "This is not the first time the president has seen this film. He's seen it twice before."

The president corrected Shriver. "I've been seeing this story not twice but for thirty years, ever since I taught in a Cotulla, Texas, school. I brought my 'Pancho' home to Johnson City for the summer. His name was Juan Gonzalez, and my mother and I gave him a home. Now Juan is a successful businessman in South Texas." The president stressed how much the investment made in Head Start would mean to others like Pancho.[4]

Today Frank Mansera—still called Pancho by many of his old friends—works as a machinist in Santa Maria, not far from Nipomo, the small town in which he attended Head Start and where he lives. On the way to Nipomo, I had seen the green rolling hills where there is still much open space, and I understood better why the Manseras had stayed in the area—and was glad they had. I probably never would have tried to find Pancho had he lived in a big city like Los Angeles.

Mansera told me he had dropped out of high school to work when he was some twenty units shy of getting his diploma and he had been determined to go back. "I wanted a diploma, not a GED," he said. "I felt that void that I needed to fill." So a few years ago he attended night school and graduated from high school. Married, he has three sons and a stepdaughter. His wife, Lorraine, works at a convalescent home and they are buying a small house at the end of a quiet cul-de-sac where the boys play basketball and other games. His wife said that he spends a lot of time with his children and makes sure they do their homework. A trim and easygoing thirty-seven-year-old, he still takes his thyroid medication every day.

I asked him what Head Start had done for him. He thought awhile as he sat in his living room and finally replied, "I want to say this right. It gave me a second chance in life. I started living life like a normal kid."

Not every turnaround in Head Start is as dramatic as Frank Mansera's. But many of the program's graduates and their parents can tell about gains in educational and social development as well.

Siretha Gentry was working at Western Electric in 1969 when she enrolled her son Henry in Head Start in Kansas City. She and Henry's father were divorced when the child was one year old, and Henry said it was important for him to be with other children. "You learn the whole world doesn't revolve around you. That's a vital lesson." For his mother's part, she liked Head Start because it gave her son "a well-protected environment" in the daytime, "yet he was still learning." She always bought him educational toys and found that "Head Start really reinforced what I was trying to do at home."

Gentry was a class officer in high school, belonged to the Chess Club, Math Club, and debate team, and was selected for the National Honor Society. He went to college on a scholarship and graduated from the University of Kansas in 1988 with a 3.4 average, which meant he was consistently on the dean's list. His favorite subject was always math. He was also president of the Minority Business Association, which helped recruit more minority students. "I'd go to high schools to tell the students about opportunities in business. You can get their attention when you remind them it's dealing with money."

When I interviewed him, he was a bank examiner for the U.S. Treasury Department's Kansas City office. Gentry had previously worked as an accountant for Price Waterhouse; he had always wanted to go into business. "I have an entrepreneurial spirit. I knew accounting was the language of business and if you're going to succeed, you need to know the language." On Monday nights when he was not on the road, he was tutoring five high school students in algebra and trigonometry through a program at his church.

I asked him the same question I asked Mansera—what did Head Start do for him?

"It created the atmosphere that learning is fun. And I've kept that attitude. I'm the kind of person who's bored if I'm not learning something. That's an attitude developed in Head Start." Later in the conversation he added, "I think Head Start based on how it has helped me should be kept intact. In this information age with the economy moving so fast, kids have got to go to school prepared. If they don't, we all end up paying for it later. Head Start has a proven track record. . . . If they send Head Start back to the states, you'll lose the consistency. Some states have better records, but some have poor records."

Out of more than 15 million children who have attended Head Start since 1965, one can easily find more Pancho Manseras and Henry Gentrys, as well as young women like Tami Torres and Rachel Jones, whom you'll meet at the end of this chapter. There are other young people who overcame aggressive behavior with the help of Head Start or who received therapy to learn to walk or talk. Many former Head Start students became the first in their families to graduate from college. There are attorneys, oculists, a tool designer, a histotechnologist, speech therapists, accountants, a park ranger, actors and playwrights, college professors, a university administrator, local politicians, military officers, psychologists, and a chef among Head Start graduates. There are some famous Head Start graduates (football and baseball star Deion Sanders, film director Mattie Rich, and member of Congress Loretta Sanchez), as well as many not as well known who teach in public schools or Head Start—or, like Tim King (see chapter 10), run Head Start programs.

Head Start is arguably the best investment this country has ever made in its young children. Its graduates hold jobs, pay taxes, raise families, buy homes, sometimes even create jobs for others. They volunteer in their communities, and they vote. Every Head Start director and teacher can tell you success stories. Was Head Start the reason for their achievement, or would they have succeeded anyway? Does Head Start work for the great bulk of children, and thus is it worth the federal investment?

If people know one "factoid" about Head Start research, it is that gains in IQ that children make as a result of attending Head Start tend to fade after two or three years in elementary school. That may indeed be correct—although there are reasons for it.[5] But IQ and what the educators call "cognitive development" are not the only functions of Head Start. Research shows gains that more than justify not only retaining the program but expanding its scope and improving its services.

One caveat: Head Start research is not as conclusive as it might be because vital opportunities were lost when the Reagan administration did not support studies to document the program's results. By 1989, only 0.11 percent of the program's budget was devoted to research, in contrast to 2.5 percent in 1974.[6] By 1995, that budget had increased only to 0.6 percent ($23 million within a total budget of $3.5 billion).[7]

In the last five years there have been two major reviews of research on Head Start and early childhood education programs. One, by Robert McCall of the University of Pittsburgh in 1993, concluded that, yes, "Head Start does help to prepare low-income children to be ready to learn when they enter school, one of the America 2000 National Educational Goals. It improves intelligence (i.e., IQ), academic readiness and achievement, self-esteem, social behavior, and physical health (including better dental and nutritional status, greater immunization rates, and periodic medical screening and treatment)."[8]

Researchers do not know with any confidence the long-term effects of Head Start on IQ, McCall wrote, adding that "one can presume they decline over the three years following Head Start attendance" just as the effects of non–Head Start preschool programs appear to wear off. Addressing this question of fade-out, McCall said that "even in immunology, only a few vaccines inoculate a person forever against a particular disease. Studies of nutritional supplementation in children also show temporary effects, with nutritional status declining after the program if the children are returned to substandard environments." So it is with education. Early intervention can improve later outcomes if the comprehensive program can be continued well into elementary school, as was tested in Head Start's transition projects (see chapter 13).[9]

McCall found that the nutritional and health benefits of Head Start were accepted and not typically challenged in public debates, so he concentrated on mental and academic performance, school achievement and the avoidance of failure, and social-behavioral outcomes. "Some studies report that Head Start graduates have better high school attendance, are less likely to be retained in grade, and use less special education services, but the evidence is less strong and consistent than for non–Head Start [preschool] programs," McCall said. "Although the data are sparse and firm conclusions cannot be drawn," he continued, "several studies show that Head Start increased parental communication with their children, participation in later school programs, satisfaction with the quality of their own lives, [and] confidence in their ability to cope."

Critics have cited Head Start's weakness vis-à-vis high-quality, intensive early education programs as a reason not to expand the program or even to reduce it. "But such results can also be used to justify funding improvements in the program that are likely to make it more effective," McCall wrote. "The research suggests that Head Start's effectiveness is likely to improve if the program were expanded to whole day, whole year and multiple years"; if current demonstration programs that seek to involve parents more intensely and keep them involved into elementary school are expanded; if Head Start teacher training is improved; and if Head Start's administration is better able to maintain program standards around the country.[10]

Like McCall's work, the other review, by W. Steven Barnett, professor at the Graduate School of Education at Rutgers University, found stronger results for model early childhood programs—those with better trained staff, closer supervision of staff by experts, smaller classes, and fewer children per teacher—than for Head Start. His review, which was reported in "The Future of Children" published by the David and Lucile Packard Foundation, covered fifteen model programs and twenty-one larger-scale public programs. Even though the model programs' results were better, Barnett added that "the weight of the evidence establishes that early childhood care and education can produce large effects on IQ during the early childhood years and sizable persistent effects on achievement, grade retention, special education, high school graduation, and socialization. In particular, the evidence for effects on grade retention and special education is overwhelming." There is a risk, he said, that public programs—Head Start and public school prekindergartens—"will not produce the desired benefits because they are lower in quality (larger classes, fewer staff members, less educated staff, poorer supervision) than the model programs." As a result, Barnett added, bringing good early childhood education to communities will not be cheap. "The important point," he concluded, "is that the nation needs to move ahead with public support for early childhood care and education. Current policies are penny wise and pound foolish, inexcusably costly in human and financial terms."[11]

Critics often overlook the fact that Head Start is a success in preparing children for school, wrote Edward Zigler, who, along with colleague Sally Styfco, conducted his own research review. "When children leave Head Start, they have better IQ test scores and school readiness skills." The criticism that they lose these academic and cognitive gains "is more appropriately directed toward the elementary schools they attend, for this is where the preschool advantage fades. To continue the momentum toward success, there must be a smooth transition from the preschool to the school environment and coordinated programming that builds upon prior learning."[12]

Or, as Sargent Shriver once put it, "If one plants a tree, for example, and gives it lots of nourishment at its beginning and then goes away and leaves it for the next five years, the tree will not grow as well as if the nourishment is continued."[13]

Head Start's effects are hard to measure. It has many variables: it's a comprehensive program that involves more than IQs and other cognitive measures, it affects children and their parents, it enrolls children of many ethnic backgrounds speaking many different languages, it is located in a wide variety of settings, and its quality is admittedly uneven. Researchers have great difficulty defining or measuring social competence and parental involvement that form a basic part of Head Start.

Nonetheless, it is worth mentioning several of the specific studies and analyses cited by McCall, Barnett, and Zigler and Styfco to get the flavor of the research. The Head Start Synthesis Project, a review of two hundred studies completed in 1985, found that the research was "virtually unanimous" that "children show significant immediate gains as a result of Head Start participation."[14] The cognitive gains did not last over the long term, however. This review also found that Head Start children were more likely to have had medical and dental examinations, vision and hearing screenings, and speech, language, and developmental screenings than non–Head Start children, and that their participation in Head Start "appears to produce a meaningful improvement in general physical health." Head Start also contributed to its communities' economic environment by hiring many local residents and encouraging parents to further their educations or job training to increase their employability.

In a study that looked at one city, researchers examining the long-term effects of Head Start in the Philadelphia school system found that "compared to control children, Head Start children more often avoided serious school problems. As they moved through the elementary grades, Head Start children were less frequently retained in grade. In later grades, they had better attendance rates and missed fewer standardized tests than comparison children. These effects, while somewhat less dramatic than those in resource-intensive research interventions, demonstrate that regular Head Start programs achieve significant and lasting changes."

The Philadelphia study also showed little or no lasting effect in achievement-test scores. "Nevertheless, as compared to non–Head Start children, Head Start graduates maintained a relatively positive and consistent relationship with the school, even when their test performance was relatively low." Speculating on what produced the positive long-term results, the researchers wrote: "Perhaps Head Start programs reduce the helplessness that parents feel in response to school. Instead of seeing the school as a mysterious and forbidding place where poor children are doomed to fail, Head Start families and children may come to see school as a place where they can hold their own. Another possibility suggested by some research findings is that Head Start children learn ways of behaving in school that work to their advantage. Children may well learn how to function more smoothly in the school environment and how to adapt to school demands. Perhaps they are trying harder; or it may be that positive early classroom experiences make children less hostile or fearful. Their parents may be supportive of their efforts in school or more comfortable and competent in parenting."

Whatever the reasons, the study concluded, "the Head Start children in the Philadelphia study did show a greater tendency than other children to 'hang in there.' They did not opt out or 'fall out' of the system as frequently as their non–Head Start counterparts. They attended school and took tests with more regularity; they were less likely to be identified as students requiring retention in grade. These may not be the dramatic transformations dreamed of by policymakers, educators and parents," the researchers said. "But they are far from trivial. The picture that emerges from the Philadelphia data, in the context of other studies in the literature is this: *The long-term impact of Head Start is in reducing school failure.*"[15]

To map directions for further study of Head Start, in 1994 the government supported establishment of the Roundtable on Head Start Research, under the auspices of the National Research Council and the Institute of Medicine (two arms of the National Academy of Sciences) and chaired by Sheldon White of the Harvard University psychology department. The panel, which included Barnett and Zigler, Head Start's national director Helen Taylor, several local providers, and other experts in child development, recommended these broad areas for future work:

- Examining the way children's families change as they grow up, the complexity of family arrangements and problems, and the manner in which Head Start responds. One example cited was the increasing need of Head Start parents for full-time, full-year care for their children.
- Moving beyond studies of cognitive development by exploring ways to measure more completely children's social and emotional development as they move through Head Start and beyond.
- Investigating the diversity of cultures and languages represented by families enrolled in Head Start. Studies indicate that 20 percent of Head Start children now speak a language other than English; by 2010, children of immigrants may account for half the growth in school-age populations.
- Ensuring that the innovative work at some Head Start centers becomes more widely known so that other centers may benefit. "Such research would fulfill the hopes of those who, in the early years of Head Start, predicted that it might become a national laboratory of early childhood education."
- Examining Head Start's impact on other community services and whether those other services, such as health care, are becoming scarcer.
- And finally, learning how to help Head Start children, families, and staff deal with the emotional aftermath of exposure to violence.[16]

Researchers and policymakers met in the summer of 1996 in Washington to explore some of these questions at a conference sponsored by the Administration on Children, Youth and Families of the Department of Health and Human Services in collaboration with the Columbia University School of Public Health and the Society for Research in Child Development. They covered topics ranging from enhancing parents' interaction with toddlers to preventing community violence. It was not the kind of meeting that generates any media coverage because shoptalk, especially about research, is hard to convert into a news story. Still, at that conference I first learned about the asthma education project in Boston (see chapter 12) and about the collaboration between the Texas Instruments Foundation, two universities, and Head Start of Greater Dallas to help children better learn to use language (see chapter 14).

More needs to be done to document not only what Head Start has (and has not) achieved but also to help it plan better what it should do to make expansion effective. Researchers also must tell the public in understandable language the results of a major program that its money is supporting.

Tami Torres described herself as a shy child when she attended Head Start in Merced, California, but you wouldn't know it now. A focused, energetic young woman, Torres had owned her own business—An American Fashion Tale boutique—on Main Street in Merced for three and a half years when we met. Her mother still worked at the cannery where she had been employed when her daughter attended Head Start, but now was a senior employee who trained forklift drivers. Her father, a former farmworker, had gotten his master's degree and taught at a local high school.

After graduating from Merced High School in 1984, Torres moved to Los Angeles to study fashion merchandising and design at the American College for the Applied Arts. After directing a San Diego modeling agency, she sank her savings into the clothing shop that served a wide range of ages in Merced, a prime tourist stop for visitors heading for Yosemite. She volunteered in her community and worked as a mentor for several young people through Golden Valley High School and a county occupational program. In 1996, Torres's community work earned her shop the business of the year award from the Hispanic Chamber of Commerce in Merced.

When she was growing up, she said, "I knew we were poor. I didn't know everybody else was." At five years old, she said she was living be-low the poverty level but "still loving life," in large part because of Head Start, where she remembered feeling carefree. "I am a prime example of why we need the federal Head Start program," she told me.

Rachel Jones is my friend. In the summer of 1965, when I was a rookie journalist writing broadcast news about Head Start and other antipoverty programs, she knew far better than I the need for them. She attended Head Start that summer in her hometown of Cairo, Illi-nois, and her family benefited from federal food programs. Her life then shaped her work, for she became a reporter covering children's issues with sensitivity and skill for the Knight-Ridder newspapers' Washing-ton bureau.

I met Rachel at the 1992 meeting of the Journalism and Women Symposium at the Sojourner Inn at Jackson Hole, Wyoming. She knew when she heard the name of the lodge that it would be a good fit be-cause Sojourner Truth, Harriet Tubman, and Ida B. Wells had long been her heroes. The group, composed as its name indicates of women in the media, meets once a year to revitalize our ideas about broadening the coverage of news and to reconnect with old friends while making new ones. Rachel's energy was boundless, and within only a few years she was on the board of directors and was then elected president of the organization.

Rachel's parents both worked—her father at a grain mill and her mother as a housekeeper. Rachel was the ninth of ten children. Her mother was active in the neighborhood, so when the first wave of social programs came to town in the mid-sixties, she knew about them. Rachel and her sister Marilyn, who was a year older, walked across the street to Sumner Elementary, where Head Start classes were held in the basement. "The only thing I really remember about Head Start was the instant mashed potatoes," she told me. "At home we'd have lumpy potatoes with no butter in them. At Head Start the mashed potatoes were creamy and smooth. I liked them almost better than ice cream."

Later she became the first child in her family to attend integrated schools from the first grade on up. Her mother had insisted that Rachel's older brother David go to Cairo High School, where he had been its first black student. Rachel spent a year at Northwestern Uni-versity, a year at Southern Illinois University, then started freelancing. She had done a piece for her freshman English class on Black English that *Newsweek* ran in its "My Turn" column. "That was it for me," she said. Her sister Marilyn wanted to be a writer, so she wanted to be a writer, too. "It was a case of hero worship," she said. The girls had always been encouraged to read, and were frequently taken to the library when they were little.

"I was a shy child, and writing was a way to express myself." From the time she was seven or eight, Rachel wrote little stories. "We were Jehovah's Witnesses, so we went to meetings four or five times a week. I would sit there at those meetings writing Bible stories and plays. Jo in *Little Women* was a role model for me."

She worked for three years for the *St. Petersburg Times* in Florida, then for several alternative publications in the Midwest, then went to the *Detroit Free Press* to do general assignment and features. The *Free Press* had just started its "Children First" project. Her assignment was to put together a panel of children across Michigan and interview them all when a story affecting children came up. "It was my first taste of public journalism, and it also put me in touch with a desire to report about them. They need a voice." Once she reached the Washington bureau for Knight-Ridder, she started covering children, not as afterthoughts or asides in stories, but rather in terms of policies that directly or indirectly affect them. Later she worked on developing Child Wire, to cover children's issues around the country.

For Rachel, her beat had "a strong connection to being born and raised in poverty, being an African American woman in a town that devalued that." She wrote frequently about poverty and race. "I think that I can honestly say that that little girl back in Cairo who wondered why people hated her because of the color of her skin or because she was poor was determined" to prove them wrong through her writing.

In the summer of 1996, Rachel wrote an op-ed piece for the *Washington Post* after listening to debates about how much help the government should give to the poor in America. "I often felt compelled to bear witness that Head Start and many of those other 'failed antipoverty programs' were a staple of my young life. And from my vantage point here in Washington writing about those Great Society experiments, I wonder how many other silent witnesses, aged 35 and younger, may be walking the halls of Congress or doing power lunches in Washington restaurants."

Rachel remembered "going to bed hungry, longing for the luxury of the hot dogs or Sloppy Joes they served at Head Start and kindergarten." It saddened her that programs that could help families feed their children might be eliminated or sharply curtailed. "And when I think of the smiles, the loving support, the hopeful, helpful moments doled out in a warm, bustling school basement 30 years ago, I know I'd gladly pay an extra dollar of taxes to provide Head Start to someone else's child."[17]

Lady Bird Johnson sent Rachel a letter after reading her article. "I wish all those who are ever to write off Head Start could read your story." Rachel framed the letter and said she gets chills down her spine just rereading it. "It brought me full circle when I thought about when I was poor and didn't know what my life would be like and if I would ever make it out of Cairo. I think now that that gratitude was not misplaced."

Tackling the
Problems

Chapter Nine

Minneapolis: Who Shall Teach?

aika and Mae were enjoying a tea party, minus the tea, in the corner of their Head Start classroom in Minneapolis. Mae, wearing a sea captain's cap that she had found in the dress-up area and pulled down almost over her eyes, had carefully set the little table with cups and plates. Then she placed several teapots on the toy stove. Maika joined her as their classmates elsewhere in the brightly modern, well-equipped room painted, constructed tall buildings with blocks, or splashed their hands in a waist-high bin of water. Erica Clark, the assistant teacher, sat down with the little girls, both from the city's large Hmong population, to talk about what they were doing. Earlier that morning, the girls had said little when their teacher asked what they wanted to do that day. They clearly understood what she asked them but were shy about replying.

Clark took a toy apple from the cupboard and asked the girls what it was. "Apple," both replied softly. Clark was doing what she had been trained to do—to discuss the children's activities with them and to help them learn the words for everyday objects. Later she nodded approvingly during cleanup time as the girls put away all the items with which they'd been playing. At all times she and the class's teacher, Sue Dopp, stayed alert to guide children away from play that wouldn't be safe—standing on chairs, putting objects in their mouths, running on a wet floor.

As the parent of a former Head Start child, Clark had participated in a model training program run by Parents In Community Action that had prepared her for a paying job at PICA's Fraser Center. And so had some seventy other teachers, assistant teachers, and bus drivers among the two hundred staff members who worked directly with the two thousand children enrolled at seven PICA centers in Hennepin County, which encompasses all of Minneapolis and some of its close-in suburbs.

Over a six-week period, parents involved in the child development training project spend ninety-six hours working as aides in Head Start classrooms. They learn by doing. They watch the head teacher and assistant teacher help the children assemble towers of blocks to develop coordination, encourage the children to try new foods, remember always to talk with children in need of discipline instead of hitting them, and learn other techniques that they can try with their own children at home. They also develop habits that they need for success on the job, such as getting to work on time, dressing appropriately, and dealing with problems with coworkers. At the end of the training period, they receive two hundred dollars to cover child-care or other expenses. They can use the experience they have gained to help their own families; if they liked working with other children and proved good at it, they may be hired as substitutes and eventually as assistant teachers. After more education and work experience, they can become head teachers.

Nationwide, almost one-third of Head Start's staff comes from the families it serves. That pattern developed when Head Start went from a gleam in planners' eyes to a full-fledged program in just a few months in 1965. The people setting up the first centers found that there were not enough university-trained teachers who specialized in preschoolers to staff the program. They also discovered that some of these teachers couldn't adapt to the Head Start approach. They were not flexible enough to welcome parents into the program, to involve themselves in children's health care and nutrition training, and to work with social service agencies as Head Start did. Head Start also could not (and most often still cannot) pay the salaries that academically credentialed teachers can earn in public school systems. Head Start turned to training its own staff for all these reasons—plus its basic philosophy that parents are their children's prime educators and that their skills should be developed as well as those of their children. Although about 19 percent of its programs are operated by public school systems and therefore usually have college-trained head teachers with parent aides, Head Start relies largely on teachers who have received a child development associate (CDA) credential based on their competence in working with children and their families.

In my travels, I saw many exceptionally skilled teachers, judging by the progress children were making toward readiness for kindergarten as well as the enthusiasm of parents who participated in the classrooms. Children had fun and emerged at the end of the year more confident and more likely to succeed in school and in life. Because I usually visited programs recommended for their strengths, I most often saw good teachers. I also saw teachers and aides who were just okay but with more training and encouragement could move to a higher level. And I saw some teachers and aides who seemed more interested in finishing their lunch or cleaning up the dishes than in talking to the children in their classrooms. Their energy seemed spent, their minds elsewhere. If they didn't feel good, it showed, and their presence did the children little good.

This uneven quality of the teaching staff must be addressed on a person-by-person, program-by-program basis or many children will not receive the benefits they should from Head Start; society also will not get its money's worth. Improving the quality of teaching and rewarding those who do an outstanding job has been a top priority of recent Head Start administrations, of the National Head Start Association, and of many local programs, but often something gets lost in the translation between national initiatives and local follow-through. Supervisors are often too busy with day-to-day concerns to go into classes to see for themselves and to encourage improvement. Some Head Start programs send their teachers to area community colleges for an uneven quality of instruction—"seat time," as one administrator put it—or hold required workshops that may not answer teachers' real on-the-job questions about discipline problems or family needs. In remote spots, Head Start programs sometimes must put their teachers down in front of instructional television courses much the way parents plop their kids down in front of the tube. Head Start should not duplicate training already available—that wastes scarce dollars. But it should monitor the community college and television courses more closely to ensure that they yield the knowledge that people need to become truly fine teachers of young children. Many teachers and supervisors told me they benefited most from in-the-classroom observation by skilled trainers. That hands-on experience can be more expensive than other forms of training, but is worth it in the long run.

Good programs looking to be better might also examine how PICA's parent training program works. It is not the only successful model, but has become one that is highly touted. For example, Nancy Spears, who runs Head Start programs in Lee and Russell Counties in Alabama (see chapter 5), has adapted aspects of the Minneapolis training to fit her center's needs. In the course of my visit, I sat in on an orientation session for three parents about to begin the training, observed classrooms in which the assistant teachers had completed the training, and talked with other staff members who had had children in Head Start and went through the training themselves.

Aubrey Puckett, for one, swears by it and by Head Start. Sure, you might expect that because she is now PICA's parent and community relations director, but life was not always so sweet. After seven years of working with corporate deposits at a local bank, Puckett was laid off in the 1980s because of increasing automation. Her husband was also unemployed because he had been hurt on his job. The couple had just purchased a house, and "all of a sudden this caved in," said Puckett, forty-four, an African American woman who grew up in Memphis and still carries a trace of the South in her speech. There was no money coming in; some days there was barely enough for food for their three children, so she and her husband went to bed hungry.

By nature outgoing, Puckett grew depressed. A friend spotted her mood and suggested that she put her daughter, Danielle, in Head Start so she could volunteer and have something to do. "The way our luck had been running," Puckett thought, "she probably wouldn't get in." But soon she received a telephone call asking her to come to orientation for Head Start. "That was the beginning of my life all over again. I felt as though a burden was lifted off of me. Even though no money was coming in, it gave me some hope that something good had come in my life again."

She and her husband both started riding the bus to Head Start as volunteers whenever they were needed. After about a month, she enrolled in the parent training program. She learned what was appropriate discipline and why children act the way they act. But in addition to learning how to work with young children, she found new determination to break out of her situation. "I learned that just because you lose out in one field doesn't mean you can't be a success in another." Head Start also provided incentive for her husband, who found a job at a mail-order firm.

After the training, Puckett substituted in the classroom. The teacher with whom she was working said she ought to apply for an assistant teacher's job. "My self-esteem had improved but it wasn't where I thought I could get a job. But the teacher went up to the office and got an application and made me fill it out." She got the job, earned her child development associate credential, and worked as a head teacher for two years before moving into administration. She has served as the president of the Minnesota Head Start Association, which represents program staff and parents from around the state. Through her job and the association, she has traveled to many programs in Minnesota as well as to Washington, D.C., Albuquerque, South Padre Island in Texas, Chicago, San Francisco, Atlanta—even Alaska.

"Had it not been for Head Start, I don't know where my life would have been." For Puckett, "Head Start is a calling, not a career. This was a way for me to give back what I gained." Her daughter Danielle was twelve years old and in seventh grade when I met Puckett. "My daughter is doing very well in school—so it *does* go beyond the third grade," she said, implicitly referring to studies that show that Head Start gains fade after the first few years in elementary school.

The child development program that Puckett and other parents have completed is on-the-job training, highly personalized and labor intensive. It takes more energy than sitting in a college classroom; it also quickly weeds out from the potential teaching pool those parents who want only to deal with their own children, not an entire roomful.

On a crisp, clear morning Puckett drove me along streets lined with trees showing off their fall colors so that we could visit the Northeast Neighborhood Early Learning Center in Minneapolis. Center director Gretchen A. Hengemuhle would be talking to three new recruits for the parent training about what they could expect and what would be expected of them. With six Head Start classes, the center had six trainees at any one time working with its 102 children. The Northeast center was one of the smaller of PICA's programs; in south Minneapolis a former high school building, now the McKnight center, housed some 1,300 children, and Fraser, the center of your dreams built with $6 million in city money in the early 1990s, enrolled 600. PICA's Head Start classes were divided into two groups: half attended two days a week, half came three days a week; then they switched schedules at midyear.

This was the first day of training for the mothers gathered around Hengemuhle in the parents' lounge at the center. One of the women had just moved to Minneapolis from North Dakota; another had had a little brother in Head Start as well as, now, her own child. She said her father had gone through the parent training years earlier. They were both white, and the third parent was Hispanic, part of a community whose growth spurt in Minneapolis was catching the program somewhat by surprise. For her, the center's receptionist translated into Spanish Hengemuhle's thorough but welcoming outline of the training.

Earlier, PICA's executive director, Alyce M. Dillon, had told me that everything in her agency evolved out of "having the belief that people are competent and then helping them develop that competency." Hengemuhle's morning of orientation underscored that premise; every aspect of her presentation was based on the understanding that the women with her that morning could and would complete the training satisfactorily and enjoy themselves in the process. Her orientation also summed up what the parents would be doing and learning more ably than I could have if I'd watched all ninety-six hours of training.

An outgoing woman of forty-nine, Hengemuhle, who is white, had been with Head Start for twenty-five years. Her son and daughter had both been in the program. She had initially volunteered by working in the kitchen and riding the bus with the children. She became more involved in the program during a fight over dismissing one of the teachers whom Hengemuhle knew to be excellent because she had often worked with her at the center. "I went to my first policy council meeting and I was hooked. I said, 'I'm in the center and I know that she's good,' " and the woman was not dismissed. "I saw that I could make a difference." Hired in 1973, she worked as a cook, assistant teacher, and head teacher before becoming a center director. She earned her CDA credential in 1976 and has taken extension courses at the University of Minnesota and a local community college.

Children should be encouraged to talk, she was telling the trainees, but they should also be urged to leave family business at home. Years ago, she told me later, some of the children might talk about their parents smoking marijuana; today they might discuss Mama's boyfriend. "You want them to talk but you tell them, 'That's your mama's business and we talk about other things here.' Kids are smart. They learn that pretty quickly."

Head Start's performance standards require its programs to provide training opportunities for parents and staff, Hengemuhle told the women seated around her on comfortable chairs. But beyond the requirements, PICA believed in creating upward mobility for parents. Parents had always volunteered, she went on, but before this program was developed, sometimes they and the teachers with whom they were paired didn't work well together. So in 1980 Alyce Dillon, Cindy White, now the program's social services director, and Hengemuhle designed the training program so that parents could learn strong child development skills and that teachers would feel more comfortable with them. Some two thousand parents have gone through the training.

"Here's what you can expect from us," Hengemuhle said. Trainees should develop skills that could help them find employment. They would be evaluated on what they had done well and in what areas they needed improvement in order to get a job in early childhood development.

"And here's what we need from trainees," she added. Trainees should behave in a professional manner in the classroom. They should not talk about adult issues in front of the children, and they should keep confidential any information about children and their families. "This is a small community," she said of the neighborhood immediately around the center. "Everybody knows everybody. You never know, if you're talking about Billy, you might be talking to Billy's grandmother. You can talk about children and the fun things you do, but remember to do so in a manner that won't offend."

The trainees' day would begin by riding the bus on which all the Head Start students travel to the center. They would be picked up first and would have responsibility for seeing that each child had his seat belt buckled and recording the times the bus reached its stops. They would also count the children and see that they didn't tamper with the emergency exits or put their arms, hands, or bodies outside the bus.

"You'll have to tell your child, 'I'm coming to school to be a trainee—you're going to have to share me.' They may cry a little but they'll get used to it." Trainees never work in their own children's classrooms. One of the women commented that that would probably suit her child just fine.

Hengemuhle cautioned the women never to leave the children alone, nor should they be left alone with the children. There should always be two paid staff members with them. "That's both for the safety of the children and for your own safety—to protect against any accusation." If anything should happen, there would always be another adult present to say what occurred.

It's often easiest to say "Don't run" or other don'ts, but Hengemuhle encouraged the trainees to speak to the children in positive ways. Instead of "Don't run," say, "Please walk." Be sure not to release the children to anyone not authorized to pick them up. Hengemuhle also said that Head Start staff members are required to report child abuse. "If you see bruises, ask the child how he got hurt but ask in a nonthreatening way. Don't automatically assume abuse." If the trainee or a teacher does suspect abuse, she or he should call the parent, ask what happened, and offer support. Many times, she added, parents will acknowledge striking a child, and the staff can offer suggestions of other ways to deal with misbehavior or their own frustrations.

"We need you. This is *your* training," Hengemuhle stressed to the women. "The more things you try, the better your training will be." First, she suggested, they should learn the daily schedule and talk to the children about what comes next. This Head Start center used a modification of the curriculum developed by the High/Scope Educational Research Foundation in Ypsilanti, Michigan, which Hengemuhle explained meant that children learned through play. The staff provided a structured environment to help the children make their choices so they could not only learn to think logically but also discover how to talk and work with other people and develop self-esteem.

When the children arrived at and left the center each day, they had to deal with coats and boots and hats because of the Minnesota climate. "Encourage the children to do as much as they can with the zipping and buttoning, but be there to help if they need it. Tell them, 'I know you can do it. Let's see you do it,' " Hengemuhle advised. "Whenever you go anywhere, always count the children to make sure you have everybody. There's nothing scarier than losing a child." The trainees could also work with the children on what are called fine motor skills (using their fingers, putting objects together, stringing beads) or large muscle skills (tumbling, running, throwing a ball, jumping). "But do watch the children. That's when we have the most accidents."

Children could learn even at mealtimes because they practiced passing and pouring at breakfast and lunch served family style. "They get real good at it," Hengemuhle said. The children are comfortable then; sometimes it is the only time they sit down to eat. "You can say take two sausages or take three sausages and that helps them learn to count," she said. "Encourage them to try new foods, to take one bite at least, but don't force them, and don't use food as a punishment."

Free play figures prominently in Head Start's schedule. "This is the time for the adults to move around the room," the director said. "Ask the children questions so the kids can learn language skills. You can use blocks to teach math. Talk about the transportation toys like cars and planes. Then during story time, sit on the carpet with the children while the teacher reads to them. Encourage the kids who are having a difficult time to sit next to you." If the trainees felt uncomfortable reading a story to the children at first, they could take the book home and read it the night before. "Think about how you can make it enjoyable for the children.

"Sing with the children," Hengemuhle added. "They don't care if we sing on key. It's fun for them to see adults do silly things."

Trainees take field trips with the children as well. While they must be watchful for the children's safety, they would find it a good time to talk to the children about what they are seeing. "She can help with Spanish and English," Hengemuhle said, smiling at the young Hispanic mother.

"We try to provide opportunities for the children to feel successful," she said. "Never use physical punishment. We don't use time-outs here"—sending a child off from the main group.

"They don't work anyway," one of the mothers interjected.

"Try to redirect their activity when they are acting up," Hengemuhle went on. "When a child hits another child, acknowledge the child who was hurt first before the one who did the hurting. Go back then to him and say, 'Tell me what's wrong.' Don't say that children are bad or naughty—say you don't like it when they do such and such. And they will respond more to a calm, kind voice than to a loud voice."

Then Hengemuhle gave the new trainees additional tips:

- Listen to the kids.
- Put their names on their papers. They love to see their names.
- Call them by name. That makes them feel good, too.
- Ask them, "How do you think that works?"
- Introduce the children to new words. Explain them.
- Try new things. "You're here to learn."

Then Hengemuhle walked the trainees to their classrooms and introduced them to the staff and the children. Hengemuhle told me later that one can never predict who the most successful trainees will be. "People all have something to offer. One of our first trainees was a Native American man who was very quiet. He could get some of the children to talk that no one else could. Some others find the job is not as easy as they thought it would be. Some people just have a natural ability with the kids. Just because you have a four-year degree doesn't mean you have that touch. These are people who are gentle, accepting, who perhaps have a kid quality themselves." They can see things from the children's perspective and therefore help them learn.

I asked Hengemuhle why she thinks the program works. "We developed it, and we believe in it. Teachers have seen the strengths of having parents coming in. I tell them, 'Keep in mind as you are working with this trainee that you may be training your next assistant. So the things you teach may be used in your classroom next year.' I think that helps get the buy-in from everybody." PICA also made its training long enough so that parents get a good taste of what it's like working with young children but not so long that they get frustrated.

As I watched former trainees in the classrooms and talked to others, I learned what they had learned. In the Glendale center in southeast Minneapolis not far from the University of Minnesota, Chesay Colson was helping the children sort through some blocks when one sneezed directly on another. Quietly Colson urged her to sneeze into her sleeve the next time so she wouldn't spray her germs on the other child. A few minutes later three children were squabbling over a plastic toy filled with colored water. Colson suggested that they talk about the best way to get a turn with the toy. "We have to share," she said. "You could say, 'May I play with that now?' You need to take turns. I'm going to take this until you learn to share it." The lesson took, at least for the moment, and the children soon were playing peaceably, as the toy gurgled and bubbled while they listened to it, once more entranced. And sharing.

Colson told me later that her in-class training had taught her techniques she could use at home with her son, who had been in Head Start. "The teachers could tell me what worked for them—like in holding a kid's attention. They get bored real quickly."

No quality is needed more than patience in working with small children. Every teacher and aide who had gone through the training told me it helped them develop longer fuses. "I think parents have high expectations. You want your children to be perfect," Gretchen Hengemuhle explained when I asked her how the training helped develop this patience. "If your child misbehaves, you think it's a reflection on you. But when you are exposed to other children the same age and you see them doing the same thing your child does, you learn to accept things. You realize it's just part of the child's natural development."

One day I had lunch at the sprawling McKnight center in south Minneapolis. There I talked with three staff members who had gotten jobs with PICA after the training and had seen their lives change beyond having employment. "I used to be real shy," said Joanie Lawrence, whose fourteen-year-old daughter had attended Head Start and who was a supervisor of one of the wings at McKnight. "I didn't speak up for myself. . . . But by being involved, I discovered I had a say-so here. I had a voice and could express my feelings here." She worked as an assistant teacher and then a head teacher at McKnight after completing the parent training and before becoming a supervisor. "The program works."

Diette Thunberg also found her voice through the Head Start training. Initially recruited to ride the school bus, Thunberg went through the parent training and also learned the need to provide political support for the program. Soon she was recruiting other parents to go to the capitol in St. Paul to encourage the state legislature not to cut programs for children. "I never knew you could go up to the Hill and protest. They never tell you on aid that you can do that." When she was receiving public aid, Thunberg, an assistant teacher, said that she would take her children to the park, go home, and do nothing else. Head Start and its training had made her more self-confident. "I've noticed a lot of changes now. It's given me a backbone." In the parent training, she also discovered how children learn through play. "I always thought you had to tell them what to do."

Like Lawrence, Geneva Taylor was a single parent and needed a job when her daughter was enrolled in Head Start. She volunteered to ride the school bus, then completed the parent training. She would help the teacher read to the children or sing songs. After finishing the training, "I decided, I spend most of my time here, I might as well become an assistant teacher." Taylor had not only completed her high school equivalency diploma, she had also gone back to school and earned two child development associate credentials, including one for working with infants and toddlers. "You can't do it all by yourself," Taylor said, "and Head Start lets you know that there is help out there for single parents."

Teachers—and women—weren't the only ones who received training at PICA. The program has worked hard to recruit fathers—or grandfathers or uncles or other significant men in children's lives—into Head Start activity. Three of the program's head teachers and four of its assistant teachers were men. PICA also employed thirty-two male bus drivers. The drivers not only picked up the children in the morning and took them home in the afternoon, they also walked them into the building, told the teachers how many they picked up, and relayed any messages the parents gave them. Drivers had desks outside the classrooms and spent an hour a day in the classroom, attended all the educational staff meetings, and went on all the field trips. They picked up the breakfast and lunch trays at the centers' kitchens and wheeled them to the classrooms as well.

Any parent with a child in Head Start could enroll in PICA's Transportation Training Project. PICA had always trained its own drivers but started a more extensive outreach and more formalized program in 1994 to try to combat a severe shortage of drivers as well as to employ more parents. Forty-eight hours of training, spread over three weeks, included classroom time, behind-the-wheel experience, and instruction in defensive driving. Parents received a one-hundred-dollar stipend during the training to cover child care and other incidental expenses. Jimmy Ferguson, a PICA employee who has had twelve grandchildren in Head Start, has been certified by the state to give the trainees their road tests. If they complete the exam successfully, they receive a commercial driver's license. In the year before my visit, PICA had trained twenty-two people as drivers, twelve of them women. PICA hired eighteen of the twenty-two as drivers.

Those driver trainees who may want to work for Head Start are interviewed by a panel that includes PICA parents and staff. "If they can't deal with children, they are not hired," Ferguson said. The panel questions the candidates about whether they are comfortable driving with seventeen to twenty children, three to five years old, on their bus. Even though there are parent monitors aboard, too, Ferguson said, "it gets to be a headache if you're not used to dealing with children. We want people that really like working with children. That's why we focus on our parents. Drivers are the first face the children see in the morning and the last face they see in the afternoon."

As such, drivers also see many parents who rarely visit the center, and so they can be powerful recruiting agents for Head Start in general, and for men's participation in particular. "Men need models for doing things," said Kenneth Macon, who was hired expressly to work on male involvement. "That's why sports figures are so popular. Men like things they can see. If they see another man doing it"—working with Head Start children—"it's okay then." In terms of raising children, "men have been socialized to become invisible and welfare gets blamed for that, too," with its requirement that there be no men in the home if a woman is to receive aid for dependent children, Macon said. "What our agency is striving for is letting those men know you don't have to be invisible. . . . We are letting them know that we do view them as parents who play a viable part in their children's education and training" (see chapter 10).

On a more limited basis than its bus driver and child development training, PICA had also begun to prepare parents to work in food service and to run modern office machines. It has also done its own training to prepare its teachers to receive the child development associate certificate that they need to become head teachers. The CDA credential, created in response to a need to improve child care quality, was developed in 1972 when Dr. Edward Zigler headed the federal Office of Child Development. In establishing the CDA, Head Start defined what teachers should be able to do, set up the means to evaluate how well they did it, and rewarded those who completed the process with a nationally recognized credential. Teachers who receive the CDA have been found competent in establishing safe and healthy classrooms, supporting children in developing their physical and mental skills, and helping children get along with others while cooperating with children's families and encouraging their involvement. They must also be effective managers and record keepers and take advantage of opportunities to improve their training. PICA has also arranged that staff members who earn their CDAs through the program's own training can receive fifteen credits toward a degree at a local community college. Where teachers at other programs often work for their CDAs largely through community colleges, all but one PICA teacher who has the credential got it through PICA's own training.

Parents are the reason PICA exists. In the early days of Head Start in Minneapolis, the program was run by the Minneapolis public schools for a community action agency. Parents rebelled because they were not involved to the degree they felt they should be under Head Start mandates. Alyce Dillon went to the parents' meeting at which Parents In Community Action was formed and has been involved ever since. At the time, she was a high school dropout, a single parent, on welfare and living in public housing. Her oldest son was enrolled in Head Start. When she attended that first meeting, she "couldn't conceive of how parents could run the program or how it could be out of the schools." But once she heard the other parents speak to the group of black, white, and American Indian parents and other community people, "I knew instantly. These people recognized what the issues were for poor people. I felt an immediate kinship." Newcomer PICA competed with the public schools to be the delegate agency running Head Start for the community action agency and won. PICA opened its program in December 1969, having hired all the staff and found the locations for the program on faith before it had any money. In 1971, the community action agency was disbanded because of mismanagement. PICA has been the Head Start grantee for Hennepin County since then.

In 1978, Dillon was named director. Since then, PICA has grown and found more permanent homes for its classes after operating out of makeshift quarters—in church basements and other donated space—for many years. In 1987, PICA almost found itself homeless when the Minneapolis school system needed the space in a building that Head Start had leased for five years. However, with the help of the mayor, a former mayor, and other city leaders, PICA negotiated the use of Regina High School's building, which the Twin Cities' archdiocese had closed because of declining enrollment and rising debts. The next year the McKnight Foundation gave PICA $2.75 million to buy the center.

From a program enrolling 214 children, PICA has grown to almost 2,000. In addition to its regular two- or three-day-a-week Head Start activities, PICA also runs full-day Head Start for children whose parents are in a job training program or children who have special needs. Hennepin County money helps provide this program. The county also helps pay for food for low-income children in Head Start. PICA has a family service center to work with parents on literacy, employability, and drug and alcohol abuse, as well as a Parent and Child Center whose staff works with pregnant teenagers, infants, toddlers, and their families. Its McKnight center also houses Project Secure, a demonstration project providing Head Start for homeless children and services for their families (see chapter 14).

Minnesota in general and the Twin Cities in particular have a populist civic tradition that has encouraged innovation and supported leaders and policies more concerned than most about the public welfare. One of these leaders, former Minneapolis mayor Donald M. Fraser, helped PICA obtain $6 million in city funds to build its state-of-the-art headquarters located just off a major freeway. The building, dedicated in 1992 and named after Fraser when he retired, houses PICA's administrative offices, Head Start classrooms, and a dental clinic. Children can have their teeth checked or filled or receive fluoride treatments and miss a minimum amount of school because the dentist's chair is just down the hall from their classrooms.

In the Fraser center, as well as at other new or remodeled buildings housing PICA programs, every two classes had an adjacent office for the advocates who help connect children and their families to needed social services. One of them, Cher Vang, said that the main concerns of the families with which she worked were finding training or jobs because of changes in welfare laws. In all, the program employed twenty of these advocates, including two who speak Spanish and four Hmong speakers.

After California, Minnesota has the second-largest population of Hmong in the United States. The Hmong are a people in transition from the rural life they knew in Laos before their employment as soldiers hired by the Central Intelligence Agency, part of the broad anticommunist offensive in Indochina. When the communists swept to control and the United States withdrew its troops from Vietnam, only those Hmong clan leaders considered most important and therefore most vulnerable were transported to safety. Thousands of Hmong perished during the decades of fighting, and thousands more knew they could no longer live safely in Laos. Ka Yeng Vang, a translator and social service aide for PICA, was among them. His father had been a soldier with the CIA, then became a farmer after the war.

As the oldest son, Ka faced a choice at fifteen that was put to him by the regime: "If I had been willing to become their soldier, I would have gone into the army. If not, they would take me to jail." So he left, as did much of his village, although his parents stayed behind. "Every child that can walk carried a package of clothing," he recalled. The Hmong refugees walked the width of Laos—"and it is as wide as Oregon," he said—to reach the border with Thailand. There Ka spent two weeks in jail while his documents were checked. Once he made it into a refugee camp, he lived with ten families in one long building. He spent six years in Thai camps, then was sponsored by a Catholic church in Sacramento, where he lived for another seven years. There he had a child in Head Start and went to the center every day.

Like many other Hmong, Ka moved to Minneapolis in the early 1990s. Once in Minneapolis, he enrolled his three younger children in Head Start and started volunteering. Speaking not only Hmong but Laotian and Thai as well as English, Ka helped interpret between the staff and parents, between children and their teachers, and for parents needing help in communicating with other public agencies. He can see how his own children have already benefited from Head Start. "Most Asian kids have to go through English as a second language programs," he said. "But mine were already advanced and didn't have to do that."

The Hmong represented a challenge for Head Start because of differences in language and culture, but such challenges were not new in Minneapolis. At PICA's Glendale center in southeast Minneapolis, there were not only Hmong but Somalian and Ethiopian children as well. Marilyn Hockert, director there, sympathized with the families seeking to hold on to their culture. Hockert, whose three children were in Head Start when she and her husband were among the working poor, is an Ojibwa Indian whose parents went to a government school. Those schools were notorious for stamping out Native American culture.

"Some parents say, 'Why don't they speak English?' " she said of the mix of children at her center. "I tell them they are trying to learn the

American way of life and hold on to their culture. I'm walking testimony that once you've lost your culture, it's gone. It's like you're an alien. I don't want these kids to feel that way."

Added to the existing mix the fall that I visited the PICA program was an influx of Hispanic children. With their arrival, 30 percent of PICA's children did not speak English as their first language. Many of the families had come directly to Minnesota from Mexico and had many of the survival problems of other poor immigrant populations. Head Start was one of the first programs they encountered. Indeed, Head Start is a microcosm of society's shifts and society's problems, which often show up among the very young first. "If you want to know what's going on in society, watch Head Start," Alyce Dillon said. "Whatever the ills are in the society—drugs, health—will show up in this population first, and before it hits the public schools and gets wider notice." So PICA geared up for more Spanish-speaking children and parents.

It is always "and parents." Every section of PICA's mission statement mentions families as well as children. Having come into Head Start as parents themselves, Dillon and her colleagues work at parent involvement in order to help the children. That is their bottom line. To get parents to participate, Dillon said, "you have to accommodate their children—that is, care for them if you have meetings. You have to provide transportation or move the meeting to a time when parents can attend. You should provide food. And you have to know your population. You have to ask what is a good day to have a meeting. Maybe toward the end of the month, when people's welfare checks have run out and a meal would draw them to the center. Parent involvement is hard work. It's a twenty-four-hour-a-day commitment. You can't do it in an eight-thirty-to-five-thirty environment."

In the early years of PICA, parents "made it work because we were committed heart and soul to making this happen. Too often," Dillon said, "poverty is equated with intelligence. People think poor people are dumb. When you get over that, it is a learning experience. I don't think we ever doubted for a moment that we could do it. Of course we were young, too. That helped."

Dillon, now fifty-two, continues to believe that the people her agency serves can do whatever they set their minds to doing. "Too often people believe, 'We don't have the credentials to ask this.' You have to believe that your organization will benefit from parents' involvement and their asking questions," she added. "It will keep you alive."

Chapter Ten

Getting Men Involved, Getting Communities Involved

ome Head Start centers hold pancake breakfasts. Some teach fatherhood skills. Some establish men's groups. Some offer mentoring. Some sponsor fishing trips or ball teams. Their aim: to involve men.

Some Head Start centers teach English to immigrant parents. Some help those who have been on welfare prepare to find jobs and hold them. Some train parents as classroom aides. Some feature special programs with children singing or dancing or dressing up in costumes. Some hold potluck lunches or dinners. Their aim: to involve parents.

Head Start prides itself on parent involvement and, indeed, parents move in and out of Head Start classrooms with far more freedom than at the typical elementary school. Parents provide thousands of volunteer hours that count toward fulfilling the federal requirement that local contributions provide a share of programs' budgets. Many parents learn how to help their children at home, and many have their lives altered by Head Start. Some of their stories fill the pages of this book.

But few Head Start programs, if they are honest with themselves, are truly happy about the level of their parent involvement. Almost all say they should do better; some fail at the task. They face a tough problem. By definition, the people they are trying to attract are poor and so are busy trying to make ends meet. Some have personal problems that isolate them and keep them down. But they cared enough to put their children in Head Start, so there is a nugget of hope, which some centers fail to exploit. Those programs do not make participation either rele-

vant to parents' lives or at a time or in a manner that is convenient for
them. Their staffs need both more time and more training to help the
many mothers who in one survey reported often feeling "sad, down and
depressed."[1] Many programs are also weak in their ability to attract men
to participate. With changes in welfare laws enacted in 1996, more low-
income parents must enroll in job training or find jobs and therefore
have less time for volunteering. The pressures that will result for Head
Start centers should provide a wake-up call for the program as a whole
to examine this key component that may no longer be all that it was
meant to be.

The main time I saw men at Head Start centers was in the morning
when the children were dropped off or in the afternoon when they were
picked up. The rest of the day, women predominated, from Westley,
California, to the West Virginia mountains. Mind you, I enjoyed seeing
women running things and mothers having positive life-changing experiences, but I took to heart the words of Sheila Tucker, who runs St.
Bernardine's Head Start in West Baltimore. "When you talk about parent involvement, it bothers me that you are talking about females," she
said, explaining later that she meant the universal "you," not me specifically. Too often, she added, "there is no conscious attempt to involve
men. When we speak of the parent as primary educator for a child, why
is it the *parent*? There seems to be an assumption that just because a
child is poor, he has one parent."

St. Bernardine's made that conscious attempt to involve men. Every
Wednesday evening a men's discussion group met upstairs at the Head
Start center, located in an African American neighborhood on a main
inner-city corridor linking Baltimore's western suburbs with its downtown. The program had hired a young man to assess the men's interests
and work with them on problems involving jobs, education, and even
relationships. It held workshops for the mostly female Head Start staff
so that if any of the women had criticisms of the approach, they could
get them out into the open. And it had a director who wanted men
involved.

I had met that director, Sheila Tucker, at seminars conducted for the
Head Start–Johnson & Johnson Management Fellows Program held at
the University of California, Los Angeles (see chapter 14). The program
brings the best Head Start directors to campus for two weeks of training
in the summertime. She was one of the dynamos in a dynamic crowd.

When I went to Baltimore to visit her program, I asked her how these efforts began. She replied that they grew out of a family therapy group that her center had been running to try to help parents solve their problems and develop self-esteem. When several men came into the group, some of the women were visibly hostile, perhaps because they felt abandoned by the men in their own lives. The discussion became an us-versus-them confrontation and wasn't helping anybody. What was needed, Tucker decided, was a forum at which men's issues could be discussed in a different atmosphere. "We only intended to do one or two forums but the men were so attracted to it that they said, 'Why don't we meet more regularly?' From that it grew into a regular group."

Tucker had also done a good deal of reading about research on the effects of fathers' absence on children and why that absence occurs. Fatherhood is often defined as a man's ability to support his family, and if he fails to meet that standard, "we have disempowered him. He does not feel that he has a place in the life of his children." Men often don't see learning how to be fathers or husbands as something they have to do. If they haven't had fathers present in their own lives, they have no reference point. "Our goal is to have the child know he has two parents, and that both parents have responsibility to their children. We have defined maleness in terms of financial position. No one looks at them as nurturer." A man feels that caring for young children is a woman's role and he'll get involved when the child is nine or ten years old, Tucker added. "But by nine or ten, the child has developed his personality. We want both parents involved so that children get a good sense of who they are."

Tucker and the women on the Head Start staff discussed how to integrate men into every aspect of the program so that they would help put the process into place. Tucker's staff wanted men in the classrooms so that boys and girls could see them as positive role models. And they wanted men to enjoy their children. Tucker also had to make sure parents were comfortable with having the men in classrooms and elsewhere because some people had questions about men who work with young children: "Are they homosexual?" "Do they like children too much?"

The Head Start staff first had the men tell stories to the children and do woodworking projects with them. "We started with things where people had a comfort level before we went into talking about child development," Tucker explained.

In its efforts to involve men, St. Bernardine's Head Start worked with whatever definitions families gave them about which males were significant in a child's life. "We're not trying to force families back together." If a man has been abusive, he's not the man they're looking for, but they will try to involve whoever the family says is significant—an uncle, a grandfather, a boyfriend. "We are redefining the role of father. You've had disciplinarian and you've had breadwinner. What about nurturing? We want him to be seen as not just a wallet but as someone with a legitimate role in the childrearing process. We want him to know that child support is more than just financial support."

One of the mainstays in involving men was St. Bernardine's men's group, where discussions were led by psychologist Henry Gregory. "I help them look at themselves and their relationships," to deal with their anger. Gregory called part of the process "decoding the patriarchy." By that, he meant that "there are some men who are on top" of the power structure and others who aren't and think it's their own fault that they're not. Anger and guilt can cause them to explode. Involving the men takes sustained effort and attention, Gregory said. "People who aren't cared for won't care for others."

The night I was at St. Bernardine's, I sat in on part of one of the sessions. The group had about half a dozen men at the outset; a few more joined as the session went on. The group is open to all the men of the neighborhood, not just those with children in Head Start. "Instead of playing rugby or football, we're doing this," one of the men said to me as he sat down in the circle of chairs. Before he started coming to the group, one man said, "it was me just being surrounded by women *all the time*. I look forward to it every Wednesday." Most of what I heard was testimonials because I had agreed I would leave before the confidential or men-only conversation really got under way. But one man told how he had gone from drug addict to productive member of the community through his involvement there; another told how things were better at home now because he was learning to listen and be more attentive.

"I'd rather be in the men's group than hanging on the corner," said Franklin Wallace, whose granddaughter Myeshia had spent two years in Head Start and was then in kindergarten. Wallace had raised the child since she was six days old because, as he put it, "my daughter was living a life she shouldn't have been." Wallace became active because Myeshia wanted him to read to her. "She made me want to go back to school if I was going to read to her. I had to better my reading skills." Once involved, he became one of the center's "volunteers of the year." He tied shoes, mopped the bathroom, escorted the children to the toilet—whatever needed doing. Wallace also enrolled in a class St. Bernardine's Head Start offered that trained security guards. Eventually he got a job at the Head Start center monitoring people signing in and out of the building, checking on the parking lot, and dealing with homeless people who sometimes caused disruptions. Before that, he had been doing construction work. "I made more money on that job but I was out in all kinds of weather." Of the benefits of volunteering, Wallace said: "It's one day a week out of your life and you can learn a lot."

For every man there was a different reason for or result of involvement. "My father was never around for me," said Brian Hawkins, whose three-year-old son was in Head Start. "My mother worked two jobs to support us." His mother made sure he didn't join a gang or pick up his knowledge from the streets. "When I had my son, I said he's going to have his father there for him." Hawkins, who went to Howard University, started his own architectural firm. In addition to Head Start activities, Hawkins, a trim sprinter, had volunteered to coach track at two local high schools. "There are a lot of role models out there on the streets," Hawkins said, "but we need to show kids that a role model can be more than just standing out on the corner dealing drugs, getting money to buy a nice car."

Yahya, a man in dreadlocks and dashiki who had had two daughters in Head Start, worked with James Worthy, the male outreach coordinator. "Basically what we do is go fishing," said Yahya. "We put on some bait. We bait the hook and throw it out there." For example, the program offered tickets to Bullets professional basketball games to the top five volunteers who had spent time in the classrooms, helped teachers, and gone on school trips with the children.

I asked Yahya what he had gotten out of being in the classroom. "I learned that I was able to learn from them, too," he replied. "Children can show adults when they're being childish." Working with the children also gave him insight into what society is up against. "You hear about inner-city youth—that's what TV calls them. I see kids whose parents are deceased, strung out on drugs, not there. Just locking these youths up is not the answer. Society's ills start with these kids. Every robber, every murderer was a child once."

Whatever the element that made each man take the bait, each found something because many approaches were used. James Worthy, the male involvement coordinator, said that about one-fourth of the 125 men identified as connected to children at St. Bernardine's Head

Start had attended two or more programs at the center that year. About 10 or 15 were there every day but his goal was to have 40 or 50 who were active. "You have to ask what are you doing for *them?* If you're not providing something for them," Worthy said, "how can you expect them to come in and volunteer if you don't make the connection?"

While female directors like Sheila Tucker can provide the initiative for involving men, this is one job that it truly takes a man to do. Programs that want to involve men cannot just sit around and think about it; they have to hire men to do it. And like St. Bernardine's, they need to find men not just to coordinate male involvement but also for jobs that might traditionally be filled by women, such as the family service coordinator. "I wanted fathers to see men in the center," Tucker said. One of the program's teachers was a man, and a former Head Start father was a teacher's aide there.

Head Start had been a family affair for Tim King, director of the South East Community Organization (SECO) Head Start program, across Baltimore from St. Bernardine's. He had attended Head Start himself in its first summer, 1965, and his mother, Frankie King, still worked at the Alabama Council on Human Relations program that I had visited in Auburn (see chapter 5).

King had also been involved in Head Start as a father. Before he finished college at Auburn University, he had had a job at a manufacturing plant but was laid off; as a result, his daughter Tiffany qualified for Head Start. His mother insisted that not only his wife but he, too, should serve on committees to do the work of Head Start. While he was still in Auburn, he had counseled homeless veterans through the ACHR's shelter. He would help them reestablish themselves in society by getting library cards, finding jobs, attending Narcotics Anonymous, whatever they needed. "I really got to know them" through the group meetings, he added. When he moved to Baltimore, he knew that Head Start was not a field for women only.

He first became family service coordinator for SECO, headquartered near Johns Hopkins Hospital, then Head Start director over five sites with 170 children. In looking at a center or a program, he would ask himself, "Is this father-friendly? Where are the welcoming signs that we want fathers in? I know that if I start a basketball team, I will get some men in. They don't know it, but before we play, we'll meet and talk."

King has succeeded in getting four men sufficiently involved to serve on his program's parent policy council. He remembered one man who said he'd volunteer one day of his vacation, then go fishing, but the man stayed the whole week. "It's amazing how the children gravitate to the men and it helps them see what their priorities are. I also say to the ladies, 'Let's not let the men off the hook. They need to know how to ask questions at the school and the doctor's office. They need to check that their child is doing his homework.' If we are successful, then the kids actually have two advocates, not just one."

As St. Bernardine's had James Worthy and SECO's centers had Tim King, so Minneapolis had Kenneth Macon, a young man who came to the Head Start program from the local Urban League. Like the Baltimore programs I visited, Parents In Community Action, the principal Head Start grantee for the Minneapolis area, had made male involvement a priority. It showed. I saw a male teacher working with the children as they tumbled on mats and played catch. I saw male bus drivers escorting the children to their classrooms and later bringing the lunch carts to each room. And I saw Macon talking to one of the fathers, asking him to come to the school as often as he could. Macon wants to help men be better men, better fathers. "If men don't have healthy relationships with their fathers, somewhere down the line that's going to prove a problem."

Central to PICA's success in attracting men to work with Head Start has been its program to train its own bus drivers. The drivers, most of whom are male, don't just bring the children to school; they work in the classroom an hour a day and confer with teachers and parents. Each driver has a desk in an alcove outside the classrooms in PICA's specially designed classroom and administration building (see chapter 9).

PICA also formed a male involvement committee. When it meets, Macon said, its members may talk about the changes in welfare laws, about voter registration, about job openings, about paternity issues. "What seems to work is really being honest with them—letting them know that we do view them as parents who play a viable part in their child's education and training."

Many times men simply haven't been asked to become involved, Macon said, echoing Sheila Tucker. "Men have been socialized to become invisible, especially because of the welfare system. What our agency is striving for is letting these men know you don't have to be invisible." For programs seeking to involve more men, Macon suggested finding out what they want to do, not what you want them to do; once you make a contact, he added, follow up so they know you really are putting out the welcome mat. Macon also encouraged men to enroll in the parent training that is another key feature of the PICA program.

Tim King had visited the PICA program from Baltimore and was impressed with the fact that the entire staff participated in training so that cooks and bus drivers as well as teachers and administrators knew everybody else's role. "Everyone there was responsible for recruiting parents," he said, adding that he had taken what he had learned in Minneapolis and incorporated it into his own staff meetings. Head Start can do some of this cross-fertilization when people from one program help review another or attend National Head Start Association or regional conferences, but many staff members said they would like more opportunities to learn about what worked at other centers. The prestigious panel that outlined directions for Head Start research in 1996 also was concerned about a dearth of these opportunities for sharing insights about innovative practices.[2]

Around the country, Head Start programs have come up with other creative ideas for involving men. James A. Levine wrote about many of these in his book, *Getting Men Involved: Strategies for Early Childhood Programs*.[3] For example, Cardinal Spellman Head Start in New York City held Father's Day celebrations, being sure to invite not only biological fathers but also guardians, uncles, older brothers, even male neighbors—whoever was significant to each child. At a Head Start program in Dayton, Ohio, the Miami Valley Child Development Centers recruited businessmen and other professional men and church members to volunteer by reading stories, talking about their hobbies, helping with computers. In Hattiesburg, Mississippi, the Pinebelt Association for Community Enhancement's Head Start staff knew that few of their children had their natural fathers living with them; they, too, found men from local businesses, churches, community organizations, and a military base as positive role models for the youngsters. And the Texas Migrant Council's Head Start program ran barbecues as fundraising events, usually having men doing the cooking. The bottom line in each case: men were directly involved in classroom or recreation activities—not just given boxes to move or asked to clean floors. One inescapable lesson emerged: involving the men took time and effort, and then more effort. But, said Sheila Tucker, the work yielded great benefits. "The biggest thing is the reconnection to their children and understanding that their children need them at this stage of their development. Having men involved also helps the communication between the men and women. Whenever that's better, it's going to be better for the children, period."

Parent involvement has several levels of meaning within Head Start.

There is parents' involvement with their children, going over lessons with them, providing them with good new experiences and helping them through bad ones. There is also parents' involvement in the classroom, reading to the children, encouraging their creativity, and helping teachers by supervising the children at play, fixing snacks, or preparing materials to color or cut. That kind of parent involvement sometimes leads to Head Start employment. And there is parents' involvement in running the programs. Head Start performance standards call for parents to help set policy as board members. At some programs, some parents really do; at some programs, it's like pulling teeth to get parents to ask about anything substantive. Often, that is not their fault.

In many places, it was difficult even to get parents to serve on local Head Start centers' parent councils. At Watts Towers, for example, Josephine Garner and Lupe Osuna urged the parents to get involved, and a few came faithfully to the meetings, but they rarely asked questions about what their children were being taught and why. Language was a problem because many of the women who at least came to the meetings were Hispanic and shy about speaking English; only women attended regularly because the meetings were held during the day. The Training and Research Foundation made sure it had a Spanish-speaking parent involvement specialist to translate at the meetings of the elected council from its three geographic regions, but the year I attended these meetings few substantive questions came up. Part of the reason, again, was acute shyness, but there also seemed to be more emphasis on teaching procedures for running meetings than actually talking about Head Start. The most heated discussion I heard was over where the group would go on its year-end social field trip.

One of the studies that came my way about parent involvement buttressed with organized observations my feeling of unease. A State University of New York at Plattsburgh professor, Jeanne Ellsworth, was invited to serve a three-year term as a community representative on a county Head Start policy council in upstate New York in the early 1990s. She and SUNY colleague Lynda Ames won the policy council's endorsement to study low-income women's priorities for schooling for their children, as well as how their involvement affected Head Start. As it turned out, they found in their observation and interviews that while "a small but important number of mothers have benefitted in important personal ways" from their involvement with policymaking, "their power was largely ceremonial—mothers had little opportunity to substantially shape the program."

The ideal of substantive involvement, they found, had been supplanted "by the notion of policy-making as compensatory education for parents. Not surprisingly, then, not once in the two-and-one-half years of our study were issues of pedagogical aims or practices brought before the policy council. Neither were questions of dilemmas of the program brought before the council to be hashed out. Virtually all issues brought to the group were brought as well-developed, budgeted, and thoroughly planned proposals to be simply voted on." It proved difficult for parents to be deeply involved because of child care and transportation problems, but also because the "experience, savvy, credentials and social class position" of the Head Start professionals inhibited the mothers who really did want to participate. Some of the staff did not consider the policy council "an authentic policy-making body at all."

Ellsworth and Ames predicted that as Head Start increasingly moves toward efficiency and tighter fiscal controls, "policy-making by parents will be seen as less and less desirable." Parent policymaking is, after all, "time-consuming, complicated and often messy—hardly the picture of efficiency and businesslike management."[4]

In another study at three rural Head Start programs, also in upstate New York, two Cornell University researchers found that many parents considered the center meetings "boring, unorganized and confusing." Their participation decreased as they were more fully employed or when they had infants to care for; however, none of the programs sought parents' help in defining the constraints working against their participation or what kind of participation would take those restrictions into consideration. Programs may have to shift their ideology, wrote Nicole M. Driebe and Moncrieff M. Cochran, "from the belief that 'good parents' fit themselves into the 'ideal involvement' mold promoted in the past by Head Start to a belief that the program must be able to respond flexibly to the needs of individual families."[5] In short, these researchers were urging Head Start to talk more to parents about how they want to participate, and not just talk to them at the beginning of the year, when they aren't likely to have many ideas yet about the program.

While some Head Start programs really do involve parents in meaningful policymaking, these two studies do not report isolated situations. If Head Start is honest with itself, it will either acknowledge that parents aren't intended to be the policymakers that its regulations stipulate, or it will renew its efforts to make participation meaningful at every level.

How, then, can Head Start involve low-income and perhaps poorly educated or depressed parents at the level of governing, or at least of suggesting policy initiatives and following up to see that they are accomplished? When a staff is busy teaching the classes and running the program, it is hard to step up efforts to tell parents what they are doing and why—in an energetic and inspired manner—and to find out what needs parents would like to see addressed. But it must be done. Attracting parents to talk with teachers or counselors about what their children are doing is a hit-and-miss proposition at every income level. It is especially important for poor people to know that they can ask questions and raise issues that trouble them. When Head Start succeeds in this area, it unlocks doors for children and their parents for the rest of the children's schooling.

One question surfaced as I saw the uneven level of parents' direct involvement in running programs: Does Head Start really want meaningful participation at the policymaking level? Or does it remember the debates of the 1960s over "maximum feasible participation of the poor" and want nothing to do with that in the more conservative 1990s? Polly Greenberg, who worked with the Child Development Group of Mississippi in the 1960s (see chapter 3), told me that one reason parents aren't more fully in charge at more programs is the conflict between experts and poor people. The best-intentioned professionals in the fields working with Head Start often find it "easier to go do it for them than to patiently stand by while others learn how to do it—others who are angry with you because you know how to do it and they don't." There is also the question of professional turf. "People who have political power and professional expertise don't give it away."

I dwell on this point because the element that struck many as so glorious about that 1960s experiment in Mississippi was that parents made so many of the decisions. They were organizing themselves for this effort, and they also benefited from civil rights organizing that was occurring in many of the same communities at the same time. Finding themselves with such influence was liberating. It may be that, early on, Head Start tapped energy and intelligence that had been dammed up for many years, and now that well is dry in many communities. But I don't believe it. Organizing for change can still be liberating.

It may be that Head Start can only be the object of organizing that yields that level of participation, not its source. Head Start could benefit so much from that kind of invigoration, but it may have to come from outside. The federal government is not about to get back into the business of subsidizing real community organizing in the concentrated, time-consuming manner it requires to succeed, although individual Head Start programs have clearly had some success when they worked hard at it. Federal money and federal rules hog-tie good organizers. As Saul Alinksy, the godfather of community organizing, warned years ago, federal antipoverty money will "suffocate militant independent leadership." Poverty can only be successfully fought, he said, when the poor have "sufficient power to threaten the status quo with disturbing alternatives so that it will induce the status quo to come through with a genuine, decent, meaningful poverty program."[6]

If the government should not (or will not) take on the organizing efforts, someone must. Communities harbor many talents, but often people have no sense of their possibilities. They don't know where to start. Where there remain active community organizers, they need to make links with Head Start, first to help find out what parents want to see done for their children, then to find out how many are willing to help do it. To be successful, they must be assured that Head Start programs with which they are working will give parents meaningful roles.

The kind of organizing I am talking about involves going door to door in a school neighborhood and building an organization from the ground up. This is not some outmoded notion from the sixties; it occurs today. The best example I have seen is the Texas Industrial Areas Foundation, a descendant of the Industrial Areas Foundation set up in 1940 by Alinksy, who had started his work in the stockyard-area neighborhoods of Chicago. Ernesto Cortes, Jr., who trained with Alinsky, launched his brand of community organizing in his hometown of San Antonio in 1974. That first successful group was called Communities Organized for Public Service (COPS), and it crusaded to win improved drainage for low-income, predominantly Hispanic west side neighborhoods that flooded every time it rained. Then COPS moved to broader campaigns to share in city improvement projects and to create meaningful job training programs. Today Texas IAF, working in collaboration with coalitions of churches, has established organizations similar to COPS in twelve Texas areas, as well as in Arizona, New Mexico, Louisiana, and Nebraska.

Texas IAF organizations have been especially active in developing what they call "alliance schools," partnerships between principals, teachers, and the community. There are now eighty-nine alliance schools in Texas, the results of a process that could be used around Head Start centers as well. It is worth exploring the process at one school in Austin, Texas, to see how hard the task is and at the same time how great the rewards could be if a Head Start program were the object of similar efforts.

Alejandro Mindiz Melton became principal of Zavala Elementary School in a poor neighborhood of East Austin in 1991 after being the school's assistant principal for five years. Zavala was in the bottom quartile for student achievement in the state. Each year almost half its staff left. Its attendance record was among the worst in the city. Only about 40 percent of the children had their immunizations. Zavala children read about two or three years below grade level. Melton knew the school had to change. "It was time to stop not being honest with the parents about student achievement," he told me. Youngsters were getting good grades but what their parents didn't know was that they were scoring poorly on the standardized tests given all public-school children. So Melton asked a parent to read aloud the test scores at a meeting. There clearly was no correlation with the grades the children had been getting. Hearing the scores depressed both the parents and the teachers.

Frustrated over the school's poor reputation and his lack of progress in motivating parents, Melton met with Joe Higgs and Kathleen Davis, organizers from Austin Interfaith, the local Texas IAF organization. He spieled off his concerns, then asked what they could do for him. "You don't understand," they replied. "We're not going to do anything for you. You're going to do it for yourself." That's the absolute iron rule of organizing: "Never do for others what they can do for themselves."

Higgs and Davis started the painstaking process that Texas IAF organizations all employ, finding the natural leaders in the community and holding house meetings with parents to learn their concerns. They heard about children going to school with colds and ear infections, that they sometimes had lice, and that they often hadn't had their shots. Parents had little time off and often couldn't take their children to the doctor; many didn't have health insurance. As a result, twenty to twenty-five children a day would need attention, overwhelming the part-time nurse. A nearby clinic was about to shut down for eight months for asbestos removal, and the Zavala parents wanted full-time health services at the school. That dovetailed with what Higgs was hearing from Zavala's teachers. They were concerned with their students' limited academic success, which seemed linked with their poor attendance because they were sick so often.

Zavala students lived in a neighborhood of small bungalows lining narrow streets and flanked by the Santa Rita and Chalmers Courts

housing projects. The parents worked at tortilla factories, meat companies, cleaning firms, hotels, and restaurants; they didn't earn much
money. They felt little connection with the elementary school situated
in their midst. That started to change when the school voted to try to
improve itself by working with Austin Interfaith. It also started to
change on a May morning in 1992 when the teachers, some of the parent leaders, and members of the congregations that formed Austin
Interfaith went house to house in that small neighborhood, talking
to parents, finding out what they wanted from the school. As they can-
vassed the neighborhood, the kids were running down the narrow streets
yelling, "Mama, the teachers are coming!"

The walk helped both the parents and the teachers. The parents saw
that the teachers wanted to know their opinions; the teachers learned
how little some of the families had but how much they wanted to be
connected to the school. The parents marshaled their facts on the
health care issue and worked with Higgs and Davis to prepare their case
for the school board. "We would role-play a lot," said Tona Vasquez,
whose daughter attended Zavala and who was one of those early leaders
identified by Austin Interfaith. "They might ask a question we weren't
prepared for so we wouldn't be caught off guard. They'd tell us who was
going to be there so we wouldn't be shocked to see all those people,
cameras, and reporters."

The parents faced a school board wary about opposition from the
religious right. "They said we had a hidden agenda, that this was going
to evolve into handing out condoms and referring kids to abortion
clinics," said Vasquez. "These were people who don't even live in the
neighborhood," she scoffed. The parents went to the school board ("I
didn't even know where it was," Vasquez later confessed), made their
speeches, and convinced the board that the city would save money in
the long run by providing health services at the school.

"You never think you can go and talk to the mayor, the city council,
the candidates. You say, 'They're not going to listen to me. I don't have
money. I live in the housing project,' " said Lourdes Zamarron, another
of the parent leaders, whose daughter also attended Zavala. But Joe
Higgs and Kathleen Davis "reminded us that power is in numbers."

Once the parents won on the health services issue, Austin Interfaith
and the school were ready to tackle the poor academic performance.
Melton got a waiver so that the school could use a new language arts
and mathematics curriculum. Teachers were trained in methods to help
students learn from one another. And the faculty members talked more

among themselves about what skills the children would need and in what grades those skills should be taught.

The parents also worked to develop an after-school program to provide their children with experiences middle-class parents routinely gave their children but which they could not afford—from learning magic to dancing, cooking to volleyball. And they wanted a richer science program so that their children could qualify to attend a science magnet school. That meant that the parents had to go to the school board again because they wanted to offer the science program for sixth graders but Zavala stopped with fifth grade. They got permission, and in the fall of 1993 the Zavala Young Scientists Program began with help from Dell Computer and the University of Texas. When I visited the following spring, six Zavala students had just been accepted to the magnet and one had won a scholarship to a private school. "My daughter loves school. Sometimes it's hard to get her to go home. She has never been as excited about science as she is now," Zamarron told me. "They've studied the planets and oceanography. There just hadn't been that much focus on science before."

The results: Zavala's attendance, once middling to poor, topped the district. Number one. Test scores up; staff turnover, way down. "Why are you working there? You're wasting your time," friends used to tell Claudia Santamaria, the after-school program coordinator. "Now people say, 'Oh, wow, you work there. How great!' It's an amazing feeling to be on both sides in so short a time." Where once he had to beg teachers to come to Zavala, one year Melton had fifty applications for one opening.

Some of the teachers at Zavala initially feared that Austin Interfaith was just another group that would drop in with more things for them to do, then fade away. When I last visited the Zavala area, it had been more than four years since the formal tie was made, and Austin Interfaith was still there. Texas IAF groups have shown the same persistence in bringing water hookups and toilets to thousands of people who lived in unincorporated areas known as the *colonias* in the Rio Grande valley and around El Paso and in building job training programs and developing better housing in San Antonio.

They needed that persistence because the parents had to go back to the school board to fight for their clinic. The board was considering contracting with a private group to provide the services because the school-based clinic wasn't seeing enough new people. That was the whole point, the parents said; school attendance was so much higher because their children were healthier. Emphasizing preventive care would help them stay healthy. The parents made their case.

And Texas IAF and the parents it mobilized needed to stay on task for another reason: the guiding force behind Zavala's turnabout, Al Melton, who had been named a Hero of American Education by the Reader's Digest Foundation, was reassigned just before school started in the fall of 1996. Zavala's parents wanted to be involved in the selection of his successor. The school administration named a nine-member committee, including three parents and three teachers from Zavala. They completed their task in five weeks, submitting three names of people who would be acceptable. They got their first choice.

I asked both Ernie Cortes and Willie Bennett, who became Austin Interfaith's lead organizer when Joe Higgs was transferred, whether their organizing tactics could work in connection with Head Start. The process, Bennett thought, was transferable. "Everything we do starts with individual meetings, sitting down one-on-one and finding out not only what people want but who you're working with, who's willing to do something." An organization may have to do something first that doesn't necessarily seem connected to academics—like the Zavala health services—but taking action on what the community wants to do is important to building the relationship. With that trust comes involvement and action.

There are several elements that must be in place for the Texas IAF process to work. The institution, be it Zavala Elementary or a local Head Start program, must see that it has a problem and want to fix it. In the case of Head Start, that problem could be lack of parent involvement in general or some specific issue. The community must be knit together, often no easy task because some areas have little sense of community. "Look," Cortes said to me, "in Dallas we're working in an area where forty percent of the kids come from homeless shelters. In Zavala, many of the families live in public housing. In some cases you're trying to reconstitute the community from the fragments. Sometimes it's a garment that's been shredded and you have to reweave it."

And you have to find the groups' natural leaders. "People have been clobbered psychologically," Cortes said. "You have to identify people who want to do these things. You never try to coerce them or intimidate them." If they don't want to get involved, you go away. Maybe they'll be involved when they see others accomplishing things. Cortes and Texas IAF also believe that other local institutions, especially churches, must be involved to back up the parents.

If these elements are present in the areas of San Antonio, El Paso, Dallas, Austin, and other cities where the Texas Industrial Areas Foundation works, they are present in any area. Head Start can apply some of the same techniques by working with local groups that understand their communities and know how to motivate people. It is not a nine-to-five job. It means working weekends and nights when you can find parents at home. It is footslogging, door-to-door, sometimes frustrating work when there are setbacks. But it could make the same kind of difference for local Head Start programs that Texas IAF has made at Zavala Elementary, a school where the parents not only go to meetings, but have accomplished great change.

Watts Towers:

The children visit the California Afro American Museum and see a skeleton. Deborah Chatman introduces her daughters, both UCLA students. And Andre wows 'em as Dr. King.

The Watts Towers Head Start center was buzzing one sunny February morning. The children were going on a field trip and the bus was late arriving. The lunches were packed and all the preparations made for the trip from Watts to Exposition Park, where the children would visit the California Afro American Museum as part of their celebration of Black History Month.

Jesús's mother had dropped him off at the center and saw Joshua pushing her son. Josephine Garner cautioned her to let the children straighten it out; they could handle it. That, she said later, was a problem when parents who hadn't visited the center much finally did come—they tended to hover. Garner steered one mother who was going on the trip around to meet some of the children, urging the parents to mingle more with the youngsters rather than keeping to themselves.

In January, the children had learned about Dr. Martin Luther King, Jr., and his efforts for black Americans. The scope of their knowledge broadened in February as the teachers put pictures on the bulletin boards of Jesse Owens, Jackie Robinson, Shirley Chisholm, Mary McLeod Bethune, Thurgood Marshall, George Washington Carver, Harriet Tubman, and Jesse Jackson.

"What about Rosie Parks—the lady who rode in the front of the bus?" Garner asked the children one morning, and Shardae walked over to the board and pointed out her picture.

Several mornings the children rehearsed for their Black History Month program for the parents; later in the year they would also observe Cinco de Mayo, the Fifth of May, commemorating the Mexican victory over an empire-minded French expeditionary force at Puebla in 1862. The Head Start teachers had selected various children to play the parts of key figures in black history. Marcus would be George Washington Carver, famous black scientist; his mother worked with him on his one-sentence recitation. Ciara would be the first black woman in Congress, Shirley Chisholm. Shardae held up a cutout of a bus; she would speak on Rosa Parks. Jackie Robinson would be portrayed by Richard, the little boy who had cried so wrenchingly the first day of school but no longer missed mom when she left. A major breakthrough: Raymound had asked if he could be Jesse Owens. He'd shake his head no, though, when asked if he wanted to practice his sentence. I had urged the teachers to add Mississippi civil rights worker Fannie Lou Hamer to their program, and Clintishabeth practiced the sentence I wrote for her to say. After one rehearsal, Garner urged the children, "Give yourself a big hand. If you get up here and don't do it, don't worry. You didn't go to drama school. Ain't nobody going to rain on your parade."

Thus primed for their trip, the children waited and waited for the bus. "Are we going to wear seat belts?" Garner asked them.

"Yes."

"Are we going to stand up?"

"No."

"Are we going to put our hands out the window?"

"No."

"Are we going to jump up and down?"

"No."

The children sang a song about a bus whose wheels went round and round, all over town. The horn on the bus went beep, beep, beep, all over town. The baby on the bus went wah, wah, wah, all over town. The teachers on the bus went shhh, shhh, shhh, all over town. The wipers on the bus went whoosh, whoosh, whoosh—with hand motions to match—all over town.

"We're not going to the animal museum. We're going to the African American Museum. You cannot run," Garner told the children. "You cannot be screaming and hollering. Hold your partner's hand. No fighting. No scratching. You have to learn to like everybody; you cannot only hold your cousin's hand." And by and large, there was no running, no fighting, and much holding of partners' hands.

The bus arrived and Garner announced she would check it to make sure there were no monsters. Back at the door with a grin, she welcomed the children on board, encouraging them to make the big step up by themselves if they could. "Come on, children, we're going on the freeway." This trip was designed not only to teach black history but also to encourage parents to take their children to this and other museums—and to show some of the especially protective parents that their children would be safe out of the neighborhood for the day. A few moms and dads stood on the sidewalk and waved as we headed on our way.

Because the bus was late and there was the inevitable traffic jam on the 110 Freeway, we were late for our tour at the museum. The children sat quietly in the unseasonable heat—the temperature reached the mid-eighties that February day—on a ledge outside the museum while Garner renegotiated and arranged for a tour at noon. With time to fill before noon, the teachers and parents took the children to the science museum nearby. The youngsters may have remembered the clear plastic torso with its visible skeleton and internal organs or the wrecked car they saw in that museum better than anything they saw later in the day. Garner used the car as a prop for urging the children not to ride with anyone who had been drinking.

Then came a long bathroom break and the walk back to the Afro American Museum. David Williams, our guide there, confessed that he "wasn't used to talking to babies," but communicated quite well. He showed us an exhibit of African American nurses that started with their service during the Civil War and included some of the weapons that had wounded the soldiers they tended. He pointed out an old-fashioned helmet worn during World War I. A larger-than-life cutout of Mary McLeod Bethune dominated one corner of the room, and Williams told the children how she had started a college in Florida. Garner responded that Bethune would be part of the children's Black History Month program.

Next, Williams took the children through a display about celebrations. One exhibit centered on births and included a wooden incubator used by midwives, leading Garner to tell me that her grandmother had been a midwife. The incubator used a lightbulb to keep the baby warm. Another exhibit dealt with parades, and Williams had the children count the buttons and pockets on a World War I uniform worn when the soldiers marched home. Some could count the buttons exactly; others just kept on reciting the numbers, not yet having grasped the concept that counting meant stopping when they reached the correct number.

While we rested in the lobby, the children were looking at a painting by African American artist John Biggers, part of an exhibit soon to open at the museum. The work showed an elderly black woman standing on the front porch of a rickety shotgun-style Southern shack. "Why isn't she happy?" one of the little boys asked Williams. It was a far more sensitive question than any I heard adults ask when I returned to see that exhibit. Thrown by the question for only a moment, Williams responded that it might be because her house was not in very good repair and she didn't have anyone to help her. But he said that Biggers painted the same lady on other days when she was happy. That seemed to make the little boy happy, too.

A week later, February 14, the Watts Towers center had its black history program for the parents. Each morning when I arrived at the center, Osuna and I had our ritual. She would ask, *"Cómo está usted?"* and I would try to reply with at least one new sentence in the Spanish I was learning. That day I was feeling *"muy triste"* over the death three days earlier of a dear friend. But kids always sense what to do—Joshua and Shardae ran over and hugged me around the knees. I almost wept.

It seemed to be a big crying day among the children. Little Karina, Cindy's three-year-old sister, was crying and Shardae, always sensitive to others' emotions, asked why. Garner told her it was because their mother had just had a baby and she wanted to be home with it; she couldn't because she might give the infant a cold. Actually, that couldn't have been the only reason; this child proved to be a crier for weeks thereafter. The next year she was back in Head Start—with no tears.

For the Black History Month program, the children who weren't portraying famous people were wearing African print cloths draped over them and bandannas on their heads. Garner had on a similar Kente cloth print dress and a bandanna on her head. Seen from the back, she wasn't immediately recognizable, and I thought someone new was there. She looked at me and laughed, "Oh, girl, this takes me back." Gloria Heyman was having trouble tying one child's scarf. "Don't you know how to do it?" Osuna asked her. "Just 'cause I'm black doesn't mean I know how to do it," Heyman said with a laugh.

The parents trickled in slowly and the children sat remarkably still for half an hour as Garner waited for the late arrivals. Donisha was crying. Jesús was crying. Andre was crying. Aide Deborah Chatman had her arm around Jesús and later several of the others; her role seemed to be comforter for the day. In the past, other Head Start teachers and aides had consoled her own children. Her daughter LaShunda Davis, a twenty-year-old communications major at UCLA when I met her, remembered her first day at Head Start. "My mother left me there and I sat in the dirt outside and cried." Chatman, a short African American woman of forty, had worked as an aide at Imperial Courts, left to sell vacuum cleaners for five years at Montgomery Ward, and returned. "I just like children." Occasionally she would tell me with pride about a paper one of her daughters had done for a college class. LaShunda and her sister Yolanda, then an eighteen-year-old freshman majoring in English at UCLA, volunteered on Saturdays for an alternative learning program for children five to twelve years old at a housing project as part of the university's African-Education Project.

Chatman dispensed tissues and hugs as Garner opened the activities by telling the children it was Valentine's Day. "This is the day to get your mama flowers or a valentine or go home and just put your arms around her and tell her you love her."

Garner assembled the children portraying the famous black Americans on chairs in front of the bulletin board as the audience assembled behind the remaining children. Addressing the parents and several visiting Training and Research Foundation staff members, Garner outlined the program, saying that each child would say one sentence. "If they say one word, that's okay. Some may say it better than others. I may have to whisper in their ears. So if they make mistakes, bear with them."

First, though, the children sang and said hello in Swahili. When they finished, Shardae clapped and the audience followed suit. "Thank you, Shardae," Garner said.

"Now, B is for Bethune," said Garner. Softly, very softly, Janette said that Mary Bethune started the first black college.

"R is for Robinson," and little Richard said his piece, his Dodgers baseball cap almost covering his big eyes. "O" was for Owens, and Raymound said, "Jesse Owens was a famous black track star." You could hear him. He did it! I almost got teary again.

"C is for Carver." Marcus, wearing a white lab coat almost to his ankles, dropped the sweet potato he was holding. "George Washington Carver was a famous black scientist."

"You did *so* good," Garner said.

Ciara was a precise Shirley Chisholm, and Wayne had to be prompted about Pele, the soccer star. Shardae spoke up, saying, "Rosie Parks sat on the front of the bus for the first time." She got a big hand from the parents. Kimberly was Charles Drew, who opened the first blood bank. Clintishabeth, aka Fannie Lou Hamer that day and wearing a special flowered dress, had an unusual attack of shyness. Osuna said, "Turn and say it to me," which she did.

Finally, Andre got up, looked his audience dead on, and said, "Dr.

sponsibility of the [program's] executive director and Head Start director," and the governing board "had abdicated and relinquished its authority to govern" the agency. "The Denver Head Start program . . . is at risk," the independent review team concluded.

The team charged, among other things, that the agency overreported by $608,904 the matching funds it raised in 1995, which meant it did not have enough money to maintain equipment and supplies for the 2,500 children enrolled. Costs were charged to Head Start that were not allowable under federal programs, the team said; Head Start funds were frequently loaned to other Child Opportunity Program accounts; the program had overspent its Head Start funds for each of the two previous years; and it did not always comply with federal procurement regulations for open, competitive bidding. Head Start named the Clayton Foundation, a nonprofit organization that ran an Early Head Start program in east Denver, to take over as an interim grantee.

Although complaints had been made for months—some say years— to the Denver regional office of Head Start, the investigation was launched following headlines in the *Denver Post* and coverage in other media set off by the firing of the thirty-two workers. *Post* reporter Paul Hutchinson talked to Child Opportunity Program staff members and was impressed with their courage in risking their jobs and by their commitment to the program. "They had a willingness to be quoted by name," Hutchinson said. He covered the issue with about thirty-five bylined stories during the year, capped on May 18 with "Heads Roll at Head Start, Feds Order Brandon and His Board Out."[2]

The Denver investigation, however belated it might have seemed to some most closely involved, was part of an effort by the national Head Start office to upgrade management and performance of local programs and shut them down if they could not be improved. "Since I've come in," said Taylor, tapped to run the program in 1994, "we've defunded seventy-six programs, and that's historic. On quality . . . I think the field has gotten the message that we're very serious about quality." New grantees were found to serve the children who had been enrolled in the failed programs; many others received technical assistance and were able to improve. Efforts to monitor Head Start quality do not yield warm and cuddly stories as visits to the program's centers do, but failure to keep tight rein on performance ends up in shoddy programs for children and headlines like those in Denver.

Reviewing Head Start programs and forcing improvements is one of the most crucial tasks facing Head Start, but one that can be lengthy and bureaucratic. Difficult, too, with a bare-bones staff of about 50 people in the Head Start national office and 160 to 180 regional employees, although local staff is recruited to help with the program reviews that occur every three years. Those reviews are supposed to provide a warning system about financial and program areas that are in poor shape. "You have to have the national-level commitment" to monitoring programs, Head Start pioneer Edward Zigler of Yale University told me, "but the real points of pressure are the regional offices. There are many programs that just need help but sometimes they can't get it. That's where I would spend some more money."

Stress on management and monitoring within Head Start could most kindly be described as uneven over the years. Until 1975 the program lacked detailed performance standards outlining what was expected of each local program. Head Start drifted for a period after its initial glory years, and it is useful to flash back again to 1970 to examine what was happening to the program. Head Start had several fights for its very survival in the late 1960s and 1970s, so weeding out poorly performing local programs was not as high on its list as it should have been.

Head Start sputtered as the Vietnam War diverted President Lyndon Johnson's attention. Increasingly, Johnson referred to the effort as "the poverty program," no longer as "my war."[3] The antipoverty program's overall budget was cut almost in half within the administration in 1966–67, and more by Congress. Between 1967 and 1968, Head Start, the program for which Johnson had predicted thousandfold results, was cut by $33 million. Complaints from local city halls against community action agencies' activities and protests from the poor who wanted a bigger role in those programs hastened Johnson's retreat. Instead of all the commotion, Johnson told aide Bill Moyers, "I thought we were just going to have the NYA.* I thought we were going to have CCC** camps and I thought we were going to have community action where a city or county or a school district or some governmental agency could sponsor projects."[4]

The Office of Economic Opportunity came under heavy fire. Rumors of Sargent Shriver's resignation as OEO's head long preceded the actual event. He stepped down in 1968 and Johnson named him ambassador to France. OEO's programs were parceled out to other agencies or

---

*National Youth Administration, for which Johnson had worked during the Depression.
**Civilian Conservation Corps, also a Depression-era agency.

killed outright. Head Start was also at risk, especially after Johnson left office. Its biggest problem was that it had been thrown together quickly with few standards and virtually no quality control. Zigler, one of its best boosters, has said repeatedly that it has been playing catch-up ever since. "The result is that Head Start programs across the nation have always been uneven in quality, with some providing excellent services, others middling, and some quite poor."[5]

Head Start's case was also weakened by early research emphasis on the program's effects on children's IQs and academic achievement test scores. Initially, the story had been upbeat. Sargent Shriver wrote with characteristic enthusiasm to Lady Bird Johnson in June 1966 as Head Start began its second summer that children were entering school "better prepared and with greater self-confidence and greater intellectual capacity than children from similar backgrounds who did not have a Head Start experience." He added that a Johns Hopkins University psychology professor, Dr. Leon Eisenberg, had found an increase of from eight to ten IQ points in the children who participated in Head Start in Baltimore, "bearing out his opinion that even a six-week project can produce significant intellectual gains in children from impoverished backgrounds."[6] Shriver also pointed to the IQ gain when asked at congressional hearings in 1966 what was the War on Poverty's greatest success that could actually be measured.[7]

Edward Zigler questioned whether Head Start had indeed made children more intelligent. In a study that he and a colleague conducted, Zigler reported that the gains weren't due to improvement in how children thought but occurred because they were more motivated; they were also more comfortable taking tests. In short, Head Start "had helped them use the intelligence they had" rather than making them more intelligent.[8] "We should have never allowed the IQ score to become the ultimate indicator of compensatory education's success or failure," Zigler later wrote. "The goal of Head Start never was to produce a cadre of geniuses to fill the teaching posts at our universities. We should reduce the confusion that I now see in this area by clearly and openly asserting that the goal of Head Start is the production of socially competent human beings."[9]

In the late 1960s, Zigler and other researchers had serious misgivings about a study the government commissioned from the Westinghouse Learning Corporation, working with Ohio University, to provide an overall Head Start assessment. They felt that Head Start should be examined not just in terms of children's intellectual development but also for the program's impact on their health and social skills and on parental involvement in their children's educations. They also argued that it was wrong to base part of the study on Head Start's chaotic first summer and that it would be difficult to provide one true picture of the program because the centers were so varied. There were also difficulties in determining whether the Head Start students being tested had comparable backgrounds to those in the control groups.

Their fears were justified. The Westinghouse report came out in 1969, and its findings were devastating: "Head Start as it is presently constituted has not provided widespread cognitive and affective gains" and "its benefits cannot be described as satisfactory." The study found little gain in test scores for children who attended the summer program its first four years compared with those who had not. For children who had attended full-year Head Start, the study reported some gain after their first year in school but not after their second and third years—what would become the fabled "fade-out effect."

The study may have been scientifically discredited in many respects—but not in the political arena. It justified for the Nixon administration its inherent suspicions of Johnson-era programs, and it caused budget and political problems for Head Start for years. President Richard M. Nixon did keep Head Start alive, but he told Congress in early 1969, just before the Westinghouse report was issued, that a major study would soon show that "the long-term effect of Head Start appears to be extremely weak." Nixon's preview and the attention the media gave the study cemented its findings in the public mind.

Not long after the Westinghouse study was released, Zigler became the first director of the federal Office of Child Development within the Department of Health, Education, and Welfare, where Head Start had been moved in 1969. He brought personal experience to his work in early childhood development. Zigler grew up in a Polish immigrant family and attended nursery school at a Kansas City, Missouri, settlement house where he also received medical care. It also had activities for his parents. "Head Start is a modern-day settlement house," Zigler told me. Later he became the first person in his family to attend college. He earned a Ph.D. from the University of Texas in 1958 and went to Yale University the next year.[10] "You couldn't have been poorer than my parents were, yet here I am a Sterling Professor at Yale. I got here through education."

Zigler knew that in the political climate of the early 1970s, Head Start would not grow. First, the program's quality needed shoring up.

Zigler assembled a team that would develop the program's first performance standards, help train teachers in what would be expected of them, and assist programs in improving their management. Zigler's team also faced the same turf battles that had begun even while Head Start was still in the Office of Economic Opportunity—threatened changes that would have weakened the program by placing it under the control of the education establishment or the states. Those battles continue to this day.

"For the most part Head Start was not in great shape in the early 1970s," said Harley Frankel, who supervised the program from 1971 until early 1975. "It had a good reputation but for the most part kids weren't getting good services. It was a great concept and in my view very important, but it didn't have meat on its bones. It's very hard to fight for something like that."

President Johnson had clearly decided "to create facts on the ground," Frankel said, but the program was operating catch-as-catch-can by the early 1970s. "No one's improved on the concept of providing disadvantaged kids with comprehensive services. Some people had picked up on it really well but others hadn't. They were all very decent people, committed to kids," but many needed a more solid idea of what they should be doing. Zigler, Frankel, and their colleagues were determined to make Head Start such an outstanding program that its critics could do nothing harmful to it. The team was directed by Frankel, an alumnus of Harvard University's Graduate School of Business Administration, and Ray Collins, a Yale graduate who held a master of public affairs degree from Princeton University.

They started with performance standards. "We did it not by sitting in Washington saying that this is what makes sense, but we went around the country and got a consensus on what it would take to make it a great program," Frankel said. Through the standards, local programs were told that they would have to make sure children received preventive health care—not just inform the parents that they should receive it. The standards spelled out what health screenings should include. Head Start programs were required to provide nutritious meals for children and to conduct several home visits each year. They had to evaluate themselves. They had to have parents on the board of directors with all the power that boards of directors have.

The planners had to ensure that there was money for the two thousand grantees to meet these standards or they would be meaningless pieces of paper. They worked out a deal with Medicaid to finance the services under its comprehensive child health program, called the Early and Periodic Screening, Diagnosis, and Testing Program, and they contracted with the American Academy of Pediatrics to find doctors in underserved areas. They convinced the Department of Agriculture to make Head Start children eligible for the school breakfast and lunch program. They designed tools so that programs could evaluate themselves. And they sent management teams to examine and shore up the practices of the fifty largest grantees.

While Zigler headed the Office of Child Development, he also introduced several concepts that are still integral elements of Head Start, in part to give the Nixon administration a stake in a program created under its predecessor.[11] For example, Head Start created a home-based option. Trained staff would work with children and their parents in their homes, a useful variation for Head Start programs in rural areas with transportation problems. It also appealed to parents who wanted to teach their children at home or who thought they were too young or not healthy enough to attend a center-based program. The Zigler era also produced the child development associate (CDA) credential, a certification of competence to work with young children (see chapter 9).

Once the performance standards had been developed, Zigler went to his boss at HEW, Secretary Elliot Richardson, and laid out what had been done. "Richardson really trusted Ed," Frankel recalled, "and that was crucial." It helped that the Nixon team liked management types, and Zigler had brought many of them on board. "Nixon's people wanted to make government work," Frankel said, "but they wanted to make government work differently."

The trust between Richardson and Zigler proved vital because once the performance standards helped Head Start become a more viable, visible program, others wanted to get their hands on it. In the past, efforts to shift Head Start to new administrative homes had been viewed as efforts to kill it. For example, in 1967 Republican senator Peter Dominick of Colorado had introduced amendments to pending legislation that would have placed Head Start under the control of the Office of Education, a move that did not reflect the fact that Head Start's mission was broader than education. In 1968, the Senate passed a Dominick amendment that would have killed Head Start and given states a lump sum of money for early childhood programs at their discretion. The attempt died in the House of Representatives, however, after Head Start supporters, alerted by director Richard Orton, flooded the members with calls opposing the move.[12]

By the mid-1970s, Head Start remained alive but still at risk of being shifted to control of the states or agencies solely concerned with education. Some Southern states were still resisting school desegregation and would have cheerfully abandoned the requirement that Head Start programs be integrated or killed the program entirely; other states were not as interested in helping their minorities, whether Latino or Indian, as was the federal program; still others might have used the money for other projects. So Head Start faced a challenge when Governor Jimmy Carter of Georgia wrote to the federal Office of Management and Budget requesting control over Head Start in Georgia under a 1974 law that allowed states more planning authority over federal programs serving their residents. Frankel and Saul Rosoff, then acting director of the Office of Child Development, felt that they could not fight the move publicly. They feared that Head Start would end up in the hands of white middle-class Southern educators who might not be sympathetic to all its broad child-development goals. But they couldn't express those fears to white middle-class members of Congress, or to Republicans who liked shifting programs to the states under Nixon's New Federalism.

Subtlety was needed. Frankel asked the lawyer for the Children's Defense Fund (CDF) to give him the best argument why the OMB directives on state planning should not apply to Head Start. Then Frankel rewrote that argument in bureaucratese and convinced the lawyers in his own agency that the directive did not apply to Head Start because Head Start's legislation authorized local control of programs. "We took it up the chain of command to Caspar Weinberger, who was by then HEW secretary, and then we knew we were on solid ground" within HEW. Meantime, "Saul Rosoff took a huge risk. He wrote Governor Carter denying him the right to take control of Head Start. It was a profile in courage. We were summoned to the White House," and were worried what would happen. There, however, "Weinberger made our case for us."

On Capitol Hill, Senator Edmund S. Muskie of Maine, who had written the legislation, let OMB know that unless it backed off its overzealous interpretation, he would see to it that Congress took away all this new authority. Since OMB was more interested in its overall program than in moving Head Start, it did indeed back off. "Had that not happened," Frankel said, "every governor in the country would have taken over the program."

Carter reached the White House in the 1976 election with the strong support of the National Education Association, having promised to create a separate Department of Education. "That was a huge threat" to Head Start, said Frankel, who by then had gone to work for the Children's Defense Fund. "All the pressure was on to have a large department and Head Start was a jewel" wanted by its planners and by Senator Abraham Ribicoff of Connecticut, who was sponsoring the legislation. Up until the morning of Senate hearings on the new department, however, Frankel had been assured that Head Start was not going to be in it. OMB had all its charts made up for testimony to that effect, but when Frankel reached the Hill, he knew something was wrong. The start of the hearing was delayed. At 7 A.M. Carter's decision had come through: he wanted Head Start in the new department. OMB was remaking its charts, retyping its testimony. Frankel and CDF president Marian Wright Edelman went to a nearby restaurant and sat there. They couldn't eat. How could they turn this around?

"Who was for it?" Frankel asked rhetorically. "Carter, Ribicoff, Senator Charles Percy, the ranking Republican on a committee that did everything by consensus. The National Education Association. A friend said, 'You're going to lose.' But we turned it into a civil rights issue." A key figure in the civil rights movement in Mississippi, Aaron Henry, who had led the Mississippi Freedom Democratic Party challenge at the 1964 Democratic convention, went to Washington to lobby to keep Head Start out of the new department. Along with Nancy Spears, a white Southerner who directed the Head Start program in Lee County, Alabama (see chapter 5), Henry visited office after office on Capitol Hill. Neither wanted the program put under the control of what were still predominantly white school boards in the South.

"We generated ten thousand pieces of mail in a day when they weren't just churned out, all the same. These were individual letters," Harley Frankel told me, remembering the fight with a nostalgic smile. "We worked the Hill. A group of Head Start mothers got on a bus from New Haven and sat in at Ribicoff's office. A similar group made a trip from Illinois to Percy's office. So in the markup session, Ribicoff made a motion that Head Start not be in the new department. It passed unanimously."

The 1970s were the decade that set the program very close to its eventual form, Frankel said. He knew that first Head Start's quality and its management needed improving. Then it would need more money if it was to maintain its momentum as well as serve more children. But Head Start had received nothing but cost-of-living increases for the entire decade. Congress still remembered the Westinghouse report. Then in the mid-1970s George Washington University issued a report summarizing 150 research studies on Head Start. The conclusion: Head Start did help children make improvements in their cognitive development and health while aiding their families as well.[13]

Frankel, still lobbying for the Children's Defense Fund, took the report—one hundred copies' worth—and almost literally ran with it to Capitol Hill. Instead of going solely to the two key men who traditionally had made the budget decisions, one on each committee staff, Frankel decided to work the entire committees. He did that for six months, "carrying that report up, educating people." For the 1978 fiscal year, Congress increased Head Start's appropriation by $150 million—from $475 million up to $625 million. The increase allowed Head Start to serve almost sixty thousand more children that year. "It was the largest percentage increase of any program in the HEW budget," Frankel said proudly.

Next he wanted the administration to commit to more substantial increases, even to cross the billion-dollar threshold. Frankel worked toward that goal from inside the administration after becoming deputy director of President Carter's personnel office in 1978. Allied with Stuart Eizenstat, a supporter of Head Start who was one of Carter's key aides, Frankel planned a celebration observing Head Start's fifteenth anniversary in 1980. Frankel wrote the president's speech, in which Carter would commit himself to the increase. But the president departed from his text. Peggy Pizzo, long associated with Head Start and then on the White House staff, recalled Frankel's anguish as he listened to the president, who was speaking eloquently about Head Start being the only fully integrated program in Georgia when he was serving on the school board in Plains. Pizzo was standing next to Frankel. "The president was wonderful, but Harley was dying. He was muttering through his teeth, 'Read the speech.'" Finally Carter returned to his text and made his pledge.

Years later, sitting at his dining-room table in California and remembering those years, Frankel recalled his last act in Head Start's behalf in an official capacity. On the first full day of the Reagan administration, Frankel was sitting at home with nothing particular to do. He thought about Reagan's campaign rhetoric about cutting social programs and he worried that all Head Start's efforts might go down the drain. He telephoned a number he knew at the Office of Management and Budget. One of the director's assistants picked up the phone. Frankel identified

himself as "the guy who had run Head Start" in the Nixon administration. " 'You're going to need a few programs that you don't cut so
you will appear humane,' I told him. 'Head Start should be one of them.
It really works, it's not that expensive, and it is well liked by middle-
class America.' I told him about the GW report. He asked for a copy
and I sent it to him." Frankel hung up. Then he asked himself whom
the man would consult, so he called several key Republican aides with
the same message.

A week later OMB director David Stockman presented his proposals
to the Reagan cabinet, with Head Start as one of the seven programs
that made up the social "safety net" that Reagan should leave in place.
Caspar Weinberger, the new defense secretary, said he agreed completely, as did Education Secretary Ted Bell. "Once we got Reagan not
to cut the program," Frankel said, "Head Start survived the eighties."

Head Start did survive the eighties. Its funds were even modestly increased several years. But one year they were cut by nearly $35 million.
The number of children served was increasing while wages fell and programs had to consolidate various staff positions, which did not help the
children. Federal food grants were reduced, which affected Head Start.
Quality control suffered because staff members could not regularly in-
spect Head Start programs, nor could they provide needed training.
Little research was done. In short, there was, in Ed Zigler's words, "a
rapid diminution in program quality from which Head Start—never
strong on quality to begin with—has yet to recover."[14]

Zigler is like a pit bull about Head Start. He can rip into it with the
best of them because he knows what it should be doing, but he will
stand and defend it when the program is threatened because he knows
what it has done. Now director of Yale's Bush Center in Child Development and Social Policy, Zigler chaired a committee that outlined Head
Start's needs for the future when it reached its fifteenth anniversary.
That report, he said, "was ignored by the outgoing administration and
shelved by the new Reagan team." He also helped a National Head
Start Association panel making recommendations for Head Start in
the 1990s on its twenty-fifth anniversary, and was appointed to a bipartisan, broadly based government advisory committee on Head Start
quality and expansion soon after the Clinton administration took office.[15] Those two reports generated concrete results in terms of both
legislation and administrative improvements.

Congress reauthorized Head Start in 1990 and set aside 10 percent
of its first year's budget increase, 25 percent for each year thereafter, to

improve program quality. Much of that money went for higher pay and increased benefits. That 1990 legislation also established pilot projects to determine what worked best in helping children make the transition from Head Start into elementary school (see chapter 13).

By 1994, Congress had in hand the advisory committee's recommendations for a program for children under three years old and their parents. "Today," the panel had said, "research suggests that for many families, providing one year of preschool for four year olds may be too late." To help programs work with younger children, Congress established the Early Head Start program in its 1994 reauthorization measure; in 1995 sixty-eight programs were awarded grants to set up Early Head Start. In 1996 Head Start managed a substantial increase in its funds despite, or perhaps because of, the bad press the budget fight had caused in late 1995 and early 1996. Many Americans weren't fond of seeing national parks padlocked, historic landmarks and museums closed, and social programs on which they or their parents depended hanging in limbo. Of the 1996 increase, $40 million was allotted for another seventy-four Early Head Start programs (see chapter 15). By 1996, salaries had also been increased by more than $3,600 a year for less-experienced teachers above what they had made in 1992 and by $4,700 for more experienced teachers, raises of more than 25 percent in four years.

The advisory committee also stressed improvements for Indian Head Start programs, and in 1994 congressional attention focused on those needs. For example, legislation allowed Indian Head Start programs to serve a higher percentage of children whose family income was above the poverty level so that parents would not be penalized when they found jobs. The employment often paid poorly but sometimes pushed families over the limit allowed.

Quality control received attention from the advisory committee, which urged that "a time-sensitive process for working to correct deficiencies and, if necessary, defunding low-performing programs" be put into place. While the advisory committee's report found that most programs complied with federal regulations, it also said that slightly over 11 percent of grantees monitored that year did not comply with performance standards in 50 or more of the 222 items reviewed. Another 18 percent needed improvement in from 26 to 50 areas. Among the areas that the report found most in need of improvement were parent participation in decision making, follow-up to assure delivery of needed social services, securing treatment of health problems, and providing staff and parent training in child development. Nearly 40 percent of the programs reported difficulty hiring adequate staff.[16]

The Department of Health and Human Services "must make clear that persistently low performance—whether fiscal, management, or programmatic—is grounds for termination of a grantee," the panel said.[17] It also should consider developing a "hard case team" for handling the toughest cases in a timely fashion, which was exactly what was sent to Denver. New performance standards, issued in 1996, also set a timetable for programs with deficiencies to submit quality-improvement plans and, if they did not take action, for termination of their grants.

Which brings us back to today's attempts to work with programs in trouble or close them down when need be. In Denver, the decision to terminate the Child Opportunity Program's Head Start grant brought cheers from beleaguered employees. The federal report had said that the program operated in a "habitual crisis mode," with the staff and teachers working in an atmosphere of "suspicion, . . . anxiety and fear." Olivia Golden, then the commissioner within the Department of Health and Human Services who supervised Head Start, went to Denver to make the termination announcement, saying at a news conference, "I believe this is an extremely serious situation." The federal investigators required that board chairman Brandon and two top accountants resign and that the program repay Head Start for loans made with its money for other purposes. The agency did not make sufficient progress toward meeting the government's conditions, so in early June its grant was terminated. The regional officer who had supervised Head Start was assigned to other duties, as were several of his subordinates. He was replaced by Beverly Turnbo, who had headed the investigative team and who had previously worked as an administrator in Dallas.

In working to find a new agency to run the Denver Head Start program, Turnbo said that the regional office was trying to find out what the community felt its program should look like. Many parents spoke up for full-day, full-year care because half-day programs weren't meeting their needs and would not under changes in the welfare laws. One of the lessons learned from the previous few years under the ousted program was "the need to build trust and respect," she said. "If people are fearful, if they're suspicious, if their needs are not being addressed—for example, the teachers would complain about the poor condition of the playgrounds—then the kids are ultimately affected. These problems distract parents and staff from the real job at hand." If people aren't heard and conflict builds, she said, it will "mushroom and then blow. Eventually, you're going to have an explosion that's going to rock the community."

In Los Angeles County in 1993, one of the middle-sized Head Start providers, Azteca Head Start of Alhambra, lost $2 million in federal funding and its approval to run a program for seven hundred children in East Los Angeles and the San Gabriel Valley. The program had a history of fiscal problems, having been ordered in 1990 to return $76,000 in mismanaged funds, including money used for unauthorized airfares and checks made out to cash. It had also violated federal regulations by refusing to accept children who were physically disabled or not toilet trained.[18]

Financial mismanagement is not the only reason to close Head Start programs. For example, in one toughly worded termination letter sent in 1995 to a local agency in Massachusetts, a regional official cited "a multitude of serious deficiencies," including classrooms that "were unsafe, unclean and lacked adequate teaching materials." Staff were poorly trained, the letter said, "and staff supervision was minimal. Parents received no support or encouragement from line staff. Parents were not viewed as an integral part of their child's education experience."

Parents who feel ignored can also bring about change. In Glendale, California, the Child and Family Services program decided to give up its Head Start classes for some three hundred children in September 1993 after parents urged the federal government to investigate program and financial issues. Parents charged that several children had been allowed to walk away from one of the centers unattended. The mother of one of the children, who had been found unharmed in a nearby park, said that although her son "could have been found dead," the program director told her it was "one of those things that happen. A child lost is not one of those things," the mother declared at a public hearing. At that hearing, a regional Head Start official said that the children's safety had been jeopardized. "We will not allow such breaches of safety that put children at risk." The parents were also upset that budget information was given to the parent policy council in "bits and pieces and without any regard to being able to provide anything other than superficial explanations." The Child and Family Services board admitted no wrongdoing when voting to drop the program, for which it had an annual budget of $1.7 million.[19] After a year under interim management, the government named an agency based in Pasadena to take over.

Some programs apparently don't believe action will be taken against them, Helen Taylor said, mentioning one in Virginia. "They didn't believe we'd do anything. We did it. We defunded them." All kinds of assistance was offered but they didn't take it, she said. They felt that they had been doing what they were doing and they were going to continue doing it. Not anymore.

Head Start officials are far happier talking about programs that have turned themselves around. They pointed to Reno, Nevada, where the Community Services Agency of Washoe County had had years of turmoil, including turnover of six Head Start directors. In March 1995 Head Start gave the agency one year to improve or be terminated. A year later, a review team reported that the program had put in place "a very capable Head Start director," and that classes are "exceptionally well run." Parent involvement was also strong and "community support was high."

In Chelsea, Massachusetts, Community Action Program Inter-City Incorporated, which a staff memo described as "a severely deficient Head Start grantee," faced loss of its federal money in 1993. To retain its grant, that program lengthened its training program, reduced its social services caseload by hiring an additional family advocate, added a nurse, and increased the scheduled work times for the mental health coordinator and nutritionist. The organization upgraded its computer system to improve monitoring of expenses and allow more efficient reporting of program information, and it improved employees' fringe benefits. The program was aided in these steps by a seventy-four-thousand-dollar federal grant.

Finally, Head Start officials tell the story of the Western Indiana Community Services program in Terre Haute. In 1994, a program review found sixty instances of noncompliance with federal regulations. Efforts to get the program to improve were unsuccessful until March 1995, when the government said that it was "seriously deficient" and gave it one year to shape up. "It was at that point the grantee began to take seriously the specter of the possible loss of the grant," a Head Start staff memo said. The regional office staff traveled to the program to help; technical support was also provided. Those efforts sent the messages to the program that Head Start would assist but not direct or mandate how the problems were to be corrected and that the local program had to take the lead in the process—or it would in fact lose its grant.

The Terre Haute program worked not only to make the necessary changes "but also set the goal of being the model program in the state."

It wanted to reverse its negative image, and did so, "as evidenced by the presence of the Mayor and media at an open house for the community, which turned out in great numbers." The follow-up review found that the Terre Haute program had achieved 100 percent compliance, adding that "the community has showered them with congratulations."

Olivia Golden, the Department of Health and Human Services official who went to Denver to announce the findings of the federal investigation into the Head Start program there, said that the Head Start community itself has been raising some of these issues about quality. "They feel that having a few bad programs endangers the rest of them and they feel that the feds act because the issue really is quality. It is based on a professional judgment, not politics or personalities. . . . The reason to have Head Start is that Head Start works. Quality does make a difference in children's lives. But it takes quality to have that impact."

Chapter Twelve

Getting Healthy, Staying Healthy

T he children in Donna Coleman's Head Start class in the Charlestown section of Boston took turns selecting a book they wanted their teacher to read to them. Four-year-old Kevin especially liked *The Lion Who Had Asthma* because he had asthma himself. The boy in Jonathan London's story would pretend that he was a lion roaring in the jungle but sometimes he had to stop because he was coughing and had difficulty breathing. He had asthma. When he started to wheeze, he strapped on a mask attached by a tube to a machine called a nebulizer, which roared like a jet plane. The little boy could pretend he was a jet pilot while the nebulizer and the medicine it sprayed into his lungs helped ease his breathing—then he could roar like a lion again.[1]

Hearing the story helped Kevin realize that other children had asthma, too—that he wasn't "different." Hearing the story helped the other children in the class understand Kevin's condition and not be scared if he or any of their classmates needed to use a nebulizer during the schoolday. Easing children's concerns was one aspect of a pathbreaking asthma education project run by Boston's ABCD Head Start program and Boston Medical Center. Asthma is the largest single cause of preventable hospitalization for children in Massachusetts, and pediatricians had found it especially difficult to reach young children and their parents with information about the condition until they teamed up with Head Start. The project reflects Head Start's holistic approach to child development—health screenings and health education are as critical as instruction in the ABCs or parent involvement.

About twice as many Americans—15 million—suffer from asthma today as did in 1980. Asthma causes 5,000 deaths each year. Nearly one-third of asthma sufferers are children.[2] For children, "asthma is the most common diagnosis in our emergency room," said Dr. Suzanne Steinbach, a pediatric asthma specialist at Boston Medical Center. Her hospital—the public-health hospital that serves many of Boston's poor—sought to educate children and parents about how to manage asthma as well as to treat its attacks, and so put a health educator in its emergency room several years ago. He did fine in reaching school-age children and their parents, but the little ones and their families were too panic-stricken when they reached the emergency room to absorb the message. When they'd leave, they'd go back to their own pediatricians or clinics, and Steinbach wasn't convinced enough education was occurring. So the pediatrics department at Boston Medical Center went where the children were: Head Start.

Head Start was increasingly aware it had a problem. Nationwide, asthma has especially increased among children, and contrary to folk wisdom, it's not something they outgrow. The year the project got under way in Boston, about 9 percent of ABCD's more than two thousand children had asthma. The next year it was 12 percent, then 14 percent overall. One-fourth of the children at one center had asthma. The national average among this age group is 5 to 7 percent. Asthma sufferers have chronically inflamed airways. When they are exposed to allergens—dust or pollen, cockroaches or animal hair, depending on the individual—those airways become even more inflamed. The muscles tighten and constrict the air that can reach the lungs. Asthmatics must then fight for every breath. Not only can asthma be life-threatening if not properly managed, it also keeps children out of school and at risk of falling behind their classmates. ABCD found that its asthmatic children missed school 30 percent more frequently than their nonasthmatic classmates.

So Head Start joined with the hospital pediatricians, directed by Dr. Barry Zuckerman, in obtaining a grant from the Maternal and Child Health Bureau of the U.S. Public Health Service to pay for supplies such as books, educational play equipment, relaxation tapes, and some staff time for the project. The project was also backed by the Healthy Tomorrows Partnership for Children Program of the American Academy of Pediatrics and the Maternal and Child Health Bureau. Jeanne McBride, a nurse who is ABCD's health coordinator, handled the Head Start side of the project.

In planning the program, the Head Start staff assumed its main mission would be to conduct basic education among parents about what triggers asthma attacks and how to manage them. But in talking with the parents, the staff found that their biggest fear was that Head Start teachers wouldn't recognize signs that their child was in difficulty, and so they were often keeping their children at home. That changed the focus. Teachers were indeed being trained to work with children with asthma, but parents needed to know that and be brought into the picture. Each child's asthma triggers are different—although dust, cat and dog hair, mold, mice, roaches, and cigarette smoke are common causes of irritation—and parents wanted to be sure that each teacher knew about each child's symptoms and medication.

"Having the focus groups helped us understand why we were doing what we were doing. The parents seemed to light up when they heard what we were doing in training the staff," Steinbach said. To stress that each case was unique and to provide information to teachers and health managers at each Head Start site, the project staff developed a booklet, "Asthma and Me," for each child. A group of parents whose children had asthma would first hear a presentation from Steinbach about the condition and talk about ways they coped with it. Then the parents and their children would assemble their own booklets. Photographs of the children and their parents were taken for the first page of the booklet. The parents and children put stickers on the next pages that identified who else was in the family, what the child liked to do, and how the child felt when making "a funny sound with a funny name called wheezing." The booklet listed the triggers that made the child "cough, and cough, and cough, and wheeze, and wheeze, and wheeze" and the medicines he or she took to relieve the coughing and wheezing. Finally, the booklet outlined the child's symptoms of difficult breathing and the relaxation exercises the child did to ease that difficulty.

"So if I stay away from my triggers, take my medicine, listen for my symptoms, drink lots of fluids, and relax, there will be fewer times when I cough, and cough, and cough, and wheeze, and wheeze, and wheeze," the booklet concluded. The project staff has also prepared booklets in Spanish and Chinese and was working on one in French.

Terri Sweatman's son Marquis especially liked the booklet "because it had his picture in it." Diagnosed with asthma at fifteen months, Marquis was having his best winter ever despite the condition, in part because his teachers at the St. James Head Start center in Roxbury knew more about what to watch for. That also increased his mother's confidence, and she sent him to school more often. "It's good to know he doesn't have to miss school because he has asthma. Other kids have to."

Head Start also obtained consent from parents and their doctors for teachers to administer asthma medicine if necessary. Some of the teachers were uncomfortable with that part of the project at first, but increasing experience and education eased those concerns.

Before the project, "all of us knew a little about asthma," said Donna Coleman, a twenty-seven-year veteran at the two-story redbrick Head Start center virtually in the shadow of the Tobin Bridge connecting Charlestown and Chelsea. The teachers there had noticed more and more children with difficulty breathing, especially when the bridge was being worked on, but they didn't know whether it was bronchitis or asthma. "We were calling up doctors and doing some research ourselves." With the beginning of the education project, the teachers learned how to keep the children calm when an attack begins. "They may panic because they're not at home or with their relatives."

Five of the children enrolled in Coleman's class had asthma. Even those who didn't sometimes asked Coleman to read the asthma- or allergy-related books. In addition to the story about the lion and the little boy, another favorite was *Furry*, by Holly Keller, about a little girl who desperately wanted a pet but was allergic to cats and dogs. Finally, she got a chameleon that she named Furry and so was happy at last.[3]

"It helps that there are books in Kevin's classroom about asthma," his mother, Kelly Paquette, said. "He knows there are other children like him—he's not the only person with it." Kevin was diagnosed with asthma at eight months and was hospitalized often when he was younger, "but he's doing a lot better now. I know how to deal with it. He can tell me himself" when he's having trouble breathing. "He helps hold his mask. He knows why he has to have it."

Paquette, who has an older daughter who was also in Head Start, had been a dental assistant for seven years but stopped working because she found Kevin's needs "more important for me than that job." For two years, she substituted in Head Start classrooms and then was employed as the center's cook. "It's a good job. I'm here. He's here." Kevin's mother was also pleased because "he can still do things other kids do for the most part."

Parents need to know "that it's their child's right to have good health," said Steinbach. "Asthma does not condemn a child to invalid status. They should be able to play hard, to sleep through the night."

She added that asthma is more prevalent among the poor than the middle class. "It cuts out the underclass from a lot of opportunities, and that's just not right."

I had noticed that several of the children in the Watts Towers Head Start missed school more often than their classmates and learned that they had asthma. This was a problem among children that I had only started hearing about in the last decade. Why, I asked Steinbach, did it seem more prevalent?

No one knows for sure, although there are many theories. Asthma seems to have increased as people have retreated indoors into insulated houses where heat and wall-to-wall carpeting produce more dust. Poor people tend to live in older, deteriorating homes, Steinbach said, "and it's the way they are deteriorating" that causes the problems. The buildings are so old that the windows are painted shut, so there's no ventilation. Often the buildings are damp, and mold develops. Landlords and some tenants don't keep buildings clean, and roaches or mice come prowling. In short, the poor face "a whole slew of badness," Steinbach concluded, and they often don't have the same access to preventive health care that better-off Americans can receive.

Both Steinbach and Jeanne McBride stressed that the asthma education project not only focused on dealing with the immediate health needs of children with asthma but also with helping their parents learn to negotiate the health care system. Their children will still have asthma once they leave Head Start and their public-school teachers may not be able to give them as much attention, so parents must be more insistent in their behalf. Sometimes parents need a little boost in that direction. Sheila Thompson, who adopted her sister's drug-exposed daughter Ashaki, had tried to take the child to an allergy clinic to see if she was doing the right things for the little girl. The nurse practitioner who did the referrals said she'd just have to wait. "She'll outgrow it," she was told.

"I can't wait for you—this is an emergency," Thompson insisted, but her plea did no good. She took her daughter home and kept her there for a week; then the Head Start center's health manager, Carol Schrank, called her. She sent her to Steinbach, who gave the child a breathing test and said she did indeed have asthma.

For her part, Thompson found a benefit in being uprooted when her federally supported housing was renovated. Instead of the carpeting where she had been living, there were wood floors in her new home, and Ashaki's breathing problems diminished. Even though Thompson would bleach everything and scrub and scrub, the radiators collected dust, so Ashaki's asthma frequently flared up and she missed school. One day when she was able to attend, the Head Start teacher was talking about mice. Did any of the children know what mice looked like? "Oh, we have a lot of them," Ashaki said with an expansive gesture. "It was embarrassing but it was cute," Thompson said as she recalled the story.

Head Start not only helped her deal with Ashaki's asthma, Thompson said, it made the little girl healthy in other ways. "From eating with the other children, she'll eat things now that I never could give her." Thompson's hopes centered on reducing the number of visits Ashaki needed to make to the emergency room and increasing her understanding of what happens when she has an asthma attack and what to do about it.

Asthma is, of course, not the only health issue with which Head Start deals, although the status of children's health has in many ways changed dramatically since Head Start began its screenings in 1965. Then, the program routinely identified children who had never seen a doctor or dentist. A sampling of 55,000 children who attended Head Start its first summer found that 70 percent were receiving their first medical or dental examinations. More than 44 percent had cavities. Many were not immunized against measles or smallpox. Shocking statistics about the state of health care of the nation's poor children emerged each year. By 1968, a count showed that of 2 million children who had been in Head Start programs, 180,000 had failed vision tests; 60,000 needed eyeglasses. Forty thousand were either mentally retarded or had learning problems that needed special attention. One million three hundred thousand had dental problems. One hundred eighty thousand were anemic.[4]

That poor children were, and still are, plagued by health problems is no surprise. Often their mothers have had little or no prenatal care. In 1989, for example, one out of four women in the United States received no prenatal care during the first trimester of her pregnancy.[5] Poverty is often linked to drug use and alcohol abuse, and using drugs or drinking during pregnancy harms infants. Children may be born too little to thrive. They may get lead poisoning from paint chips where they live or from breathing the air. Their parents often cannot afford to feed them nutritious meals. They may not have health insurance. A study conducted for the Head Start program during the 1993–94 school year found that serious health conditions were reported for 20 percent of the children in the program: ear problems, speech and language development problems, gastrointestinal conditions, and asthma. No single condition was reported by more than 10 percent of the children.[6]

To identify these health conditions, Head Start conducts its medical and dental screenings as the children enroll as well as checking their vision, hearing, and speech and language development. The screenings identify many children who speak very little or whose speech is unintelligible or those whose language development is not what it should be for their age. There are also problems like asthma or anemia that may not be universal but are significant for those children whom they do affect and for which Head Start can be helpful, said Dr. Mireille Kanda, director of health, disabilities, and Early Head Start for the national program.

By now, there are far fewer children who have never seen a doctor. Many are already enrolled in Medicaid when their parents sign them up for Head Start, Kanda said. There are also more community clinics available for these families. But Kanda, a pediatrician who worked at Children's Hospital in Washington, D.C., before joining Head Start, voiced concern about potential reductions in health care, especially for mental health, as more families are switched into managed care organizations, which may limit services. Children who witness violence, either in their homes or in their communities, often need intensive counseling, but "we are still dealing with a stigma in mental health services," Kanda said. "There's still a lot of educating that needs to be done. Because someone needs these services doesn't mean they're crazy. I think we must do as Head Start is doing and stress the wellness approach to mental health. We need to keep pushing prevention."

Beyond children's specific health problems, Kanda said that Head Start is focusing on families' access to care and ensuring that they have a "medical home" so there will be continuity in their care after the children leave the program. Local Head Start programs are working hard, she said, to forge relationships with health care providers in their communities to make sure families can find and continue to receive health care, no matter their income level.

Many of Head Start's boosters have said that if the program did nothing else but uncover health problems through its screenings and ensure follow-up treatment, it would have earned its keep. But a disturbing report by the Office of Inspector General of the Department of Health and Human Services in 1993 found that Head Start programs were not completing the minimum health requirements as they said they were. For example, the inspector general's staff checked the records of 3,100 children at eighty different Head Start programs and found that there were complete immunizations for 43 percent of the children, not the 88 percent that Head Start said were fully immunized. The report indicated that one key factor in the discrepancy between what the inspector general's staff found and what Head Start was reporting was the difficulty programs had in hiring staff to keep up with the rapid expansion that Head Start had just undergone.[7]

Kanda, who was not health director when the survey was made, explained that some of the problems stemmed from conflicting definitions of what it meant for children to be fully immunized. What Head Start is trying to assure, she said, is that each child has a regular health care provider so that all the required shots and other tests are done in a timely fashion—and that that care will continue as the child moves through school.

Research on Head Start has tended to focus on children's educational gains, so studies of the program's impact on health are uneven. More research is especially needed on Head Start's effectiveness in making sure that children receive their immunizations and on its mental health services. An analysis published in 1994 in the *Annual Review of Public Health* concluded that "children in Head Start receive more and better preventive health services and treatment than low-income children not in Head Start. Nutrition, medical and dental screenings, and the integration of children with disabilities are especially strong components of the program." Head Start, said the article by Edward Zigler, C. S. Piotrkowski of the National Council of Jewish Women's Center for the Child, and consultant Ray Collins, "not only provides some services directly, but it also helps link children and families to a community network of health services and to a 'medical home' that may lead to ongoing participation in preventive and remedial health activities."[8]

Perhaps the most visible symbol of Head Start's health effort, aside from mobile units that visited many centers to provide the required screenings and some of the immunizations, was the toothbrush. At Fort Belknap, Montana, in Crum, West Virginia, and in the Watts Towers center, I saw the children brush their teeth every morning. Some centers, like several I visited in Minneapolis, even had their own dental clinic.

Education usually accompanied the health care, whether one was talking about asthma or tooth decay. In Boston, Sara Monajem, a clinical instructor at the Forsyth School for Dental Hygienists, was visiting a Head Start program in Dorchester the same day I did. She was accompanied by some of her students, who later would talk to the rest of the center's classes. Monajem, who formerly was director of community health services for the Children's Aid Society in New York City, said that Head Start sees few children today who have never been to the dentist. The big dental problem that Head Start sees now is a result of nursing-bottle syndrome. The sugar in milk rots children's teeth because they may have a bottle in their mouths overnight.

In the class she visited, Monajem told a story about a tooth that didn't feel good and so went to the dentist. She had cutouts of a male and female dentist that she held up for the children. "I pick one and because I'm a woman, the woman usually wins." The tooth sits in a magic chair in the middle of the dentist's office, she told the children. There's a button that makes the chair go up and down. Monajem, preparing the children for what it would be like to go to the dentist, held a mirror over their mouths to see if she could quickly spot any cavities. "I found two today," she said. In her story, the dentist gave the tooth a toothbrush and the tooth was happy once again.

Maria goes to the zoo. The children have a fire drill. TRF conducts its annual review. Yaneth speaks more English. And Wayne almost cleans his plate.

Maria hadn't wanted to go to the zoo when the day came in March for the Watts Towers center trip. "Miz Osuna, you'll have to hold my hand," she said, fearing the unknown. Once she reached the zoo, she forgot her wariness. "I didn't cry," she announced to me in both Spanish and English the next morning. Shardae rushed up to tell me that she had seen a giraffe drinking milk from its mama. Clintishabeth said she saw an elephant with a long trunk. "And she didn't even go," teacher Lupe Osuna told me with a wink. But at least she knew about elephants.

"Where did we go?" Osuna asked the children. "To the zoo. We went up and down the hill. How many waterfalls did you see?"

"A lot of them," answered Ciara.

"How were the giraffes? Did they have a small neck, or a big neck? Were the elephants skinny or fat?" Andre made a wide gesture with his hands.

"There were all kinds of snakes," Osuna added.

"There were pythons this wide," said aide Deborah Chatman, demonstrating as though she were holding a basketball. "They were a foot wide and still growing."

"What's missing here?" said Osuna, pointing to the drawing on the bulletin board behind her. It said: "Welcome to the zoo" and showed the walkways passing by the animals' cages. "When you walk in here? Flamingos! What color are flamingos?"

"Pink. And the water was falling on them," one child answered.

"What was the animal in the water?"

"An alligator."

"What is this animal?" Osuna asked, going, "Oomph, oomph, oomph" and strutting around the carpet. The children clapped and laughed because it was a good imitation of a gorilla.

"Who was asleep and wouldn't wake up?"

Joshua guessed a lion. No, that wasn't it.

Osuna hopped a few hops, patted her stomach, and asked, "What carries its baby right here?"

"A kangaroo!"

Andre stood up and imitated a gorilla.

At that moment, a bell clanged. Fire drill! The children filed outside and stood next to the chain-link fence. "What do we do?" teacher Josephine Garner asked them. "Do we stay inside? If the school is on fire, we get outside." The teachers called roll.

"My coat would burn," Anthony said.

"Your coat can burn. For you to come back and get your coat, you would burn up," Garner told the child.

Once the children went back inside, Garner turned off the lights and started shaking the tables. Earthquake drill! The children scrambled under the tables, except for Raymound. "Raymound, you're dead," Garner called out to him. "Get down."

Periodically, the Head Start teachers also urged parents to conduct similar drills at home. They wanted children to know the safest exit route and to learn to stand under a doorway during an earthquake if they could. Safety was a subtle but constant concern at each Head Start program I visited. Garner always made sure there was an aisle cleared so people could leave the building quickly if they needed to, and all the teachers attended safety workshops and learned cardiopulmonary resuscitation.

That morning Faye Bell, site director at the Training and Research Foundation's center at Fairview Heights, and Yolanda Schaeffer, a parent from another site in Inglewood, were visiting to review the Watts Tower operations as part of TRF's annual look at its own program. It conducted these reviews to stay primed for the official reviews every three years. The committees checked whether permits were properly displayed and children's folders were complete, plus how staff and children related to one another.

Committee members met with the TRF education supervisors to report their findings. Yolanda Schaeffer said she felt so comfortable talking with Josephine Garner, "I felt like we had church." Michael Odom, a parent volunteer from Imperial Courts who had visited Fairview Heights, liked the idea that the teachers had two helpers each day to do tasks like setting the table. "It got the kids involved." If the committee reported anything questionable, the supervisors took up the matter with the staff. That year, for example, the administrators found that the teachers and other staff needed to refresh themselves about the basic performance standards Head Start's national office expected them to meet. They know what they are but they get used to them; they forget why they do what they do. "We need to go back to basics," said Elaine Atlow, TRF's Head Start director.

Amid the visit of the review committee and the safety drills and Mr. Joe's lunch delivery, the children's routine continued. Chatman was reading the story "Turnips for Dinner" to one small group of children as lunch was being served.

The zebra said, "I don't like turnips."

"He eats grass," Raymound said.

Chatman pointed to a wolf. "*Un perro*," Karina said.

"That's right, Karina, it looks like a dog. Here's a red coyote. Do you think he likes turnips, Donisha?" She shook her head no. "The elephant says he'll eat the turnips. They taste like grass. He ate up all the turnips."

"And he got sick," Ciara volunteered.

Across the room, Garner led a small group singing one of the children's favorite songs about five little monkeys sitting in a tree, teasing Mr. Crocodile. "You can't catch me, you can't catch me. Along came Mr. Crocodile as quiet as he can be, and he snapped that monkey right out of that tree." The kids especially loved making the vigorous snapping motions of Mr. Crocodile's jaws as five monkeys became four, then three, and so on.

"You have to remember not to tease the animals. They'll eat you. Do you tease the dog?"

"No, he'll bite you," one child answered as Shardae jumped up and emphatically declared, "You do not tease the animals!"

Everything becomes a lesson in Head Start. Taking trips to the zoo. Having fire drills. Talking about neighborhood helpers such as doctors, police officers, and firefighters. Eating fruits and vegetables. Enjoying holidays. Learning safety. Checking the weather. Observing Black History Month. And always the alphabet, numbers, and shapes. If the children from the Watts Towers Head Start center had gone home and announced that they played all day, their teachers would have accomplished their goal—to make learning fun.

Sometimes my travels became a small part of the lesson. Once when I returned from a trip to the East Coast, I told the children at the Watts Towers center in sunny Southern California that I had been in the snow. My focus was on the blizzard that had kept me from business appointments in New York. Their concern? "Did you make a snowman?"

"Miss Kay went on a plane back from Washington," Garner told the children one April morning when transportation was the topic. "She also took a taxi. She had to use her feet. She used a car, too. But today we're going to talk about a boat. Stand back, Clintishabeth," the teacher said as the little girl crowded up next to a dishpan containing water about four inches deep that Garner had set up for floating several plastic boats. "You'll drown." Someone laughed. "Don't laugh," Garner admonished. "I know a baby who drowned in less water than this."

The children gathered around. "Can a boat travel on the street?" Garner asked. "No. Can it travel on tracks? No."

"Only in the water," one of the children said.

"Can it travel in the air?"

"Only an airplane can do that," Ciara said.

Garner talked about a plane that could land on water. "But a boat can't fly. You can go to the train station to see trains. You've been on a bus. So you're going to see pictures of different kinds of ships. You can go to Long Beach and ride on this ship called the *Queen Mary* for just a little money. You can have a birthday party and look at all the nice things." Clintishabeth allowed that she'd been to Long Beach.

The children sat down in pairs, feet to feet, pretending that they were row, row, rowing their boats gently down the stream. Josefina and Andre were paired, Ciara and Edwin, Maria and Shardae, and Garner with Michael. "Where do you want to go?" Garner asked the rowing children. "Mexico," said Ciara. "Mexico, too," said Maria. "El Salvador," said Edwin. Andre couldn't make up his mind but got up and pointed to an ocean liner on a poster.

"What letter does boat start with? B is for boat." The alphabet remained a principal focus because Garner wanted the children not just to be able to recite their letters but to recognize them out of sequence. Marcus, for example, could sing the alphabet song but didn't recognize the letter C standing alone. "You have to pay attention," Garner interjected. "You can sing 'em but you don't know them."

Wayne couldn't recognize some of the letters, either. "When you get to kindergarten," Garner warned, "they're going to send you back to baby school."

Turning to another child, Garner said, "Andre, you did a very good job. I'm proud of you."

"I know my alphabet," Ciara reminded Garner.

"I know you do. That's why I'm not going to call you up."

So here's the problem: What do you do to keep Ciara interested while Wayne and Marcus catch up? What happens in fourth or fifth grade when this bright child gets bored? Will there be a teacher along the way who pushes her to excel, or will she just feel she's been there, done that?

At midmorning each day, the children surged out onto the small play yard outside their center. This particular morning they had an over-abundance of energy and chased each other around the yard on foot and on tricycles. "It's all that Easter candy," Lupe Osuna told me. Watching them was a study in group dynamics. One moment Andre would be playing with Raven in the sandbox, the next he'd be leading a cavalcade of tricycle riders around the sidewalk. Donisha, often shy, played happily with Clintishabeth and Ciara. "Push me, Miss Kay, push me," Shardae or Maria would call to me from the swings. Push one, you push all.

Shardae and Maria held my hands on the way back into the building. Waiting inside, Kimberly touched Maria's cheek lightly and Maria drew back. "My mother says you're not supposed to do that," she said quietly. To distract them, I pointed to my Hawaiian-style shirt and asked them what colors I had on. They identified "pink" and "blue" and "white." Thereafter, Maria would call out to me when I arrived, "Miss Kay, I have on pink today," as she pointed to her little warm-up suit, or "Miss Kay, I have on blue today." The exchange would barely have been noticed by an outsider, but Maria, like the other children, was starting to be more outgoing.

Andre was still having his good days and his bad days, sometimes the same day. He'd crawl under the lunch tables while the rest of the children were resting before lunch. Some days Garner would separate him from the rest of the children several times; other days he blended happily into the group.

By April, more and more children were speaking audibly; the Hispanic children also spoke more English. While the children were eating roast beef, carrots, bread and butter, rice, milk, and pineapple one day, Yaneth, who usually chattered nonstop in Spanish with several other little girls, proudly told me in English that she'd eaten all her carrots, then all her rice, then her fruit. She told me her parents didn't speak English and she was urging her father to try it. Just then, Wayne called out for me to look at how much he'd eaten. The children seemed to finish more of the food than they had in the fall, but some were still picky or slow eaters.

There were still some children whose words I couldn't always make out. After lunch, Maria walked over to me with a small piece of clay in her hand. She wanted me to do something with it that I couldn't understand. It sounded like "rumble." Rumble? Rumble?

She was becoming frustrated at how slow I was. "Show me," I suggested.

She took the clay and rolled it in her hands. Oh, rumble, ruhm-ball, round ball. So we sat conspiratorially making rumbles together, two friends with complete understanding at last.

Chapter Thirteen

Keeping It Together

ead Start and elementary school can mesh like well-oiled gears—or children and parents can find themselves abruptly jolted into a world that is not as welcoming, comprehensive, and caring as the best Head Start programs. Kindergarten teachers generally have larger classes and less time for each child. Will a Maria continue to receive the attention a more assertive child might demand and on which she was thriving? Will the elementary-school teachers continue to work with a Raymound or an Andre to bring them along, or will the progress they made in Head Start lapse? Some teachers see parents in the classroom as distractions, not helpers. Will they encourage the mothers of a Janette or a Joshua to participate? And how many public school systems will help families maintain the connections with social services they need, whether that is counseling about domestic violence or children's health, classes to build the self-reliance many poor parents lack, job training, whatever?

To keep the comprehensive Head Start approach alive in the early years of elementary school, the program's transition project was created. Included by Congress in Head Start's 1990 reauthorization under the sponsorship of Massachusetts senator Edward M. Kennedy, this project examined how Head Start and selected elementary schools could keep children interested in learning and parents involved with their progress. Congress clearly had in mind the "fade-out effect" when it set up the transition effort. So did Head Start when it requested project proposals to test the hypothesis that providing "continuous and comprehensive services, developmentally appropriate curriculum, and parent involvement" would "sustain the gains" of Head Start after children left the program. As one local transition project report put it, "This so called 'fade-out effect' has been attributed to a lack of continuity in philosophy, methods, services and environment between Head Start and the public schools."[1] In many respects, the transition project was a school reform effort under an alias. Public schools rather than Head Start should be addressing the question of sustaining preschool gains, but Head Start nonetheless took the initiative.

At the outset, there were thirty-two projects accompanied by a massive nationwide research study as well as local evaluations. The national study posed two questions: What really affects children's successful development in the early years of schooling, and would these transition efforts help? Would prolonging the intensive attention families normally receive for only the year their children are in Head Start cement the health, educational, and social gains the children made that year?

The local sites enrolled some 8,400 former Head Start children and families at 450 schools in 85 school districts. "What is strikingly apparent is that there is no 'typical' Head Start family," according to the interim report on the transition project from the Civitan International Research Center at the University of Alabama in Birmingham. It found that about 40 percent of the former Head Start families had both parents present in the home and not on welfare, while another 40 percent received Aid to Families with Dependent Children. About 20 percent of the families lived in public housing. More than 15 percent of the primary caregivers were born outside the United States; just over 10 percent spoke a language other than English at home. And "the most serious [health] problem reported by primary caregivers (about 50 percent) is that of depression."[2]

That research is not yet complete. But the practical experience is. The part of the project directly involving children and their families concluded in the spring of 1997. The Head Start transition projects found that it was sometimes tough to alter the public school culture; it took hours and hours of meetings and training to bring even receptive school systems to understand and accommodate Head Start's way of operating and to help Head Start programs learn how to work best with the schools. The attitude of the school principals was critical to this project, yet the principals had so many demands on their time that they were not always available when needed. Learning whom a principal most relied on to speak and act in his or her place and gaining that person's ear could be a long but vital process; it was one of the lessons the research projects passed on for future Head Start transition efforts.

To compare approaches and problems, I traveled to three transition projects: in rural Crum, West Virginia; urban San Jose, California; and suburban Montgomery County, Maryland. And I went with the children of Watts Towers Head Start on their kindergarten visit. I saw the benefits of concentrating on this transition process and the problems in making and maintaining any real changes, as well as the drawbacks of having comparatively few meaningful transition activities and the reasons why that happens.

I went to West Virginia not only because it had a transition project, but also because I wanted to see what Head Start was like in Appalachia, the region that had stirred so much national concern about "the other America" in the 1960s. In West Virginia, presidential candidate John F. Kennedy had been, in the words of aide Theodore C. Sorensen, "appalled by the pitiful conditions he saw, by the children of poverty, by the families living on surplus lard and corn meal, by the waste of human resources." West Virginia made him understand, "as the distressed areas of Massachusetts had never made him understand," the problems of the unemployed, those on pensions, and those on relief.[3] Seeking to lay to rest the issue of his Catholic religion in the 1960 primaries, Kennedy had campaigned in the cities and in the "hollers," saying, "I am the only presidential candidate since 1924, when a West Virginian ran for the presidency, who knows where Slab Fork is and has been there."

Thirty-six years, almost to the day, after that pivotal May 1960 primary, I drove not to Slab Fork but to Crum, another coal-country community that Kennedy could just as easily have cited in his campaign speeches. Towns like Crum and Kermit and others on the way south on U.S. 52 from Huntington in the westernmost part of West Virginia share the bottomland with the railroad tracks, the two-lane highway, and the Big Sandy or Tug Fork Rivers. There's not room for much else—maybe a school or a filling station, sometimes a few stores and a bar or pizza place—in these narrow valleys, literally wide places around the road. Settlements are scattered along off the highway—a family cluster of two or three small houses or trailers on one hillside, a few more around another bend. More houses and trailers are tucked away in the hollows down dirt roads off the highway. Nearly two-thirds of West Virginia is rural, and the area on the way to Crum is not heavily populated; women and children may be especially isolated if the father takes the family's only car to get to work. Those people able to make their living in this area do so either in the mines, driving trucks from the mines, teaching the miners' children, pumping their gas, or slaking their thirst. Many do not make a living here. Wayne County, in which Crum is located, has around 10 percent unemployment.

As I came over the hill into Crum, it was raining, adding to the grimness of the gray stone elementary school and its bare blacktop playground sitting hard by the railroad tracks. The school looked like a prison; it could make you weep. Unlike the gray weather outside, though, inside the Head Start center a block away all was cheerful—the place was alive with the sounds of children playing before they sat down to breakfast.

Ada Johnson, one of the staff members, was sitting on the floor reading a story to four of the younger children in one of the two classrooms. Like many a Head Start room, this one had a housekeeping area with a small table displaying plastic fruit and vegetables, an area for working with blocks, a dress-up area where a firefighter's hat and a sombrero were hanging, and hooks over a sink in the corner that held toothbrushes with the children's names on them. Decorating the walls were outlines of the children's bodies that they had painted earlier in the month while they were learning the words for their arms and legs, knees and elbows. The children had taken a field trip to the Huntington airport the previous week, no small occasion when many rarely have transportation to go very far from Crum. "We went to the fire truck and it squirted water," one of the little girls said. Another reminded her teacher she hadn't wanted to get on the truck; it was too big and it scared her.

This center's graduates attend the elementary school just a few minutes' walk away, where students in the lower grades are part of the national transition pilot study. The Crum Head Start center and the transition project were run by the Southwestern Community Action Council, a nonprofit agency operating Head Start (613 children in 1996) and parent-child centers for younger children (100 in 1996) in four of West Virginia's most westerly counties: Cabell, Lincoln, Mason, and Wayne. West Virginia's population is 96 percent white, a figure reflected in the region's 92 percent white Head Start population. The Southwestern Community Action Council's headquarters are in Huntington on the Ohio River where Kentucky, Ohio, and West Virginia meet.

Out of twenty-four children enrolled for the half-day, four-day-a-week Head Start program in Crum, only thirteen attended the day of my visit. Poor attendance was a problem, sometimes caused by bad weather (the Crum center would be closed the next day because of flooding), sometimes by the distances the children must come by bus, and sometimes by indifference on the parents' part. In addition to Head Start for three- and four-year-olds, Crum also had a parent and child center for younger children, in which twenty-eight infants and toddlers were enrolled. These children came to the center one day a week; several times each month staff members visited their homes to help parents learn more about caring for their babies and about stimulating them mentally and physically.

Diane Ray, a parent volunteer, had been hooked on Head Start by the parent and child center. A slender woman wearing glasses, Ray said she had heard about the center through her sister-in-law when her oldest child, a boy, was little. "If I don't like it, I can always drop out," she thought to herself then. "I've been here six years," she added with a gentle laugh. She had two daughters, Stacy, four, and Rosalie, three, in the program when I visited. "Stacy used to be really shy," said Ray, a quiet woman herself. "When they would play, she would go by herself. She doesn't do that anymore." Her son adjusted well to kindergarten, too, said Ray, whose husband was a coal miner. "He said it was harder but he was learning a lot." He was in first grade, and part of the transition project, when I was in Crum.

When you visit a Head Start center, you look for its sense of purpose, a sense that there is a reason for what the children are doing. It can be deceptive—children may look as though they're "just playing"—but in the good centers they're learning virtually every step of the way. Take painting, for example. That morning Heather, R. J., Luster, and the rest learned about red and blue and green as they created rainbows or sunny skies—whatever they hoped to see after the storms ended. Whenever there were disputes over a chair or a box of paints, they also learned about sharing. "Who had his hand on it first?" the teacher asked when two boys were trying to place their bottoms in one chair. "Okay, Chris had it first. Luster, you can come over here." Then Heather complained that the child next to her was using her paint. "They've got their own," she whined. So there was a little more instruction that the boy needed to share Heather's paint because he was too small to reach across the table.

Like so many Head Start staff members, those at Crum started as volunteers when their children were enrolled, then were hired to work full-time. Sandy Justice, a hearty redhead originally from neighboring Kentucky who explained that she "married across the river," had been associated with the program for seven or eight years. Through Head Start, she learned ways to help her two sons at home. "I was young and didn't pay attention" at first. "I learned what they could do. I guess I was lazy at first till I learned."

Children don't always move smoothly into elementary school from a small, personalized program like this Head Start, where their parents were welcome—indeed, encouraged with open arms—to help out in the classroom, on the playground, and on field trips. The transition grant enabled the Southwestern Community Action Council program to hire six social workers (called family service parent specialists) at the five schools (including Crum) involved in its pilot project as well as a registered nurse to help train parents and check the children's health. The program also paid several parents part-time wages to keep open a room at each of the schools where parents could meet and help prepare materials for some of the children's teachers to use. Everyone worked toward the common goal of keeping Head Start parents involved with their children's education when they moved into kindergarten and beyond, as well as getting those parents whose children hadn't been in Head Start to work more with their children.

Paula Thompson, the parent assistant at Crum Elementary, had been a volunteer at the Head Start center near Fort Gay, a small town off the highway between Huntington and Crum, when her twin daughters were enrolled. The family became eligible for Head Start after Thompson's husband got hurt on his railroad job. Because the family had no close neighbors with children her daughters' age, "there's a lot of twindom at my house," Thompson said. Head Start helped create some independence in the girls, who were in third grade at the time of my visit.

In her job at Crum, Thompson worked at involving the parents in craftwork—sewing, for example—and gradually they would talk about their concerns. What is popular with the parents, she added, is the ball teams. Moms and dads and grandparents turn out to see the children play. "They feel comfortable with athletics but they are still trying to be comfortable with academics." Thompson kept the parent resources room on the second floor of the Crum Elementary School building open for the parents to socialize and to prepare teachers' bulletin board materials, grade papers, or otherwise help out. She and the other parent assistants may have been better able to find points of contact with hard-to-reach parents than the professionals. Her presence at the resource room also freed David Colley, the full-time family service parent specialist, to make home visits and do other liaison work between the school and the parents.

One of his big tasks, Colley said, was finding parents to come and pick up their children if they got sick or had head lice and could not stay in school. "Many of the families don't have phones, so I have to go out and get them to come in for the child." People in this mountain area stay to themselves and have always been suspicious of strangers; the men often jealously watch their wives, so Colley found that some of the women's husbands wouldn't allow them to get into a car with him (or any other men for that matter), an added complication.

The transition project was breaking down some parents' wariness about the schools. Ernestine Smith, whose husband drove a coal truck, always had dropped her children off at school but never went inside. "Before, I didn't think parents were welcome." But lately she had been at the school almost every day, either in the parent resource center preparing worksheets or helping a first-grade teacher who always found something for parents to do, "even if you only have fifteen minutes," Smith said. "Then if you get involved, you know what to do at home to help your children."

Parents became involved big-time through the transition project at Fort Gay Elementary, another of the schools working with the Southwestern Community Action Council's Head Start. At a picnic at the school in 1993, a group of parents asked that site's family services specialist, Joann Spence, a retired teacher and administrator, for help building a playground. "They didn't know exactly what they wanted but they wanted something better for their kids." The playground equipment was old, broken, and unsafe. There was no color on the playground, no trees, no grass, "no nothin'." Ten or fifteen years had probably elapsed since anyone had done any work on the area.

One mother who was involved, Elaine Stilner, remembered how many times her son came home from school with torn pants and skinned knees because of the playground's condition. "I don't know how many pairs of pants Brandon ruined on the playground but it was too many," Stilner told a local reporter. "I just thought kids should have a safer place to play at school."[4]

Joann Spence knew the philosophy of organizing parents around what *they* wanted to do, so she told them to get ten signatures from people who would form a committee for the playground. They did. First, they cleaned up the playground, filling a box with bits of broken glass they picked up the night before the children were to return to school. The committee researched safety regulations and handicapped-access rules. Committee members brought in others from the community, and they wrote letters to Congress, political leaders, and agency heads to find financial help or professional guidance. An organization that works on conservation and recreation adopted their project.

Spence told the parents that they needed to earn enough money themselves to prove to potential allies and donors that they were serious. They held spaghetti dinners and solicited contributions, raising five thousand dollars the first year. The board of education said that whatever the parents earned by a certain date, it would match. "So we earned eighteen thousand dollars and they weren't prepared for that. They gave ten thousand dollars." On June 1, 1995, the parents broke ground for the new playground. They put in a drainage system and foundation on the acre and a half of land. Today there are basketball backboards, swings, a gaily colored slide, and a climbing apparatus down the hill from the school.

In addition to improving the playground, another goal was to train parents to deal with agencies so that when the transition project left, they could do for themselves, Spence said. "These people have been talked at, preached at, told how to live their lives for so many years that they just turn you off."

Despite its successes, the West Virginia transition project, like each of the others, was not without its problems. Head Start wants children to learn what is appropriate for their stage of ability—taught through what educators call "developmentally appropriate curriculum." The transition staff was surprised at how much time it took to sell the notion that how children learn is at least as important as what they learn. Despite the transition project's best efforts, it still faced the reality that because children moved through the grades without learning how to read and write well, the school system was under increasing pressure to stress test scores. Teachers taught for the tests, not for what children were ready to learn. As I walked through Crum Elementary one day with Lynn Bolen, the transition director, some of the teachers told us how one of the grades had dramatically raised its test scores. That was a big deal. When teachers try to adapt to a Head Start–style curriculum while administrators place emphasis on testing, "some teachers feel betrayed," a transition project report said.

Nationwide, implementing this requirement for developmentally appropriate educational curricula was "perhaps the single greatest challenge for many sites," according to Civitan's interim research report. This emphasis "often represented a major change in classroom practice, and not all teachers and administrators [had] previous training in the philosophy and practice."[5]

At about the midpoint of West Virginia's transition project, the Republican-controlled Congress threatened cuts in the Head Start budget, sending Head Start and transition directors scurrying for public support and into drawing up contingency plans. Funds were slow in coming through because of fights over the federal budget, and the delays took the director's time and energy away from other tasks. Because the transition project would last only a limited time, it also had understandable difficulty retaining staff, especially nurses, who sought more permanent, better-paying positions. There was also a shuffling of teaching positions at the beginning of each school year, so the transition project constantly had to acquaint new teachers with its curriculum and its desire to get parents involved.

If the project was expected to achieve higher test scores for the children, "this has not yet become a reality and we know all the reasons why," a transition report said. Tests don't measure what Head Start does and cannot pick up the social aspects of the program. Many of the children served by the transition project in West Virginia lived in isolated areas, perhaps having regular contact only with family and a few neighbors. To enter Head Start and successfully become part of a group of children was a big difference in their lives—but not one that's easily measurable.

"We do not, however, consider higher test scores an indication of our success," the transition report added. "As teachers have become more aware of the importance of everything they do, children are becoming more interested and involved in school activities and for the most part, they love school and their teachers." The families that seemed to have benefited most, not surprisingly, were those that were easily motivated. "We hope that the active parents will lead us to the next layer of families, who may be less ready and so on down the line until we get to those who are hardest to reach, of which we have many," the transition staff reported.

And what change did the transition project make in any of the schools? "The involvement of parents may be one systematic change which has the best hope of success as parents begin to see themselves as actively involved in their children's educations and as educators see the value of involving parents," the West Virginia transition report concluded. "Principals especially have become aware of the importance of parent involvement and they have been delighted at parental responses to a satisfaction rating form which asks how they feel about their children's school."

Nationally, many principals and teachers changed their attitude about the merits of involving parents through the transition project. "This is the piece that will hang around because teachers now value it," said Michele A. Plutro, national Head Start staff member who served as the program's project officer for its duration. "They know that with parents in the classroom they have extra eyes, extra hands, extra feet. The principals value it, too."

Another element of the West Virginia transition project that was most successful, and therefore most likely to be retained wherever possible, was placing a social worker in the school. "Nurses could get the health problems taken care of," transition director Bolen said, but when families needed social services, they often didn't know where to turn. If there had been no social worker in the school, the teacher would have had to try to find out what was wrong and what was needed; often she really didn't have time to do that adequately. The social worker could guide the families in finding help and aid in working through the problems. "That's the strength of this whole thing—the importance of the social worker in the school," Bolen said.

Civitan's interim report buttressed what both Bolen and Plutro discovered. "The highly qualified family service coordinators are viewed by most sites as being 'at the heart' of the project," it said. "Many sites attribute their successes to the quality, dedication, cultural sensitivity, and creativity of these family support workers. The ability to maintain continuity in the family support staff may be a key factor in maintaining close and effective relationships with both families and teachers."[6]

The national transition project began with thirty-two local programs. One, in San Jose, California, was dropped from the nationwide study because of questions about its research component, not because of its effectiveness. That did not diminish its findings about the process of linking Head Start with elementary schools, especially the value of hiring family advocates. Across the board, Michele Plutro told me, family advocates were consistently used in the transition projects, and they were the element that principals did not want to lose. "They can't be everywhere at once," she said, and the advocates expanded their capacity to deal with families' situations.

One vignette from my visit to the San Jose transition program illustrated why family advocates were the soul of this project. The scene: a classroom in which drawings of houses, obviously kindergartners' work, adorned the walls. A handsome Cambodian man, Tin Hout, sat in one of the pint-sized chairs in which parents inevitably find themselves when they confer with their child's teacher. His five-year-old daughter, Marina, stood shyly but attentively beside him as Santee School teacher Margie Oyama gave them the child's progress report, a good one. Marina, who had attended Head Start the previous year, could count almost to thirty, knew her colors, recognized shapes. If she had a roomful of Marinas, Oyama told me later, teaching would be a dream.

There was one more person in what otherwise would have been a typical parent-conference picture. Nisseth Sath, a refugee from Cambodia like many of the families he was helping, translated Oyama's report into the Khmer language that Marina's father spoke. It was logical for Sath to attend because he's the one who telephoned many of the parents to schedule these conferences, then called to remind them. He also helped families negotiate government bureaucracies and sometimes even transported them to doctor appointments.

The San Jose project, administered by the Santa Clara County Office of Education, focused on Santee and McKinley Elementary Schools and their three feeder Head Start programs in the east central area of the city. The schools operated year-round, and the first group of Head Start "alumni" moved into kindergarten during the summer of 1992. By the time of my visit, 360 students were involved. The original group was in second grade, and other Head Start children had moved into kindergarten and first grade. Not all of them had attended Head Start; the law specified that all children in a transition-project classroom with former Head Start students receive the same services.

Don Bolce, the project director, and I spoke about the project over lattes at a downtown coffee shop the first afternoon I was in San Jose. A lanky forty-seven-year-old who first served with Head Start as a janitor while he was in college, Bolce went to work for the program in 1973 after he earned his early childhood education credential. Later he headed programs in Mendocino and Alameda Counties, and most recently had been the director of governmental affairs at the National Head Start Association, the group that represents parents and Head Start staff in Washington. He was still doing what he could nationally to prevent conservatives from taking aim at Head Start and was busy as president of the California Head Start Association.

I asked Bolce how much had been spent on his pilot project during its four-year life. His estimate: $2 million on screening the children for medical and dental problems, giving teachers curriculum training, providing classroom supplies, allowing the schools to have full-time nurses, and paying the family advocates.

The San Jose project tackled one of the toughest areas of the city in terms of people's poverty and inability to speak English. Yet anecdotal evidence suggested that it helped many Cambodian, Vietnamese, and Latino families become better adjusted to American life and helped their children know better what to expect in public school. Education officials were optimistic that these children were also more likely to stay in school. This, despite the fact that the children moved frequently; their parents were unemployed or poorly paid because they spoke little English. Some were not literate even in their native languages. Many of the adults had fled war and refugee camps in Southeast Asia or economic hardships in Mexico. The Cambodians, for example, spoke of Thai bandits in the same manner that you or I might mention a grocery clerk, violence was such an ordinary aspect of their life. Nisseth Sath, who was about ten years old when war broke out in Cambodia, told me that he and his brother routinely saw soldiers carrying dead bodies. Shelling, whether from the Khmer Rouge or the Thais, was commonplace.

The idea behind the San Jose project and those elsewhere around the country was to hire family advocates to work with families not only in Head Start but in the early grades of elementary school—and to give them lower caseloads than they might ordinarily have had in Head Start. They helped involve parents in the children's schooling. Meantime, teachers received extra training in a special curriculum to help reinforce children's Head Start experiences.

But the best-intentioned plans face strains in going from policy papers to the messy world of reality. Federal money came in irregular cycles because Congress did not always complete its appropriations measures in timely fashion. Supplies that teachers ordered in the fall still weren't there by midwinter. A trailer intended as a transition-project office and parent center didn't arrive on schedule. One school changed principals. The county also tried to move the family advocates from the McKinley School into the central Head Start office until the principal put his foot down. Some children planning to go to one of the participating schools found they couldn't because it was overcrowded. Some of the communication and early enthusiasm bogged down as the program was drawing to a close. "The program went gangbusters the first year," said one teacher, but afterward she never saw some of the key staff. And the director was not always accessible because of his other activities.

Ken Van Otten, a hearty gray-haired man who was principal at McKinley Elementary, told me much that he thought was wrong with the transition project, but he remained high on it. "Transition was so effective initially that coupled with its potential, I wanted it to go, go, go." In fact, he thought the services the project provided should last until fifth grade rather than stopping with second grade. "This is a program of great promise, that has far more right than wrong with it. It is richly human as opposed to something written down in a proposal or guidelines."

Van Otten was the kind of principal who was willing to take time to go into detail about the makeup of his student body and the pluses and minuses of the program. He told me that his school, which included preschool through fifth grade and ran year-round, usually had between 720 and 730 students. He couldn't say any more definitely than that because there was such turnover. A parent would get a job and off the family went. Or a parent lost a job or a couple split up and off the children went to live with relatives somewhere else. The student population was 72 percent Hispanic, mostly from Mexico—largely Catholic, rural, Indian. Eighteen to 20 percent were Asian, most of those Cambodians who spoke Khmer. "The Cambodians were virtually all directly affected by the killing fields," he said. Students enrolled at McKinley spoke ten different languages: Spanish, Khmer, Vietnamese, English, Thai, Pilipino, two dialects of Chinese, Hindi, and Lao.

Van Otten, in his fourth year as McKinley's principal and his thirtieth as an educator when I visited, said he knew only the basics about this project when his former superintendent asked him to get involved. It was to focus on parent literacy, health care, family advocacy, parenting. "It appealed," especially when his superintendent told him at the close of that initial conversation, " 'Kiddo, this will get you about a million dollars.' That perks up a principal's ears." It didn't get the million dollars—and Van Otten called the financing "a confounding cycle"— but it did bring in many resources.

Among the things that the transition money allowed was creation of a parent center in the kind of prefabricated trailers that schools often must use as extra classrooms. There was one at McKinley, and the transition office near Santee School doubled as a parent center there. Spending several mornings in the parents' center next to either school—they are about a mile apart in an area of stucco strip malls and small apartment buildings in various states of repair—demonstrated what Van Otten meant about the project being more than just something written down on paper. At Santee's center, Gretchen Biswell was teaching English to seven women, all but one of them Spanish speakers, one morning; another morning Latina women were creating colorful Mexican craftwork at the McKinley parent center. The family advocates worked in these trailers, ready if someone needed to translate an undecipherable government form or just sought a sympathetic ear.

At the English class, Biswell was showing the women pictures from magazines and having them describe the scene in English, enabling Teresa Alvarez to try out her growing English vocabulary. Alvarez, who came to the United States permanently in 1988 from Irapuato, an industrial city in Mexico, had worked as a secretary at a technical secondary school at home. When she first came to the United States, she said, she was *"muy triste."* She felt she was doing nothing. When the transition program started, she met Santee kindergarten teacher Diana Gallegos, who asked her to help in her classroom.

Alvarez also took parenting classes, which helped her learn patience with her family. Her self-esteem returned. Then she signed up to study English. She was clearly an energetic, outgoing woman who joked with her friends and was firm about shortcomings she saw in the project, such as an art class that the women had no say in selecting. She and other parents were perturbed that the project was winding down; they voiced the disappointment of generations of others who have participated in social experiments that inevitably end. "I know how to deal with the school now. I know about its responsibility. What about the parents who follow us? How will they know?

"Some of the friendships will disappear. We won't have as much chance to get together. Now we can say, 'See you on Thursday.' Or 'See you in class.' We have potlucks. This is a place where you can rest; you don't bring your problems." Project officials realized by then that they should have done a better job spelling out what would happen at the end of their work, that they hoped parents would take over the initiatives.

I asked the family advocates and one of the principals what they would say if they were called to testify before a congressional committee and grilled on why government money should be spent on these parents and children. "Let 'em learn English," critics would say.

"I would put it right back on them," said Melissa Casas, one of the family advocates. "How would they feel if they went to a brand-new country—France, for example—and they didn't know French, didn't know their way around? You have to learn to become independent. This [help] is not a life-long process. We are teaching them to be independent. You can't just turn your back on poor mothers and innocent children."

"Before Head Start and the transition project, we felt like a social service agency," said Barbara Anderson, the former principal at Santee who had moved to another school not far away. "The families would come in with PG&E [Pacific Gas & Electric] bills they couldn't pay and with other problems. We would make contacts for them."

Sometimes people would need transportation, so the school nurses would go out to the bus, show them how to use it, show them how to get to the clinic, and go with them. "So we weren't just enabling them. A lot of teaching was going on. Counselors would help parents find places to get free food and show them how to get it. I think we empowered a lot of parents to do that. You can say, 'You go figure it out,' and some of them will and some never will," Anderson added. "You have to help educate them. Even if they aren't going to become strong citizens themselves, if they instill that in their children, we're helping everybody."

"Before the project started, I thought the goal should be engaging parents in their children's education," said Margo Maida, who supervised the family advocates. "Once we started, I realized our immediate goal was to stabilize families. It was impossible to get them involved in children's educations when they were worried about getting food on the table." I had heard the same refrain in Alabama, in Maryland, in Texas.

Many parents felt isolated. There was domestic violence, some parents were selling drugs, some were illegal immigrants worried about their status, some had problems with landlords or finding inexpensive clothing and food. Some parents even needed to be made aware that they should do laundry and taught how to operate the washing machines, as well as helped to budget money for laundry supplies. "The most efficient mechanism to get parents involved in children's education is listening to the parents first. They want attention, opportunities to socialize. Once they trust you more," Maida added, "once they know they've captured your attention, then it's okay to go into other areas, such as how they parent their child."

Nisseth Sath was one of those family advocates who listened to the parents. Sath, a thirty-year-old, had come to this country fifteen years earlier, speaking no English. His father had been a local judge in Cambodia but kept quiet about that when the Khmer Rouge came to his community because they were particularly vicious toward those who were educated. When the war started, Sath said his family hid in a camp in the jungle where, he recalled, "there was no safe place." He had been in third grade when the war started and had no more schooling until he came to the United States. Eventually he went to San Jose State University and earned a bachelor's degree in business. He started working for Project Crackdown, a gang program in the area, and then heard about the family advocate job.

One of the people who sought Sath's help was Pok Mao, who came to the United States in 1984 after enduring the Khmer Rouge regime and war in Cambodia. Unlike Teresa Alvarez, she had had no schooling in the rural area where her father was a rice farmer. She and her husband, who is handicapped and cannot work, have five children, two of whom have been in the Head Start transition project. She and her friends, Sokharan Uth, Chandy Kauth, and Savy Hem, had studied English in a class offered before the transition project began but they liked the project's class better. They learned more, and it was close to home and held during the day while their children were in school. All of them had children who had been in Head Start, and all said that had the transition program existed when they first came to America, they might have already learned enough English and found jobs.

Pok Mao had a sparkle in her eye and said quietly but proudly that she had moved up to a more advanced class. "If I know more English, I like to be a nurse," she said.

For Teresa Alvarez's children and for those of the Cambodian women, the transition project's most visible change was one they wouldn't have noticed: their Head Start and elementary teachers used the same curriculum and therefore their classrooms were arranged the same way. Once again, it's called "developmentally appropriate curriculum," in this case developed by the High/Scope Educational Research Foundation in Ypsilanti, Michigan.

Using High/Scope meant children were encouraged to choose at least some of their learning activities during the day and to move at their own pace, always with guidance but without teachers constantly lecturing and children passively listening. One administrator called it "management by walking around." It was hard work setting up the rooms, planning what would work where, labeling everything from building blocks to light switches so that students could learn vocabulary. Jan White, who taught kindergarten the project's first year at McKinley, said she and fellow teacher Concha Garcia rearranged their room three times before they got it right.

Head Start children, therefore, went into kindergarten classrooms that looked familiar, so they knew what to do, even on a visit to the elementary school before classes began. Kindergarten teachers also visited the Head Start class—one read the children a story—and talked with them about what to expect. As a result, said Margie Oyama, the children were able to take more responsibility when they got to kindergarten. "If they haven't been to preschool, they tend to cry a lot. Of course, a few cry a lot anyway. With this program, they know how to learn, how to listen, how to interact with other children."

Evaluators from the county education office regularly conducted extensive interviews with children, parents, and educators. They concluded that the transition students had fewer nonexcused absences than those not in the program, became more confident during the school year, and had received free health and dental care as planned, while their parents increased their involvement in the classroom and with children's homework.

But "if you say, I don't have numbers, that's right, I don't have numbers," said researcher Gretchen Wehrle. "Measuring change is not just about test scores, especially given this population" with limited English. For example, "now if a parent goes to a doctor or nurse, they know what questions to ask. How do you measure that?"

The local assessment would be the only one completed for the San Jose project; the other thirty-one pilot projects across the country were evaluated by affiliated universities and the Civitan International Research Center. The San Jose project was not able to set up transition and control groups at random, as national criteria dictated, explained Craig Ramey, Civitan's director, and so couldn't be included. "If you see differences, do you know whether they were there already?" he said. "But that doesn't mean it's not a good program."

Nonetheless, Ken Van Otten saw a lasting legacy. Children were in school longer and liking it more. They were healthier because of the screenings that were conducted. "We have come to see how much parents can do—how much difference they make—in reality. They also tend to stay in the community, largely because they have a tie to the school and they can see the difference a school can make."

Mary Garcia, new as Santee's principal the year I visited, said that "given the condition of public schools not just in California but across the country, it's obviously a big plus" to have received the additional manpower, material, and training brought by the transition project. On the downside, she thought the program should have concentrated more on giving children language skills. "I would rather see the money and resources concentrated on three or four Head Start preschool programs." With seven hundred students at Santee, the number who had had Head Start was "not even a drop in the bucket. That is a big need."

Looking to the future, project director Bolce was at once frustrated and optimistic. "I don't feel we've made institutional change. On the other hand, what institutional change can you expect" in just a few years? At the same time, it was clear to Bolce that the project has had "an impact on a relatively sizable number of parents. In both schools, there is a core of people who've experienced change and will continue to be a force at schools for themselves and their families."

In as different a setting as suburban Montgomery County, Maryland, the Head Start transition project faced some of the same problems encountered in San Jose—even though the Head Start classes were often in the same elementary-school building where the children would attend kindergarten and first, second, and third grades. Some teachers simply weren't as accommodating to parents as others. Lois Bell, the county's Head Start director, said that the degree of participation depended on the principal at each school. A former principal herself, Bell said, "What we're about now is educating principals that we have this cadre of parents that wants to work with them. All the principals *say* they favor parent involvement," but she guessed that about half made it happen. Some "parents do report having doors closed," she said.

Maryvale, where Sheila Levine's Head Start class met (see chapter 8), was one of four schools involved in the transition project in Montgomery County. That meant, among other things, that a family services worker was available to help parents and children from kindergarten through third grade, whether the child had been in Head Start or not. Working with all the families—not just those of Head Start children— was done so that the Head Start children weren't considered "different" from the other kids, something no child wants. Non–Head Start children were also included in the transition project because Head Start had found that their parents, too, had difficulty finding needed social services or had never been encouraged to play a more active role in their children's educations.

Gerald Johnson, the principal at Maryvale, was realistic about what the families of his students could do: while involvement of the parent in a child's education "is the key and should be the goal," he said, some families simply don't value education or can't take the time to be involved. "Sometimes circumstances mean that families are focusing more on survival than on education." The benefit he had seen from the transition project was that its staff spent more time working with parents, saying, "We want you to see the value of continuing your involvement throughout the child's education." The transition program had also improved teachers' perceptions of children's ability because it encouraged parents to get more involved. "If you know the parent is going to be there, then the attitude of the teacher is a more positive one."

The transition program had also increased the interaction between families, Johnson said. "Having them get together in after-school programs wipes out barriers between people," he said. He had found that the way to encourage parents to participate in activities at the school at night was either to have children in the program or to serve food. "It's better to have some chicken and thirty parents than nothing and six parents," he said. Because the school was working with the transition project, it was also encouraged to apply for several small local grants to finance these activities, including one from the *Washington Post's* foundation.

Parents gave the schools mixed grades. Debbie Sewell had had three children in Head Start, including her daughter Dreamma, a third grader at the time of my visit. Head Start, she said, always made parents feel welcome. "It wasn't the same when they went on to kindergarten. The teacher didn't want you there as much." In Head Start, Sewell said, "you can walk in anytime. But in kindergarten they say you have to make an appointment, let them know you're coming. You may not know you're going to have time to come and all of a sudden you do. Even now they ask for volunteers but you feel you're not wanted in the classroom." But that's changing. "Since transition, you're more welcome. Now I can just drop by more. It's still not like Head Start but it's getting a lot easier."

Here again the family service workers were a fundamental part of the transition project. Gail Leonard, the family service worker at Maryvale, "has helped us get to doctor appointments," Sewell said. "Any kind of resource you need, she can show you how to get it." Each of the four schools in the transition project had a family service worker. Like the rest, Leonard was a former Head Start parent. Years ago, her youngest children, twins, qualified for Head Start because hers was the large family of a government worker earning only ten thousand dollars annually. She served on the parent policy council, was hired to ride the bus with the children, then was an instructional aide. For fifteen years she had worked on the social services side of Head Start, meantime earning her bachelor's degree from Marymount College. She became a family services worker for the transition project in 1991.

I asked Leonard why the people with whom she worked couldn't find the services on their own. In some cases, she replied, it's lack of confidence in themselves, but in many instances it's simply that people don't know the resources their communities offer—counseling, job training, housing assistance, transportation—and it's her job to know them. "I hope I haven't fostered a dependency," she said, but added that she has seen parents starting to stick up for themselves and make their own inquiries. She added that she felt confident that, with the families' many strengths, "if I'm not here, they'll figure out how to do it."

Before the transition project began, Leonard worked at several schools that had Head Start programs, including one in which Diane Wilkins's daughter was enrolled. Wilkins, an African American woman in her mid-thirties, sang the praises of both Leonard and her successor at the Beall Elementary School Head Start transition program, Gaye Monaghan. Monaghan had been a Head Start parent—her husband was on disability retirement from the police force at the time—then a volunteer, then a substitute, then an aide. She returned to school, and received a bachelor's degree in human services from George Washington University and a master's degree in guidance and counseling from Johns Hopkins University. Because the program helped her so much, she especially wanted to help Head Start families as a family services worker, and she met Diane Wilkins and her family when the transition project began.

Wilkins had grown up in comfortable, middle-class surroundings in Washington, D.C. Her father ran several service stations and used to buy a new car every three years; her mother was a teacher. She had married her elementary-school sweetheart, but later left him and lived in a homeless shelter. She enrolled her daughter, Diamond, in Head Start in Takoma Park, a Montgomery County suburb near the District of Columbia. Later she moved to Rockville, and Diamond became part of Beall's transition project.

"I was depressed. I watched everything I had be destroyed." Wilkins had spent about five years on and off welfare. When she heard about the Head Start transition project, she found that "for once somebody cared about me and cared about my entire family. I came to depend on Gail Leonard and I was crushed when I learned there would be a new advocate.

"How God sent a second angel to me I don't know. Here came Gaye, who was all smiles and busy. Gaye and Gail loved you for who you are regardless. The more crises we were in, the more they provided help. They provided emotional support for my son [also a Head Start student]. . . . He was angry. Head Start paid for a therapeutic summer camp for him. He was thrown out of Head Start every day for biting or hitting. They worked with him. There's not been one incident this year. They kept me from committing suicide or abusing my child." When I last spoke with Wilkins, Diamond was in fourth grade, regularly on the honor roll and a safety patrol. David was in first grade and, his mother said proudly, doing third-grade-level math.

Wilkins and her husband were back together. He served on the Head Start parent policy council and was trying to get more men involved. Too many of them think volunteering in the classroom is just for women. Wilkins said that she can tell a father, "You've got to get off your butt and get involved," but that won't necessarily do any good. "But another father can say, 'Man, it's important for you to be involved. These are our kids. Don't let them be like us,' and the other guy will say, 'Oh, okay, that's a cool thing.'

"If those services would have been taken away after one year," she added, that would not have been enough for her family. "I did have the belief by then that someone else believed in me, but I would have been still asking for emergency food. I was doing that three times a month. There's no way one year was enough. I didn't have enough belief in myself, in my marriage. I didn't have a belief that I could keep a job. It would have been easy for me to slip back on welfare. The help goes on—from the hugs to the talk."

Wilkins was working in a Montgomery County government office, and she and her husband had just bought their first house, ending what Wilkins described as nine years of dependency on housing subsidies. They'd also purchased a used minivan so the family could take trips. She was enrolled at Montgomery College, working toward an A.A. degree, and hoped eventually to get a degree in sociology from the University of Maryland so she could work with families in crisis.

In the spring of 1996, the Wilkinses testified before the Montgomery County Board of Education about the value of the Head Start transition project. They were both encouraged to participate in Head Start, with child care and bus rides provided, David Wilkins told the board. "For every obstacle you could put in the way, they removed it so there was no excuse that you could not come into the classroom and participate. For a guy like me that made it easier to come in." The transition team often helped them cut red tape to get food assistance; in helping them, the team helped other families because then they could tell others what they had learned about finding services.

"My children look at us as role models today. Back then I can't say that they looked at their father as a role model. . . . It's been a struggle, but without the transition team behind us—showing us that we can improve, that there are people out there willing to help us as long as we were willing to help ourselves—that made a lot of difference in our lives."

After the Wilkinses spoke, board of education president Ana Sol Gutierrez raised a point that is key to implementing the lessons learned from the transition project. Head Start is applauded, she said, for its holistic approach to children and their families. But the minute that that approach "went in to our regular school there was resistance— there was resistance by principals, there was resistance by teachers— that this was not the way we did business and there was a huge clash in the two philosophies. That, to me, was the reason HHS [the Department of Health and Human Services] was funding this thing was to see how can you move this philosophy into the classroom." She urged the Head Start staff to develop strategies to help address these attitudes so that the transition way of operating can be "the way we do business" in the schools.[7]

She had put her finger on the next step. Each of the transition teams around the country hopes to use what it learned about how schools are organized and how parents can be involved to aid others as transition activities are developed for all Head Start programs. When the project was nearing its end, Head Start was finishing its new performance standards, which included a requirement for increased transition efforts at all centers, not just those in the pilot project. That requirement said that Head Start staff should initiate meetings between its teachers and parents and kindergarten and elementary-school teachers to discuss children's progress and continue to work together.

The national Head Start office provided a pool of $35 million to which programs could apply to aid their transition process. Based on early research results, the national office suggested that local agencies consider employing a transition coordinator. That person would do the kind of bridge-building work that teachers at both Head Start and in elementary schools lack the time to initiate. The task of strengthening these ties will be enormous, given the obstacles the transition project uncovered.

"Many sites are facing challenges related to ensuring that the project's goals, objectives, and activities will be continued after the current funding is discontinued," Civitan's interim research report said. They operate at a time when school resources are shrinking, leading to cuts in programs and staff, and when the public wants more accountability— "most often defined as improved scores on standardized achievement tests." Balancing the conflicting pressures makes the transition process difficult for everyone, but especially those who have not had the experience of the demonstration projects.[8]

For their part, the public schools should consider using some of their Chapter 1 federal aid or whatever other funds they can raise to hire family advocates. Having such aides not only helps the principals and teachers concentrate more on their own jobs; their assistance can also allow parents to spend more time with their children because they aren't forever struggling through bureaucracies to locate health care or other services. If these workers have small enough caseloads to enable them to work closely with the families, they may prove as valuable as the aides did in the transition project to its children and to parents like Teresa Alvarez, Pok Mao, and Diane and David Wilkins.

Watts Towers:

We visit kindergarten. Suddenly elementary-school children look huge.

It was one of those mornings in Los Angeles when you could smell the air. Certainly you could see it—the power lines, even the exit signs on the Century Freeway disappeared behind a gray scrim. It was going to be hot. Amend that: it was already hot when I arrived at the Watts Towers Head Start center. The main event of the day was visiting the kindergarten at 102nd Street School.

At 8:30 that morning only three children had been sitting having their snack at Site 05. Usually there were far more at that hour. Whether people were slow getting up because of the heat or because it was Monday morning or because they knew about the kindergarten visit, who knew? Gradually the children trickled in. Maria didn't want to go on the trip. She didn't want to take off her white coat. She hid behind teacher Lupe Osuna, and this time she wasn't playing. So she didn't go.

At 8:45 teacher Josephine Garner lined up the children and corralled Raymound's mother Candy and Fabiola's mother to walk along with her and Heyman as we headed off down 105th Street. There were nineteen children, plus two younger brothers walking along with their mothers. Garner was at the head of the line with little Marcus, with Wayne and his partner behind them. Garner decided Wayne must ride everywhere in a car because he certainly wasn't walking very fast. We made it to the yellow stucco school only a few minutes after nine, the appointed time. When we arrived, it looked for a moment as if nobody knew we were coming.

We stepped inside the cool lobby, where there was a table manned by two parent volunteers assigned to register any visiting parents or just keep tabs on movement around the building. One was Precious Andrews, one of Watts Towers' stalwart parents, who had just started this volunteer job the Thursday before. She pointed out her son Richard to the other woman at the table.

Soon Helen Little, a kindergarten teacher and chair of the preschool section, came out to talk with Garner and take the children on a tour.

Nothing special had been planned; it wasn't her fault—there had evidently been a mix-up in the office. In past years, one of the kindergarten teachers had read a story to the Head Start children. I thought of the hundreds of hours other Head Start programs with special transition projects were expending in trying to keep parents involved and children motivated as they made the move from Head Start into elementary school. Head Start officials in Washington had mandated transition efforts in every program, but good intentions easily faltered in the face of staffing realities.

The teacher in the first room was going over the alphabet with the children gathered around her on the carpet. "I'm thinking of a word that starts with W that tells time." A little boy responded: "A clock." The teacher replied that when it was on the wall it was a clock and when you wore it on your wrist, it was a watch. That started with W. As the Head Starters filed out, the teacher commended her students, telling them, "The visitors came and you showed how you can sit down quietly and learn." In the next classroom, the teacher was going over shapes and numbers that looked alike and might be confusing. Some of the Head Start youngsters were mesmerized watching the teacher and the older children.

Outside room 39, Helen Little's classroom, were pictures of the celebrations during the year. Inside, the children were reading a poem called "The Little Turtle." The Head Start class rounded the corner of the building and as they were entering room 36 Raven twisted Andre's hand and he called out, "*Stop!*"

One classroom had first graders as well as kindergartners. I realized I had been hanging out a long time with little four-year-olds: these children looked huge to me.

As we came out of room 35, Garner said to Little that she had taught about three of the children in each of the classrooms. She hadn't said anything to them in order not to disrupt the classroom. As if to reinforce the point, at just that moment a little girl came along and gave Garner a big hug.

Not much was said to the children about what they were seeing as they were seeing it. Little told Garner, "We can see the difference when the children come from Head Start. They come in ready—and we can move on." As the children left, Little waved good-bye. They waved back. Perhaps the children benefited from seeing the classrooms and gaining familiarity with this school, so much larger than Site 05. However, I did not sense much effort on either side to keep alive some of the Head

Start principles. Hard to do, of course, without staff specifically assigned to do that task as the transition programs had.

On our return trip to the Watts Towers center, we walked down
Grape Street at a more leisurely pace than when we were rushing
toward the school. At one house, there was a small child watching us
from his porch, and Garner prompted Candy, Raymound's mother, to
ask his mother if the little boy was in school. The women spoke in
Spanish and Candy translated that the woman was going to enroll him
at the 102nd Street School. Garner asked Candy to tell her about Head
Start because she was starting to recruit the fall class. Garner sometimes walked through the neighborhood to find children for the program, and if she saw a tricycle in the yard, she'd head for the front door.

Meantime, Andre and Edwin had both raised their fists. Garner
broke up the fight and tried to get them to hold hands. No way. We
walked on down 105th, passing dogs barking and one sleeping in the
sun—it was broiling hot by then. Some yards were neat, some ne-
glected. Garner called out greetings to people she knew. When we
neared the center, Raymound ran ahead and climbed up on the gate to
undo the latch. We were back by 10:05.

Garner had all the children lie down on the carpet for a few minutes
to cool off and calm down. Lunch arrived at 10:25—sloppy joes, salad,
celery, honeydew melon. The boys played outside as Lupe Osuna and
Marisol's mom and Veronica Perez helped the girls try on their costumes and shoes for the big International Awareness Day event. The
Training and Research Foundation held a parade each year with children costumed to represent countries around the world. This year Watts
Towers children would portray Egyptians; the preparations had been
under way for months.

The "good mornings" started at 10:50 A.M. "Where did we go this
morning?" Garner asked. "We went to the big school. We saw kindergarten. Did you see all the animals they had on the wall? The zoo animals? Did you see boys and girls working at the tables by themselves?
Everybody had their own pencil. Were they playing in the classroom?
Noooo. Did the teacher have to tell them to go sit down? When you get
to the big school, you can't jump up and down and go to the bathroom
every five minutes."

About a year later, I asked Elaine Atlow, the Training and Research
Foundation's Head Start director, what her program was doing to enhance its transition efforts. That year, she said, the program's administrative office had sent letters to each of the schools that its Head Start

children would be attending to call attention to the importance of the transition process. Individual meetings were also being set up between the Head Start parents and kindergarten teachers. And the program used some of its transition grant to buy a VCR to show the children and their parents special tapes about what to expect in kindergarten.

A few days after I had been on the Head Start children's kindergarten visit, I returned to the 102nd Street School for a conversation with Helen Little, a trim woman who is a graduate of Spelman College with a master's degree from Mount St. Mary's College in Los Angeles. It was her tenth year at 102nd Street, part of the Los Angeles Unified School District. We sat in the staff lunchroom and chatted.

"The way we usually recognize Head Start or preschool children is that they are more in tune with school," she told me. "They usually know their numbers, they usually know their alphabet, they can often write their names, and they can express themselves a little better. They are more adjusted to being in school and away from their mothers. They've had more socialization experiences. Quite often children come to school who've never been away from home, never been away from their mothers. They cry. Their separation anxiety is very prevalent until they realize that they are not being abandoned, that mother went away and she came back."

Students primed for school by Head Start "are really the students that we need in order to do our mission," she added. "We are expected to do more with the students in kindergarten now than in years past." There is more emphasis on reading, less on social activity. "We are being pushed to teach the children to read. Head Start is focusing on the readiness that we focused on years ago."

All the children are very capable of learning, Little said; "it is just that some have had experiences that others haven't had. For example, we talk about animals all the time. If they've never seen a big elephant, it's just not as meaningful to them. If we talk about a peacock spreading its feathers and how beautiful it is, it's much more meaningful if they've seen a peacock spreading its feathers.

"We can definitely see the difference, those of us who get students from what we call prekindergarten. When they come to us, it's just very obvious those who have had that experience. They just have that readiness—readiness for learning."

How, I asked her, can the public schools keep alive the kind of parent involvement that Head Start tries to foster?

"Parent education" was her quick answer. Parents really need to be aware of what they can do and how to do it. "With a great focus on parent education, we could see great progress. Parents would do more volunteering."

But many parents, she added, seem to feel that once the child gets into elementary school, their responsibility is over, that the teachers know what to do. Having parents involved "is one of the crucial things in helping students be more successful." It may be, she added, that having those parents who do get involved brainstorm on how to encourage others would be an effective technique for stimulating participation.

Her school has some parents who volunteer their time but the teachers usually have to ask. The attitude is, " 'If you ask me, you're going to tell me what you want,' " Little said. "With parent education, they would already know. They would be more comfortable, more willing to come into the classroom, and would catch the excitement of children learning."

Considering the
Prospects

Chapter Fourteen

Ways to Serve More
Children, Longer

What the KCMC Child Development Corporation, which runs thirteen Head Start centers in Kansas City, Missouri, found when it surveyed its communities in 1992 was hardly unusual: more and more parents worked and needed full-day child care but couldn't afford it. Dwayne Crompton, KCMC's executive director, and his staff came up with a plan to stretch their Head Start dollars to give children that full-day, full-year care while maintaining the program's comprehensive services. They launched their Full Start effort the following fall, working with existing day care centers and helped by state and local agencies and local foundations.

In the early days of Head Start, many centers offered full-day programs. Then Head Start expanded and emphasis was placed on serving more children, not on serving them longer hours. Most Head Start programs today are half-day as a result; many close their doors in the summertime. But as even more women have entered the workforce, needs have changed. However, money for full-day services has not always seemed readily available. Building partnerships like those constructed by KCMC can be a time-consuming process, as other programs around the country have also found. But they are one way to respond to these changing needs. They are also vital to Head Start's survival as a pathbreaking child development program in an era when Congress has insisted that many welfare recipients find jobs—without providing enough financial support to meet the increased demand anticipated for child care once they do. If Head Start cannot provide daylong, year-round care, someone else will, and that someone may provide care lacking Head Start's comprehensive approach. And the poor may not be able to afford it anyway.

"I'm an old community organizer," Dwayne Crompton said. "I believe anybody can do it, neighborhood by neighborhood. You start out by knowing your community, what it needs."

A visit to Lollipop Land Child Care Center on Kansas City's east side demonstrated what KCMC had done. The hilly neighborhood was a picture of urban blight—some of the once substantial houses were boarded up although others were neatly kept. Clunker cars filled some yards and abandoned sofas or mattresses graced more than one curbside. But inside the blue-gray building at the top of a hill, I stepped into a different world.

Lollipop Land stayed open from 6 A.M. and until 6 P.M. year-round except for a few holidays. The center served children from two to fourteen years old. The program accommodated children as old as fourteen, before and after school, because, as director Willie Burke said, "How many parents are really comfortable with an eleven-year-old home alone?"

This center has long been run by KCMC, which has operated both Head Start centers and day care centers not affiliated with Head Start. Lollipop Land had been one of the latter. When Crompton and his staff decided to try their new approach to stretch Head Start dollars, they did it at one of their own centers first, starting at Lollipop Land in 1993. With the lessons they learned there, they branched out to other agencies. One of these was St. Mark's, run by St. Mark's/United Inner City Services in a church basement near the redbrick apartments of a public housing project. Both were already full-day programs but without many of Head Start's hallmarks, such as more thorough health screenings and more intensive teacher training.

KCMC Day Care Corporation had been established in 1970 under the federal Model Cities Program to provide child care in inner-city neighborhoods. It changed its name to KCMC Child Development Corporation in 1979 to reflect an expanded mission to help families, conduct research and educational activities about early childhood, and advocate for improved child care. For twenty years, Dwayne Crompton has been KCMC's executive director and a national force for change as well. Tall, with graying short hair, Crompton, fifty, is in frequent demand as a speaker about the Full Start approach; he has chaired the Black Caucus of the National Association for the Education of Young

Children and he served on the Department of Health and Human Services' most recent advisory committee on Head Start quality and expansion. He grew up in Kansas City and was a sixth-grade teacher before joining KCMC. He knew that what he did made a difference at that level, he said, but if he was really going to have an impact, he had to start working with younger children.

When Congress began increasing Head Start funding in the early 1990s so that local programs could serve more children, Crompton and his staff started to think about how to leverage that additional money for maximum benefit for children. KCMC therefore was well under way with its efforts to increase the amount of full-day, Head Start–quality care when Congress changed the welfare laws in 1996.

KCMC checked local inner-city day care centers and found that from 30 to 70 percent of their enrollments were eligible for Head Start because of their parents' low income but were not receiving the program's comprehensive services. KCMC then spent hours and hours, months and months, constructing partnerships that would stretch Head Start dollars to serve more children longer. The results: KCMC spent Head Start dollars that would cover, let's say, sixty eligible children at Lollipop Land. Other money was still coming in to the program—some of it from fees paid by parents who could afford the services, some of it from state day care funding through the Missouri Department of Social Services, some from Kansas City and Jackson County funds. The addition of Head Start funds freed some of that other money to improve the educational program, buy more art materials and play equipment, and enhance teacher training. The state and the city, as well as United Way, which also helped pay for child care services at St. Mark's, agreed not to reduce their funding despite the addition of Head Start money at the two centers. The approach was christened Full Start.

Services were improved for all the children at the centers, not just the 60 children eligible for Head Start funding the first year at Lollipop Land and 50 at St. Mark's. Willie Burke, a tall, poised African American woman who had worked for KCMC for almost twenty years, told me about the changes that Full Start brought to her center. First, teacher training was more frequent and hands-on. Second, the center could provide more nutritious food for the children. Third, health screenings became more thorough—not just for the 60 Head Start children (who are not separated in any way from the rest of the children) but for all 167 enrolled. Finally, the advent of Head Start as well as Jackson County funding brought two family advocates to work with parents, making them more aware, for example, of health services that might be available if they didn't have insurance.

The first floor of the Lollipop Land center was a big, open room, toddlers on one side and older children on the other, but the children could roam anywhere. Each teacher was responsible for all the children, especially those who went into his or her area, although for report or field-trip purposes, teachers were assigned to a set number of children. The center used a modified version of the High/Scope curriculum that allows children to select an area in which they want to work—blocks, dress-up, manipulative toys, art. The 125 preschoolers were upstairs, and 42 of the school-age children were occupied downstairs.

Supporting KCMC as it moved to expand services were two major Kansas City foundations. Jan Kreamer of the Greater Kansas City Community Foundation brought most of the major funders to the table to back KCMC. The Ewing Marion Kauffman Foundation gave KCMC a three-year, eight-hundred-thousand-dollar grant to support Full Start and make plans for child care services at a center connected with the new Swope Parkway Community Health Center in southeast Kansas City. Kauffman has evaluated the Full Start approach. Preliminary data showed the program made a marked difference in how children learned to work together and in how well teachers interacted with the children, for example, engaging them in conversation that helped them use language better instead of simply watching over them or giving them orders. The biggest difference showed up at the center that has had the program the longest, Lollipop Land. A later study compared Full Start centers with traditional full-day Head Start and concluded that "community child care centers can meet quality standards of strong Head Start programs if they have access to Full Start's staff training, equipment/building enhancements and financial resources."

The St. Mark's center is located in a church basement near one of Kansas City's main north-south thoroughfares, The Paseo. It was in its third year as a Full Start program when I visited. Full Start helped increase the number of preschoolers at St. Mark's from 40 to 65, 50 of whom were eligible for Head Start. "We had the basic equipment but we just didn't have enough," said director Bobbye Fuller. Lighting in the classrooms was improved, furniture was repainted, and more storage cabinets were added. Teachers also started to use the High/Scope curriculum. Addition of Head Start dollars for health screenings enabled the center to identify children with hearing problems or needing glasses.

St. Mark's has undergone a 100 percent staff turnover. When Full Start began, none of the teachers had the required child development associate credential. They weren't used to being evaluated, so some resigned. With more planning time, Fuller said, she might have been able to weed out some of the staff before they went through expensive training. Or more might have been done to encourage staff to stick with it. On the plus side, pay has gone up for teachers, who are better trained.

At the George Washington Carver Full Start Child Care Center, director Dawnetta Jones was in her first year with a Full Start program when I visited. She was decidedly upbeat. This center, open from 6 A.M. to 5:30 P.M., had 119 children, 89 of them all day. Thirty-four of the children were enrolled in Head Start. There was a waiting list of about 65 children. What made Full Start so special, Jones said, was that parents had somewhere reliable to leave their children all day. Before Full Start, her budget had been very tight. "Since our partnership [with KCMC] we've been able to participate in remarkable training and to receive new equipment. Staff morale is better; my morale has become better. It was an emotional change that the teachers and staff went through," but Jones said the physical changes helped the self-esteem of both the children and the teachers.

"We had some toys but now the shelves are filled. In the baby room, we have new mattresses and bumper pads. The kitchen has been totally redone with new countertops and new equipment. Even the food situation is better—we were having a lot of beans and other things that were less expensive. Now we have lots of chicken. KCMC did an assessment on what we needed. Soon after that, new equipment started to come."

KCMC operated half-day Head Start as well. The Northland Center served an area about ten miles north of the Missouri River in a new building that had brought together many county services—employment and domestic violence counseling, YMCA child care—on the Maple Wood Community College campus. Children at this center were mainly white whereas enrollments at Lollipop Land and St. Mark's were predominantly African American. KCMC's Guinotte Center, a stone's throw from the river, had a heavy Vietnamese enrollment in a World War II–vintage housing project.

Because research was showing that the project worked, the KCMC staff planned to expand the concept into other child care programs in the community as funding allowed. I asked planning and development director Shirley Stubbs-Gillette how other programs might clone the Full Start approach. "The short answer," she said, "is that you can't

clone it. Every community is different. The feds are pushing collaboration so I often go to other areas to talk about our program and people
will tell me, 'That won't work in our community.' And I say, 'You take
the pieces of it that will work for you, but always know your own community.' There has to be a stable community agency to run the program
and there has to be some outside funding to help improve the services
for the children." Many of the problems in building collaborative arrangements seem to be concerns over turf; child care programs may be
jealous of Head Start because it typically receives more money, and
some Head Start staff may see the child care agencies as having lower
standards. But Stubbs-Gillette said there is evidence that some of these
barriers are coming down.

With the creation of Full Start, one asks, "Are more children being
cared for who wouldn't have been otherwise?" No, and yes. The children eligible for Head Start would have been at Lollipop Land anyway,
but not with the quality of education, breadth of health screenings, or
degree of parent involvement that Head Start can bring. And because
there are 167 children altogether at Lollipop Land, all 167—not just
the 60 who bring in the Head Start funds—benefit from the improved
program. So, yes, at the three Full Start centers, more children are now
served by full-day, full-year Head Start. Said one parent: "The program
teaches my child more than other child care she's been in. . . . The
teachers take more time with her." As important, social service agencies, state, county, and local governments, and major foundations have
new ties that can only help them in bringing services to more families.

Across the country, as in Kansas City, Head Start centers have used
several approaches to provide full-day programs, as reported in a 1995
study for the government by the Pelavin Research Institute and The
Urban Institute.[1] Some find outside sources of money to expand their
own programs. This is often called "wraparound care." Others provide
"wrap-in care," meaning a Head Start program contracts with another
child care program and helps it expand its services to meet Head Start
performance standards. Some use "connected care" for children before
or after Head Start's day; these programs do not have to meet the performance standards.

One would not think that efforts to provide more full-day programs
would erupt into a debate within the Head Start community, but that is
what happened in the spring of 1997. The Head Start bureau said it
would use expansion funds for the first time to encourage partnerships
with child care providers for full-day Head Start services. KCMC's ef-

forts were cited as one of its models. The national office may well have been reacting to members of Congress and governors as well as to its advisory committees, who have urged Head Start to work more closely with the child care community. But the leadership of the National Head Start Association, which represents program directors, staff, and parents, reacted sharply to the proposal, bristling at the idea that Head Start programs weren't capable of providing full-day care on their own if provided the resources. Ron Herndon, NHSA president whose own program in Portland, Oregon, operated full-day, said that the Head Start bureau's action threatened the work that had been done to improve quality. "Child care is in an abysmal state, not because the child care people don't care but because it is not adequately subsidized and has no national standards." Herndon and the NHSA were also miffed because "the decision was made from the top . . . without much input from people in communities."

"While NHSA wholeheartedly supports partnerships," NHSA executive director Sarah M. Greene said in a letter concerning the action, "we do not support mandating a particular model. If a program's community needs assessment demonstrates the need for blended funding or partnerships in order to extend the day or serve more children, it is the program's decision. Programs must retain the flexibility to make those decisions at the local level."

Helen Taylor, who herself ran full-day Head Start in the District of Columbia before directing the national program, disagreed. It would be wonderful if local programs could decide for themselves how they want to expand, she said, "but we can't do that because we have limited resources in this country. Our job is to maximize the resources we have available to serve children and families well." The HHS announcement made it clear, she said, that programs would have to meet Head Start's performance standards.

As the debate went on concerning how Head Start should expand, the state of Ohio continued on its own initiative to try to serve all eligible children who wanted to enroll. In 1990, Head Start enrolled about 36 percent of the three- and four-year-olds eligible in Ohio, about par with the national average, and the state was contributing $5.4 million to the federal government's $74.3 million. Since then, operating with bipartisan support, the state government has poured millions of its own dollars into Head Start to try to reach all eligible children. By mid-1997, 75 percent of the three- and four-year-olds eligible for Head Start were enrolled, the most in any state, and Ohio was contributing $77 million to the federal government's $139.5 million a year.

The Ohio effort began with Democratic governor Richard Celeste and continued and grew under Republican governor George Voinovich. In the late 1980s, the Committee for Economic Development, a national roundtable of the leaders of major corporations, helped stimulate the state effort when it recommended increased investment in education for young children. In 1988, Celeste created a blue-ribbon commission of Ohio business executives, state legislators, and educators to develop a plan to try to move the state's public education system from one that was perceived as about average to one of the best in the nation. Owen "Brad" Butler, retired chairman of Procter & Gamble, chaired this Education 2000 Commission. After the panel heard public testimony around the state, it recommended, among other things, that all disadvantaged three- and four-year-olds should have access to a high-quality preschool program and that state money be used to expand Head Start. The governor then appointed a staff-level commission to report to him on specific actions.

The effort had bipartisan appeal, said Carla Edlefson, Celeste's executive assistant for education, who served on the Education 2000 Commission. The economic arguments for investing in young children presented by an earlier High/Scope study of the Perry Preschool project in Ypsilanti, Michigan, were compelling; in a report that made a splash in the mid-1980s, the Perry Preschool study had found that a dollar spent on its program saved seven down the line because its graduates had jobs instead of going to jail or needing various social services. Preventing problems made a lot of sense to the business executives, most of them Republicans. Investing in Head Start had a strong constituency among minorities, a base of Democratic support.

Meantime, the National Governors' Association promulgated its Goals 2000 Initiative, the first of which was that all young children should start school better prepared to learn by the year 2000. George Voinovich continued the efforts Celeste had begun after his election in 1990 because, as a former mayor of Cleveland, he knew big-city problems and he also saw Head Start as successful.

Outside forces had helped in laying the groundwork for the increase in state support. In 1982, the Children's Defense Fund opened an Ohio office to try to provide a voice for children. Two years later, the Ohio Department of Education created a commission to study the issues of early childhood education. The Ohio Head Start Association was also working to help improve its staff training and to be an advocate for its programs. Each group helped increase the visibility of children's issues and worked toward generating more state money for early childhood programs.

By 1990 the pieces were in place. Many leaders in Ohio's business community saw the importance of Head Start, the Department of Education was on board, and a revenue recalculation meant there was money in the state's coffers. The legislature approved $19.2 million in its two-year budget to expand both Head Start and preschool in the public schools. The federal government was also expanding Head Start at that time. That same year, the Ohio Head Start Association, the Children's Defense Fund, and other organizations sponsored a conference on early childhood that helped frame questions for gubernatorial and legislative candidates in that fall's election. Voinovich pledged to expand the state's Head Start contribution and did so.

The Ohio Head Start Summit in 1993 kept the momentum alive by exploring the challenges the program faced and developing coordinated efforts within Head Start and state government to try to solve them. That led to creation by Voinovich of the Governor's Head Start Task Force to propose ways to improve quality, expand facilities, and streamline licensing. Mark Real of the Ohio office of the Children's Defense Fund chaired the group.

In Ohio's two-year budget enacted in 1997, Head Start received an increase of $6.7 million for 1998 and more for the following year. The money would be put into existing child care centers to give them the comprehensive services of Head Start and make more full-day care available to working parents in much the same way KCMC has done in Kansas City. These additional funds would allow Head Start in Ohio to serve an additional 4,000 children, or 80 percent of the youngsters estimated as eligible for the program—virtually the saturation point. While many forces came together in Ohio to win this unprecedented commitment to Head Start, the key has been the leadership in the governor's office. The question now is whether other states can win similar commitment to advancing the agenda for young children—or if many are even trying.

Chapter Fifteen

Meeting Conditions—
Head Start Adapts

ead Start has survived more than thirty years by constantly reinventing itself. In the past, meeting changing conditions led to creating parent and child centers to work with mothers and fathers who needed help learning how to care for their children and to encourage their development. It meant Head Start working with other organizations to find pediatricians for programs in areas lacking them. It caused Head Start programs to start training their own teachers. And it led Congress to set up transition programs to explore how best to help Head Start children make the move into elementary school.

Today there are still adaptations to be made, partnerships to be formed, new sources of money to be found. Children continue to come into Head Start from homes where no one has read to them or even talked to them much, so they may not be ready to learn to read themselves. Parents may work hours other than the traditional nine-to-five, especially in the low-wage jobs they find when leaving the welfare rolls. Thousands more children will need full-day programs because more parents must find work or go to school as a result of changes in federal welfare laws. Teenage pregnancy remains at high levels, and young mothers and fathers need help learning how to be mothers and fathers. Head Start demands many skills of its managers, who need new techniques and revitalization. And Head Start always struggles to find good classroom space, especially in times of expansion. This chapter will introduce people and programs meeting these conditions.

The headline on the first story: the Texas Instruments Foundation not only helped finance the Margaret Cone Head Start Center in a poor neighborhood of Dallas where Head Start had not existed, it also involved two local universities in its project and stayed with the program when initial results were poor. It supported development of a language-enrichment curriculum and turned those poor results around.

The Texas Instruments Foundation (TIF) was established in 1964 to invest some of the profits from one of the world's foremost technology companies to improve life in the communities where it operates. In 1988 the board members, made up almost entirely of Texas Instruments employees, were sitting in the spacious meeting room at corporate headquarters in Dallas going over some of the hundreds of grant applications the foundation receives each year. Members were asking, "What is it in Dallas that we can get our arms around and really make a difference?" Some of the applications, for example, were from programs to help battered women and battered children and the homeless; over and over again, board members saw the importance of early intervention to prevent these conditions from arising. In Dallas as elsewhere, foundation president Mike Rice told me, there were so many children brought up in an atmosphere where there was practically no intellectual stimulation. Families seemed stuck in poverty. The foundation wanted to find strategies that could have an impact on the problem. "The place to solve it is working with young children," he added.

Someone mentioned a program that had made the kind of difference they were looking for: the Perry Preschool program in Ypsilanti, Michigan. So a foundation staff member went to Ypsilanti to see the program. Afterward, TIF contacted Mary Fulbright, director of the Community Services Development Center, the service arm of the School of Social Work at the University of Texas at Arlington. The foundation commissioned her and a team of specialists to study whether preschool was effective in Dallas, and if so, to design a quality program and help determine where to locate it. Fulbright's team visited Head Start and public and private preschools and decided that the public schools appeared to be too structured to experiment in the way the foundation wanted. Fulbright concluded that "Head Start helps children—but not enough." The next question: What would it take to help them enough? The team did not model its program on Head Start, but rather considered what would best meet the needs of four-year-olds; it ended up designing something close to the theoretical model of Head Start—a comprehensive year-round, all-day program with two social workers and a nurse practitioner as well as five teachers and five aides for ninety children.

The Texas Instruments Foundation wanted its program located in a neighborhood where the center's attendance zone would match that of a nearby elementary school so that there could be an ongoing relationship with the children. It also wanted to go into an area of Dallas where there had been no preschool so the new center wouldn't drive someone out of business and thus reduce services to children. It identified a neighborhood southeast of downtown in the Julia Frazier Elementary School area as a likely site, and discovered that Head Start of Greater Dallas had done so as well. Head Start entered into a partnership with the Texas Instruments Foundation and the university. The Dallas Housing Authority, which operates the Frazier Courts housing project in which many of the children live, gave Head Start a long-term lease on the land. The Meadows Foundation and the Communities Foundation gave $50,000 apiece to help build the new center.

Margaret Cone Preschool, named after the first official director of Head Start of Greater Dallas, opened in 1990. It was housed in a buff-colored building just across from the redbrick apartments of the housing project. Over 90 percent of its children were African American and most lived with just one parent who earned less than $7,500 a year. Fewer than half of the parents had graduated from high school. The children generally were about eight months to two years behind other kids their age in language skills. Test results after the first year were not good. Planners said, "Okay, you can't judge from one year." But the second year was no better than the first. When the children who had attended Cone finished kindergarten, they were scoring in the bottom one-third of the nation's children on the Iowa Test of Basic Skills, a widely used standardized test of school achievement. "It was not a happy two years," Fulbright said.

TIF considered its options. "We asked, 'Do we get in for the long haul or do we quit?'" said Ann Minnis, TIF's grant administrator and now a foundation board member.

"TIF faced it squarely when it heard the results," Fulbright told me. "Neither Mike nor Ann said the word dollar. Mike said, 'Mary, we've lost another group of children.' They were not committed to showing their model worked but to having a model that works."

Eventually they linked up with Southern Methodist University's Learning Therapy Program, which specialized in working with children who had difficulty learning. Its staff observed Cone's teachers and children in 1993. They saw few objects in the classrooms that would stimu-late language and little conversation between teachers and children. They tested the children and found four-year-olds who were function-ing at about the level of two-and-a-half-year-olds in terms of language skills, that is, what they understood when people spoke to them.

To change that situation, Nell Carvell and Jamie Williams of SMU designed the Language Enrichment Activities Program (LEAP) for the Cone center. Helping implement that curriculum, the Texas Instru-ments Foundation put more books into each classroom—five new books a week, hardcover, some classics, some newer works showing children from many ethnic groups. Each class also received plastic letters for the children to play with and posters with pictures of everyday objects and occupations for the children to identify and discuss. Instruction also in-cluded helping the children become aware that words are the basic building blocks of language. The Texas Instruments Foundation also paid for Cone's five teachers, five aides, and its director to receive six weeks of training at SMU on the structure of language and on using the new techniques and materials.

By spring of the first year that they were using the new materials, teachers saw a change in the children. That helped them buy into the new program. Test scores started to go up. The fourth group of Cone center graduates—the first to use the new curriculum for a substantial amount of time—scored twice as high as the first two groups (in the sixtieth percentile as opposed to the twentieth or thirtieth) and signifi-cantly higher than the third.

SMU also lined up volunteers to work at Cone and one other center each Monday morning to provide extra support for the teachers. Often volunteers were former teachers themselves. They always took a book to read with the children—the ones paid for by the foundation—then left the books in the classrooms, where the teachers could use them again and again. This part of the program placed 100 books in the center. Nell Carvell, director of SMU's Learning Therapy Program, said that the volunteers also conducted other activities in the classrooms, such as helping the children learn concepts like positions ("behind," "on top of," "in front of") or shapes. SMU's planners also wanted to teach par-ents what they could do at home, but they have not been as successful in getting the parents to come to the center for the training. They've tried handing out Golden Books, plastic alphabets, and Play-Doh but still don't attract many parents.

One weekday morning during my visit to the Cone center I watched teacher Marilyn Martin putting this curriculum into action. She sat on the floor with five children while others worked with the classroom aide or on their own. The book of the day was *Vegetable Garden*, and Martin read to the children about how the seeds were planted, how the rain and bright sunshine helped the garden grow, how rabbits nibbled on the sprouts. The book had big, bright pictures. Martin asked the children questions as she read, and helped them answer in short but complete sentences, not just single words. "What is this?" she asked. "This is a pumpkin," a little boy responded. "That's a tomato," another child said when she pointed to a picture of a plump red vegetable. If a child did not use a complete sentence, Martin would say encouragingly, "What is this? This is a string bean," to give the child a model of how to answer.

The story mentioned harvesttime. "What does 'harvesttime' mean?" Martin asked. "That's when you pick the food," said one boy, who had grasped a rather sophisticated concept for a four-year-old. "And these kids have just started" in Head Start, Martin told me.

"What is this?"

"This is a sweet potato."

"Where do vegetables grow?"

"Vegetables grow in a garden."

"And some vegetables grow on a vine. Give yourself a big hand, boys and girls," Martin said, concluding that part of the lesson. Then she got out a little bag. This was a P bag, she said, so the children could learn the sound of the letter P. "What would I have in this bag?"

"A pumpkin?"

She reached in and pulled out a small pumpkin. "This is a pumpkin," she said, emphasizing the *p*. She passed the pumpkin around, and then pulled out a potato and a peanut. One little boy suggested a pea. Martin peered into the bag. "No, there are no peas in here."

"What about a pig?"

"No, I don't think a pig would fit in here."

Before this curriculum went into use, Cone's Head Start director, Lue Alma Sumlin, said, "We had children who were not talking. They would nod their heads or point and their parents were accepting that. We said they had to talk to the children, not at the children. Parents think a four-year-old is still a baby. One was talking baby talk instead of talking as you would to another adult."

Sumlin started a toy- and book-lending library so that the children and their parents could work and play together at home. Through a "Read to Me" Book Club, the parent who had read the most books to her child within a month won a prize, usually an educational toy. One grand prize was a battery-operated toy computer that helped children learn about animals. Through such projects, children got reinforcement at home that reading was important, and the parents found out how much their child could really learn, Sumlin said.

Sumlin has tried to involve more parents because she knows from experience how the program can change lives. Her son had been in Head Start. She was working as a keypunch operator at the time, and she didn't like keypunching, so she quit to take a job as an assistant teacher with Head Start. She went back to school and earned an associate of arts degree in early childhood development; she was heading the Sunnyview Head Start Center when Mary Fulbright's team arrived to do its analysis. When the Margaret Cone center grew out of that study, Sumlin applied for the director's job and got it. Meantime, her son had become an Eagle Scout and started college.

Each year the Cone program collaborators have studied their results, received feedback from the teachers, and adjusted the curriculum to correct weaknesses. For example, they realized that children need help developing the grip for holding a pencil and learning to write. Children go through a sequence of motions when they pick up pencils or crayons—first grabbing, then grasping, then squeezing, and finally pinching in the way one holds a pencil—so the curriculum was enlarged to include activities to help children develop their hand muscles and coordination, both in play and at snack time. The Cone program also extended the length of time the language enrichment curriculum was used for the fifth group to go through the program, and the children made even more gains in their language skills that year. Another year they added the section of the curriculum concerning concepts to teach the ideas of rhyming, opposites, and plurals as well as size, shape, color, and number.

The program at the Cone center costs more than other Head Starts. Each year it spends $5,700 per child while Head Start at other Dallas centers costs about $3,300 per child. Nationwide, the average cost per child was $4,534 in the mid-1990s. Since the Texas Instruments Foundation started exploring the possibility of creating a model preschool program, it has contributed a total of $1.41 million for the Cone center project.

The investment has reaped rewards. At a research conference in Washington in 1996, the collaborators presented these conclusions: Results from a variety of tests of the groups that attended Cone from the second through the sixth years "reveal a pattern of improved performance in vocabulary, language skills, concept development and social-adaptive skills during the years of the language enrichment program. The children who participated in the LEAP curriculum, in addition to a nurturing environment, received better scores on the Iowa Test of Basic Skills and report cards than those children who did not." The curriculum helped children enter kindergarten at grade level and strengthened their chances for success in school.

Frazier Elementary is working to sustain the gains the Head Start children bring with them. "When we first started, the school was a sad place. The old principal had retired on the job. There was no excitement," Mike Rice said. The school got a new principal and within a matter of weeks, it started to turn around. "All of a sudden there were posters all over the place. All of a sudden there were people walking in the halls smiling. All of a sudden there was a sign inside the door urging parents that if they had any questions, they should ask the principal, and her office is this way." The new principal looked at how the kindergarten classes were performing. She found some good teachers, some bad, and retrained or got rid of the bad ones.

The Cone center program has affected not only its own children and families but also the Dallas Head Start program in general. Seeing the differences that smaller caseloads made for social workers' ability to work with families, Head Start of Greater Dallas hired more social workers and aides. That enabled them to cut in half the number of families with whom each deals at other Head Start centers, improving the program's ability to connect people to the services they need and to help the families resolve issues that concern them, a Head Start spokesman said. The program also hired two more nurses to serve other areas.

Head Start is also using the language curriculum at the Rosie M. Harris Center in south Dallas. The SMU curriculum writers had tested their curriculum there, and its director said, "When are you coming back?" That expansion was financed by Head Start. A third center (and the second financed in part by the Texas Instruments Foundation) opened in 1997. Between them, TIF, the Patrick and Beatrice Haggerty Foundation, and the Eugene McDermott Foundation contributed nine hundred thousand dollars to build the Jerry R. Junkins Child Development Center in a Hispanic neighborhood on the far west side of Dallas. The center is named for a former chief executive officer of Texas Instruments. Parents in the neighborhood were anxious to have the program because as many as 65 percent of the students in that area dropped out of school before graduating from high school. The College of Education at Texas A&M created a dual language development program for the center because the children's first language was Spanish. The San Marcos Civic Foundation supported the teacher training at SMU for the new center's staff.

I asked people who have worked with the program how it might best be duplicated elsewhere. "The first thing you have to do," director Lue Alma Sumlin said, "is get to know the people who live in the community, find out what the parents would like." That provides a basis for trust and ideas for building parent involvement. In terms of curriculum, she felt the key elements were the books, the posters, and the frequent questioning of the children so they speak as well as are spoken to.

"You can't really put a template down and copy the program," Ann Minnis said. "You have to take what you can use." Organizations that want to undertake any similar effort have to realize they're in it for the long haul and stay focused on the goal. "When you work in communities like these, so many other needs arise, but you must stay focused on your goal. Sure, you try to connect families with social services they need, but you can get derailed so quickly by those other needs. You have to focus on the goal, that is, to get the children ready to learn." A project like the Cone center is labor-intensive, Minnis added. The partners in the work hold quarterly meetings usually involving about twenty-five people. "This is a coordinating thing. If you just let it evolve," she said, "it won't happen."

Mike Rice came from an engineering background before becoming manager of corporate communications for Texas Instruments, then TIF president in 1984. Any corporation or foundation considering undertaking a similar project, he said, must get actively involved in the process. He's never missed one of Cone's quarterly meetings, for example. "You have to get in there and get your hands on. Most foundations write a check and that's the end of it."

By itself, Head Start probably would never have had the money or the time to do the study conducted by the team from the University of Texas at Arlington, nor to develop the curriculum and the teacher training that the SMU center did. Nor could it have stayed with an approach that, early on, wasn't showing the desired results. But in partnership with those universities and backed by the Texas Instruments Foundation, the Cone center has shown that poor children, given the tools, can start school ready to learn. Rice thought it was not mainly a matter of money, however, but a matter of setting goals and staying with them.

Head Start of Greater Dallas was also involved in another effort to meet contemporary conditions, a national program to serve younger children. Early Head Start is based on accumulating research that shows the importance of intervention even before children reach three or four years old; it was launched through the 1994 legislation extending Head Start's life for four years. The first year, the Department of Health and Human Services announced sixty-eight grants for programs to serve infants and toddlers up to three years old. Dallas and the KCMC Child Development Corporation of Kansas City, Missouri (see chapter 14) were included; seventy-four grants were awarded the second year. In addition to the education, nutrition, and family development aspects of Head Start, these programs also worked on health concerns for newborns, on ways grandparents as well as parents can help very young children, and on the needs of teenage parents or migrant families.

Anyone who has watched a healthy baby grow has seen him explore his surroundings, learn language, play with whatever is at hand. The pace of development can be astounding. Research and common sense both demonstrate the need for good health and caring relationships to support children physically and emotionally so that they can learn, adjust to other children, and deal with their environment. Many poor families lack decent prenatal health care; some suffer malnutrition or abuse drugs or alcohol, which can lead to low-birthweight babies, birth defects, or undeveloped brain growth. Sometimes these conditions kill children; sometimes they harm them in school or in relating to others.

Early Head Start programs employ a variety of formats. Some provide full-day, center-based care, while others are helping develop family day care for infants and toddlers. Some are based near schools and thus work more with teenage parents. Some, like the Early Head Start program run by the Venice Family Clinic near Los Angeles, are home-based. That program, which had approval to serve one hundred families with about 275 children, employed ten home visitors who spent an hour and a half each week with the families. They helped first-time parents learn what was normal in their child's stages of development and what they should expect in terms of speech or physical abilities. Most of the Venice program's children came from two-parent families; most were Latino, with a few from the Middle East. Many of the parents worked in hotels or restaurants or for gardening services.

Being near the ocean, Venice can be an expensive place to live, especially for the working poor, said program director Manuel Castellanos. Early Head Start staff can help connect the families with needed services. The clinic, a local institution since 1970, serves the low-income population that traditionally has had a difficult time finding and paying for health care. It branched into Early Head Start, Castellanos said, because "we see health as going beyond the medical."

Early Head Start is nothing new to programs for migrant children (see chapter 6), which have been providing services to infants and toddlers since 1969. The alternative was for the children to spend their days in parked cars while their parents worked or out in the fields and orchards with them.

Around the country there have been other initiatives by Head Start programs tackling unique circumstances in their communities or collaborating with other agencies to broaden their reach:

■ In Seattle, ground was broken in August 1996 for a $19.5 million International District Village Square project including housing for elderly Asians in a neglected section near Interstate 5, which cuts through the city. The project, located where once a bus barn stood, included a Head Start center, the Asian Counseling and Referral Service for mental health services, a job training program, and a health clinic.[1] The new space will allow the Denise Louie Head Start program to serve more children or expand into full-day care.

■ In San Diego, the Neighborhood House Association was working with the San Diego Unified School District, Children's Hospital, the San Diego Health Department, and local community colleges on what it called Twilight Head Start. Located in a school building in mid-city, the program used classrooms that otherwise would have sat idle after the state preschool's morning program ended. It also allowed Head Start to fulfill more of the demand for its services. Many immigrants—Hispanic, Vietnamese, Samoan—lived in the area, so the school also offered English classes for parents during the time children were in Head Start. Parents could also make field trips outside the neighborhood for grocery shopping because few stores existed in the immediate area.

■ In Huntington, West Virginia, Southwestern Community Action Council, Incorporated, had to find new space for some of its Head Start children because a school in which it had had classes was being torn

down. Other schools needed some of the space Head Start had been using because the state had recently required them to offer full-day
kindergarten. One solution was already near at hand to provide two of
the classrooms. Southwestern Community Action Council had been
working with the city, other community groups, Marshall University,
and local banks to convert an abandoned school into thirty-seven one-
bedroom apartments for elderly people. A small building next door,
which had been used to provide lunches for senior citizens, continued
in that role, but Head Start converted its gymnasium into two classrooms. Agency director Thomas Hargis, Jr., hoped the older generation
that ate lunch at the center would mingle with the younger generation to
the benefit of both.

■ In Des Moines, Iowa, Head Start faced the reality that many poor
people work the second shift, and so began a night program from 6 P.M.
to 9:30 P.M. in a downtown building. The parents of the children were
maids at local hotels, data entry operators at insurance companies, ad-
mitting clerks and nursing aides at hospitals, and factory workers. Some
were single mothers taking night classes to get off welfare. The children
already kept different schedules, sleeping later in the morning than
many of their friends, and so weren't too tired to learn at night.[2]

■ In the San Jose area, Head Start operated two centers for homeless
children in local shelters. In one case, the Santa Clara County Office of
Education, the Head Start grantee, had worked since 1985 with the
Emergency Housing Consortium to provide services for children at the
Family Living Center in Santa Clara. The center, part of a sprawling
complex near U.S. 101 that was once a mental hospital, housed families for longer than many shelters could while the parents received job
training.

As part of a demonstration project, the national Head Start office financed sixteen projects around the country from 1993 to 1996 to serve
growing homeless populations and their unique problems. Homeless
children live in surroundings that provide little privacy, often don't eat
regularly, and may have few clothes, toys, or books. As a result, they may
be slow to develop language skills, show intense aggression or depression, have trouble sleeping, and be in poor health. Their parents often
don't have jobs and lack the skills to get them.

One of the projects, Inn-Circle, was developed in 1990 by the Hawk-
eye Area Community Action Program in Cedar Rapids, Iowa. It provided transitional housing and Head Start classrooms for forty-four

families in what had been a motel. In addition to the usual factors that contribute to homelessness such as domestic abuse or the loss of low-skill jobs, the situation was exacerbated in Cedar Rapids by the loss of some low-income housing near the city's two hospitals when those apartments were converted into doctors' offices. In addition to Head Start support for its project, the community action agency received money from the Department of Housing and Urban Development. In partnership with several local businessmen, it bought the motel. The Hall Foundation helped finance major renovation; local organizations donated time and money to the work. Kirkwood Community College students also held dances to raise funds for the project. The state contributed funds for at-risk children to help support the Inn-Circle Head Start program.

Head Start has also worked with the Johnson & Johnson Foundation since 1991 to provide management training for Head Start directors in a partnership with the University of California, Los Angeles's Anderson Graduate School of Management. About 40 directors participate in each two-week seminar as Head Start–Johnson & Johnson Management Fellows; in the first seven years of the program, 444 people received the training. The program, headed by Dr. Alfred E. Osborne, Jr., who also directs UCLA's Entrepreneurial Studies Center, includes lectures, group discussions, and workshops on human resource management, finance, computers and information systems, operations, and marketing—areas in which many Head Start directors have said they felt weak. They are also areas in which competence is essential as Head Start expands.

Working with teaching associates, the fellows develop management improvement projects to help them tackle problems when they return to their centers. When I visited one seminar, Margaret Adams of Westfield, Massachusetts, had as her goal improving her program's ability to handle children's inappropriate behavior—what we once called "acting up" but which often takes on more serious overtones today because of the underlying problems it can reveal. She developed a plan that incorporated teacher training and mental health counseling. Beverly Graywater, project director for Early Head Start in Fort Totten, North Dakota, wanted to reduce duplication of social services for the Devil's Lake Sioux tribe her Head Start program served. "Our families often have more than one case manager," she told her colleagues. "The families get frustrated. We cannot afford to waste any of the social services we have," so she sought to reduce the number of case managers and increase cooperation. Betty Toney of Dayton, Ohio, had fourteen new Head Start classrooms but difficulty obtaining quality staff, so she was developing a training program for Head Start parents.

"The program is designed to provide directors with a strategic management perspective," Osborne said. It helps them see the challenges they face and align their organizations to meet them. "Rather than believe, 'Woe is me,' they can be able to say, 'We've got a challenge here—how are we going to meet it?'

"We try to help them think strategically, to learn that they're in control of their future—to look at marketing, operations, their own role, how they work with their staff, how they feel about accounting or financial statements. These Head Start directors are resourceful, as entrepreneurs often have to be. They have to find matching funds. They may be trying to make do in a basement that's not working. Their resourcefulness is great. They are people with a heart. All we're trying to do is say it's great to have a heart, but sometimes you need to have a hard head about what you're doing when you allocate resources or make business decisions about which groups of children to serve.

"They need to know, for example, how to evaluate a lease. Is this a good lease or a bad lease? They don't need to know everything about the subject but they need to be able to ask their leasing agent key questions," Osborne said. "We try to buttress their ability to better serve children and families.

"We also make every effort to be sure the Head Start director is treated as an executive here. Too often people think of them as somebody's nursemaid. They are the leader and strategic person. By doing the program the way we do it, I think we get an extra bonus making people really feel good about themselves because they are doing important stuff."

Watts Towers:

Michael breaks the piñata for Cinco de Mayo. Veronica Perez reflects on her experiences as a volunteer. The teachers and children, looking straight out of *Cleopatra*, go on parade. Shardae, Andre, and the rest help milk a cow.

Every year the Training and Research Foundation's Head Start centers held an International Awareness Day parade, featuring children dressed in costumes from countries around the world. Preparations began during the winter with costume designs, discussions of how much money to spend, recruitment of seamstresses, costume fittings, and, almost parenthetically, lessons for the children about the countries they would be portraying. Parenthetically, because more emphasis seemed to be placed on the costumes than on the cultures. So many events were scheduled for the spring, so much pressure was on the teachers, that the educational aspect of the event seemed lost in the shuffle.

As preparations continued, the centers observed Cinco de Mayo. That is a major day for festivities in Hispanic portions of the United States, commemorating a key Mexican victory in 1862 over the French, who threatened their independence. As they had during Black History Month, the Watts Towers children rehearsed a program for their parents. Teachers Josephine Garner and Lupe Osuna were firm believers that the children needed to know about and appreciate each other's cultures.

On the morning of the Cinco de Mayo program, Osuna was busy helping the girls slip on white skirts trimmed in red and green, the Mexican national colors. The girls practiced holding their skirts out like giant fans for the dancing later. Maria said no, she didn't want to dance, but eventually she did put on one of the skirts. She was promised that she wouldn't have to perform. Two little girls from the afternoon Head Start class, both named Aurora, were outfitted as different versions of Selena Quintanilla Perez, the Tejano pop singer killed by an admirer a year earlier and already an icon to many Latino families. During the year, I had frequently seen several of the little girls wearing Selena

T-shirts. One of the Selenas-for-a-Day wore a lacy pink frock and the other had on a tight black shirt and white short skirt. They lip-synched with a Selena record as they swayed in front of applauding parents, who particularly cheered when they sobbed out *"bebé"* in one of the songs.

The children picked partners to dance, and Wayne rushed to ask Janette to dance. Raymound's mother tried to talk him into dancing, but he would have none of that. After Kimberly and Karina sang a favorite song with gusto, the Auroras wanted to do an encore. They spun around while they sang, then curtsied, knowing they were the hit of the day.

The children went outside to attack the piñata that Garner had strung up under a sunroof. She told the children that on the first round they shouldn't hit the piñata too hard so that everyone would have a turn. A father who was delivering a set of loudspeakers for the afternoon program argued that Garner should let whoever could break it to do so. "We do it for fun," Garner explained to him, trying not to lose her patience as he kept hectoring her. "We want everybody to have a turn. This isn't a party. This is school." They did it her way and each of the children had several turns. Michael—remember, he was one of the bigger boys—took several mighty whacks at the piñata. The second time around it started to tear and eventually broke. The parents divided the candy inside for the children to take home.

Twenty parents, several with babies in tow, attended the program. As we chatted in the back of the room, Veronica Perez contrasted the attendance for Cinco de Mayo with the cancellation of two TRF parenting workshops the week before because nobody showed up. Food and children's performances seemed the only guarantees of a turnout for some, except for Perez and half a dozen other faithful volunteers. Perez had been at the center virtually every day I was there and many others besides.

"I didn't plan on volunteering," she said, thinking back over her four years of involvement with Head Start. Her oldest daughter, Cynthia, had cried when she was left at the center, so Perez started staying with her and learning what she could do to help the program. "One of the main reasons I put her in Head Start was to learn English. I didn't want her in bilingual classes. I didn't want that to hold her back. Even so, when she was tested, she was given English as a second language. But I got her into an English-only class in second grade. Diana [her second daughter] had two years of Head Start so when she was tested, she went right into English-only."

Head Start also helped Perez become more involved in her children's educations. "Nobody is going to be able to tell me what they know and don't know. I know because I work with them at home. Or if they don't know something, I know that. For example, Diana's teacher was doing numbers with them and told me Diana didn't know a 6. She tried to make me think that she was playing, that she really did know it. I said, no, she doesn't know 6, she gets it confused with a 9. I try to have them do their homework when I'm not cooking or cleaning. I want to be there. I make sure they're really learning it." They were. Cynthia was later identified as gifted, which made her parents very proud.

"Head Start is not for kids only but for the whole family," Perez added. Head Start had helped her overcome some of her shyness about talking to her neighbors. "I still get a little nervous in meetings. Until I started volunteering, I'd be in my pajamas all day. I had no place to go." The year after her youngest child, Janette, left Head Start, Perez was volunteering at the girls' elementary school.

Whole families—several hundred of them—lined the children's parade route a week later for TRF's International Awareness Day at Jesse Owens Park, a short bus ride from the Watts Towers center. Even though I remained concerned about how much the children were learning amid all the hoopla, I had to admit it was quite a show. Boosting morale for families and the staff does have its place. Purple jacarandas were blooming, and they combined with the children's aqua, red, and blue costumes to produce a riot of color. Wearing a blue-and-white Hawaiian-style dress, TRF's Head Start director, Elaine Atlow, announced each group as it paraded by. First came Jordan Downs children in the elegant outfits of India. Parents were snapping pictures and videotaping the banners from each center and the costumed children and teachers. Then came Watts Towers. Dressed in floor-length gold sheaths, Garner, Osuna, Gloria Heyman, and Deborah Chatman all looked as though they had stepped out of the movie *Cleopatra*. The children in their Egyptian costumes stepped along, waving to people they knew. Some of the girls had on long purple dresses, some wore white. The boys were handsome in short white outfits with blue trim and aqua fezzes that looked straight out of a picture book on the land of the pharaohs. Annette Russell led the children of the Imperial Courts center in Mexican costumes, and then came Guatemala and Somalia, American Indians and Hawaiians, Germans and others from around the world.

Once the children walked the short parade route, they crossed a grassy field where there was a display of objects from each country. I found myself hoping they had absorbed something about Egypt, Mexico, Guatemala, and the other countries. It wasn't that I didn't like a good time—but I wasn't sure this program was anything more than a big show that had preoccupied the teachers and parents far too long.

The children seemed as interested in a fire truck and a police car brought to the park for them to explore as they had been in the parade. Garner boosted children up the big step into the cab of the fire truck while across the field Los Angeles Police Department officer Tim Wunderlich let the children turn on the siren and speak into the microphone. Some said "Hi" or an authoritative "Pull over!" Andre had his turn, and soon it was Shardae's time at the mike. "I love you, Miz Garner" blared out.

Site 05's year was winding down, but there were two more field trips, one to see farm animals and one to Chuck E. Cheese for pizza. I opted for the farm animals. We climbed aboard a school bus, this time driving north and east to the Ernest Debs Park in Monterey Park, where Green Meadows had set up its animal pens and corrals. I sat with Michael and Maria, still a shy child, who had been persuaded to go on this trip after missing several earlier adventures. Lupe Osuna had sent Maria's mother a pamphlet about what the children would see at Green Meadows and written a letter in Spanish urging that she encourage her daughter to go along. "I said it would be good for her to go."

So that morning Maria had walked into the center and announced proudly that she was going and she wasn't going to cry. Several times on the bus, she called out, "Miz Garner, I'm not crying," or "Miz Osuna, I'm not crying." School buses lined the lane as we pulled into the park. We were met by "Farmer Francesca," her name tag said, a personable young woman who urged the children to use their "walking feet" as they moved from animal enclosure to animal enclosure. Josephine Garner translated that to mean "don't run." All around the park were fenced-in areas where pigs, chickens, cows, and horses grazed or slept.

First, the children saw the pigs. Francesca explained that pigs rolled in the mud to stay cool. She asked the children not to pet the baby pigs, who were sleeping. The children moved easily and unafraid among the animals. Then they headed for the chickens' enclosure. "Pick them up and hold their wings so they don't flap and then don't drop them," Francesca instructed. "Put them down gently." Little Jenyffer, one of the youngest of the children, with the biggest, most beautiful eyes, headed right for one of the chickens and picked it up easily. Her mother took several photographs. Behind Jenyffer, Andre was getting pecked by one of the chickens. He giggled.

After the children petted two camels through a fence and Osuna made faces at the camels, much to the children's delight, we went to see Angie the black-and-white cow. The *patient* black-and-white cow, because Francesca had each of the children squeeze Angie's teat lightly and "help" milk her. Francesca warned the children not to step behind Angie because she might kick them. Patience does have its limits.

Eight parents accompanied the children, including Joshua's mother, Jenyffer's, and Anthony and César's, plus the teachers and aides. The parents watched with special pleasure as each child climbed aboard a horse to be walked on a brief ride around a ring. One little girl held on for dear life but the rest were pleased as punch, looking as though they'd been in the saddle for a lifetime. Andre grinned. Raymound grinned. Maria grinned. She still wasn't crying. We picnicked at tables under nearby trees. Then, as the children started to get restless, Osuna gathered some of them around her, and one spontaneously began singing "Old MacDonald Had a Farm." The children made all the animal noises with new enthusiasm.

Back on the bus, I joined Jameisha, and we talked about the animals she had seen. Soon she was nodding off. It had been a full morning. Would she like to take a nap? She nodded, put her head down on my lap, and zonked out immediately, sleeping so soundly I had trouble waking her when the bus pulled up at the center. We had a busload of tired but happy children, including Maria, sound asleep on Garner's lap. And yes, still not crying.

Chapter Sixteen

Summing Up and Looking Ahead

ead Start works. Head Start can work better.

Head Start performs its mission of preparing children to enter kindergarten ready to learn. Research supports that conclusion (see chapter 8). Whether the clear immediate gains in cognitive abilities and self-confidence are sustained over the longer term into the elementary-school years is a matter of debate. Sometimes they are; sometimes they aren't. The quality of the elementary schools, not of Head Start, should be the focus of that debate, however.

There are excellent Head Start programs. There are ordinary Head Start programs. And there are bad Head Start programs. The Clinton administration has moved to improve quality, but any state governor, any regional Head Start administrator, can take you to poor programs. These programs generally need either more inspired leadership, better teacher training and pay, more community support, increased parent involvement, or better buildings—or all of the above. In short, they need some kind of shot in the arm. Improving quality should be the number one task ahead, and it should not be compromised as Head Start seeks to serve more children and serve them for longer hours each day.

Head Start has been working to improve children's transition into elementary school, to upgrade its teaching staff, and to serve younger children and those who need full-day care. But Head Start staffs are not miracle workers: they need congressional support, not continual congressional carping. For their part, Head Start centers should be doing more congressional consciousness-raising. They must make sure their members of Congress know where they are, whom they serve, what they do, and what their program's needs are. By now, there are enough Head Start graduates of voting age who should identify themselves and speak up for the program that helped them.

Head Start parents also should become more politically involved; unless they vote and raise their issues with lawmakers, they will be overlooked in favor of those with louder voices or deeper pockets. They do have allies in Congress—from Democratic senator Edward M. Kennedy of Massachusetts, a longtime supporter, to Republican representative Frank Riggs of California, who helped head off major cuts to the program in 1995. Two California members of Congress even have firsthand Head Start experience—Loretta Sanchez, as a student, and Maxine Waters, as a staff member. Many Head Start parents might find that their children have shared experiences with Sanchez. The daughter of Mexican immigrants, she attended Head Start in the summer of 1965 and has called it "one of the most fundamental experiences of my life." An extremely shy child, Sanchez remembered that she was frightened of the English-speaking environment, but Head Start's snack time helped stop her crying. "If you come from a Latino family," she said, "you never have celery and peanut butter." That did the trick.[1]

Historical perspective is important in thinking about Head Start. This program has affected America's schools as well as the children it has served directly. Whereas some states did not even offer kindergartens when Head Start began, today twenty-eight states have public *pre*kindergarten programs of their own, often directed at children with special needs, including poverty. That's a product of many strands of development within early childhood care and education, but Head Start is key. It has served as the most visible national laboratory demonstrating the benefits of early intervention. Head Start has also shown many teachers and principals the value of having parents in the classroom and more directly involved with their children's educations. Good teachers and good principals already knew that, of course, but sometimes they had difficulty overcoming the wariness some parents felt. Head Start was in many cases a comfortable venue through which parents who might not have done well in school themselves could establish new ties for the sake of their children.

From late 1994 into 1997, I visited Head Start centers across the country. I saw toddlers learning to explore their surroundings and four-year-olds learning to write and gaining confidence. I heard parents' stories of their new abilities to work with their children and their own expanding horizons. I found out what teachers and administrators felt that they needed to do their jobs better. Much of my evidence is anecdotal, journalistic. To help myself frame the discussion of the issues ahead for Head Start, I also spoke with two experts who have written extensively about early childhood programs. Both testified at the 1994 Senate hearings about legislation, later passed, reauthorizing Head Start until September 1998: Douglas Besharov, resident scholar at the American Enterprise Institute,[2] and Yale University psychology professor Edward Zigler.[3] I knew in advance that I would hear contrasting views, which is what I wanted in order to illustrate the nature of the debate.

At the time of their 1994 testimony, the government had just released a report on the future of Head Start prepared by a forty-seven-member committee on which both Besharov and Zigler had served. Besharov warned that the panel had prepared "a wish list of expensive 'quality enhancements' to the program." By so doing, "we have fed those forces that are making Head Start too expensive for its own good." He estimated that if a majority of the improvements the committee had recommended were adopted, it would cost about ten thousand dollars to deliver twelve months of full-time Head Start. "Other publicly supported child care programs—of roughly comparable quality—cost about six thousand dollars," he added. He repeated that concern when we spoke. Whether you accept Besharov's figures or his assertion about quality—and not everyone does—keeping Head Start from pricing itself out of the market will remain a focus each time Congress considers extending the life of the program.

Besharov has also written that Head Start is too big, so quality control is a problem. I think it's not big enough *and* quality control is a problem. Zigler has urged improving Head Start's quality for decades. Agreeing on the quality-control point, then, where do we go from there?

The way Head Start is funded—the same programs receive money each year, virtually unchallenged unless the reviews every three years have found major flaws—does not provide incentives for initiatives and improvement, Besharov told me. There is no competition for the grants, therefore no incentive for improvement, he added. His argument is supported by the National Governors' Association, which would like to see states that want to provide these services allowed to compete for Head Start grants. There are "many poorly performing centers," Besharov said—and the governors privately agree—and parents should be able to vote with their feet by enrolling their children somewhere else.

Head Start has recognized the problem of quality control but, Besharov added, it seems unwilling to accept the idea that the process has to be changed. Head Start must have a competitive process that allows programs to go out of operation if they aren't performing, he said. Head Start, of course, will tell you that programs do go out of business—the process is written into the most recent performance standards—but it is clear that the program's small national and regional staffs cannot check local centers often enough and thoroughly enough to ensure quality in every single center. That process may need changing—but to a system in which every annual budget and its supporting documentation from every grantee is given the careful scrutiny it deserves and sometimes does not receive. Head Start directors sometimes feel as though they send their reports into a great void. If the government must hire inspectors and pay for their travel, then it should do so; otherwise, it is only paying lip service to quality.

Besharov testified about the need for more coordination between federal programs like Head Start and state preschool programs to avoid needless duplication and better mesh performance standards and practices. "If you had your druthers," I asked him, "would you like to see states managing Head Start?"

"Yes."

"Why?"

"State-run Head Start would be better coordinated with other child care programs," he replied. As the system is now, child care programs are age-segregated. The state's basic child care money covers younger children and Head Start usually serves three- and four-year-olds. They bounce from program to program, Besharov said. The only way to ensure coordination, he added, is to have states running Head Start. Moving Head Start to the states is not an argument to destroy it, he maintained, but rather to protect it and to regularize the interaction between it and other programs.

I asked Edward Zigler the same questions about what remains to be done to improve Head Start quality and whether authority over the program should be shifted to the states. "Quality control is a daily task that Head Start has got to do as far into the future as I can see," he replied. "With the diversity of programs, there's still a long way to go. One study of Head Start programs in North Carolina, for example, showed only eight percent of high quality. Having said that, I couldn't be more impressed with what the Clinton administration has done" in trying to raise the level of performance. He had urged similar improvements during the Reagan and Bush administrations, he said, and no one listened. "In the past," Zigler went on, "if you had a really rotten program and Head Start tried to lift your grant, you'd just call your congressman. They have to be very courageous to do what they've done."

Where any competition should enter the picture is during expansion or launching new parts of the program, such as Early Head Start, Zigler said. That's the time to visit the sites, learn who the people are who'll be running the programs, and pick the best ones. But he disagreed with Besharov on requiring wider competition for existing programs. "If you have people having to reapply every three years, you don't have the kind of permanence that you need. That's the downside of that idea." If everyone has to face frequent competition, he added, "then we'll spend more money reviewing applications than on the program."

Should the states run Head Start?

"If the states did the Head Start model—," Zigler began, then stopped, saying that what he cared about was the services families received. "Do they have medical services? Do they have social services" in the state preschool programs? He had been reviewing the states that have preschool programs and "so far it looks to me as though Head Start is superior to what they offer. They don't have the comprehensive services. They don't have the parental involvement that Head Start does. None of them have that degree of involvement. If I thought the states were going to do that—I don't believe that's going to happen. If we give Head Start to the states, the governors are going to take the Head Start money and continue programs that are marginal programs."

This debate led me to the National Governors' Association. Some governors doubtless would like access to Head Start money as they wrestle with increasing need for child care brought on by changes in the welfare laws. But a 1996 issue brief and policy statement applicable into 1998 places the governors, publicly at least, on the side of collaboration, not takeover. It's clear from the statement that the governors see barriers to such collaboration because child care and Head Start programs have traditionally competed for some of the same children and remain reluctant to cooperate. These programs see themselves as having different missions and different standards. Colorado's governor, Roy Romer, an advocate of early childhood education who is also chairman of the Democratic National Committee, is one who thinks Head Start is ill-advised in resisting coordination with more traditional day care. Speaking in March 1997 before a meeting of child-care experts, Romer said, to Head Start administrators who say, " 'Don't touch us because you're going to pollute our program,' I say, 'You're wrong.' Don't put walls around yourselves so that you're so pristine but so far from the working people."[4]

Undaunted, the governors have urged more incentives for collaboration. The national Head Start office appeared to have heard the governors when it said that it would use expansion money for the first time for programs that formed partnerships with other state and local agencies to provide full-day services (see chapter 15).

Throughout the 1990s, in Congress and elsewhere, the principal issues surrounding Head Start have concerned the quality control that both Besharov and Zigler addressed as well as questions about expansion. Should the program serve younger children? The government has said yes in launching its Early Head Start programs for infants and toddlers. More and more research indicates the impact on brain development of talking to children and bonding with them in their first months of life; these findings may increase pressures to offer more Early Head Start programs. Should Head Start expand to serve all eligible children? That seemed the direction the Bush administration preferred. Should it use its money to provide full-day, full-year services, or should it stay with the children it already has served as they go into elementary school, as the transition projects did?

These issues will only be magnified by the 1996 changes in the welfare laws—what the headline on an *Atlantic Monthly* article by former administration official Peter Edelman called "The Worst Thing Bill Clinton Has Done."[5] There may not be enough money from federal and state sources to cover the child care needs of all those who must find work instead of receiving welfare. Those needs could be enormous. In California, for example, a children's advocacy group has estimated that while the current system meets only about one-third of the need for subsidized child care, that need will more than double in the next three years—from 240,000 children to 560,000.[6]

President Clinton wants to expand Head Start to serve 1 million children by the year 2002. That's a big leap from the nearly 800,000 enrolled in 1997, but one that can and must be made. The move can best be accomplished by learning from recent history and planning with more foresight. The program expanded from 451,000 to 714,000 during George Bush's presidency and it is still recovering. Head Start is not like a soft-drink machine, where you put in your money and out comes a can; you also must have the factory, the workers, the transportation, the ingredients, and the formula. A report by the Department of Health and Human Services' Office of Inspector General in 1993 after the earlier expansion found that sound planning and timely funding did not always occur. Interviews with eighty Head Start grantees revealed that there weren't enough buildings available to provide the necessary classrooms for expansion, they weren't in good shape, or the rent was too high. Forty percent of the programs had difficulty finding the additional qualified staff that they needed, and some ran into problems paying for more transportation as well. Expansion also increased the demands on social services because children were enrolled who had behavioral problems or special needs and they came from families that had more drug or alcohol abuse. The warning lights are there in the report. In Head Start, children learn through experience; Congress and the president must do the same when contemplating expansion.

It is obvious from the thrust of this book that I would like to see far more children benefit from Head Start. Congress and the White House should give Head Start and local programs time to draw up a strategic plan that outlines the regions of the country and the groups of children who most need additional Head Start slots, Early Head Start, or full-day, year-round programs. They should do so with the assurance that the money will still be there when the need is identified, the classroom space found, the teachers trained.

We know what to do to improve Head Start while expanding it. In report after report, experts have also outlined what children and their families need to improve their opportunities in life. It's time for national political leaders to stop nibbling around the edges and pledge to do the job, not just for 40 percent of America's eligible children but for all of them. That is a Contract with America that would truly benefit its families.

The people who must tackle these issues—quality control, expansion and its attendant problems, the effect of new welfare laws—by and large will not be those who launched the program. Many of the pioneering adults of Head Start have reached or are nearing retirement age. The mission that they felt may become "just a job" among some staff members, especially administrators who have never worked in a Head Start center. Keeping that spirit alive is more vital than ever so that poor parents can continue to discover their possibilities and poor children can see that someone cares about them and their education. Keeping that spirit alive is difficult, however, for a program that must constantly recruit or train new teachers because of turnover and expansion. Head Start needs more hands-on, well-supervised training to give new teachers techniques that work with young children and build in that sense of enthusiasm that carried the program through its early days. The public has an important role, too: it must recognize that what those teachers are doing is important, and reward them for doing it, so they'll stay the distance.

In addition to maintaining its sense of mission in changing times, there are three other critical areas that involve Head Start's vision of itself. First, parent involvement; second, language; third, public perceptions.

Parent involvement is a hallmark of Head Start. It seems far more successful in bringing parents into more contact with its centers than the public schools are, perhaps because the children are little and parents are still enthusiastic when they're so young. Changes in the welfare laws and the entry of more mothers into the workforce means that Head Start must work more creatively to keep parents involved. Perhaps by working with other community organizations (see chapter 10), Head Start can learn what parents need and what activities would increase their level of participation. Toward this end, the family advocates employed by many of the programs I visited can provide invaluable links with parents. There should be more of them, and they should have smaller caseloads.

Head Start also must acknowledge in its hiring practices and in its training that it increasingly serves the children of immigrants who do not speak English. Usually they speak Spanish at home, but sometimes it's a Southeast Asian language, even Creole or an African language. Yes, these children need to learn English and they do, but their frustrations are eased when someone in the classroom can talk freely to them in their own language. Many Head Start programs must find or train more truly bilingual teachers—no easy task when bilingual people are in great demand. Training more parents who speak Spanish or Asian languages as classroom aides would also help the children cope better.

It is to Head Start's credit that it has concentrated on its program, not its public relations. But at budget time and other periods of crisis, that low profile works to Head Start's disadvantage. Who beyond the world of Head Start knows what its staff does every day, what they seek to achieve? The National Head Start Association, the professional organization of program directors and staff members, works toward the goal of telling the public and policymakers what they do, but, given limited federal resources, it may need to do more in its home communities to remind people that Head Start still exists. Local Head Start directors need to establish more links with the media, to showcase good programs and teachers, to highlight their innovations as well as families' success stories. Americans rarely see anything in the media about Head Start, unless a presidential candidate visits a local center in an election year. If they have heard of Head Start, members of the public and even policymakers often have no idea of its comprehensive nature, its impact on families as well as children.

The media are at fault for this inattention as much as Head Start. Head Start falls between the cracks of education and welfare coverage. Yet in one recent year, Head Start contributed almost $400 million to the California economy through program salaries and other expenses, almost $150 million to Illinois programs, even $7.6 million in Vermont. Would other grants of similar magnitude receive better news coverage? It's hard to interview four-year-olds, so Head Start doesn't generate the media attention that a gang fight at a high school does or even a successful advanced math class. Most Americans know more about the O. J. Simpson trials than about the children at their local Head Start center. Is it losing children because their parents need full-day care? How does it train its teachers? Who runs it? Do your local newspapers or television stations ever tell you?

Head Start needs everyone's attention, not just that of the children and families it serves. As Edward Zigler said, "Head Start will prosper to the extent that it is always being reevaluated. From the beginning, it has been an evolving process." One of the biggest lessons has been that Head Start cannot do it alone. No one program could, and this one is hardly perfect. No one today would dare announce that Head Start would end poverty as we know it. Too many hazards face children and their families while they are in Head Start and after they leave. Head Start is only that, a start. People need jobs so they can buy their way out of poverty, and to get jobs they need better education. They need transportation to reach the jobs that are no longer in their own neighborhoods. And they need those neighborhoods to be safer so they feel secure going to a Head Start meeting. What is still needed is war on the real causes of poverty, not our current war on those in poverty.

A word now about what I personally have learned through examining Head Start for the last three years. My journey taught me how near the edge many in America live today. It reminded me again and again not to stereotype people, never to anticipate someone's words or attitudes by his or her station in life. The poor are not one formless clump of people but a collection of remarkable, resilient individuals—yes, and some who are violent or lazy or crazy, just like the rest of the world. I saw how people make do with what they have—and how much more they would like to do for their children. I met people with little to sell in the marketplace but strong backs and willing hands because they had no education, and I was so thankful I had always enjoyed reading and writing and could make a living with those tools.

For all my caveats, I saw something the federal government has been doing right—sometimes despite itself. The Head Start program that Lyndon Johnson and Sargent Shriver launched has been tempered by thousands of hands. It has faced threats to its very existence, and it has endured, in large measure because of broadly based local support. This program has transcended the nation's ambivalence about federal involvement in education and care for poor children. It has helped families so that they in turn may help build something better for their children. It may undergo stress as never before in helping meet the increasing need of services for poor children and their families, but it is still there, trying.

Epilogue

The Last Day of School at Watts Towers Center

Year's end. I had grown attached to these children at Watts Towers. Teachers get used to children moving on. They always have another class entering in the summer or the fall. I didn't. I had seen the children at the Watts Towers center becoming more confident, more comfortable in the outside world. Yes, you could have told me how Raymound started to join the games or flashed a winning smile, but seeing that happen for myself was a rare opportunity for a journalist. Too often we must take a snapshot of the garden rather than having the chance to watch it grow. You could have told me how Marisol started to speak or Maria didn't cry on field trips or Andre comforted Jesús instead of being restless himself, but seeing for myself showed me what Head Start does.

Sadly, I also saw some loving children who, confronted with school's definition of success, will fail. Who cannot pay attention and may never learn how, who will fall behind unless someone lights a spark that so far seems nonexistent. Performing that miracle requires teachers and counselors who have more time and smaller classes than they now have, and it has to happen early or the child becomes too frustrated to hang on. I saw others who were so bright that they might not be sufficiently challenged by overworked or apathetic public-school teachers and so would lose that wonderful light that I had seen in their eyes. I wondered which among these thirty-two children might someday invite their Head Start teachers to their high school or college graduations. Or which would pay the taxes to help run programs like Head Start in the future. Or which might be teenage moms or unemployed. They do not face an easy world there in Watts.

I discovered how good teachers can pull out of children words that are there but as yet unspoken, activity that is there but as yet untapped. On a very basic level, I was reminded how difficult a concept the word s-h-a-r-e can be for a four-year-old and how vital getting along with the child next to you is for success in school.

I saw mothers learning what they could do for their children—and for themselves; learning that they had talents and ideas that were worthy. I had seen others with just as much potential who simply dropped their children off in the morning, not to be seen again until noon—just like the BMW set in wealthier neighborhoods. "Drop and run," a PTA president I know had called them. I had seen only two fathers directly involved with their children's Head Start centers in this Los Angeles–area program in this particular year.

And I attended the year-end activities and watched the preparations for the children's next school year. Teachers Josephine Garner and Lupe Osuna showed each parent her child's individual education plan and talked with the parents about whether their goals had been met. The Training and Research Foundation stored these files at its office in case the next school the children attended had any questions. Wayne, for example, still needed help recognizing certain letters in the alphabet. Marisol was doing better with speech but still needed to work on it. Garner was encouraging Shardae to develop better eating habits. Osuna translated into Spanish the material in the children's health reports for some of the mothers and helped them collect the documentation they would need to enroll their children in kindergarten.

Garner was stepping up her efforts to make sure the children knew their colors, numbers, and shapes. She worked one morning at a little table with Raven, Andre, Ciara, Edwin, Wayne, and Jesús, who by this time was missing several front baby teeth, as were several of the other children. Most of this group did well although Jesús could count only to three. "That's why you need to pay attention," Garner told him. Another morning she asked him to bring her four crayons; he brought three. But he did know all his colors when she had him pick them out.

Ciara twisted in her chair. "Ciara, I took you out of the circle because you weren't paying attention," Garner said. Ciara tried to coach Andre as he picked out the shapes but Garner cautioned her, "Ciara, he needs to know himself because he's going to be going to school in Long Beach and you are not going to be there."

One early June morning there was time for one more walk around
the block to Watts Towers. A workman twenty-five feet high on scaffolding for the tower renovation waved at the children below as they
gazed at the inlaid stones and picked out familiar shapes. On the walk
back, Marcus aimed an imaginary pistol—his finger—at a barking dog.
"Marcus," Osuna called out, "we don't have guns." As we headed back
to the classroom, Donisha and Clintishabeth wrapped their arms around
my knees, making it slow going. Clintishabeth had always been given to
hugging, but this was new for Donisha. Osuna nodded at the scene,
saying that Clintishabeth had helped bring Donisha out of her shell.

Counselor Julie Kammerer arrived and worked with Wayne and Richard to see if they recognized colors and drawings of common objects.
"This is the only site I have," she said, "where all the kids know their
colors. This is what it's all about in Head Start—at the end of the year
the kids know their colors and so many things. They are so much better
prepared for school. They've made the transition from home, learned to
be a bit more on their own. It makes such a big difference."

Garner was talking with the children about kindergarten, whereupon
Shardae announced out of the blue, "I'm getting tired of this school."
Her father came in a few minutes later and told her she should still listen to her teacher because she had always liked this school. He knew
she was ready to move on after two years, he told her quietly, but for
now she was still at this center and she needed to behave. Meantime,
Anthony was sitting on a beanbag chair next to me, telling me what he
was going to learn in kindergarten. "I'm going to learn everything.
When I go, I'm going to be good or they'll take me to the office." Anthony's mother, who volunteered often, told me that he didn't speak
any English when he began in Head Start. "He's learned a lot. He used
to be . . . separate," she said, trying to find the right word in English
herelf. "Now he has lots of friends and is friendly." César, her younger
son, "had just a few words. Now he talks. He's more social."

Raymound's three-year-old brother Jovanny had just started Head
Start. A big boy, although not yet as tall as his brother, Jovanny previously had been the free spirit able to roam around the center while his
mother volunteered. Now that he was enrolled, he had to do what the
other children did, and he hadn't completely switched roles in his mind
yet. He'd punch the boy next to him or start outside when everyone
else was inside. His wandering made me realize how much the other
children had changed since fall and settled down into the routine.

Several of the children were writing their names on little slates. Kimberly, one of the two Karinas, and Janette could write their whole names, first and last. Marisol did an M and an S, Jesús made a J and an e, and Garner oohed and aahed over them. Later she worked with some of the children on their numbers, especially to see if they recognized them out of order. "That's easy," Ciara said, while the others—Janette, Raven, Cindy, Raymound, Clintishabeth, and Donisha—spoke more quietly; but all seemed to know their numbers well.

Another June morning, several days before the children were to go to Chuck E. Cheese for pizza, Maria and her grandmother came into the center very early. Maria was afraid they would go to Chuck E. Cheese without her. When she converted, she converted. When the other children arrived, they sang, "If You're Happy and You Know It, Clap Your Hands," clapping and then stomping their feet and whistling with as much enthusiasm as they had the first day of school in September.

"Donisha says she knows her numbers," Garner said with a note of joy in her voice. She put large wooden numbers on each of six chairs and asked one of the children to go to the chair with a five on it. "Fabiola, you find three," and she did. Marisol couldn't find the number 2 right away, so Garner coached, "*Dos! Dos!*" and she found it. Richard couldn't find number 1 and several of the children laughed. Garner told them not to do that and turned to encourage him: "Number one, baby," and he found it.

Then Garner had Clintishabeth, Kimberly, Karina, and Andre sit in chairs in front of their classmates. She handed each a square or a circle or a triangle or a rectangle. She told the square to stand up, the circle to sit down, and so on, testing them not only on shapes but also on following directions. Andre listened and took his cues flawlessly.

Finally, Garner had several other children sit up front as she put a piece of colored plastic under each chair. "This is a hard game," she told the children, instructing them to tell her what color they had and then to find a toy on the shelves that was the same color. While she was giving directions, Travell and Marcus were tugging on each other, so when she asked them what they were supposed to do, they couldn't tell her. "You know what happens when you don't listen." But Marcus found something orange right away, and little César, still only three years old, went straight to something yellow to match his piece of plastic, so Garner shook his hand and the children applauded.

As the year ended, it was time to honor the parents who had volunteered. Many of the mothers, mostly Hispanic but also Joshua's mom,

Linda, would do everything from preparing elaborate seasonal decorations for the center to cutting paper towels in half to stretch a package and to make the towels kid-sized. At Parent Appreciation Day in June, Garner told the parents: "We can't pay you. We can't buy you a Rolls-Royce. We can't buy you a diamond ring. But we do want to thank you."

She looked around at the twenty mothers in the center that day. "We don't have fifty-two parents in here. We have fifty-two children [in the morning and afternoon classes]. Some parents just come in and pick up their kids and I hardly even know they've been here. But you all come and help or you go on field trips. Veronica is leaving after four years. I'm going to cry. I hope next year many of you can come in and help." Veronica Perez translated Garner's message into Spanish for the mothers.

While we had been waiting for the parents to assemble, Shardae and Ciara wrote part of the alphabet for me. Then Ciara and Maria drew pictures in my notebook. Maria wanted to draw her family—mother and daddy, grandma and grandpa, everybody. "Now I'm going to draw God," she said solemnly, drawing a large circle above the family. "God is very big."

Finally came graduation day. The Training and Research Foundation's leadership frowned on graduation ceremonies with caps and gowns because the occasion became too elaborate, too much for the parents and not meaningful for four- and five-year-olds. Still, there were balloons and festive food at the centers across the city on June 19. The Watts Towers staff displayed the trophy they had just been awarded for the center that rated best in the most areas. The trophy had been presented at a Parent Awards Night ceremony that drew several hundred people at a local hotel ballroom. Veronica Perez had won several trophies for parent participation as well. They, too, were on display.

Garner had urged parents to dress their children in black and white for graduation, even if was a white T-shirt and black pants, and most got the message. Joshua wore a black suit and white shirt, looking very spiffy. When he went to wash his hands, his mother took his jacket off. "I certainly don't want to get this wet," she said. Marcus had on a gray suit, tie, and suspenders to match, but the clip-on tie soon ended up on Deborah Chatman's T-shirt so it wouldn't get lost. Maria wore a frilly white dress with a white picture hat; her hair, usually pulled back, hung loosely around her face.

Two dozen parents arrived for the graduation. It was clear to me which ones were accustomed to being there. They were helping out, while the rest just stood around. Garner started the children off with a rendition of "If You're Happy and You Know It, Clap Your Hands," then asked the children how they were that day. "Good morning, Raymound, how are you?"

"Fine!" he replied, loud and clear.

"All right, children. Today is Wednesday. There are three days in a week. . . ." She paused.

"Seven," Andre quickly corrected her. He had been listening, which was of course the point.

The teachers presented little badges to each of the graduates. About seven of the younger children would be coming back for another year, but the rest would be scattering to several area elementary schools. Then the children gave their mothers flowers that the teachers supplied. The teachers urged the children to call out their mother's first name so they'd know it when they went to kindergarten. Some said, "Mama," but Andre announced: "My mother's name is Andreda," and she came up and gave him a big hug. Cameras flashed and videotapes whirred as the children received certificates that they had completed Head Start. Andre and his cousin Raven posed with Andre's mother with huge smiles across their faces. Maria posed for her mother's video camera. Then the children ate cheese sandwiches, Fritos, lettuce, carrots— singing, "Thank you for my lunch. *Gracias por las comidas*" one last time. For the special occasion, they had cake and ice cream as well.

Amid the farewell hugs, Michael's mother, Bianca, thanked Garner for all she had done for her son. Other parents who hadn't attended the graduation picked up their children as though nothing special had happened. But it had.

ACKNOWLEDGMENTS

Head Start is a family-oriented program; for a year, I became part of the Watts Towers Head Start family. I could not have written this book without the hospitality, openness, and insights of the staff at that center and of the Training and Research Foundation that operates it. Thanks especially to Josephine Garner, Lupe Osuna, Deborah Chatman, and Gloria Heyman as well as Elaine Atlow and Paul DeVan. I would not have found them without the good counsel of Congresswoman Maxine Waters. Parents and staff everywhere were unfailingly gracious and candid about talking about their lives. I appreciate all their help, especially that of Debra Alexander and Veronica Perez, whose daughters attended the Watts Towers center.

During the several years that I worked on this book, I visited centers at Santo Domingo and Isleta pueblos near Albuquerque, New Mexico; San Jose, Westley, Patterson, Ceres, Planada, and Los Banos, California, as well as many TRF centers in the Los Angeles area; Fort Belknap, Montana; Stonewall and Dallas, Texas; Mayersville, Anguilla, and Belzoni, Mississippi; Auburn, Opelika, and Hurtsboro, Alabama; Silver Spring, Rockville, and Baltimore, Maryland; Biglerville, Pennsylvania; Minneapolis, Minnesota; Huntington and Crum, West Virginia; Boston, Massachusetts; and Kansas City, Missouri. Many of the people I interviewed there are quoted in this book; many are not. Nonetheless, every interview informed what I wrote. Many people taxied me around, shared meals with me, or set up appointments for me; their help made my travels most rewarding. Thanks, then, not only to all those quoted in the book but also to Beatrice Aguilar, Lucy Gutierrez, Joan Lawler, Barbara Lovelace, Jennifer Tollefson y Chavez, Ann Stubbs, Francie Erikson, Carolyn Reid-Green, Nancy Goldsmith, and Myra Brown.

Even though he has written books of his own about Head Start, Edward Zigler of Yale University constantly encouraged my work and helped me fight my way through the thicket of research about the program. At the Head Start office in Washington, Gilda Lambert fielded endless questions and connected me with those who knew the answers when she didn't. Helen Blank at the Children's Defense Fund steered me toward many of the programs that I visited. Danielle Ewen at the National Child Care Information Center provided useful background papers.

In 1995, I received an Alicia Patterson Journalism Fellowship to report on Head Start. I deeply appreciate both the financial support and the encouragement of knowing that this topic was deemed important by a prestigious selection panel. I thank the foundation and its director, Margaret Engel. The articles that I did as part of that year's work form the core of several chapters in this book. My first travel to work on this book was made possible by a grant from the Freedom Forum through the help of one of its board members, the late Nancy Woodhull. I am but one of many people who know Nancy was always there to support fellow journalists' work. I also received a Moody Grant from the Lyndon Baines Johnson Foundation for research at the LBJ Library in Austin. At the library, I especially thank Linda Hanson, Allen Fisher, and E. Philip Scott. Liz Carpenter had coincidentally organized a gathering of Texas Hill Country Head Start teachers to visit the library while I was there, and my conversations with those staff members helped reenergize me.

My first agent, Diane Cleaver, died suddenly as I was beginning work on this project. She thought it was the best idea for a book that I had had. Heide Lange carried forth the project with ideas that helped me expand my sense of the context within which Head Start operates. It was with great delight that I worked for the third time with Deb Brody at Dutton, an editor who is also a writer's friend and fellow baseball fan.

You can never adequately thank anyone who reads part of your manuscript. Dean Mills, Eileen Shanahan, and my mother, Mary S. Mills, urged me toward more description where that was needed and less where less was needed. And they asked questions that had not occurred to me. Harley Frankel and Wendy Lazarus reassured me repeatedly about the importance of this work. Friends around the country heard my joys and laments, always boosting my morale and often feeding or housing me on my travels. Thanks, therefore, also to Sue Mills, Connie Koenenn, Susan Henry, Ann Reiss Lane, Christine S. Conaway, Geraldine Kennedy, Jordan Mo, Hal and Pam Fuson, Pam Pettee, Matt and Jeannine Herron, Celia Morris, Bill and Teddye Clayton, Cheryl Arvidson, Cheryl Fields, Betty Anne Williams, Claudia Levy, Laurie Lipper, Leola Johnson, Glenda and Pete Holste, Melinda Voss, Richard and Susana O'Mara, Melissa Ludtke, Pamela Moreland, Jane Bernard-Powers, Molly Ivins, Saralee Tiede, Dan and Faith Sullivan, Patricia Sullivan, Sharon Rosenhause, Winifred Green, Connie Curry, Gina Setser, Leine Stuart, Jane and Ned Cabot, and Julia Kagan.

Mostly, though, I appreciate the time I spent with the children at Site 05, Watts Towers Head Start. Talking with them, eating lunch with them, taking field trips with them, watching them grow, I learned the most about what Head Start accomplishes.

NOTES

Introduction

1. U.S. Bureau of the Census, *Poverty in the United States: 1996* (Washington, D.C., 1995), table 2, p. 2.

2. U.S. House of Representatives, Poverty Rates for Individuals in Selected Demographic Groups, 1959–1994, *1996 Green Book: Background Material and Data on Programs within the Jurisdiction of the Committee on Ways and Means* (Washington, D.C.: U.S. Government Printing Office, 1996), table H-4, p. 1226, and Steven A. Holmes, "U.S. Census Finds First Income Rise in Past Six Years," *New York Times*, September 27, 1996.

Chapter One: The First Day of School at Watts Towers Center

1. Kay Mills, "Maxine Waters: The Sassy Legislator Who Knows There's More Than One Way to Make a Political Statement," *Governing*, March 1988, p. 28.

2. Joe Domanick, "The Browning of L.A.," *Los Angeles Magazine*, May 1996, pp. 74–79, 172. Background on the history of African Americans and Latinos in Los Angeles comes from Carey McWilliams, *Southern California: An Island on the Land* (Santa Barbara, Calif.: Peregrine Smith, 1973); John Weaver, *Los Angeles: The Enormous Village, 1781–1981* (Santa Barbara, Calif.: Capra Press, 1980); Walton Bean, *California: An Interpretive History* (New York: McGraw-Hill, 1978); and David E. Hayes-Bautista and Gregory Rodriguez, *Latino South Central* (Los Angeles: Alta California Policy Research Center, 1994).

Chapter Two: Stonewall, Texas: How It All Began

1. "Joint Church Services Open Head Start Program Sunday; President and First Lady Attend," *Fredericksburg Standard*, December 18, 1968.

2. Associated Press, "President Hears Head Start Plan," December 15, 1968.

3. Mrs. Lyndon B. Johnson contributed her recollections to Edward Zigler and Jeanette Valentine, eds. *Project Head Start: A Legacy of the War on Poverty* (New York: Free Press, 1979), p. 48.

4. Hugh Davis Graham, *The Uncertain Triumph: Federal Education Policy in the Kennedy and Johnson Years* (Chapel Hill, N.C.: University of North Carolina Press, 1984), p. xvii.

5. Zigler and Valentine, eds. *Project Head Start*, p. 5.

6. Hugh Davis Graham, *The Uncertain Triumph*, pp. 44–51.

7. Theda Skocpol, *Protecting Soldiers and Mothers: The Political Origins of Social Policy in the United States* (Cambridge, Mass.: Belknap Press of Harvard University Press, 1992), pp. 480–524.

8. Background material on the history of child care in America from Margaret G. Weiser, *Infant/Toddler Care and Education*, 2nd ed. (New York: Macmillan, 1991), pp. 3–18; Catherine J. Ross, "Early Skirmishes with Poverty: The Historical Roots of Head Start," in Edward Zigler and Jeanette Valentine, eds. *Project Head Start*, pp. 21–42; and Edward F. Zigler and Mary E. Lang, *Child Care Choices: Balancing the Needs of Children, Families and Society* (New York: Free Press, 1991), pp. 28–41.

9. Michael Katz, *In the Shadow of the Poorhouse: A Social History of Welfare in America* (New York: Basic Books, 1986), is an excellent summary of America's ambivalent treatment of the poor.

10. James L. Sundquist, *Politics and Policy: The Eisenhower, Kennedy and Johnson Years* (Washington, D.C.: Brookings Institution, 1968).

11. Michael Harrington, *The Other America: Poverty in the United States* (New York: Collier Books, 1962).

12. Dwight Macdonald, "Our Invisible Poor," *The New Yorker*, January 19, 1963, pp. 82–132.

13. Daniel P. Moynihan, *Maximum Feasible Misunderstanding: Community Action in the War on Poverty* (New York: Free Press,1969), pp. 7–19.

14. Ibid., pp. 34–59.

15. Homer Bigart, "Kentucky Miners: A Grim Winter," *New York Times*, October 20, 1963, p. 1.

16. Bennett Schiff and Stephen Goodell, "The Office of Economic Opportunity During the Administration of President Lyndon B. Johnson, November 1963–January 1969," White House Special Files, Administrative Histories, box 1, vol. 1, p. 17, Lyndon B. Johnson Library.

17. Schiff and Goodell, "Office of Economic Opportunity," p. 19.

18. Nicholas Lemann, "The Unfinished War," *Atlantic Monthly*, December 1988, p. 39.

19. Schiff and Goodell, "Office of Economic Opportunity," p. 19.

20. Remarks of the president at the Welhausen Elementary School, Cotulla, Texas, November 7, 1966, Statements of Lyndon B. Johnson, box 221, Lyndon B. Johnson Library. Johnson knew Cotulla well and had changed his speech text accordingly. Where the prepared text said children there had been taught that the end of life is a beet row or a cotton field, Johnson had written in "spinach patch" instead of cotton field.

21. Lemann, "The Unfinished War," p. 39.

22. Schiff and Goodell, "Office of Economic Opportunity," p. 21.

23. Harris Wofford, *Of Kennedys and Kings: Making Sense of the Sixties* (Pittsburgh, Pa.: University of Pittsburgh, 1992), p. 295.

24. Schiff and Goodell, "Office of Economic Opportunity," pp. 29–30.

25. Sundquist, *Politics and Policy*, p. 141.

26. Adam Yarmolinsky oral history, quoted in Michael L. Gillette, *Launching the War on Poverty: An Oral History* (New York: Twayne Publishers, 1996), p. 91.

27. Schiff and Goodell, "Office of Economic Opportunity," p. 44.

28. Schiff and Goodell, "Office of Economic Opportunity," vol. 1, part 2, p. 231.

29. Polly Greenberg, "Before the Beginning: A Participant's View," *Young Children*, September 1990, p. 42.

30. Sargent Shriver oral history, cited in Michael L. Gillette, *Launching the War on Poverty*, pp. 215–216.

31. Zigler and Valentine, eds., *Project Head Start*, p. 51.

32. Sargent Shriver's recollections come from an interview conducted in May 1977 in Washington, D.C., by Jeanette Valentine, and published in Zigler and Valentine, eds., *Project Head Start*, pp. 49–67.

33. Margaret G. Weiser, *Infant/Toddler Care and Education*, pp. 14–17, and Edward Zigler and Karen Anderson, "An Idea Whose Time Had Come: The Intellectual and Political Climate for Head Start," in Zigler and Valentine, eds., *Project Head Start*, pp. 9–11.

34. Sargent Shriver interview in Zigler and Valentine, eds., *Project Head Start*, pp. 54–55.

35. Wofford, *Of Kennedys and Kings*, p. 287.

36. Ibid., p. 12.

37. Jule Sugarman oral history by Stephen Goodell, March 14, 1969, in Washington, D.C., Oral History Collection, Lyndon B. Johnson Library.

38. Schiff and Goodell, "Office of Economic Opportunity," pp. 229–230. Shriver liked positive-sounding names: Head Start, VISTA, Upward Bound. He didn't want the alphabet-soup agencies created during the Depression. Only OEO was called by its initials, and that sounded like a Swiss yodel, according to an antipoverty aide quoted in *The New York Times*. OEO had almost been officially named the War on Poverty or the War Against Poverty, but those titles were scrapped because the former's initials might offend Italians and the latter might sound like pop art. From "New Era in Naming Projects; Shriver Puts Accent on the Positive—Scorns Alphabet," *The New York Times*, February 13, 1966.

39. Sargent Shriver interview in Zigler and Valentine, eds., *Project Head Start*, p. 53.

40. Mrs. Lyndon Johnson in Zigler and Valentine, eds., *Project Head Start*, p. 44.

41. Ibid.

42. Jule M. Sugarman, "History," in Zigler and Valentine, eds., *Project Head Start*, p. 117.

43. Julius Richmond oral history with Michael L. Gillette, October 5, 1981, Boston, Mass., Oral History Collection, Lyndon B. Johnson Library, pp. 2–3.

44. Polly Greenberg, *The Devil Has Slippery Shoes: A Biased Biography of the Child Development Group of Mississippi (CDGM)* (Washington, D.C.: Youth Policy Institute, 1990), pp. 778–781. Greenberg's book was originally published by Macmillan in 1969.

45. Jule Sugarman oral history, p. 17, and Julius Richmond oral history, pp. 9–10.

46. Julius Richmond oral history, pp. 12–13.

47. Schiff and Goodell, "Office of Economic Opportunity," p. 235.

48. Julius Richmond oral history, pp. 13–14.

49. Thomas E. Mullaney, "Another Historic Year in the Making, *The New York Times*, January 11, 1965, p. 47.

50. Sargent Shriver interview in Zigler and Valentine, eds., *Project Head Start*, p. 56.

51. Norbert Schlei oral history, quoted in Michael L. Gillette, *Launching the War on Poverty*, p. 77.

52. Sundquist, *Politics and Policy*, p. 151.

53. Julius Richmond oral history, p. 15.

54. Charles Mohr, " 'Head Start' Plan for Pupils Begun," *New York Times*, May 19, 1965, p. 1.

55. White House Special Files, Remarks of the President, May 17, 1965, Statements of Lyndon B. Johnson, box 147, Lyndon B. Johnson Library.

56. John C. Donovan, *The Politics of Poverty* (Washington, D.C.: University Press of America, 1980), p. 89.

57. John W. Gardner, "Lyndon Johnson As I Knew Him," in *The Johnson Years: The Difference He Made*, ed. Robert L. Hardesty (Austin, Tex.: Lyndon Baines Johnson Library, 1993), p. 25.

58. Memos from Jack Watson to the President and from James Jones to Liz Carpenter, White House Central Files, Subject File, WE 9–1, box 45, Lyndon B. Johnson Library.

59. Jule Sugarman oral history, p. 19.

60. Remarks of Mrs. Lyndon Johnson, June 30, 1965, White House Social Files, Liz Carpenter's Subject Files, box 82, Lyndon B. Johnson Library.

Chapter Three: Mississippi: *The Fight for Control*

1. The Carter family's personal fight against school segregation is movingly told by Constance Curry in *Silver Rights* (Chapel Hill, N.C.: Algonquin Books, 1995).

2. Polly Greenberg, *The Devil Has Slippery Shoes*, pp. 3–14.

3. Two excellent books include sections on CDGM: John Dittmer's *Local People: The Struggle for Civil Rights in Mississippi* (Urbana, Ill.: University of Illinois Press, 1994), and Charles M. Payne's *I've Got the Light of Freedom: The Organizing Tradition and the Mississippi Freedom Struggle* (Berkeley, Calif.: University of California Press, 1995).

4. Greenberg, *The Devil Has Slippery Shoes*, p. 230.

5. Ibid., p. 244.

6. Julius Richmond oral history, p. 28.

7. Ibid., pp. 29–30.

8. Letter from Governor Paul Johnson to Sargent Shriver, June 29,1965, with letter from the Reverend M. L. Young, White House Central Files, WE 9-1, box 46, Lyndon B. Johnson Library.

9. Senate Committee on Labor and Public Welfare, *Examination of the War on Poverty: Hearings Before the Subcommittee on Employment, Manpower, and Poverty*, 90th Congress, first session, Jackson, Miss., April 10, 1967, p. 782.

10. All five of Young's children went to Head Start. One became a power company lineman, one a nurse, one a science teacher with a master's degree, one a college student majoring in business, and one was still in grade school when I met Young.

11. Greenberg, *The Devil Has Slippery Shoes*, pp. 447–451, and Joseph A. Loftus, "Youthful Lobby Asks School Fund," *New York Times*, February 12, 1966.

12. Schiff and Goodell, "Office of Economic Opportunity," p. 71.

13. CDGM Fact Sheet, "Examination of the War on Poverty," p. 776.

14. Robert Analavage, "Bolivar Head Start Not Funded," *The Southern Patriot*, April 1966, p. 4.

15. Mary Coleman, "Exits from Poverty in Sunflower County: Shelters in Times of Storm" (paper loaned by the author), pp. 77–78.

16. Bob Boyd, "Sunflower Head Start Protest Is Persistent, Quiet," *Delta Democrat-Times*, August 18, 1968. For more on the Sunflower County Head Start struggle and Hamer's work in general, see Kay Mills, *This Little Light of Mine: The Life of Fannie Lou Hamer* (New York: NAL/Dutton, 1993).

17. Coleman, "Exits from Poverty," p. 84.

18. Schiff and Goodell, "Office of Economic Opportunity," p. 75.

19. Nicholas von Hoffman, "Manna from OEO Falls on Mississippi," *Washington Post*, October 13, 1966.

20. Nicholas von Hoffman, "3000 Jackson Negroes Flay Head Start Cutoff," *Washington Post*, October 9, 1966.

21. Schiff and Goodell, "Office of Economic Opportunity," p. 77.

22. Aaron Henry oral history interview with Neil McMillen and George Burson, Clarksdale, Miss., May 1, 1972, Mississippi Oral History Program of the University of Southern Mississippi, Hattiesburg.

23. CDGM Situation Report of September 27, 1966, "Examination of the War on Poverty," p. 774.

24. "Say It Isn't So, Sargent Shriver," *New York Times*, October 19, 1966.

25. Letter to the Editor of *New York Times*, "Examination of the War on Poverty," p. 801.

26. Jule M. Sugarman oral history, p. 34.

27. Greenberg, *The Devil Has Slippery Shoes*, p. 657.

28. Ibid., p. 311.

29. Friends of Children of Mississippi, "History of Friends of Children of Mississippi, Inc." updated pamphlet.

Chapter Four: Fort Belknap, Montana: A Powwow to Preserve a Culture

1. The Hays/Lodge Pole Staff and Students, *Creating a Better Understanding of Tribal Government and History Concerning the Fort Belknap Indian Reservation* (Billings, Montana: Sign Talker Lithographic Service, undated), pp. 3–9.

2. Senate Committees on Indian Affairs and Labor and Human Resources, *Indian Issues Regarding Head Start Reauthorization*, 103rd Congress, second session, March 25, 1994, p. 120.

3. Senate Committees, *Indian Issues Regarding Head Start Reauthorization*, p. 9.

Chapter Five: Auburn, Alabama: Reaching Beyond the Classroom

1. Voices for Alabama's Children, *Alabama Kids Count: 1995 Report* (Birmingham, Ala.: Voices for Alabama's Children, 1995), pp. 93–94.

2. Alabama Council on Human Relations, "ACHR, *Inc. Lee County Community Needs Assessment,* Demographic and Socioeconomic Characteristics of Lee County—1994," unpublished report, p. 2.

3. Voices for Alabama's Children, *Alabama Kids Count 1995 Report,* pp. 125–126.

Chapter Seven: Montgomery County, Maryland: Head Start in a Suburban School System

1. Winnie Johnson died of pneumonia in January 1997.

Chapter Eight: Where Are They Now?

1. *Pancho,* 16 mm., 25 min., Robert K. Sharpe Productions, made for the Office of Economic Opportunity, from the audiovisual collection at the Lyndon Baines Johnson Library.

2. Robert Hansen, "Head Start Rescues Little Pancho," *San Luis Obispo County Telegram-Tribune,* July 15, 1966.

3. "Remarks of Mrs. Lyndon B. Johnson at beginning of 'Adventure in Learning' trip and showing of 'Pancho' film, the White House, March 13, 1967, White House Social Files, Liz Carpenter's Subject Files, box 33–34, Lyndon Baines Johnson Library.

4. Liz Carpenter, *Ruffles and Flourishes* (New York: Doubleday, 1970), p. 78.

5. In their own policy review, Dr. Edward Zigler of Yale University and his colleague Sally J. Styfco wrote: "There are several reasons why children leave the program testing well and then may lose this advantage. One is that performance on an IQ test reflects not only formal cognitive processes but achievement and personality variables as well. The IQ gains apparent after Head Start are not necessarily due to expanded intellectual capacity but may instead be explained by improved motivation, familiarity with test content, and comfort in the testing situation. Thus, participation in Head Start can enable children to develop the skills and attitudes needed to apply their abilities more fully. When they enter school, however, the environment may not continue to encourage full use of their potential; for example, there may be a poor curriculum or teaching practices that lower self-confidence and ignore individual learning styles. Another explanation for fade-out, advanced by early childhood educators, is that the paper-and-pencil, standardized group achievement tests used in many studies are inappropriate for children in the primary grades." Edward Zigler and Sally J. Styfco, "Using Research and Theory to Justify and Inform Head Start Expansion," in *Social Policy Report,* a quarterly publication of the Society for Research in Child Development, Vol. VII, No. 2, 1993, p. 6.

6. Robert McCall, *Head Start, Its Potential, Its Achievements, Its Future: A Briefing Paper for Policymakers* (Pittsburgh, Pa.: University of Pittsburgh, 1993), p. 2, and Edward Zigler and Sally J. Styfco, "Using Research and Theory," p. 4.

7. Deborah A. Phillips and Natasha J. Cabrera, eds., *Beyond the Blueprint: Directions for Research on Head Start's Families* (Washington, D.C.: National Academy Press, 1996), p. 4.

8. Robert McCall, *Head Start,* p. 3.

9. Ibid., pp. 1–7.

10. Ibid., p. 8.

11. W. Steven Barnett, "Long-Term Effects of Early Childhood Programs on Cognitive and School Outcomes," in Richard E. Behrman, ed., *The Future of Children: Long-Term Outcomes of Early Childhood Programs* (Los Altos, Calif.: Center for the Future of Children, the David and Lucile Packard Foundation), pp. 43–46.

12. Edward Zigler and Sally Styfco, "Using Research and Theory," p. 7.

13. Edward Zigler and Jeanette Valentine, eds., *Project Head Start*, p. 65.

14. Ruth Hubbell McKey, Larry Condelli, Harriet Ganson, Barbara Barrett, Catherine McConkey, and Margaret C. Plantz, *The Impact of Head Start on Children, Families and Communities: Final Report of the Head Start Evaluation, Synthesis and Utilization Project* (Washington, D.C.: Department of Health and Human Services, 1985), p. 7.

15. Carol E. Copple, Marvin G. Cline, and Allen N. Smith, *Path to the Future: Long-Term Effects of Head Start in the Philadelphia School District* (Washington, D. C.: U.S. Department of Health and Human Services, 1987), pp. 3–4.

16. Deborah Phillips and Natasha J. Cabrera, eds., *Beyond the Blueprint*, pp. ix–xiii, and the publication announcement for the report, "Head Start Research Should Address Changing Conditions of Poor Families," National Research Council News, Washington, D.C., April 15, 1996.

17. Rachel Jones, "When You Have to Pretend You're Not Hungry," *Washington Post*, August 23, 1996.

Chapter Ten: Getting Men Involved, Getting Communities Involved

1. Faith Lamb Parker, Chaya S. Piotrkowski, Wade F. Horn, and Sarah M. Greene, "The Challenge for Head Start: Realizing Its Vision as a Two-Generation Program," in I. Sigel (series ed.) and S. Smith (vol. ed.), *Advances in Applied Developmental Psychology: Vol. 9, Two Generation Programs for Families in Poverty* (New Jersey: Albex Publishing Corp.), p. 152.

2. Deborah A. Phillips and Natasha J. Cabrera, eds., *Beyond the Blueprint*, pp. 51–54.

3. James A. Levine, Dennis T. Murphy, and Sherrill Wilson, *Getting Men Involved: Strategies for Early Childhood Programs* (New York: Scholastic, 1993).

4. Jeanne Ellsworth and Lynda J. Ames, "Power and Ceremony: Low-Income Mothers as Policy Makers in Head Start," *Educational Foundations*, fall 1995, pp. 5–23.

5. Nicole M. Driebe and Moncrieff M. Cochran, "Barriers to Parent Involvement in Head Start Programs," presented at the Third Head Start research conference, June 20–23, 1996, Washington, D.C.

6. Erwin Knoll, "Profess on Poverty," *The Progressive*, July 1965, cited in Schiff and Goodell, "Office of Economic Opportunity," p. 65.

Chapter Eleven: Getting It Together

1. Bill Scanlon, "Head Start Starts Over; Program Reorganized After Tumultuous Year," *Rocky Mountain News*, September 10, 1996.

2. A selection of stories by Paul Hutchinson includes "Child Agency's Donors Hold Off; Dispute Clouds Head Start," *Denver Post*, March 14, 1996; "Head of Head Start Runs Things His Way," *Denver Post*, March 17, 1996; "Head Start Shuts Its Doors, Denver Program out of Money; Kids Stranded," *Denver Post*, May 15, 1996; "Heads Roll at Head Start, Feds Order Brandon and His Board Out," *Denver Post*, May 18, 1996; "Fed-

eral Role in Head Start Questioned, Answers Are Few in Denver Situation," *Denver Post*, June 2, 1996; and "Head Start Shakeup Continues, Regional Overseers Relieved of Their Duties," *Denver Post*, June 18, 1996.

3. Harris Wofford, *Of Kennedys and Kings*, p. 319.

4. Quoted in Wofford, *Of Kennedys and Kings*, p. 321.

5. Edward Zigler and Sally J. Styfco, "Preface to the Paperback Edition," Zigler and Valentine, eds., *Project Head Start: A Legacy of the War on Poverty* (Alexandria, Va.: National Head Start Association, 1997, p. xix.

6. Schiff and Goodell, "Office of Economic Opportunity," pp. 242–243.

7. Edward Zigler and Susan Muenchow, *Head Start: The Inside Story of America's Most Successful Educational Experiment* (New York: Basic Books, 1992), p. 26.

8. Ibid., p. 59.

9. Edward Zigler and Jeanette Valentine, eds., *Project Head Start*, p. 369.

10. Melissa Ludtke, "At the Heart of Head Start," *America's Agenda*, winter 1994, p. 31.

11. Zigler and Muenchow, *Head Start: The Inside Story*, p. 158.

12. Ibid., p. 175.

13. Ada J. Mann, Adele Harrell, and Maure Hunt, Jr., *A Review of Head Start Research Since 1969 and An Annotated Bibliography* (Washington, D.C.: Social Research Group, George Washington University, May 1977).

14. Zigler and Styfco, "Preface to the Paperback Edition," p. xix.

15. National Head Start Association (Alexandria, Va.: National Head Start Association, 1990); *Head Start: The Nation's Pride, A Nation's Challenge: Recommendations for Head Start in the 1990s* and Advisory Committee on Head Start Quality and Expansion, *Creating A 21st Century Head Start: Final Report of the Advisory Committee on Head Start Quality and Expansion* (Washington, D.C.: Department of Health and Human Services, 1993). The advisory committee included not only Zigler, Harley Frankel, and Julius Richmond but also representatives of the Clinton administration, key Capitol Hill staff members from both sides of the political aisle, staff from the Children's Defense Fund, the National Head Start Association, the National Black Child Development Institute, the National Migrant Head Start Directors Association, the National Governors' Association, and the National Association for the Education of Young Children, as well as Douglas J. Besharov of the American Enterprise Institute (see chapter 16), Dwayne Crompton of the KCMC Child Development Corporation (see chapter 14), Yolanda Garcia from Santa Clara County, California (see chapter 13), and Sheldon White, a Harvard University psychologist who chaired a key research panel in the 1990s.

16. Advisory Committee on Head Start Quality, *Creating a 21st Century Head Start*, pp. 9–10.

17. Ibid., p. 34.

18. Tracey Kaplan, "2 Head Start Providers Lose $7 Million in Funding," *Los Angeles Times*, February 24, 1993. The second program mentioned in the headline subsequently corrected its deficiencies and still offers Head Start services.

19. Ed Kamian, "Head Start Assailed at Meeting," *Glendale News-Press*, August 26, 1993; Ed Kamian, "Oversight Agency's Board Cuts Ties with Head Start," *Glendale News-Press*, September 1, 1993; as well as brief items by Tommy Li in the *Los Angeles Times*, September 1 and 17, 1993.

Chapter Twelve: Getting Healthy, Staying Healthy

1. Jonathan London, *The Lion Who Had Asthma* (Morton Grove, Ill.: Albert Whitman & Co., 1992).

2. Thomas H. Maugh II, "Cockroaches Tied to Asthma in Inner Cities," *Los Angeles Times*, May 8, 1997, and Warren E. Leary, "Cockroaches Cited as Big Cause of Asthma," *New York Times*, May 8, 1997.

3. Holly Keller, *Furry* (New York: Greenwillow Books, 1992).

4. Schiff and Goodell, "Office of Economic Opportunity," pp. 237–239.

5. Edward Zigler, C. S. Piotrkowski, and Ray Collins, "Health Services in Head Start," in *Annual Review of Public Health*, 1994, p. 516. By 1995, that figure had improved; 81 percent of pregnant women were receiving prenatal care in their first trimester, the highest level in the nation's history.

6. Robert W. O'Brien, Michael K. Keane, David B. Connell, James A. Griffin, and Nicole C. Close, "A Descriptive Study of the Head Start Health Component," poster presentation at the 1997 conference of the Society for Research in Child Development in Washington, D.C.

7. Office of Inspector General, "Evaluating Head Start Expansion Through Performance Indicators," report from the Department of Health and Human Services, May 1993, pp. i–ii, 1–9.

8. Zigler, Piotrkowski, and Collins, "Health Services in Head Start, pp. 530–531.

Chapter Thirteen: Keeping It Together

1. Santa Clara Office of Education, Children's Services Department, "Bridges to the Future," Head Start transition project staff manual, San Jose, California, 1992, p. 3.

2. Sharon Landesman Ramey, Craig T. Ramey, and Martha M. Phillips, *Head Start Children's Entry into Public School: An Interim Report on the National Head Start-Public School Early Childhood Transition Demonstration Study* (Birmingham, Ala.: Civitan International Research Center, 1996), pp. vii, xii, and xiii.

3. Theodore C. Sorensen, *Kennedy* (New York: Harper & Row, 1965), p. 140.

4. Tim R. Massey, "Play Area Rooted in Mother's Concern," *The Herald Dispatch*, Huntington, West Virginia, February 1997.

5. Ramey, Ramey, and Phillips, *Head Start Children's Entry into Public School*, pp. 61–62.

6. Ibid., p. 47.

7. The comments of David Wilkins and Ana Sol Gutierrez came from a tape of the April 22, 1996, meeting of the Montgomery County Board of Education meeting.

8. Ramey, Ramey, and Phillips, *Head Start Children's Entry into Public School*, pp. 63–64.

Chapter Fourteen: Ways to Serve More Children, Longer

1. Lorelei Brush, Sharon Deich, Kerry Traylor, and Nancy Pindus, *Options for Full-Day Services for Children Participating in Head Start* (Washington, D.C.: Pelavin Research Institute and The Urban Institute,1995).

Chapter Fifteen: Meeting Conditions—Head Start Adapts

1. Bruce Ramsey, "A Place Asian Elders Can Call Home," *Seattle Post-Intelligencer,* August 27, 1996.

2. Anne Carothers-Kay, "Head Start Gets a Fresh Start—at Night," *Des Moines Register,* January 26, 1996.

Chapter Sixteen: Summing Up and Looking Ahead

1. Ethan G. Salwen, "From Head Start to Capitol Hill: How Head Start helped transform a shy, first generation Mexican American into a confident Congresswoman," *Children and Families,* Spring 1997, pp. 34–38.

2. Among Douglas Besharov's work on Head Start: "Why Head Start Needs a Re-Start; Poverty, Violence Threaten the Gains," *Washington Post,* February 2, 1992, p. C1; "New Directions for Head Start," *The Education Digest,* September 1992, pp. 7–11; and "Fresh Start: What Works in Head Start?" *The New Republic,* June 14, 1993, pp. 14–16. He also edited *Enhancing Early Childhood Programs: Burdens and Opportunities* (Washington, D.C.: Child Welfare League of America Press and American Enterprise Institute, 1996).

3. Edward Zigler's writing about Head Start includes *Project Head Start: A Legacy of the War on Poverty,* edited with Jeanette Valentine (New York: Free Press, 1979); *Head Start: The Inside Story of America's Most Successful Educational Experiment,* with Susan Muenchow (New York, Basic Books, 1992); *Head Start and Beyond,* edited with Sally J. Styfco (New Haven, Conn.: Yale University Press, 1993); and "Using Research and Theory to Justify and Inform Head Start Expansion," *Social Policy Report,* with Sally J. Styfco, Society for Research in Child Development, 1993. See also Melissa Ludtke, "At the Heart of Head Start," *America's Agenda,* winter 1994, and Kay Mills, "Edward Zigler: Head Start's Architect Reflects on Building Achievements," *Los Angeles Times,* April 4, 1993.

4. Melissa Healy, "Clinton Seeks Head Start Enhancement," *Los Angeles Times,* March 26, 1997.

5. Peter Edelman, "The Worst Thing Bill Clinton Has Done," *Atlantic Monthly,* March 1997, pp. 43–58.

6. Dave Lesher, "Cost of Child Care Puts Welfare Reform at Risk, Study Says," *Los Angeles Times,* February 13, 1997.

INDEX

· A NOTE ON THE TYPE ·

The typeface used in this book, Transitional, is a digitized version of Fairfield, which was designed in 1937–40 by artist Rudolph Ruzicka (1883–1978), on a commission from Linotype. The assignment was the occasion for a well-known essay in the form of a letter from W. A. Dwiggins to Ruzicka, in response to the latter's request for advice. Dwiggins, who had recently designed Electra and Caledonia, relates that he would start by making very large scale drawings (10 and 64 times the size you are reading) and having test cuttings made, which were used to print on a variety of papers. "By looking at all these for two or three days I get an idea of how to go forward—or, if the result is a dud, how to start over again." At this stage he took *parts* of letters that satisfied him and made cardboard cutouts, which he then used to assemble other letters. This "template" method anticipated one that many contemporary computer type designers use.